CYRIAC OF ANCONA
LATER TRAVELS

ITRL 10

CYRIAC OF ANCONA
· · ·
LATER TRAVELS

EDITED AND TRANSLATED BY

EDWARD W. BODNAR

with Clive Foss

THE I TATTI RENAISSANCE LIBRARY

HARVARD UNIVERSITY PRESS

CAMBRIDGE, MASSACHUSETTS

LONDON, ENGLAND

2003

Series design by Dean Bornstein

Library of Congress Cataloging-in-Publication Data

Ciriaco, d'Ancona, 1391–1452.
Later travels / edited and translated by Edward W. Bodnar with Clive Foss.
p. cm. — (The I Tatti Renaissance library ; 10)
Fifty-three letters, brief diary excerpts,
and five extensive fragments of travel diaries.
Includes bibliographical references (p.) and index.
ISBN 0-674-00758-1 (alk. paper)
1. Ciriaco, d'Ancona, 1391–1452—Correspondence.
2. Ciriaco, d'Ancona, 1391–1452—Journeys.
3. Archaeologists—Italy—Correspondence.
4. Classical antiquities—Early works to 1880.
5. Voyages and travels—Early works to 1880.
6. Classicists—Italy—Correspondence.
I. Bodnar, Edward W.   II. Foss, Clive.   III. Title.   IV. Series.
CC115.C57A4 2003
938'.007'202—dc21   [B]   2003051107

Contents

᭖᭡᭞᭡᭖

Introduction   ix

Map   xxiv

Illustrations   xxvi

December 1443 to 4 May 1444:
Ascoli Piceno to Foglia Nuova

1. To Emperor John VIII Palaiologos, after
   26 February 1444, off Euboea   3

2. To Cardinal Giuliano Cesarini, 3 December 1443,
   Ragusa   9

3. To Andreolo Giustiniani-Banca, 29 March 1444,
   Chios   15

4. To Andreolo, 2 April 1444, Foglia Nuova   21

5. To Andreolo, 27 March 1444, Manisa   25

6. To Andreolo, 24 April 1444, Foglia Nuova   25

7. To Andreolo, 4 May 1444, Foglia Nuova   31

22 May to 21 July 1444:
Adrianople and Constantinople

8. To Andreolo, 22 May 1444, Adrianople   35

9, 9a, 9b1. To ?Andreolo, 12 June 1444, Adrianople   37

9b2. To Andreolo, 18 June 1444, Adrianople   45

10. To ?John Hunyadi, 12 June 1444, Adrianople   49

11. To ?John Hunyadi, 24 June 1444, Galata/Pera   51

12. To ?Andreolo, 19 July 1444, Constantinople   53

13. To Andreolo, 21 July 1444, Constantinople   59

25 July 1444 to 25 February 1445:
The Propontis and Northern Aegean

Diary I: Travels in the Propontis, 25 July to
12 August 1444 (including letter 14)   61

14. To Raffaele Castiglione, 12 August 1444, Perinthus   83

15. To Andreolo, 27 August 1444, ?Constantinople   85

16. To Giuliano Cesarini, 12 and 19 September 1444,
Constantinople   87

Diary II: Travels in the Northern Aegean,
20 September 1444 to January 1445
(including letters 17 and 18)   91

17. To George Scholarios, 29 September 1444, Imbros   95

18. To an unknown addressee, 29 September 1444,
Imbros   99

19. To Giovanni Pedemontano, January 1445, Ainos   141

20. To Boruele Grimaldi, 19 January 1445, Ainos   145

21. To Andreolo, 25 February 1445, Lemnos   145

April to December 1445: The Cyclades and Crete

22. To Andreolo, 4 April 1445, Mykonos   149

Diary III: Travels in the Cyclades, April 1445   151

23. To Niccolò Zancarolo, 5 July 1445, Cydonia, Crete   179

24. To ?Andreolo, 15 July 1445, Cydonia   183

Diary IV: Travels in Crete, July to October 1445
(including letters 25 and 26)   187

25. To Melchiore Bandino, 12 August 1445, Candia, Crete   193

26. To M. Lepomagno, ?October 1445, Candia   197

27. To Andreolo, 7 November 1445, Candia   207

28. To Andreolo, December 1445, Paros   209

13 January to 8 April 1446:
Chios, Miletus, Lesbos, Foglia Nuova

29. To Andreolo, after 13 January 1446, Chios   213

30. To Andreolo, after 1 February 1446, ?Miletus   217

31. From Andreolo to Buonaccorso Grimani,
    12 February 1446, Chios   227

32. To Andreolo, 2 March 1446, Khardamyla, Chios   229

33. To Andreolo, 6 March 1446, Kalloni, Lesbos   235

34. To Andreolo, 13 March 1446, Mytilene, Lesbos   237

35. To Andreolo, 8 April 1446, Foglia Nuova   239

20 April to August 1446:
Manisa, Foglia Nuova, Galata/Pera

36. To Andreolo, 20 April 1446, Manisa   247

37. To Andreolo, 11 May 1446, Foglia Nuova   251

38. To Franzesco di Drapieri, 15 August 1446,
    Galata/Pera   253

39. To Baldassarre Maruffo, after 21 August 1446,
    ?Galata/Pera   257

13 February to 18 May 1447: Chios and Environs

40. To Andreolo, 13 February 1447, Foglia Nuova   275

41. To Andreolo, 20 February 1447, Foglia Nuova   285

42. To Andreolo, 22 February 1447, Foglia Nuova   287

43. To Andreolo, 16 April 1447, Homerica, Chios   289

44. To Cyriac in Chios from Domenico Grimani,
    20 May 1447, Rhodes   293

45. To Andreolo, 28 May 1447, Chios   295

30 July 1447 to October 1448:
The Peloponnesus, Epirus

Diary V: Travels in the Peloponnesus, 30 July 1447 to
17 April 1448   299

46. Diary fragment: Account of a royal hunt,
8–13 September 1448, Arta in Epirus   343

47. To Niccolò Ansalone from Pasquale Sorgo,
11 September 1448, copied by Cyriac in Arta   349

48. Diary fragment: Dodona and Rhogous,
18 October 1448, Arta   349

49. To Egidio of Megara, after 19 October 1448, Arta   355

24 June to 8 July 1449: Return to Italy

50. To Roberto Valturio, 24 June 1449, Ravenna   359

51. To Roberto Valturio, after 24 June 1449, Ravenna   361

52. On Donatello's statue of Gattamelata, ?June 1449,
Padua   363

53. In praise of Rogier van der Weyden, 8 July 1449,
Ferrara   365

Biographical Notes 371

Note on the Texts 379

Notes to the Text 383

Notes to the Translation 403

Bibliography 439

Index 441

Introduction

✷✺✺✷

Cyriac of Ancona (1391–1452)[1] was the most enterprising and prolific recorder of Greek and Roman antiquities, particularly inscriptions, in the fifteenth century, and the general accuracy of his records entitles him to be called the founding father of modern classical archeology. Raised and educated to be a merchant, he became, like most of the early humanists, a born-again convert, so to speak, to the revived interest in ancient Greek and Roman culture that we call the Renaissance. But unlike such humanists as Francesco Filelfo, Leonardo Bruni and Poggio Bracciolini, with whom he was well acquainted, his conversion came about, not only through the rediscovery of classical manuscripts, but especially by his continued personal encounter, during his voyages aboard merchant ships that did business in the Levant, with the decaying physical remains of classical antiquity that littered both the Italian landscape and the islands and mainland of Greece and Asia Minor. From these travels, undertaken increasingly to serve his antiquarian rather than mercantile interests, came his diaries and letters, which he filled with accounts of his wanderings. These verbal descriptions were often illustrated with amateurish drawings of the temples and other buildings, statues and city walls he had seen, many of which today either no longer exist or survive only in a far more deteriorated state.

Perhaps his most widely known contributions to classical research are his copies of about a thousand Latin and Greek inscriptions, many of which have disappeared between his time and ours, copies made on the spot, under whatever conditions he found them in at the time he visited the site (e.g., worn and weathered, broken, some embedded in later walls, even upside down, partially obscured by later buildings), at whatever time of day he happened

to be there, and, of course, without the aid of modern "squeezes" or photography.

We now know the exact day he was born, 31 July 1391, of a patrician mercantile family in Ancona, and that he lost his father Filippo when he was six years old, shortly after the family had suffered financial ruin caused by three shipwrecks and two pirate raids. His mother Masiella (née Selvatico), although reduced to poverty, raised him and his two siblings, Cincio and Nicolosa, and "by working day and night, did whatever was possible to educate them in good manners and letters."[2]

Already as a teenage apprentice Cyriac proved to be accomplished in business, managing the home office of an importer-exporter in Ancona. Before he was thirty he had run the finances of an ambitious project of the city's papal governor, Cardinal Gabriele Condulmer (the future Pope Eugene IV), to restore the city's ancient harbor.

At the entrance to that harbor there stands even today a commemorative arch placed there by the Roman Emperor Trajan, whose inscriptions can still be read, even though all the bronze letters have long since been pried away. It was this arch that sparked his interest in the physical remains of classical antiquity, and in particular, in ancient inscriptions, which he recognized as historical documents contemporary with the events and persons of antiquity. Since these monuments and inscriptions had deteriorated — owing, as he often complained, to the ravages of time and the neglect of later inhabitants — he saw it as his calling to record their current state and to lobby with local authorities for their preservation and protection from further despoiling.

His travels began early, when he was nine years old. His grandfather and namesake, Cyriac Selvatico, took him on extended journeys in Italy, first to the Veneto, then, for a year and a half, to various cities in the Kingdom of Naples. After his apprenticeship in Ancona and before the harbor project, he passed over further op-

portunities at home and signed on as a clerk in a relative's ship because, as he said, he "wanted to see the world." In this, the first of his travels to the Levant, he did see Crete, Alexandria in Egypt, some of the Greek islands, as well as some sites of the ancient Greek settlements on the Ionic (western) coast of Asia Minor and in Sicily. Later he would be absent from Ancona for four years (1427–1431) as the agent for a Venetian relative's businesses abroad, sailing on commercial trading ships that made the rounds of ports in the eastern Mediterranean, including Damascus, Cyprus, Constantinople, Adrianople (or Edirne, the Turkish European capital in Thrace), and Gallipoli, where in 1431 he learned that his friend and former employer from the harbor renovation project, Cardinal Gabriele Condulmer, had been elected pope with the name Eugene IV.

All this time he was gaining experience, not only in trade, but also in politics, governance, and diplomacy. Early on, he was chosen to be one of six *anziani* or "elders" who governed the city of Ancona, and he was appointed to the senate although he was below the minimum age at the time. While passing through Cyprus, he paused for a month to govern the city of Famagusta in the absence of its *podestà*,[3] making decisions based on Roman Law. Later, in 1440, he was chosen as one of six *regolatori* to renegotiate a commercial treaty with Ancona's friendly rival, the free city of Ragusa (modern Dubrovnik) across the Adriatic from Ancona.

In Adrianople he witnessed the pageantry of the sultan's court and the misery of thousands of Greek prisoners of war whom the Turks had captured and enslaved when they took Thessalonica in 1431. This empathy did not stop him from buying some of the spoils, including one of those prisoners, a girl from Epirus, whom he sent home to serve his mother. Out of this experience came an ambitious plan that he rushed back to Rome to urge upon the new pope shortly after Eugene's election, a two-pronged initiative to (1) convoke a council of the Church that would effect a reunion of the

Greek Orthodox and Roman Catholic Churches, healing a schism that went back to the tenth century; and (2) to proclaim a crusade whose purpose would be to relieve the pressure on Constantinople by driving the Turks out of European Thrace.[4] Eugene did both eventually, convoking the council of Ferrara-Florence in 1437 and proclaiming a crusade in January 1443.

It is this complex web of interests and skills—antiquarian, political, religious, and commercial—that runs through the letters and diaries of 1443 to 1449, the content of the present volume. At one moment he is measuring the then-deteriorating, now almost completely vanished temple of Hadrian in Cyzicus or marveling at the mammoth temples of Ephesus and Didyma in Asia Minor, all the while lamenting the ruined state of these monuments of the past; at another, he is listening in on the gossip in Adrianople about negotiations going on between Sultan Murad II and representatives of young King Ladislas II of Poland and Hungary, leader of the allied crusader army that was to descend from Hungary, fight its way through the Balkans, and confront the Turkish army on the European side of the Bosporus, while a papal fleet was to prevent the bulk of the Turkish army from crossing over from Asia to Europe. Even after the disastrous defeat in November 1444 of the crusader army at Varna by a vastly superior force of Turks, who had gotten across the Bosporus despite the papal fleet, he continues to keep track of the Hungarian general John Hunyadi's attempts, after reconstituting his army, to resume his offensive against the Turks, until his final defeat at the second battle of Kosovo in the fall of 1448, just a few months before Cyriac's return to Italy.

Yet he is still the merchant during this, the last of his journeys through the Levant, dealing, at least occasionally, in antiquities—shopping for manuscripts, ancient gems, coins and the occasional bit of sculpture, rummaging through the libraries of the monasteries on Mount Athos for old manuscripts and buying some of

them. He is a kind of naval hitchhiker now, catching rides on the merchant ships of Venice and Genoa, carrying in his knapsack personally-owned manuscripts of Pliny's *Natural History*, Thucydides, and the ancient geographers Ptolemy, Pomponius Mela and Strabo. These he reads and annotates to keep himself busy while waiting for a ship to carry him to his next destination. Also in that copious bag are his precious notebooks, ever growing in number, in which he records what he has just seen in his travels, along with copies of the ancient inscriptions he finds on these sites, often illustrating them in his own untutored hand.

The travels documented in this book draw to a conclusion on the mainland of Greece, where he spends the fall of 1447 visiting ancient sites in Messenia, the Tainaron peninsula, and Laconia; the winter of 1447–1448 in and around ancient Sparta and Mistra, the Byzantine capitol of the Morea (the Peloponnese), where his host, Constantine, the lord of the Morea, is soon to be crowned the (last) emperor of Byzantium on the death of his brother John VIII. In the spring of 1448 he is in Acrocorinth. All this is recorded in the only portion of his diaries that has survived in his own hand, identified in 1910 by the great Remigio Sabbadini in the Ambrosian library of Milan.[5]

The fall of 1448 finds him visiting his friend, Carlo II Tocco, lord of Arta in Acarnania, in northwest Greece, who sadly dies during Cyriac's visit. We know from a letter of Francesco Filelfo that by the beginning of winter 1448–1449 he is back on Italian soil, in Venice. Two letters to Roberto Valturio in late June locate him in Ravenna; shortly afterwards he is in Padua composing an inscription for Donatello's equestrian statue of Gattamelata; and on 8 July 1449 he is in Ferrara admiring a diptych by Rogier van der Weyden proudly shown him by Duke Leonello d'Este.

Records in Genoa dated 31 August 1449 confirm that Cyriac's request for a safe-conduct to travel to the west and south was granted, but whether he actually ever traveled to Spain, as some

have thought, we do not know. The manuscripts preserve a few other writings of his that might be assigned to this period, but they are not included in this volume because they cannot be securely dated.

From this point on we lose sight of Cyriac. The only document is an isolated note in one manuscript, that he died in Cremona in 1452, a year before the fall of Constantinople, an event marking the end of the Roman Empire in the East and sealing the doom of the short-lived reunion of the Eastern and Western Churches.[6]

A word must be said about Cyriac's much-maligned, undeniably difficult, and sometimes pretentious Latin. Although the *Vita Kyriaci* of Scalamonti leaves little room in his life for formal schooling—a year and a half as a boy while traveling with his grandfather in the kingdom of Naples (*Vita*, §11) and half a year in Ancona reading Virgil with a private tutor (§53)—it is clear from a careful reading of the texts in this volume that, however idiosyncratic his style of writing, he certainly knew the rudiments of grammar. His sentences, often extraordinarily complex, almost always construe (and when they do not, the flaws can usually be laid at the door of copyists, to judge from the few autograph texts that have survived); and he had at his fingertips a much more extensive vocabulary than is commonly thought.[7]

Cyriac's religious language is syncretistic—semi-pagan, semi-Christian, in the manner of the Renaissance. A Christian and an ardent supporter of the papacy, he is equally at home in a Greek Orthodox church, especially after the reunion of 1439: for example, on August 15th, 1446, the Marian feast of the Assumption in the Latin church and of the Dormition (her "Falling Asleep") in the Greek, he attends both the Byzantine liturgy in Constantinople and the Latin-rite Mass in the Genoese colony of Galata/Pera across the Golden Horn. But his language is syncretistic. The deity or tutelary spirit to whom he prays at the beginning of his journeys is Mercury, the god of merchants; and Mercury's day,

Wednesday, is Cyriac's special day. He is devoted to the Muses and the Nymphs, whom he mixes together, and especially to his protective water nymph, Cymodocea (in Greek, "wave-receiver"), who in one letter rescues a dinghy from disaster by turning it into a nymph, a concept borrowed from Book IX of Vergil's *Aeneid*. In another letter his intention to sail from Chios to the island of Lesbos is at first frustrated by the nymphs of Chios, who cause contrary winds because they want to keep him there so he can discover an interesting ancient temple on the northern coast of Chios. Only then are the nymphs of Lesbos allowed to receive him into their island. Finally, he consistently refers to the incarnate Christ as *Jupiter humanatus* (Jove incarnate).

His manner of dating his letters and the entries in his diaries conforms to the ancient Roman way: e.g., *pridie Kalendas Decembris* means the day before the Kalends (1st) of December, i.e., November 30th. In syncretistic language similar to that of English and Italian, he calls Sunday *dies Kyriaceus* (equivalent to the Latin *dies dominica* "the day of the Lord"); Monday, *dies Lunae*, is Diana's day, as goddess of the moon (Italian, *lunedì*); Tuesday is Mars' day (Latin *dies Martis*, Italian *martedì*); Wednesday *dies Mercurii*, Mercury's day (Italian *mercoledì*); Thursday *dies Iovis*, Jupiter's day (Italian *giovedì*); Friday *dies Veneris*, Venus' day (Italian *venerdì*); Saturday *dies Saturni*, Saturn's day. It is important for dating his letters and the entries in his diaries that, although he does not always give the year, he does name the date and the day of the week, from which the year can usually be inferred.

The texts of most of the inscriptions that Cyriac copied in the course of his travels, including those that no longer exist, have found their way, through the medium of epigraphical manuscripts of the late fifteenth century, into the great modern collections of classical inscriptions: the *Corpus Inscriptionum Latinarum* and *Inscriptiones Christianae* and their Greek counterparts, the *Corpus Inscriptionum Graecarum* and the *Inscriptiones Graecae*, as well as

other, more specialized collections. It is through the authors and editors of those volumes, especially Theodor Mommsen and Giovanni Battista de' Rossi, that we know of the existence and whereabouts of the manuscripts that preserve Cyriac's letters and fragmentary excerpts from his diaries.

The great classical scholar Theodor Mommsen compared the remains of Cyriac's once-voluminous notebooks and correspondence to the Sibyl's scattered leaves. Only twenty folios of his journals (Diary V in this collection) and comparatively few of his letters and presentation pieces actually survive in his own hand. Fortunately, however, from the mid-1460s, scribes and scholars began excerpting inscriptions, drawings, letters and descriptive passages from his notebooks to satisfy their avid interest in everything connected with the *realia* of classical antiquity — an interest that Cyriac himself had helped to awaken.[8]

From the point of view of written evidence, Cyriac's career falls unevenly into three distinct parts. The first consists of the forty-five years from Cyriac's birth to 1435, covered by Francesco Scalamonti's *Vita Kyriaci Anconitani* and supplemented by only a very few letters.[9] The second part, the "middle years" (1435–1443), is represented by two extensive excerpts from his travel diaries that were printed in the seventeenth and eighteenth centuries from now-lost manuscripts, as well as a significant number of letters. The first of these diaries, printed around 1660, recounts a journey through Dalmatia and mainland Greece beginning in November 1435 and ending back in the Veneto in August 1436, followed by several entries relating to the Peloponnesus and the neighboring islands of Cythera and Zante, dated June to September 1437.[10] The second printed diary recounts journeys through Tuscany and Liguria, radiating out from Florence, then north to Milan and east to the Veneto, with many stops along the way, from August 1442

to March 1443.[11] Both diaries include drafts of numerous letters, usually with dates and places.

For the years between September 1437 and August 1442, because he was either in Ancona engaged in official business or at the Council of Ferrara-Florence as an interested observer and, one supposes, occasional translator, there are no extant diaries, and only a few letters.

It is the third and last period of Cyriac's life, his final years from 1443 to 1452, that is documented in this volume. It begins with his departure in October 1443 from Italy for Ragusa (now Dubrovnik), whence in January 1444 he sets out on a journey to the Levant that will keep him in the eastern Mediterranean until the summer of 1449, a sojourn of a little more than five years. His itinerary, dictated by diplomatic as well as antiquarian purposes, will take him along Venetian and Genoese shipping routes to the mainland of Greece, the islands of the Aegean (especially Chios, the hub of the Genoese mercantile empire), Turkish-held Anatolia and Thrace, Mount Athos, Constantinople, the Cyclades and Crete.

From these last travels there survive 53 letters and brief diary excerpts, designated here by arabic numerals. Most, but not all, of them are addressed to Andreolo Giustiniani-Banca, a Genoese humanist residing in Chios. Woven in among them chronologically in this volume are five more extensive fragments of his travel diaries, designated by Roman numerals. These diary-fragments record: (I) visits to several sites on the Propontis (Perinthus, Erdek, and the site of ancient Cyzicus), setting out from Constantinople on 25 July 1444 and returning to the Byzantine capital in early September; (II) visits to many of the islands and coastal cities of the northern Aegean, starting out from Constantinople on 20 September 1444, stopping at the island of Proconnesus in the Propontis, and, after passing through the Dardanelles, visiting

the islands of Imbros, Samothrace and Thasos, the neighboring coastal cities of Ainos and Maroneia, as well as several monasteries on Mount Athos, and breaking off in January 1445 during a visit to Ainos;[12] (iii) a tour in April 1445 of the Cycladic islands, arriving at Mykonos from Chios on 4 April, proceeding from Mykonos to Delos, then sailing on to Naxos, Paros and Andros, and eventually back to Chios.[13] Less generous excerpts and letters survive from (iv), the Cretan diary of July to October 1445;[14] and finally there is the well-known fragment (v), in Cyriac's own hand, of the Peloponnesian journal composed in the winter and spring of 1448–49, which gives us the best evidence of what Cyriac's *commentaria* originally looked like — a mixture of narrative and descriptive texts interspersed with drawings, Greek and Latin inscriptions, and occasional brief literary *testimonia* pertinent to the location just described.[15]

The late Charles Mitchell and I worked together, on and off, for over 35 years on the corpus of Cyriac's letters, diaries and opuscula. Together we published the texts of the Propontic and Aegean Diaries in 1976, re-published here under a slightly different format with the permission of the American Philosophical Society. With regard to the letters, it was Kenneth Setton who alerted me to the careful transcriptions by the late James Morton Paton of the letters in **Fn8**, the difficult-to-read manuscript in which the majority of the letters in this volume are preserved, and of a few other manuscripts containing some of the diary fragments and related letters. With permission of the Paton family and the Houghton Library, where his papers are kept, I copied these transcriptions and compared them with the manuscripts, all of which I have seen. I am deeply grateful to the librarians and keepers of manuscript collections in the various libraries in Italy, Germany, and England for allowing me to study them first hand and to have them photographed.

Clive Foss is the sole translator of all the inscriptions that appear in this volume. The translations of all the letters and diaries are mine, with the invaluable assistance of Professor Foss, who voluntarily vetted my translations with great care and a heavy investment of his time, comparing them with the difficult and complex Latin texts and catching mistakes and omissions that might otherwise have gone unnoticed.

The poems in Cyriac's regional Italian were both edited and translated by Nelia Saxby. I am grateful also to Dennis J. McAuliffe for his initial assistance with the poems and in initiating contact with Prof. Saxby.

The Penrose Fund of the American Philosophical Society enabled me to examine Ciriacan manuscripts in twenty-two Italian libraries (Summer, 1961). The Gennadeion Fellowship of the American School of Classical Studies in Athens (1963–1964) enabled me to see many of the ruins and extant inscriptions reported by Cyriac in mainland Greece, Turkey, and on the Greek islands. A Senior Fellowship at Harvard University's Dumbarton Oaks Center for Byzantine Studies (1975) gave me the opportunity to make preliminary translations of most of the letters. The Translations Program of the National Endowment for the Humanities (1979–1980) enabled me to do the research for an extensive commentary, which remains unpublished, on the letters in this book. The American Council of Learned Societies provided travel grants in 1971 and 1983 which subsidized summer travel to England and to the Cyriacan sites in Croatia.

I owe a deep debt of gratitude to the late Benjamin D. Meritt, the late Antony E. Raubitschek, and the late Homer Thompson, for sponsoring me as a Summer Visitor at the American School of Classical Studies in Athens during the course of thirteen summers between 1958 and 1976; to the Maryland Province of the Society of Jesus and the Jesuit communities at the Novitiate of St. Isaac Jogues and at Georgetown University, for financial and moral sup-

port over many decades, including a year's leave of absence in 1978–79 to work on the letters of Cyriac; to Georgetown University, for sabbatical leaves in 1974–75, 1983–84, and 1989–90.

This book is dedicated to the memory of the late Charles Mitchell, the late Kenneth M. Setton, and the late James Morton Paton.

NOTES

1. Called Cyriacus in Latin, German, and sometimes in English; Cyriaque in French; and Ciriaco de' Pizzecolli in Italian. He usually signed himself as Kyriacus Anconitanus de Picenicollibus (abbreviated to K.A.P.) or, occasionally in his later years, in Greek as Κυριακός ὁ ἐξ Ἀγκῶνος.

2. This information is now available to us through the discovery by Filippo di Benedetto in ms. 534/8 in the Biblioteca Comunale of Treviso of a copy of the first two-thirds of the *Vita Kyriaci Anconitani* of Scalamonti made in 1590 by Dr. Giovanni Antonio Oliva from ms. I-138 of the Biblioteca Capitolare of Treviso, before the older manuscript had lost fol. 21 (the beginning of Scalamonti's narrative). See F. di Benedetto, "Il punto su alcune questioni riguardanti Ciriaco," in *Atti*, pp. 18–21 and 38n. In their edition of Scalamonti's *Vita Kyriaci*, Mitchell and Bodnar, p. 145, notes 5 and 6, infer some of this information from the ensuing context of the older manuscript, but not the exact day of Cyriac's birth or the name of his brother or the date and circumstances of his father's misfortune and death.

3. Or chief magistrate. In many towns of Italy, the *podestà* was the chief judicial officer of the town, usually a doctor of laws and a non-native of the town who was brought in by the civic administration for a six-month term of office. In other cities and towns, the *podestà* was more like a mayor, often appointed by the town's overlord.

4. For the political nature of these journeys see Setton, 2: 70–72, ch. 3, passim, and Bodnar 1988.

5. Several other documents written in Cyriac's own hand have survived, but they are either letters or selected specimens of his work prepared for presentation to potential sponsors.

6. The elaborate hypothesis of Jacobs, which I once favored, that in 1453 Cyriac was in the camp of Mehmed II during the siege of Constantinople, tutoring him in the great writings of the West and entering the vanquished city with the Conqueror, has been thoroughly refuted, and can no longer be accepted. See Raby (q.v.) for a summary and refutation of Jacobs' arguments.

7. For a careful study of Cyriac's Latin see Piergiorgio Parroni, "Il latino di Ciriaco," in *Atti*, pp. 269–289.

8. The comparison to the Sibyl's leaves is in *CIL* V, 322. Through the tireless investigations of Mommsen, de Rossi, Sabbadini, Ziebarth, Kristeller, and others, we do know what ultimately happened to these fragments and where they are now. What we do not know — so far — is where the complete, intact notebooks of Cyriac were between the time of his death in 1452 and the first appearance of fragmentary excerpts in the mid-1460s.

9. Edited by Charles Mitchell and Edward W. Bodnar in 1996 in a publication referred to in this volume as "Scalamonti" (see Notes to the Translation).

10. Because this edition lacks a title page, the editor, Carlo Moroni (the librarian of the Barberini collection in Rome), is not named and the date and place of publication (Rome, ca. 1660) have to be inferred from the extant correspondence. It is usually referred to by the title of its initial section, *Epigrammata reperta per Illyricum a Cyriaco Anconitano*. See Bodnar 1960a, pp. 78–87, for a summary of the contents of the diary, with generous excerpts, and ibid., pp. 23–49; for other manuscripts containing long excerpts from this diary and for bibliographical details, ibid., pp. 87–95.

11. The *Commentariorum Cyriaci Anconitani nova fragmenta notis illustrata*, edited by Annibale Olivieri degli Abbati (Pesaro 1763), referred to as *Nova Fragmenta* in this volume. For a discussion of the lost manuscript

from which this edition was made, see Olivieri's prefatory remarks *erudito lectori*, pp. 7–9.

12. On the drawings see especially Ashmole 1956 and 1957 and Lehmann 1973. See now Andrea Barattolo, "Ciriaco de' Pizzecolli e il tempio di 'Proserpina' a Cizico: per una nuova lettura della descrizione dell'Anconitano," in *Atti*, pp. 103–140, and Michele Polverari, "Ciriaco a Samotracia," in *Atti*, pp. 141–144.

13. See Bodnar 1998.

14. First published in Cornelius, I: 37, 38, from **VL5** and **VL7**.

15. See Sabbadini 1910, 1933.

Padua
Ferrara
Ravenna
Rimini
Florence
Arezzo
Ancona
Ascoli
Rome
Ragusa
Naples
Dodona
Arta in Acarnania
Nicopolis

Adriatic Sea

Ionian Sea

MEDITERRANEAN

0   100   200 miles

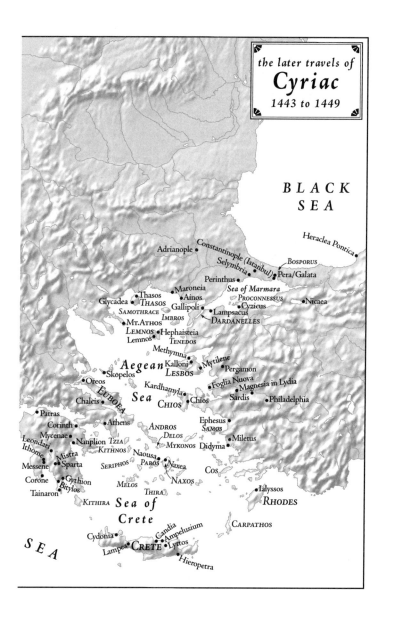

the later travels of
Cyriac
1443 to 1449

BLACK
SEA

Heraclea Pontica

Adrianople
Constantinople (Istanbul)
Selymbria
BOSPORUS
Pera/Galata
Perinthus
Sea of Marmara
PROCONNESSUS
Nicaea
Maroneia
Ainos
Cyzicus
Thasos
THASOS
Gallipoli
Lampsacus
Glycadea
SAMOTHRACE
IMBROS
DARDANELLES
Mt.ATHOS
LEMNOS
Hephaisteia
Lemnos
TENEDOS
Methymna
Aegean
Kalloni
Mytilene
Skopelos
LESBOS
Pergamon
Oreos
Kardhamyla
Foglia Nuova
Magnesia in Lydia
Chalcis
EUBOEA
Sea
CHIOS
Chios
Sardis
Philadelphia
Patras
Athens
Ephesus
Corinth
ANDROS
SAMOS
Mycenae
DELOS
Leondari
Nauplion
Tzia
MYKONOS
Miletus
Ithome
KITHNOS
Naousa
Didyma
Mistra
SERIPHOS
PAROS
Naxea
Messene
Sparta
Cos
Corone
Gythion
MELOS
NAXOS
Tainaron
Bitylos
THIRA
Ialyssos
KITHIRA
Sea of
RHODES
Crete
CARPATHOS
Cydonia
Candia
Ampelusium
Lampea
CRETE
Lyrtos
SEA
Hieropetra

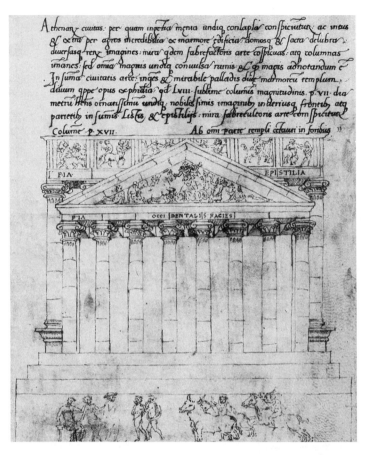

PLATE I. *Athens, the Parthenon (Letter 3, 5–10). Copy by Giuliano da Sangallo of Cyriac's drawing: the west façade, Doric columns with Composite capitals; six metopes from the south side superimposed. Belows, parts of the Panathenaic frieze; above, descriptive text. Vb2, fol. 28v.*

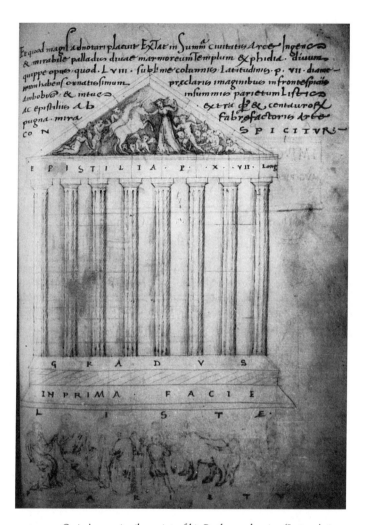

PLATE II. *Cyriac's copy, in silverpoint, of his Parthenon drawing (Letter 3), in a presentation sample of his work made for Pietro Donato, bishop of Padua. Columns are properly Doric, but proportions are not classical; the pedimental sculpture is transformed fancifully. B1, fol. 85r.*

PLATE III. *Constantinople (Letters 12-16 and 38–39). Copies by Giuliano da Sangallo of Cyriac's drawings, showing the interior and exterior of Hagia Sofia, and a fanciful drawing of the nymph Cymodocea (see Letter 4). Vb2, fol. 28r.*

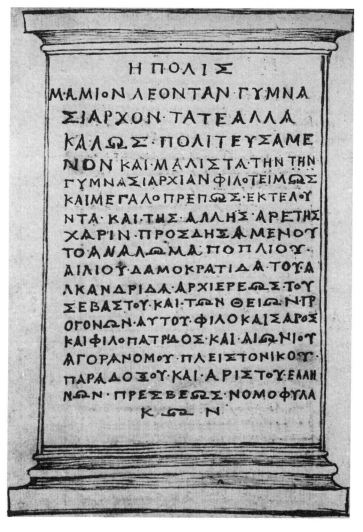

PLATE IV. *Greek inscription recorded by Cyriac in the ruins of ancient Sparta (Diary V, 5). Ma5, fol. 103v.*

PLATE V. *Cyriac's drawing of an ancient sculpted and inscribed sarcophagus used to adorn the altar of a church in the village of Kairia, on the Tainaron peninsula in the Peloponnese (Diary V, 26). Ma5, fol. 107r.*

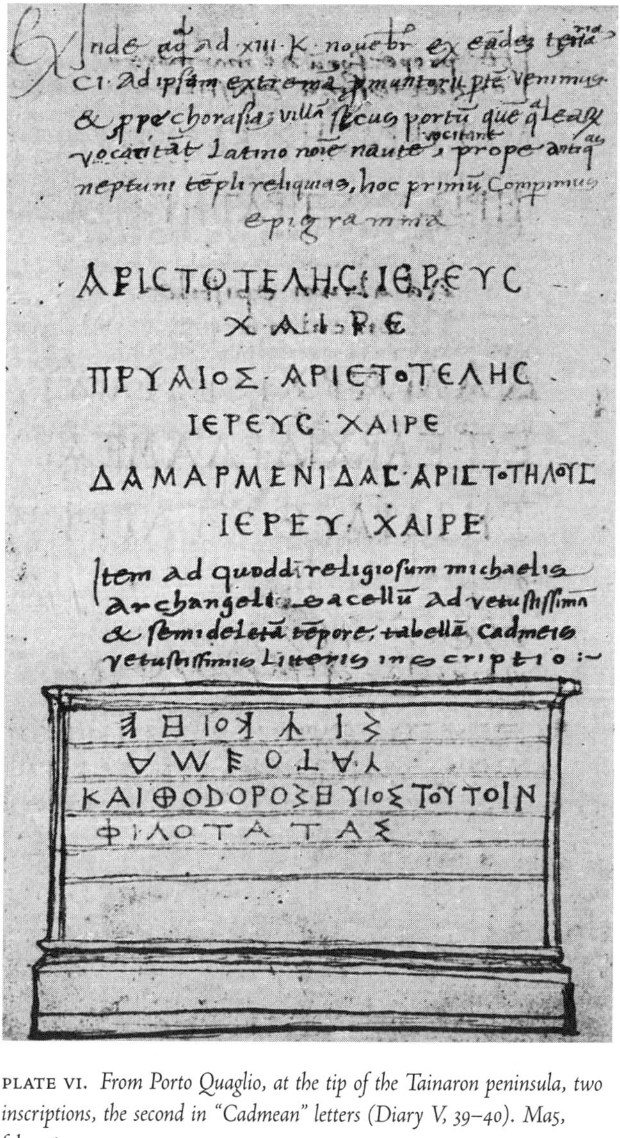

Inde eo ad xiii. K. nouebr ex eade̅s ter̅ia
ci. Ad ip̅s̅am extre̅m̅a̅ R̅m̅an̅t̅o̅r̅ui ̅pte venimus:
& ppe chorasias villa̅ s̅ecu̅s portu̅ que q̅ leax
vocat̅ iat latino noi̅e naute̅ prope antiq̅
neptuni te̅pl̅i reliquias, hoc primu̅ compimus
epigramma

ΑΡΙϹΤΟΤΕΛΗϹ ΙΕΡΕΥϹ
Χ ΑΙ Ρ Ε

ΠΡΥΛΙΟϹ · ΑΡΙϹΤΟΤΕΛΗϹ ·
ΙΕΡΕΥϹ · ΧΑΙΡΕ

ΔΑΜΑΡΜΕΝΙΔΑϹ · ΑΡΙϹΤΟΤΗΛΟΥϹ
ΙΕΡΕΥ · ΧΑΙΡΕ

Item ad quodd̅ religiosum michaelis
archangeli sacellu̅ ad vetustissim̅a
& semideleta̅ te̅pore, tabella̅ cadmeis
vetustissimis Litteris inscripti o :~

ΚΑΙΘΟΔΟΡΟϹ Η ΥΙΟϹ ΤΟΥ ΤΟΙΝ
ΦΙΛΟΤΑΤΑϹ

PLATE VI. *From Porto Quaglio, at the tip of the Tainaron peninsula, two inscriptions, the second in "Cadmean" letters (Diary V, 39–40). Ma5, fol. 116v.*

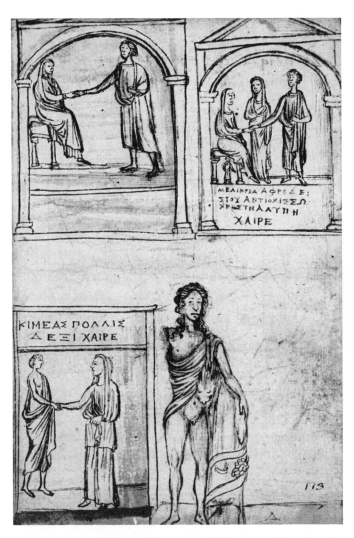

MEΛIKPEA AΦPOΔE:
ΣIOY ANTIOXIΣEΩ·
XPHΣTHΛΛΥΠΗ
XAIPE

KIMEAΣ ΠOΛΛIΣ
Δ E ΞI XAIPE

PLATE VII. *Cyriac's drawings of three funeral reliefs, two inscribed, and a sculpture in the round, seen at Nauplion in the Peloponnese (Diary V, 61–62). Ma5, fol. 113r.*

Apud eandem   Naupliam
arcem .   antiqua
in Lapidea   tabella

ΕΛΙΣΣΑ ΑΝΕΘΗΚΕ

ad alium Lapidem semifractum antique Cadmea
ue Litere :—

ΜΙΚΡΙΑΣ   ·   ΘΕΟΧΣΕΝ
ΙΣΧΡΟΝΟΣ ·   ΑΦΘΟΝΕΤ

PLATE VIII. *Drawing of a dedicatory relief and a partially preserved inscription in "Cadmean" letters, at the citadel of Nauplion (Diary V, 63–64). Ma5, fol. 114r.*

Ad alium antiquũ & semifractũ ab ipso Capite,
Lapidem doricis egregiis Litt. inscriptio.

ΤΑΣ·ΕΣ·ΤΟΝ·ΔΑΜΟΝ ΤΩΝ ΤΡΟΣΑΝΙΩΝ ΚΑΙ
ΤΑΣ ΕΙΣ ΠΡΟΤΕΡΟΝ Δ ΩΡΕΑΣ ΔΕΔΟΜΕΝΑΣ ΕΙΜΕΝ
ΑΥΤΩΙ ΔΕ ΔΟΣΘΑΙ ΑΥΤΩΙ ΚΑΙ ΕΜΠΡΥΤΑΝΙΩΙ ΣΙΤΗΣΙΝ
ΚΑΙ ΕΣ ΤΟΥΣ ΑΓΩΝΑΣ ΕΣ ΚΑΡΥΣΣΕΣΘΑΙ ΕΣ ΠΡΟΕΔΡΙΑΝ
ΑΥΤΟΝ ΚΑΙ ΕΚΓΟΝΟΥΣ ΕΜΠΡΟΣΘΑΙ ΔΙΕ ΤΟΝ ΙΑΡΗΤΩΝ
ΔΙΩ ΔΕ ΚΑ ΘΕΚΑ ΘΕΩΝ ΣΗΝΟΔΟΤΩΙ ΚΑΙ ΕΚΓΟΝΟΙΣ
ΠΟΛΛΑ ΚΑΙ ΑΓΑΘΑ Ο ΚΑΙ ΠΑΝ ΔΑΜΟΡΓΙΑ ΚΑΡΙΣΤΑΤΑΙ
ΚΑΙ ΕΙ ΤΙΝΟΣ ΚΑ ΑΛΛΟΥ ΔΕ Η ΤΑΙ ΤΟΥ ΔΑΜΟΥ ΤΟΥ ΤΡΟ
ΣΑΝΙΩΝ ΥΠΗΡΕΤΕΝ ΑΥΤΩΙ ΚΑΙ ΕΚΓΟΝΟΙΣ ΑΝ ΓΡΑ
ΤΑΙ Δ ΩΤΟ ΔΕ ΤΟ ΨΑΦΙΣΜΑ ΕΝ ΣΤΑΛΛΑΙ · ΟΙΝΑΙ
ΚΑΙ Σ ΩΣΑΙ ΕΣ ΤΟ ΙΑΡΟΝ ΤΟ ΑΠΟΛΛΩΝΟΣ ΤΟΥ ΘΕ
ΡΙΑΤΟΝ ΔΕ ΒΟΥΛΛΑΝ ΤΑ ΤΑΝ ΥΠΟΡΓΙΑΝ ΠΑΡΕΧΕΝ
ΤΙΜΑΝ ΕΙΓΕ ΠΡΟΕΣΤΑΙ ΕΙ ΒΟΥΛΑΣ ΔΑΜΕΑΣ ΑΡΚΦΙ
ΕΓΡΑΦΟ ΦΙΛΟΤΟ ΚΑΛΟ ΔΑΜΟΥ

Ad X Kal. apriliũ fausti resurrectionis humanati ipuis
die pmiũ cũ nauplium reuississem & p. rangam us
scribam Iohanne q: bendramen Amicissimos magna
cũ hilaritate peuissimus, & postridie si d delere
mycenas Ạrbis, ũ nra; ad die reliquũ extare uideř
desiderano, idem comitantib; plera q: primũ argua
in campo uidimus ueterũ Insignia monumenta. &
inter potiora, no nullas pulcherrima ũ imaginũ m
candenti ex marmore tabellas, olis iunonis exantiss.
templo ex Insignib; polycleti ut putandũ operibs, ad posteras
relligionis nře edes, a spicelis ornamento deductas
quas ad primaria & spectanhore ad stm, dirutũ lapidẽ
hoc Latinis quoq: Litteris antiquũ epigrama comperimus.

Q·CAECILIO·C·F·METELO
IMPERATORI·ITALICI
Q·VEI·ARGEIS·NEGOTIANTVR.

PLATE IX. *Cyriac's copy of a proxeny decree, seen in the Peloponnese at
?Troezen, and a Latin inscription still extant in the apse of a church in Merbaka
(Diary V, 67). Maş, fol. 114v.*

PLATE X. *Three grave reliefs seen by Cyriac embedded in the church of the Panaghia in Merbaka (Diary V, 67). Ma5, fol. 115r.*

LATER TRAVELS

1 Ad Ιωannem Palaeologum, divum augustum pium felicem Byzantianum Imperatorem, Kyriacus Anconitanus.

2   Posteaquam ex Italia, sanctissima illa peracta fidelium unione summa tui cum laude, concessisti, πολύαινε 'Ιωάννη βασιλεῦ, maiestatem felicissimam tuam Βyζantiana inclyta ipsa tua in regia revisere, multis eximiisque suadentibus meritis, desiderabam, excolendissime princeps. Verum etsi occiduas ad partes me conferre omnimode maluissem, ut, quod de more optabam, si quid hisdem nobilibus locis nostram ad diem vetustatis dignum extaret inspectaremus, non absque te primum viso tuisve felicibus auspiciis iter ipsum coeptare constitui.

[Ascoli Piceno, 14 September 1443]

3 Interea vero cum Idibus Septembribus exactis Alphonsus ille Hispanus et inclytus Ausoniae rex, inito cum pontifice Eugenio foedere, nostram in Picenam provinciam cum copiis adventasset et eam ecclesiae potiori ex parte deditam restituisset, dum Asculum premeret, ex Ancona patria ad eum una cum domino cardinale Firmano, eadem in provincia pontificia potestate legato, me quam avidissime contuli.

4   Ubi cum brevem hanc hisce vobis transmissam orationem suis coram principibus regiis in tentoriis habuissem, ac inde alia inter digna relatu de ingenti Pannonum in Turcas motu eximia cum car-

December 1443 to 4 May 1444
Ascoli Piceno to Foglia Nuova

: 1 :

To Emperor John VIII Palaiologos, shortly after 26 February [1444], off Euboea

To John Palaiologos, the divine, august, devout, successful Byzantine emperor, from Cyriac of Ancona. 1

After the most holy union of the faithful was achieved,[1] to your 2 great credit, and you left Italy, much-praised King John, I wanted, for many extraordinarily persuasive reasons, to visit your fortunate majesty in your famous palace in Byzantium, most worshipful prince. Indeed, although I had every desire to go to the west in order to see, as is my habit, whether any worthwhile antiquities have survived in these noble lands until our own day, I decided not to begin that journey without first visiting you and receiving your blessing.

[Ascoli Piceno, 14 September 1443]

Meanwhile, on the 14th of September, Alfonso, the renowned 3 Spanish king of [southern] Italy, having entered into a treaty with Pope Eugene, had entered our province of Picenum with his army and restored it for the most part to the church.[2] From my native Ancona I went to him most eagerly while he was besieging Ascoli, accompanied by the lord cardinal of Fermo, who was legate with papal authority in the same province.[3]

In the presence of his courtiers, I delivered the enclosed brief 4 address[4] in the royal tent and added, among other matters worth mentioning, a good bit more about the Hungarians' massive action

3

dinalis Sancti Angeli laude pleraque digna oratione relata fuissent,
summe desideranti gloriam principi pro viribus suadere conabar,
ut ad quiescendum Italiam et eum ipsum optimum patrem hac in
sanctissima expeditione favitandum nobilem intendere animum
maluisset. Suaserat et idipsum sibi Byζantianus ille Theodorus
Charistenus, egregius orator tuus, qui superioribus diebus ex eadem urbe regia tua hanc ob rem ipsam ad Venetos et occidentales
principes legatus tua providentia missus adierat.

5   Cui bonus ille rex mihique non alienum ab hac re animum os-
tentarat; quin et summo se desiderio rem ipsam affectare auxi-
liaque interim daturum classeque tibi opitulaturum pro posse et e
Baliaribus usque Insulis ex Ebyssaque pollicebatur.

[Ragusa, October 1443]

6   Ego praeterea, cum inde post Idus Octobres cessissem, et ob id ipsum et tui potissimum gratia Byζantium petens, Rhagusium, Illy-
ricam Epidauri coloniam, divertissem, continuo iisdem ipsis de rebus nuper ab inclyto Pannonum rege Ladislao in barbaros bene
gestis felices adventare nuntios video non exigua cum eiusdem
cardinalis et Coniati Iani fortissimi ducis laude, quorum certas vidimus Ragusaeorum ad ordinem epistolas et alias ad pontificem
ipsum et caeteros in Italia principes providentissime missas inspeximus.

7   Quibus et nos utique principibus hac ipsa de subitanea barbarorum invasione litteras plerasque ex Illyrico dedimus, ut ex iis denique bonis piisque coeptis rebus et tam laudatissime motis mo-
veant et se demum Itali praecellentissimi potentatus et heroes
clari: cohibeant denique illa saeva Latinorum invicem praelia et
detestanda bella nullos hercle triumphos habitura, pudeantque ex

against the Turks, with special praise for the cardinal of Sant'
Angelo. I tried with all my powers to persuade this prince, who
has a great appetite for glory, to focus his noble attention on the
pacification of Italy and the support of our excellent pope in this
most holy campaign.[5] He was also urged to the same end by Theodore Charystenos of Byzantium, your distinguished emissary,
who had arrived a few days before from your royal city, providen-
tially sent by you as your envoy on this very matter to the Venetians and the western leaders.

To him and to me that good king displayed an attitude not in-   5
disposed to this enterprise; indeed, he even said he felt strongly
drawn to it; and he promised that, meanwhile, he would provide
aid and would assist you as far as he could with a fleet from Ibiza
in the Balearic Islands.

[Ragusa, October 1443]

To go on, in the middle of October I departed for Byzantium on   6
this very mission primarily for your sake. Stopping off at Ragusa,
the Illyrian colony of Epidauros, I learned immediately that good
news had arrived about this very same matter, the recent successes
achieved against the barbarians[6] by Ladislas the illustrious king of
the Hungarians, including no small praise for the above mentioned cardinal and for that brave general, János Hunyadi. We saw
certain of their letters to the senate of Ragusa, and we examined
others addressed to the pope himself and, with great forethought,
to the other Italian rulers.

To these very same rulers I also wrote a number of letters from   7
Illyricum concerning this sudden descent upon the barbarians, to
the effect that the eminent potentates and illustrious heroes of Italy should at last take action after these good and holy beginnings
of a praiseworthy campaign: let them check the cruel fighting and
hateful warring of Latins among themselves, which are certain to

iis penitus ab externis Parthicae expeditionis trophaei palmam subripi. Quin etsi hos tandem aliqua movet pietatis imago, in tam truces Christicolum voratores animadvertendum curent.

8   Ego etenim cum inde ad coeptum peragendum iter cessissem, Raguseae civitatis principes et celsitudini tuae dicatissimi viri litteras fide dignas ad maiestatem tuam et illustres despotas fratres Theodorum et Constantinum dedere, ut ego vobis dicatissimus et tamdiu fidelissimus observator et vestrum apprime cupidissimus gloriae vos ipsos tam fideles, catholicos et Christianissimos principes ad hanc ipsam adversus barbareos hostes expeditionem favendam excitarem, et ut aiunt, calcaria currentibus addere summo studio solertiaque conarer.

[Patras. Corinth]

9   Et tandem cum ad Achaicam Peloponesiacamve Patrarum ad urbem venissem, ilico fratri tuo illustrissimo Constantino scripsi et hac ipsa utique de re quae digna visa sunt detexi; et cum inde Corinthum venissem, a Demetrio Axanio praefecto suo percepimus eum, nuper magnis undique collectis ex Peloponnesso copiis, una optimo cum Thoma germano ex Lacedaemonia Spartanave Misistrate ad Isthmon cum exercitu adventurum; ubi iterum longo murorum aggere restituto Isthmoque fatali rursus utique turritis moenibus vallato, exinde per Megaridem copias traducturum Achaiamque totam, Thebarum iam urbe nuper in deditionem recepta, Lebadeam Parnaseamque Dauliam sacram et Delphorum urbem singulis cohortibus invasurum et a barbaris praedigne liberaturum, optimo iuvante Deo.

result in no one's triumph; let them be ashamed that foreigners have snatched completely out of their hands the triumphant palm of an expedition against the Parthians. Furthermore, if they are moved at all by the faintest shadow of piety, they should take the pains to punish these cruel devourers of Christians.

When I left there to resume the journey I had begun, the city 8 of Ragusa's leading men, who are very devoted to your Highness, gave me trustworthy letters to your Majesty and to your brothers, the illustrious despots Theodore and Constantine, [with instructions] that, completely committed to you as I am and being a long-time faithful observer [of events] and primarily eager for your glory, I might stir you, faithful, catholic, and deeply Christian princes, to support this campaign against a barbaric foe, and that I should try earnestly and skillfully "to spur a willing horse," as they say.[7]

[Patras. Corinth]

At length I arrived at Patras, a city of Achaea in the Peloponnesus, 9 where I wrote immediately to your distinguished brother Constantine and disclosed what I thought he ought to know concerning this project. From there I went to Corinth, where I learned from Demetrios Asan, his deputy, that Constantine had recently gathered a large force from everywhere in the Peloponnesus and was about to march with his excellent brother, Thomas, from Lacedemonian Mistra to the Isthmus. There the long line of earthworks has been restored and the fateful Isthmus has again been fortified with turreted walls.[8] From there he intends to lead his entire force through the Megarid and all of Achaea, and, now that the city of Thebes has recently been received in surrender, to invade Lebadea, Parnassian Daulis and the sacred city of Delphi, sending one division to each, and, with the good Lord's help, to free them from the barbarians, a worthy task indeed.

[Chalcis. Oreos]

10 Ego sed enim interea cum Euripeam Chalcidiam insignem Euboeae civitatem advenissem, ut tute magis tuam versus regiam urbem navigarem, ad v Calendas Martias Euripeam triremem conscendens, Maphio Molino Veneto viro nobili navarcho, coepimus navigare, ipse quidem ut Aegeum ab infestis Cyothalanis pyratisque liberaret, ego vero ut ex itinere sacram Delon caeterasque sparsas per aequor Cycladas indagarem, et ex Chio denique tutiorem per navim regiam ipsam tuam Constantinopolim adventare curarem, optimo iuvante Deo nec non genio sanctissimo nostro favitante Mercurio.

11 Ex eadem trireme ex Orea, antiqua Euboicae insulae et vetustate deleta civitate, excolendissimae serenissimaeque regiae maiestati tuae dicatissimus Kyriacus Anconitanus.

: 2 :

1 Ad Cardinalem Sancti Angeli legatum Kyriacus Anconitanus.

2 Posteaquam e Florentina urbe ad tuam hanc piam felicemque legationem profectus es, optime Iuliane pater, saepe tuis de successibus optimis plura undique pergrata audivimus voce litterisque delata, et feliciores in dies de te angelos advolare videmus et meliora semper intelligimus allaturos, angelice et vere Iuliane atque Caesaree verendissime vir.

3 Equidem vero cum superioribus diebus Alphonsus ille Hispanus et inclytus Ausoniae rex, inito cum pontifice foedere, nostra in Picenam provinciam [...]¹

8

[Chalcis. Oreos]

Meanwhile, on 26 February, after visiting Chalcis, a noble city of   10
Euboea on the Euripus,[9] in order more safely to sail towards your
royal city, I boarded a trireme in the Euripus whose captain was a
fine Venetian named Maphio Molin, and we began to sail—he to
free the Aegean from pirates and the dangerous ?Catalans,[10] I to
investigate along the way sacred Delos and the other Cyclades
scattered over the sea; and finally, from Chios on a safer ship, with
almighty God's help and the favor of our most holy *genius* Mercury, to arrive at your royal [city of] Constantinople.

From the previously mentioned trireme off Oreos, an ancient   11
city of the island of Euboea which has been destroyed by the passage of time, Cyriac of Ancona, your worshipful and serene royal
majesty's dedicated servant.

∴ 2 ∴

To Cardinal Giuliano Cesarini, 3 December 1443, Ragusa

Cyriac of Ancona to the Cardinal Legate of Sant'Angelo.   1

Excellent father Giuliano, ever since you set out from the city   2
of Florence on this, your holy and auspicious mission, I have been
receiving frequent, most gratifying reports from every source, both
written and oral, about your very commendable successes. Day by
day these "angelic" messengers fly in to us, and we anticipate they
will bring increasingly better tidings concerning you, O angelic,
most reverend sir, true Julian that you are, most worthy Caesar.

For my part, when, a short while ago, Alfonso, that Spanish   3
King of [southern] Italy, after making a pact with the pope, [came
with his army] to our province of Piceno [...].[1]

4   Quin etsi hos tandem aliqua movet humanae pietatis imago, in tam truces Christicolum voratores ad nostrum imperium nostramque propagandam religionem te, pium et optimum patrem, hac tua in sanctissima conspiratione secundent, et ut pluries maiores nostri praeclarissime fecerant, insignes ex his triumphos ducere laudatissime curent.

5   Nec minus interea Ladislaum optimum ipsum Pannoniae regem tibi hac in tam piissima re optemperaturum videre, summe laudare atque attollere cogor, nec equidem iniuria eum ipsum pium et religiosissimum regem ad praedignam hanc in Teucros expeditionem exequendam magnum intendisse animum existimandum puto, quom et olim Romae Caesareo quoque tempore Sibyllinis fatalibus in libris compertum fuisse tradatur: numquam nisi a rege Parthos subiici posse. Teucrorum namque genus et Achaemenidum originem a Parthis duxisse notum satis est καὶ ἐκφανέστατον² πάντῃ.

6   Nec non fortissimum illum equitum magistrum et insignem peregrinae militiae ducem, Konyati Ianum, inclytam omnifariamque per laudem extollendum censui, qui perstrenua virtute sua suique florentissimi exercitus probitate tam modici temporis spacio, tot egregiis victoriis, tam saevi perniciosique almae religionis nostrae hostis inveteratam diu audaciam ita depresserat, ut quod paulo antea Murath Beg truculentissimi principis nomen undique Christicolis formidandum memorabatur, hodie tergiversatum, fugax, deiectum, peneque extinctum videatur habeaturque.

7   Laudandum utique magnopere duco Georgium ipsum pientissimum despoten, qui a tam violentissimo hoste Moesiae Servianae provinciae suae imperio pulsus, ob eam ipsam digne in pristinam potestatem redigendam tam provide solerterque hanc ipsam di-

Further, if these [Italian princes],[2] are moved at all by the faint- 4
est shadow of human loyalty [to take action] against these cruel
devourers of Christians, let them help you, excellent holy father, in
this, your holy alliance, toward the spread of our empire and religion; and let them see to it that they celebrate most laudably
[your] signal victories over them, as did our ancestors, most gloriously, on more than one occasion.

Likewise, I am equally compelled to observe, praise, and extol 5
greatly the fact that the excellent king of Hungary, Ladislas,[3] will
obey you in the most holy enterprise; indeed, for my part, I believe it would be unjust to suppose that this loyal and most devout
king has not applied his great spirit to the successful execution of
this most worthy campaign against the Turks, since tradition tells
us that, long ago at Rome, in the time of the Caesars, the fateful
books of the Sibyl revealed that the Parthians could be subjected
only by a king. For it is well known and altogether clear that the
Turks and Achaemenids take their origins from the Parthians.[4]

I also feel that I should heap all manner of praise on that coura- 6
geous cavalier and outstanding general of [our] foreign forces,
John Hunyadi. By his vigorous valor and the quality of his highly
effective army, in such a short space of time, with so many splendid victories, he has so subdued the long-ingrained arrogance of a
cruel and dangerous foe of our nurturing faith, that the name of
that savage prince Murad Bey, which, only a short while ago was
spoken in fear by Christians, is today seen and held to be [the
name of one who] turned back in abject flight, and on the brink of
annihilation.

I also feel strongly that I should praise the very dependable 7
Despot George [Branković], who, because he was driven from his
sovereignty over his province of Serbian Moesia by this most vio-
lent foe, and is determined to regain his own power over it, has
providently and skillfully devoted his own fortune to setting in

gnissimam expeditionem aere potissimum suo excitandam, parandam prosequendamque curavit.

8   Sed in primis et ante alios omnes probare laudareque constitui divinum illud Eugenii sanctissimi pontificis ingenium et admirabilem providentiam, qui tot tantosque inter celeberrimos patres te unum dignum et optimum atque angelicum hominem huic tam piae laboriosaeque et honorificentissimae rei praefecerat antistitem designatum benemeritumque pontificia potestate legatum, utque semper quibusque in rebus et ecclesiae Dei maximis et in illa potissimum tot externarum gentium compositione provide, constanter, aeque, pie magnanimiterque gessisse cognoverat.

9   At et quis tam expers humanae pietatis esset qui in tam profanum, invisum et penitus execrandum Teucrorum genus hunc ipsum pium, dignum opportunumque motum non summopere laudare, benedicere et praedicare potuisset? Equidem vero cum profanorum iisdem perniciosis in locis saepius fuerim et per nobilissimas Asiae et Europae per orientem urbes perque Iωnicas insulas et Aegeas, miserabilem Graecorum plurigenumque fidei nostrae gentium calamitatem aspexissem, quis foedam illorum cladem, quis funera fando explicet, aut lacrimis possit aequare dolorem?

10   Vidimus enim Christicolas homines puerosque simul et innuptas pueras ac ingentes omnigenum matronarum globos a Teucris longo ordine praeda ferreis sub catenis verberibusque afflictos per Threicias et Macedonias urbes miserandum in modum saepenumero ductitari[3] ac eos denique per vicos foraque et Hellespontiaca littora infande turpiter et obscene, more ut ita dixerim pecudum, venumdari.[4] Proh scelus! Nam et haec ipsa tam immania barbaricave facinora et a sacra praeditis religione generosis quoque principibus intolleranda ad praedignum hoc ipsum insigne facinus conspirandum humanissimam vestrum utrorumque pietatem plu-

motion the mustering, preparation, and pursuance of this most worthwhile expedition.

But primarily and before all others, I am resolved to commend 8 and praise the divine genius and admirable providence of his Holiness, Pope Eugene, who among so many and such famous fathers, appointed you alone as the worthy, excellent, and 'angelic' person, as bishop-designate and well-deserving legate with papal power to take charge of such a religious, toilsome and supremely honorable enterprise. And he knew that in every undertaking, both in important affairs pertaining to the church of God, and most especially in your well-known reputation for settling numerous differences between foreign peoples, you had always conducted yourself with foresight, steadfastness, justice, loyalty and nobility of spirit.

Who would be so devoid of human kindness as to be unable 9 to praise greatly, bless, and proclaim this holy, appropriate, and timely campaign against that unholy, hateful, and thoroughly execrable tribe of Turks? I myself, since I have been rather often in the same dangerous lands of the infidel throughout the famed cities of the east, both those of Asia and of Europe as well as those of the Ionian and Aegean islands, and have witnessed the wretched state of the Greeks and of various peoples of our own faith, [ask], "Who could express in words their vile massacre, who their obsequies, or shed tears equal to their pain?"[5]

For on numerous occasions we saw Christians — boys as well as 10 unmarried girls and masses of married women of every description — paraded pitiably by the Turks in long lines throughout the cities of Thrace and Macedonia bound by iron chains, and lashed by whips, and in the end put up for sale in villages and markets and along the shore of the Hellespont, an unspeakably shameful and obscene sight, like a cattle market, so to speak. What an enormity! For what prudent man would doubt that such monstrous, barbaric deeds as these, unendurable by noble princes gifted with the holy faith, should likewise fire the deepest sense of human loy-

rimum accendere debere vestramque virtutis magnitudinem excitare, prudentum quisnam ambigerit?

11   Vestris his igitur bonis felicissimisque coeptis magna illa caeli-
colum numina faveant et aspirent, quorum optimis auspiciis
Christiana alma religio, sublatis superstitionibus per orbem omnibus et perfidiis, profanum infandumque genus omne valuit pes-
sumdare, quorumque sanctissimo auxilio fugatis, pressis et truci-
datis profanis undique hostibus, non modo ab his Moesiam,
Graeciam, Macedoniam, Epyrum Illyriamque liberam per vos
atque restitutam ⟨videre⟩, quin et extra per Asiam atque Libyam
nostrum ipsum pium et religiosum imperium nostraeque almae religionis cultum super et Aethiopas atque Garamantas et Indos
proferre insigniter fauste atque felicissime videamus.

12   Opto bene valeatis. Ex Ragusio, Nonas Decembres, Eugenii
pontificatus anno XIII.

∶ 3 ∶

1 Athenis. Kyriacus Andreolo Iustiniano Musarum cultori. Minervae templum ex Phidia. Descriptio.

2   Revisimus et octogonam Aeoliam de marmore aedem octo ali-
geras ventorum imagines suis cum insignibus mira fabrefactoris[1]
arte consculptas summis angulorum parietibus habentem, et quaelibet imago suum desuper nomen magnis Attico de more litteris[2]
habet, ut prope conspeximus:

ΖΕΦΥΡΟΣ ΛΙΨ | ΝΟΤΟΣ ΕΥΡΟΣ Α|ΠΗΛΙΟΤΗΣ
ΒΟΡΕ|ΑΣ ΑΠΑΡΚΤΙΑΣ ΘΡΑ|ΣΚΙΑΣ

alty in both of you to join together for this worthy and extraordinary campaign and arouse the full intensity of your courage?

Therefore, may those great powers who dwell in heaven favor   11
and assist this, your good and most felicitous undertaking, under whose excellent auspices our fostering Christian faith, having done away with all false beliefs and faithlessness throughout the world, has been able to put an end to all manner of unspeakable sacrilege. By their most holy assistance may the impious foe be everywhere put to flight, overpowered, and butchered. May we see not only Moesia, Greece, Macedonia, Epirus, and Illyria freed and restored by them through your agency, but may we also see, in good fortune and happiness, our upright and holy dominion and the practice of our bountiful religion spread notably beyond [those regions], throughout Asia and Libya and into Ethiopia, Africa and the Indies.

I wish you good health. From Ragusa, the third of December,   12
in the thirteenth year of the pontificate of Eugene.

: 3 :

To Andreolo Giustiniani-Banca, 29 March [1444], Chios

Athens. To Andreolo Giustiniani, devotee of the Muses. Description of the temple of Minerva by Phidias.[1]   1

We went back to see the octagonal marble temple of Aeolus,[2]   2
which bears eight winged representations of the winds with their attributes, one at the top of each angled wall, carved with the artisan's admirable skill. Each figure has his name written above it in large, Attic-style lettering, as we observed from close at hand:[3]

Zephyr, Lips, Notos, Euros, Apeliotes, Boreas, Aparktias, Thraskias.[4]

3   Et cum ad Nerium Acciaiolum, Florentinum et Athenarum ea tempestate principem, una suo cum germano Nerio me contulissem, eum in acropoli, summa civitatis arce, comperimus. Sed quod magis adnotari placuit, cum eiusdem praecellentis aulae nobilissimum opus diligentius aspexissem, vidimus eiusdem mirificum porticum quatuor expolitis de marmore columnis decemque desuper ex ordine marmoreis trabibus constare.

4   Sed postquam ad ipsam et praecipuam venimus aulam, sex ingentes bino ordine columnae³ trium pedum diametri latitudine marmorea laquearia xxiiiique terno ordine trabes polito utique de marmore substentabant; quaelibet vero trabes pedum xxiiii° longitudine, latitudo vero iii fuisse videntur; et ipsi⁴ utique nobiles de marmore parietes aequa magnitudine expoliti lapidis constant, ad quas per unicam ingentem et mirificam portam patet ingressus.

5   Sed potissimum eadem ipsa in praeclara arce iterum revisere ac omni ex parte diligentius vestigare malueram nobilissimam illam divae Palladis aedem, quam solido et expolito marmore Phydiae mirificum opus extitisse Aristotheles ad Alexandrum regem Pliniusque noster et alii plerique nobiles testantur auctores.

6   Nam ubi phylosophus de mundi compositione ad ipsum regem scribere propensius maluisset, talia eo in opere lectitavimus verba: φασι δὲ τὸν ἀγαλματοποιὸν Φειδίαν κατασκευαζομένον τὴν ἐς ἀκροπόλει Ἀθήναν et reliqua. Nam et continuo subdiderat, quam magnus opifex deus ad omnem et indissolubilem contextae mundi compositionis armoniam optimam rationem habuerat, eandem ipsam in Minervae praeclari operis artificiosam compaginem architectum insignem illum Phydia habuisse.

7   C. vero Plinius in eum quem De naturali hystoria librum inscripsit, in eo de architectorum laudibus loco, inquit

When I went to see Neri Acciaiuoli, a Florentine who was 3
Prince of Athens at the time — [I went] with his cousin, also called
Neri — I found him on the acropolis, the topmost citadel of the
city. But what I deemed more important to record is that, when I
had rather carefully inspected the very imposing workmanship of
the same prince's exceptional palace,[5] I saw that its admirable
porch consists of four finished marble columns and, above, ten
marble [roof] beams in a row.

But after we had come into the main hall itself, [we saw that] 4
six huge columns, arranged in two rows, three feet wide in diameter, supported a marble, coffered ceiling and twenty-four beams,
entirely of polished marble, arranged in three rows. Each beam is
twenty-four feet long and three feet wide, in my estimation. The
stately marble walls themselves consist of finished stone equally
large, entrance through which is by a single, remarkably big door.[6]

But my special preference was to revisit on that very same 5
bright citadel that greatly celebrated temple of the divine Pallas
and to examine it more carefully from every angle. Built of solid, [PLATES I–II]
finished marble, it was the admirable work of Phidias, as we know
from the testimony of Aristotle's instructions to king Alexander as
well as from our own Pliny and a host of other notable authors.

For in the passage where the Philosopher chose willingly to 6
write to the king about the composition of the universe, we read
the following words in his work: "They say that the sculptor
Phidias built the Athena on the Acropolis," and so on.[7] For he immediately added that, just as the great creator God exercised the
utmost rationality to [bring about] complete and indestructible
harmony in the arrangement of the complex universe, so that outstanding architect Phidias himself exercised the very same [ratio-
nality] to [bring about] the artistic structure of his preeminent
achievement, the Minerva.

Gaius Pliny, in that part of his *Natural History* which is given 7
over to the praise of architects, wrote,

Phydiam clarum esse per omnes gentes quae Iovis Olimpi famam intelligunt nemo dubitat. Sed ut merito laudari sciant etiam qui opera eius non viderunt, adducimus[5] argumenta parva et ingenii tantum nec ad hoc Iovis Olympi pulchrytudine utemur, non Minervae Athenis factae amplitudine, cum sit ea cubitorum xxvi (ebore et auro constat), sed in scuto eius in quo Amazonum proelium caelavit ambitu parmae,[6]

et reliqua.

8   Extat enim nostram ad diem eximium illud et mirabile templum octo et L sublime columnis, xii scilicet ab utroque fronte, vi videlicet in medio duplici ordine, et extra parietes in lateribus ab utraque parte xvii numero, quaelibet magnitudine diametri pedum v et inter ipsas hinc inde pro lateribus columnas et praeclaros parietes deambulatoria viii pedum amplitudine constant.

9   Habent et columnae epistilia longitudine pedum viiii cum dimidio, altitudine vero iiii, in quis Thessalica Centaurorum et Laphitarum pugna mirifice consculpta videtur.[7] Et in summis parietum listis, duorum fere cubitum a cacumine discretas, Athenarum Periclis tempore victorias artifex ille peregregie fabrefecerat, pene decennis pueri staturae. In frontibus vero tota re velaminis dimensione magnis colosseisve simulachris hominum et equorum tam ingentis delubri ornamenta atque decora alta videntur.

10   Cuiusce magnificentissimi operis figuram hiisce nostris et hac tempestate per Graeciam comentariis, quoad licuit, reponendam curavimus et hodie, iiii Kalendas Aprilium, fausto, sereno Kyriaceoque die, apud Chyum, Asianam insignem Aegaeo in pelago insulam et dilectissimam nobis urbem, Andreolo Iustiniano, amico

Throughout all the peoples who know the fame of Olympian Jove no one doubts that Phidias is brilliant. But, that even those who have not seen his works may know that he is praised deservedly, we bring to bear only small proofs of his genius. We shall not adduce the beauty of Olympian Jove, nor the size of the Minerva made in Athens, though it was 26 cubits high (it was made of ivory and gold), but on her shield, on which he carved a battle of Amazons around its edge,[8]

and so forth.

This extraordinary, marvelous temple has survived to our own day. It is raised up on 58 columns: 12 at each of its two fronts, two rows of six in the middle and, outside the walls, seventeen along each side. Each column has a diameter of five feet. There are ambulatories eight feet wide between the lateral columns and the splendid walls on either side. 8

The columns support entablatures nine and one-half feet long and four feet high, on which one sees the battle in Thessaly between centaurs and Lapiths, sculptured with amazing skill. On the topmost friezes of the walls, separated from the top by about two cubits, the noted artist fashioned with outstanding skill [representations of] Athens' victories in Pericles' time, about the height of a ten-year old boy. On the two facades one sees, high up, in the whole space measured by their roofs, beautiful embellishments for such a prodigious place of worship consisting of large, indeed colossal, statues of people and horses. 9

I took pains to include a drawing of this absolutely splendid building, as far as in me lay, in this notebook that I am keeping of my current [travels] through Greece; and today, the 29th of March, a calm Sunday of good omen, in Chios, that remarkable Asian island in the Aegean sea and a city most dear to us, most fittingly and with great pleasure we presented it to Andreolo 10

incomparabili nostro et viro rerum omnigenum peritissimo curio-
sissimoque dignissime atque libentissime dedimus.

: 4 :

1 Ad Andreolum Iustinianum, virum clarissimum et amicum incomparabilem suum, Kyriacus Anconitanus salutem.

2   Ad Kalendas Aprilium, faustum genialemque nostrum Atlan-
tiadeum diem, una viris cum praestantissimis Francisco Drapperio, Paride Visconteque Iustinianis, cum vestro e portu cetea
quidem et oneraria navi, Uberto Grimaldo Ienuensi viro nobili
praefecto, aurora iam albescente, concederemus, secundis aspirantibus euris, eodem ipso felicissimo die, plenis et aequatis transiecto
aequore velis, Phocaeam expetitam venimus, novum in Ionia alu-
minemque Phocaeae veternissimae civitatis emporium, omnes et
incolumes, optimo iuvante Iove et genio illo sanctissimo nostro
ductitante Mercurio, nec non nympharum Nereydum nimirum
praeclarissima favitante et alto aequore modulante nivea doctissi-
maque Cymodocea.

3   Verum enimvero ita bonis avibus hoc et Aegaeum ipsum transiecimus aequor, ut omnia nobis felicia mirificaque secundarent.
Nam, ut alia praetermittamus tam et honorificae insignia syn-
odiae, dum nostrum ipsum per aequoreum iter, bonis crebrescentibus Aeolis, tumescentibus omnibus proveheremur velis, cym-
baeque puppi alligatae binae pone subsequerentur, cum, iam
medio transiecto itinere, maior erecta cervice, veluti superbam in
pystrim versa, sororem, quae[1] nos subvehendo ad matrem in portu
perduxerat, haemulans, dum minorem ante se leniter fluctum se-
cantem vidisset, duroque pectore impetu non mediocriter lacessis-

20

Giustiniani, our incomparable friend, a man expert and most eager for knowledge of every kind.

: 4 :

To Andreolo, 2 April [1444], Foglia Nuova

Cyriac of Ancona sends greetings to his distinguished, incomparable friend, Andreolo Giustiniani. 1

On the first of April, the favorable day of our protecting deity 2
Mercury,[1] we left your port[2] on a huge cargo ship[3] along with the eminent Franzesco di Drapieri and Paride and Visconte Giustiniani.[4] The ship's noble Genoese captain was Oberto Grimaldi. The dawn was just growing bright and a following southeast wind was blowing. Our sails were full and smooth as we crossed the sea, and we arrived on the same favorable day at our destination, Foglia [Nuova], the new center of the alum trade for the ancient city of Phocaea. All of us arrived safely thanks to supreme Jove's help, our most holy protector Mercury's guidance, and the favor of white-clad, learned Cymodocea, the brightest of [PLATE III] Nereus' sea-nymph daughters, who kept the deep sea calm.

Indeed, we crossed this and the Aegean Sea with such good 3
omens that all kinds of lucky marvels combined to favor our journey. For, to pass over other such marks of harmonious companionship, we were proceeding by sea under increasingly good winds, all sails swelling and the two tenders following along behind, tied to the stern. The voyage had passed mid-point when the larger of them raised her neck, as if she had turned into a proud sea-mammal jealous of her sister, who had conveyed us to their mother in harbor, when she saw the smaller boat riding gently ahead of her on the waves while she herself struck them amidships with no lit-

set, eam miserans optima Cymodocea, cum illam suis illico lacertis niveis amplexisset, et amplo aperto sinu suis illam mediis in visceribus protectam occulisset, delphynum more demerso lato sub aequore rostro, eam ipsam sororum augendo numerum mutavit in *νύμφαν*.

4   Et ita Amphitrite capaci omni ex parte abluta, matrem nosque candidissima subsequebatur,

>   qualis diva illa Nereyda Loto[2]
>   et Galathea secant spumante[3] pectore pontum.

Et denique, cum eam, pientissime manu extensa, mater suum adhaerentem laevum latus paulisper incumbens, ab aequore suspensam substulisset, et quam imbiberat Nereydum e visceribus partem, amplissimo Tethidis alveo restituisset, abluta, detersa et expolita levis, et pristinam in faciem restituta, ab invida illa sorore spatio paulisper disiuncta, cum de more iterum placidi Neptuni liquidum sulcare campum cepisset, postquam cetea mater, paulo ab emporio distans, alto in aequore anchora se fundarat, nos nostrasque res et suppellectile carum optatum ad portum bona cum salute incolumesque perduxit.

5   Opto quidem te tua cum praeclarissima et pudicissima domna cumque dulcissimis natis et omnem domum bene diu felicioremque valere. Et omnes tuos necessarios et affines bene valere scito. Tuis praeterea amplissimo ex ordine collegis et clarissimo praetori vicarioque egregio suo me saepe commissum memoremque facere velis. Ex eodem emporio et postero quo ad ipsum venimus IIII Nonarum Aprilis Ioviali die, iterum vale.

6   Praeterea quae nostra de Scyllea preciosissima gemma, quam nobis Urbini principem servasse diximus, perdocti Graece Latineque scripsere viri, lectitare potestis. Et scias hodie Italianam navim his

tle force. Most kind Cymodocea,[5] taking pity on her, embraced her immediately with white arms and, opening her copious bosom, hid and protected her deep within her body, immersing her beak in the broad sea the way dolphins do, increasing the number of her sisters by changing her into a nymph.

And so Amphitrite, washed thoroughly to sparkling brightness, followed closely after her mother and us,   4

> just as the divine daughters of Nereus, Loto
> and Galatea, cut the foaming sea with their breasts.[6]

Finally, her mother thrust out her hand most devotedly, bent her left side forward a bit towards her [daughter], raised her up from the sea as she clung to her, and restored to the capacious channel of Tethys from her [daughter's] stomach that part [of the sea] that the Nereid had swallowed, whilst she, washed, dried, polished smooth, and restored to her original appearance, separated from her grudging sister by a little space, began to plough the liquid plain of peaceful Neptune again in her usual manner. After her enormous mother ship had cast anchor in the deep sea a short distance from the mart, she brought us and our effects and our precious cargo safely and unharmed to the port we had sought.

I wish you and your brilliant, modest wife, along with your de-   5
lightful children and your whole household, long good health and good fortune. Be assured that all your friends and relations are well. Remember me to your colleagues in the senate and to the illustrious *podestà* and his distinguished deputy. Farewell again from the same emporium on Thursday, April 2nd, the day after we arrived.

[*Postscript:*] You can read what deeply learned men have written in   6
Greek and Latin about our most precious gem that depicts a Scylla, which we said the prince of Urbino[7] has kept for us. Know

horis applicuisse et anchora se Phocaeo hoc in portu firmasse. Πάλιν ἀνδρὸν πανάριστε, ΧΑΙΡΕ.

∶ 5 ∶

1 Insigni viro, Andreolo Iustiniano Maonensi, amico suo incomparabili.

2   Scripsi ad te pridie, karissime Andreole, et aliquid nostra de io-
cunda navigatione latiori nempe ordine solatii loco dixi. Verum
hodie illud unum difficile mihi erit explicare, quanta scilicet hylaritate iocunditateque perceperim illas Paridis nostri ad Antonium
Bocconem litteras perlegere. E quis vos inter inclitos Genuenses et
Alphonsum, Ausonicum potentissimum regem, decennale optimum oportunumque et exoptabile foedus initum significabat, ex
quo vobis et illi bona melioraque successura putamus nec non
Italiae ferme omni feliciora speramus eventura.

3   Vale. Ex Magnesia postero quo ad eam venimus, vi Kalendas
Aprilium die, Kyriacus Anconitanus tuus.

∶ 6 ∶

1 Andreolo Nicolai filio Iustiniano, viro insigni.

[Mytilene]

2 Reversus ex Lydia, karissime Andreole, et Sardiana Croesi regia
Phyladelphia Magnesiaque nobilibus et olim potentissimis urbibus

also that today, at this very hour, an Italian ship has put in and anchored in this port of Foglia. Farewell again, O best of men.

: 5 :

To Andreolo, 27 March [1444], Manisa

To the distinguished Andreolo Giustiniani, member of the 1 *Maona*,[1] my incomparable friend.

Yesterday, dearest Andreolo, I wrote to you and, to cheer you 2 up, described our joyful voyage in a rather expansive composition. Today, however, there is just this one matter, though it will be hard for me to express it, namely, how happy and delighted I was to receive and peruse that letter our Paride sent to Antonio Boccone, with its news of the excellent, timely and desirable ten years' treaty into which you renowned Genoese have entered with Alfonso, the powerful king of southern Italy. We think it will prove good, nay better, for both you and him and we hope it will turn out to be more beneficial to almost all of Italy.

Farewell, from Magnesia, the day after our arrival, the 8th of 3 April. Your Cyriac of Ancona.

: 6 :

To Andreolo, 24 April [1444], Foglia Nuova

To the eminent Andreolo Giustiniani, son of Niccolò. 1

[Mytilene]

After returning from Lydia, my very dear Andreolo, where I saw 2 Croesus' royal city Sardis as well as Philadelphia and Magnesia, fa-

visis, ad Lesbiam Mytilenem me quam avidissime contuli, ubi Dorinus optimus princeps cum me meaque perbenigne vidisset honoreque non exiguo suscepisset, mihi denique in recessu non aspernenda quidem praeclara suae in nos benivolentiae insignia declaravit.

3 Vidimus et inter praeclaros eo loco viros Leonardum, venerandum religione ac divinarum et humanarum litterarum peritissimum hominem, quocum multis cum nobilibus splendido in symposio fuimus.

[Sardis]

4 Et alias tibi in eo dicta referenda servavi, et hisce de Croesi regia urbe aliquid te meque dignum rescribendum censui. Ibi enim maiora longe quam antea fama perceperam suae priscae nobilitatis monumenta conspexi. Sed inter clariora mirifici de marmore Sardiani Iovis templi eximiae expolitaeque parietis partem inspexi, et quae nostram ad diem extant, XII rotundas et immanes columnas suo ordine vidimus erectas, altitudine pedum XLV, periferie vero XV.

5 Vidimus et statuae marmoream basim quondam cuiusdam in honorem pontificis conscriptam, ut hisce, quoad licuit, rescribendum et beatitudini tuae utique transmittendum curavi:

ΛΕΥΚΙΟΝ ΙΟΥΛΙΟΝ [ΛΙ]ΒΩΝ[Ι]ΑΝΟΝ ΑΝΔΡΑ Ε[Κ
ΠΡΟ|ΓΟΝΩΝ ΜΕΓΑΝ ΚΑΙ ΦΙΛΟΠΑΤΡΙΝ ΑΡΧΙΕΡΕ|Α
ΤΗΣ ΑΣΙΑΣ ΝΑΩΝ ΤΩΝ ΕΝ ΛΥΔΙΑ ΣΑΡ|ΔΙΑΝΩΝ
ΚΑΙ ΙΕΡΕΑ ΜΕΓΙΣΤΟΥ ΠΟΛΙΕΩΣ | ΔΙΟΣ ΔΙΣ
ΑΡΧΙΕΡΕΑ ΤΩΝ ΤΡΙΣΑ ΠΟΛΕΩΝ | ΚΑΙ
ΣΤ[Ε]ΦΑΝΗΦΟΡ[Ω]Ν ΚΑΙ ΙΕΡΕΑ ΤΙΒΕΡΙΟΥ |
ΚΑΙΣΑΡΟΣ ΚΑΙ ΣΤΡΑΤΗΓΟΝ ΠΡΩΤΟΝ ΔΙΣ ΚΑΙ |
ΑΓΩΝΟΘΕΤΗΝ ΔΙΑ [Β]ΙΟΥ ΕΝΔΕΙΑΣ ΔΕ
ΓΕ|ΝΟΜΕΝΗΣ ΚΑΤΑ ΤΟΝ ΔΗΜΟΝ ΜΕΓΑΛΟΨΥ|ΧΙΑ
ΧΡΗΣΑΜΕΝΟΣ ΕΚ ΤΩΝ ΙΔΙΩΝ ΕΙΣ |

mous and once very powerful cities, I went on quite eagerly to Mytilene on the island of Lesbos. There the most excellent prince Dorino[1] looked very kindly on me and my wares, received me with no scant ceremony, and, on my departure, displayed splendid, undeniable evidence of his good will to us.

Among the distinguished men we saw there was Leonardo,[2] a man to be revered for his spirituality and an unqualified expert in divine and humane studies, who was my fellow guest, along with many luminaries, at a dazzling banquet.   3

[Sardis]

Saving for another time my account of what was said on that occasion, I thought that here I should tell you something about the royal city of Croesus, a subject appropriate to our mutual interests. For I saw there remnants of its ancient nobility far more extensive than previous reports had led me to suppose. But among the more striking [of these], I observed a portion of an extraordinarily elegant wall belonging to the impressive temple of Sardian Jove, and, surviving to our own day, twelve round, huge columns 45 feet tall and 15 feet in circumference, standing in their [original] positions.[3]   4

We also saw the marble base of a statue, inscribed long ago in honor of a certain priest; I have undertaken, to the best of my ability, to write it down here and to send it off for your enjoyment: 5

[Dedication to] Leukios Ioulios Libonianos, a man of great ancestry and a lover of his country, high priest of Asia of the temples of Sardis in Lydia, twice priest of the greatest Zeus Polios, high priest of the Thirteen Cities, and crown-wearer [magistrate] and priest of Tiberius Caesar and twice first magistrate and president of the games for life. When the

ΕΠΙΚΟΤΦΙΣΜΟΝ ΕΚΑΣΤΩ ΠΟΛΙΤΗ ΕΧΑΡΙ|ΣΑΤΟ |
ΜΟΔΙΟΝ ΚΑΙ ΠΑΣΑΣ ΤΑΣ ΑΡΧΑΣ ΦΙ|ΛΟΤΙΜ[Ω]Σ
ΤΕΤΕΛΕΚΟΤΑ ΤΗ ΠΑ|ΤΡΙΔ[Ι]¹

Habeas Crytem Canabuzium vel Graeci alium quempiam eruditum, ut tibi insignem hanc inscriptionem eximiae intelligentiae
tuae faciliorem reddat.

6   Verum et ne dignum aliquod praetermittamus, cum primum
Sardianam urbem adventaremus, pro moenibus decurrentem perspeximus Pactolum illum exiguum amnem, sed omnium precio
clariorem, harenam quippe aurigenam perferentem, ex qua olim
Croesus, auri coagolandi arte fretus, maximas sibi opes compa-
rasse fertur. Cuiusce nos harenae partiunculam, Canabuzio magistro Phocense indicante, detulimus, quae sane minutis plerisque
atomis enitescere videtur aureis.

7   Vale et quas Antonio, monacho seraphici ordinis claro et devo-
tissimo virtutis tuae, litteras mitto, legere primum et inde sibi reddere curabis. Exopto bene valeatis et clarae Clarentiae domnae
sanctissimae tuae ex me salutem plurimam dare velitis nec non natis caris et ingenuis tuis. Ex Phocarum emporio, viii Kalendas
Maias.

8   Scribam et in tergo nondum finitum Orestem. Te enim sermone
rogo Vesconti digna aliqua verba facere sua de optima in me exhi-
bita benivolentiae ostensione et ex me honore ei semper quaque in
re tributo, nam virtutem suam non parum existimandam duxi.

9   Iterum atque iterum vale. Kyriacus Anconitanus tuus.

people were in need, with greatness of spirit, he gave a *modius* [of wheat] for relief to each citizen out of his own funds, and he honorably fulfilled all the offices of his city.

Please have Crytes Canabuzios or some other learned Greek interpret this noteworthy inscription to your exceptionally keen understanding.

But also, not to pass over something important, the first thing 6 we noticed when we arrived at the city of Sardis was the Pactolus river flowing downhill in front of the city walls;[4] a tiny stream, but more famous than all others for its monetary worth as it carries the gold-bearing sand from which, it is said, Croesus once acquired enormous wealth, relying on a technique for causing gold to coagulate.[5] We carried off a small sample of this sand which Canabuzios, the teacher from Foglia, pointed out. It seems to glitter with numerous tiny particles of gold.

Farewell. I enclose a letter to Antonio, a brilliant friar of the se- 7 raphic order,[6] greatly dedicated to your spiritual well-being. Please read it first, and then pass it on to him. I wish you good health. Please give my sincerest greetings to your brilliant and most devout wife Carenza and to your dear, noble children. From the mart of Foglia [Nuova], the 24th of April.

[*Postscript:*] I shall copy my "Orestes," not yet finished, on the back 8 [of this letter]. In your conversations with Visconte, I beg you to drop a few appropriate remarks about his very helpful display of good will toward me and about the respect in which I have always held him, for I place no small value on his steadfast character.

Again and again, farewell. Your Cyriac of Ancona. 9

1 Andreolo Nicolai filio Iustiniano, incomparabili amico suo.

[Chryse]

2 Cum hisce diebus, clare Andreole, ad perscrutandum Chrysoneae urbis antiquitatem me una comitatus indigena contulissem, pleraque tantae veternitatis magnalia vidi et inter potiora conspicua et magnis condita lapidibus moenia, et quamvis ob ignaviam nostrae aetatis hominum et immensam lucri cupiditatem in dies magna ex parte desolari videantur, tamen suae magnitudinis mole plurimi adhuc lapides suo ordine muro congesti maiestatis priscae et eximiae suae architecturae splendorem ostentant. Sed de hoc alias, nam et latiori calamo tantam gentium aevi nostri incuriam, desidiam et inhumanitatem exclamandum, detestandum, improbandum et penitus execrandum erit.

3 Praeterea, ut quid dignum tantae civitatis monumenti conspectare queas, avem aeneam, quam colubrum rostro stringentem eumque sinuato volumine ab alto tereti cervice reflexum collum eiusdem lacessentis momordentem vides, Antonio Bocchoni nostro dedi, ut tibi redderet; eamque mihi tu, vir digne, digniora tua inter eiusdem generis suppellectilia servare velis.

4 At et cum latius eo de simulachro vetustissimo tuae claritati declararim, non aes parvum parvifaciundum censebis. Nam et ipsa de fatali ave fatidicoque serpente magnum apud vatem Homerum

: 7 :

To Andreolo, 4 May [1444], Foglia Nuova

To Andreolo Giustiniani, son of Niccolò, his incomparable friend.   1

[Chryse]

The other day, renowned Andreolo, I went with a local inhabitant   2
to explore the city of Chrysonea's antiquities,[1] where I saw many
grand works of great age, and, among the more important of
these, clearly visible walls built of large stones. Although, owing to
the laziness of the men of our age and their boundless appetite for
gain, they appear to be mostly neglected from day to day, yet, very
many stones, still assembled in courses to form a wall, reveal, by
the sheer mass of their size, the brilliance of their extraordinary,
ancient architecture. But of that another time, for one needs a
more expansive genre in which to cry out against, despise, con-
demn and thoroughly curse such great negligence, slothfulness and
lack of humane culture on the part of our contemporaries.[2]

Moreover, that you may be able to look upon a worthy souvenir   3
of that city, I have given to Antonio Boccone, to deliver to you, a
bronze bird, which you see grazing a snake with its beak, and you
see the snake, with curved coil and highly-arched, smooth neck
biting the bent-back neck of the bird that is attacking it.[3] Be
pleased to keep it for me, worthy sir, in your collection of more
noteworthy items of the same sort.

When I explain to your excellency in greater detail about this   4
very old image, you will conclude that this tiny bronze [coin]
should not be thought insignificant. For concerning this same fateful bird and fate-prophesying serpent, there is in the great poet
Homer a reference that should not be overlooked.[4] And indeed

mentio habetur haud aspernenda. Ipsum etenim pridie nostri ut puto gratia, ductitante Mercurio indigenae satyri, qui pretio lapides (heu, generositas prisca!) solo ab immo effodiunt, invenere.

5   Vale et sanctissimae coniugi Clarentiae ceterisque tuis ex me salutem dabis et nos cras una nostro cum Drapperio, viro claro, iter nostrum peragendum curabimus. Ex Phocarum novo emporio, IIII Nonas Maias.

native "satyrs," who dig stones from the depths of the earth for a fee (alas for the nobility of other days!) found it for our sake, as I believe, under Mercury's guidance.

Farewell, and greet for me your devout wife Carenza and the 5 rest of your household. Tomorrow, with our illustrious Drapieri, we shall try to continue our journey. From the new trading mart of Foglia [Nuova], on the 4th of May.

1 Ad Andreolum Iustinianum, virum praestantem et amicum suum incomparabilem, Kyriacus Andreolo suo felicitatem dicit.

2   Postquam unas ad te hac ex urbe litteras dedimus, suavissime Andreole, ad xii Kalendas Iuniarum faustum Iovialem Iovisque humanati ascensione ad caelum mirifica solempnem venerandumque diem, una nostro cum clarissimo Drapperio Raphaeleque Castelleoneo, ad regiam soltanei principis Murath Bey, magni regis Asiae, praestantiam ascendimus, amplissimae aulae regia patente porta, ingenti splendore et apparatu frequentissima hinc inde suorum barbarica spectatione praestante regeque, stratis de more tapetis, primis cum et eximiis principibus suis iuxtaque Cialaby filio, splendore regio et barbarico more sedente.

3   Hic primum ex Galatia Synopei principis Hysmael Bey, magni quondam Spendiar Bey regii soceri nepotis, oratores dona eximia sua regi detulerant: quinque cilicos et alipedes equos, binas nitentes galeas totidemque rigentes hamis loricas et ornatas totidem ex Adiabenico ferro clavas, et alii plerique diversa regione legati sua quaeque munera principi magno dedere.

4   Sed ultimo, quod et lubentius spectare placuerat, Franciscum ipsum nostrum purpureas et elaboratas auro vestes, pretiosius quidem suppellectile suum, regi ipsi potentissimo deferentem vidimus. Et denique ministri delicata fercula regi barbarisque suis ex-

22 May to 21 July 1444
Adrianople and Constantinople

: 8 :

To Andreolo, 22 May 1444, Adrianople[1]

To the distinguished Andreolo Giustiniani, his friend beyond 1
compare, Cyriac wishes good fortune.

After sending you one letter from this city, dear Andreolo, on 2
the 21st of May, Jove's lucky day and the feast of Jove Incarnate's
miraculous ascension to heaven, a solemn and worshipful day, I
ascended to the royal palace of the Sultan, Prince Murad Bey, the
great King of Asia, along with my friends, the illustrious Drapieri
and Raffaele Castiglione. The royal door opened to an enormous
hall full of vast brilliance and pomp, and, around the room, a great
throng of magnificently exotic courtiers and the king, seated on
carpets strewn in the usual manner, with his leading men and distinguished princes, and beside him, his son Çelebi, in the splendid
manner of exotic royalty.[2]

Here, first of all, emissaries from Galatia of Ismail-Beg, prince 3
of Sinop on the Black Sea, grandson of the Sultan's once-great fa-
ther-in-law, Isfendiyar Beg, brought choice gifts to the Sultan: five
wing-footed Cilician horses, two gleaming helmets and the same
number of cuirasses stiff with hooks and as many ceremonial cud-
gels made of iron from Adiabene.[3] Many other emissaries from
different localities gave the great prince their several gifts.

Finally, a sight that rather pleased me, we saw our very own 4
Francesco bringing to this most powerful king purple garments
worked with gold, his own rather costly material. At length, servants brought to the king and his barbarian [courtiers] luxurious
dishes of food in polished vessels [set] on this side and on that;

politis hinc inde vasis detulere, mox vero, libatis poculis epulisve obesis, multitudines ex aula concessere.

5   Vale ex Andrianupoli, xi Kalendas Iunii mccccxliiii.

: 9 :

1   [...] Praeterea cum ex Hadrianupoli recedere et abitum Byζantium adornassem, ex Pannonia legatos propediem eodem ad magnum ipsum regem adventuros percepimus. Quos cum expectare delegissem, non multos post dies quattuor hic oratores ad lx equitum comitatos vidimus advenisse: unum scilicet Stoyca Gisdanich a Polloniae Pannoniaeque inclyto rege Ladislao; alterum Vitislaum ab illo praecellenti equitum magistro, Coniati Iano; et duos a Georgio, argentigenae Moesiae Servianaeque provinciae despota, quorum alter *metropolites* Athanasius religione venerandus erat, alter vero nomine *logothetes*.

2   Qui cum post biduum ad superbam tyranni praesentiam se contulissent, regius orator primum, deinde despotei et ultimus ex primario bellica virtute Iano Latinis, Graecis Servianisque litteris epistolas de fide et sua quaeque modesta munera principi magno dedere.

3   Et ad posteram diem, cum apud regios bassianos collegas rem tantae legationis agitassent et ablata iampridem occupatave eorum in provinciis oppida, repetita maiori ex parte concessa, denique post triduum excepissent, nonnullis ad pacem componendam conditionibus acceptis, ad principes eorum et patriam remeare cu-

soon, though, cups drained and food devoured, the throng left the hall.

Farewell from Adrianople, 22 May 1444.   5

: 9 :

Fragment of a letter to ?Andreolo, [12 June 1444], Adrianople

[...] Moreover, when I was packed and ready to leave Adrianople   1
and to depart for Byzantium, I learned that delegates from Hungary to the great king himself would arrive here shortly, so I decided to wait around. Not many days later, we observed that four emissaries had arrived here, accompanied by sixty knights. One is Stojka Gisdanić, representing Ladislas, the famed king of Poland and Hungary; the second is Vitislao, representing that superb master of the horse, John Hunyadi; in addition, there are two [others], representing George [Branković], despot of the silver-producing province of Serbian Moesia: one was the metropolitan A[tanasije], revered for his religious authority, and the other has the title of chancellor.[1]

Two days later they entered the proud presence of the tyrant —   2
first the king's emissary, then the despot's [two envoys], and last, the one from John [Hunyadi], foremost in martial courage — and presented letters of credence written in Latin, Greek and Serbian, and each presented his modest gift to the great prince.

On the next day, they dealt with the group of royal pashas on   3
the substance of this important embassy and after three days they had regained the majority of the towns in their provinces that they had asked for, [towns] that had been seized and taken from them. In return, they accepted certain conditions for establishing a peace and made ready to return to their sovereigns and their homeland.

rarunt. Sed cum expetitum praecipue oppidum illud insigne Columbarium, quod ad Danubii meatum *Peristerion* Graece dicunt,
barbarus occupatum iterum detinere maluerat, non omne ab rege
foedus sociisve ratum fore putandum.

4   Nec ea forte quae tam late reddiderat princeps hic superbus
amisisset ni nuper adversus Charamannum suo potiori cum exercitu profecturus esset. Nam ingens bellum potens ille in Asia princeps in ipsum Teucrorum regem parasse suasque iam provincias
vastatum iri oppidaque occupare coepisse perceperat. Quas ob res
non multos post dies relicto in Thracia Cialaby nonnullis cum le-
gionibus filio et Chalil Bassia collega primario Hellespontum
transfretare et in Asiam copias enixe ductitare decreverat.

5   Postridie vero cum legati, ut Columbarium recuperarent, hac in
urbe morantes insisterent, id ipsum hodie sibi regem reddidisse
cognovimus, et suos utique barbarum, Solymambegh, et Vranam,
Graecae nationis, legatos ad firmanda Christianis cum principibus
foedera in Pannoniam misisse [...].

: 9A :

Copia litterarum regis Pannoniae ad Teucrorum regem

1 Excellenti principi et magno imperatori soltano Murath Beg, tanquam fratri et amico syncere praeferendo, Wladislaus Dei gratia
Hungariae Polloniaeque, Dalmatiae, Croatiae etc. rex, Litouiaeque
princeps suppremus et heres Rasiae etc., salutem ac fraternitatis et
amicitiae prosperum incrementum.

But since the Turk wanted, and especially sought to hold back, the important town of Golubac (in Greek *Peristerion*)² at the crossing of the Danube, which he had again seized, they thought the king and his allies would not ratify the entire treaty.

And perhaps this proud prince would not have lost those towns 4 that he so broadly restored had he not been just on the point of setting out against Karaman³ with the better part of his army. For he had learned that this puissant prince in Asia was prepared [to wage] a mighty war against the Turkish sultan himself and was already poised to lay waste his provinces and had begun to seize his towns. This was why, a few days later, he decided to cross the Hellespont and lead his forces vigorously into Asia, leaving his son Çelebi in Thrace with a few legions and with Halil Pasha⁴ as his principal associate.

So today I learned that, when the emissaries remained in the 5 city the next day to press for the recovery of Golubac, the sultan returned it to them and dispatched two legates to Hungary, a Turk named Suleiman-Beg and one Vranas, a Greek, to ratify the treaty with the Christian princes [...].

: 9A :

[Enclosure:] Copy of a letter of the King of Hungary to the King of the Turks¹

To the excellent prince and grand sovereign, Sultan Murad-Beg, 1 sincerely as to a brother and preferred friend, Ladislas, by the grace of God King of Hungary, Poland, Dalmatia, Croatia etc., supreme prince of Lithuania and heir of Russia, wishes health and a favorable increase in brotherhood and friendship.

2   Noverit vestra excellentia nos nobilem et egregium Stoyka Gisdanich dictum, hominem nostrum fidelem in factis et negotiis cum vestra excellentia nostri parte tractandis plene informatum et per nos sufficienter eruditum, cum totali nostra auctoritate et potestatis plenitudine ad vestram excellentiam destinasse, ut cum ipsa vestra excellentia nostri parte valeat tractare, disponere et concludere auctoritate ac in persona nostri. Cuius quidem verbis et dictis nec non relatibus nostri ex parte vestrae excellentiae referendis, placeat magnitudini vestrae fidem credentiae adhibere, tanquam nostrae propriae personae.

3   Velit igitur magnitudo vestra suos nuntios solemni ⟨cum⟩ praefato nuntio nostro, videlicet Stoyka, ad nos dirigere et transmittere. Et quicquid ipse Stoyka noster fidelis cum vestra magnitudine disposuerit et concluserit, fidem et vinculum quodcumque volueritis, promittimus praefatis vestris nuntiis dare et conferre. Vestra igitur magnitudo velit modo simili fidem et vinculum dare iam fato nostro nuntio, quod omnia illa quae disposueritis et concluseritis, observabitis inconcusse, ut certi sumus in vobis.

4   Datum Budae, secundo die festi Sancti Georgii martyris, anno Domini 1444.

: 9BI :

Responsio Teucri ad ipsum Pannoniae regem

1   Magno ac excellenti principi, magno imperatori Wladislao, imperatori Ungariae regique Polloniae etc. tanquam fratri et amico dilectissimo, Amurath Beg, magnus dominus, magnus Amorath, soltani filius magni imperatoris, magni soltani Machmeth Beg, salutem atque fraternitatis et amicitiae prosperum incrementum.

Be it known to your excellency that we have appointed the no- 2
ble and distinguished Stojka Gisdanić to deal with your excellency
on our behalf. He is a man faithful to us in deed and enterprise,
fully instructed and adequately informed to negotiate on our behalf with all our authority and the fullness of our power, so that
he may be able to negotiate, draw up and conclude [an agreement]
with your excellency with the authority of our own person. May it
please your highness to lend credence to the message from our
side, both oral and written, that he is required to convey to your
excellency, as [you would] to our own person.

May your highness be willing to appoint and send us envoys to 3
accompany our aforesaid envoy, Stojka. And whatever our faithful
Stojka shall arrange and conclude with your highness, whatever
binding promise you shall require, we promise to give and bestow
upon your aforesaid envoys. May your Highness in a similar fashion give your binding promise to our aforesaid envoy that you will
firmly abide by what you shall have arranged and concluded, as we
are sure you will.

Given at Buda, the day after the feast of St. George the Martyr, 4
in the year of our Lord 1444.[2]

: 9BI :

Reply of the King of the Turks to the King of Hungary

To the great and excellent prince, the great ruler Ladislas, ruler of 1
Hungary, king of Poland, etc., as to a brother and very dear
friend, Murad-Beg, great lord, great Murad, son of a sultan, a
great ruler, the great sultan Mehmed-Beg,[1] wishes health and a favorable increase in brotherhood and friendship.

2   Noverit vestra excellentia quod nobilem virum ac egregium nuntium, Stojka vestrum fidelem, nobis placitam et dilectam litteram ex parte excellentiae vestrae conduxit; per quam litteram excellentia vestra narravit quod, quicquid fidelis ac vester nuntius Stoyka vestri parte tractabit, tanquam vestrae personae propriae credamus.

3   Narramus dominationi vestrae quod dictus nuntius Stoyka nobis dixit in primo de domino despota Georgio, videlicet quod dare debeam filios atque loca sua et quod ipse Georgius sit obligatus in omnibus servitiis nostris sicut pro praeterito erat. De quo pro fraternitate excellentiae vestrae concessi.

4   Ac etiam nobis narravit quod domino Blado vayvoda Velacho placeat mihi pacem secum agere in hoc modo: quod ipse Blado vayvoda mihi det tributum ad solitum primum ac in omnibus servitiis nostris, sicut primo erat obligatus, quod noviter sit, nisi quod non personaliter ad nostram curiam veniat.

5   De quo amore excellentiae vestrae contenti sumus, videlicet quod Blado vayvoda det tributum et omnia quae in nostris negotiis erat obligatus etiam noviter faciat, ac contenti sumus quod ipse personaliter non veniat in curia nostra, nisi quod nobis mittat ostagium; ac etiam si nostri in locis suis fugiant, quod nobis mittant; et etiam nos sic faciamus, si de illis hic fugient.

6   Et ista intelligitur hoc modo, videlicet quod excellentia vestra nobiscum pacem atque fraternitatem et amicitiam bonam simul habeamus. Ex qua causa nos iuravimus coram nuntio excellentiae vestrae, videlicet Stoycae, quod nos cum excellentia vestra bonam et solidam pacem habeamus sine aliquo dolo vel fraude usque ad annos decem.

7   De quo nos mittimus nostrum fidelem, nobilem et egregium Solyman Beg, videlicet quod placeat excellentiae vestrae personaliter iurare recte et fideliter sine aliquo dolo quod per annos decem bonam et solidam pacem nobiscum habebitis.

8   Datum Hadrianupoli, XII Iunii

May your excellency know that your noble, distinguished, and 2
trustworthy envoy, Stojka, brought us on your excellency's behalf
a letter that wins my approval and affection. In this letter your
excellency told us that, whatever negotiations your loyal envoy,
Stojka, shall make on your behalf, we are to trust as we trust your
own person.

We relate to your lordship that the aforesaid envoy, Stojka, spoke 3
to us first of all concerning the lord despot, George,[2] to the effect
that I should give back his sons and his territories and that George
himself should be bound entirely to our service, as he was in the
past. This I granted to your excellency in view of our brotherhood.

He also stipulated that I should be pleased to make peace with 4
Lord Vlad, the voivode of Walachia[3] under the following conditions: that first, the voivode Vlad should pay me the usual tribute
and do everything he is bound to do in our service, as before, except that he need not come in person to our court.

Out of love for your Excellency we are content with this [re- 5
quest], to wit, that the voivode Vlad shall pay tribute and once
more do everything he has been bound to do in our service, and
we agree that he need not come in person to our court, except that
he must send us a hostage; and also, that if our people should take
refuge in his territories, they must send them back to us, and that
we must do the same if any persons flee here from those lands.

The understanding behind these concessions is that your excel- 6
lency and I will observe a mutual good peace, fraternity and
friendship. Therefore we have sworn before your excellency's envoy, Stojka, that we will maintain a good and unbroken peace with
your excellency without any guile or deceit for ten years.

And we are sending our trustworthy, noble and distinguished 7
Suleiman-Beg,[4] to wit, that it may please your excellency to swear
in person duly and sincerely without any guile that you will observe a good and unbroken peace with us for ten years.[5]

Given at Adrianople, 12 June. 8

1   Praestantissimo Andreolo Iustiniano, amico incomparabili suo.

2   Praecellentissimo principi Ladislao, Pannoniae Poloniaeque serenissimo regi, perinde ac fratri et amico excolendissimo nostro,
Amorath Beg, sultani Machmeth Beg magni olim regnatoris Asiae
filius, magnus Asiae rex Thracumque et Macedonum potentissi-
mus imperator, salutem et sincerae devotionis affectum.

3   Sthoyka, fidelem celsitudinis tuae hominem, nuntium orato-
remque legatum egregium, lubenter vidimus; et quas nobis praecellentiae tuae pergratas litteras obtulerat libentius quidem inspeximus, e quis te velle cognovimus nos praefato Sthoyka omni in
re perinde ac tuae propriae personae fidem credulam adhibere.

4   Quem primo tuae celsitudinis nomine de re Georgii despotis
exposuisse scito, ut et sibi filios et sua quaeque loca restituere
velim et ipse tamen Georgius, quemadmodum nobis quibusque
nostris in rebus opitulatum iri exacto tempore tenebatur, sic et
deinceps pariter teneretur. Quae omnia celsitudinis tuae et regiae
fraternitatis intuitu quam placide largiti sumus.

5   Idem praeterea tuus orator tuae serenitatis nomine flagitabat ut
Blado vayovode principive Flaccorum pacem dare hisce conditionibus dignaremur, quod ipse Blado ea quae nobis primo in foedere
vectigalia quot annis tribuere tenebatur in futurum utique teneatur, sed nostram ad curiam se more solito personaliter conferre ab-
solutus sit.

6   Quae omnia lubens regiae tuae fraternitatis gratia concedere
hoc pacto decrevimus, ut ipse quot annis obsidem quempiam nobis transmittere teneatur, ac etiam, si qui nostratum homines suis

44

: 9B2 :

Cyriac's "enhanced" Latin translation of 9B1, with a covering note to Andreolo, dated 18 June 1444, Adrianople

To the eminent Andreolo Giustiniani, incomparable friend.   1

To the preeminent prince Ladislas, most serene king of Hun-   2
gary and Poland, as to our brother whose friendship is worth
keeping, Murad-Beg, great king of Asia, son of Sultan Mehmed-
Beg, the former great king of Asia, and most puissant ruler of
Thrace and Macedonia, wishes health and a sense of our genuine
fidelity.

We were pleased to see Stojka, a man loyal to your highness, an   3
envoy, ambassador, and emissary extraordinary; and we were even
more pleased to study your eminence's welcome letter that he presented to us. From it we learned that you wish us in every respect
to place the same implicit trust in the aforesaid Stojka as we would
in your very own person.

Know that in your highness' name he first proposed concerning   4
the despot, George, that I willingly return to him his sons and his
several territories, and that George himself be obliged in the future to assist us in each of our needs, just as he was in the past.
All this we have granted with ease in consideration of your highness and brotherhood in royalty.

In addition, your emissary also demanded, in the name of your   5
Serenity, that we deign to make peace with the Vlad, voivode of
Wallachia, on the following conditions, that Vlad himself also be
required to pay in the future the annual tribute that he was required to pay under our former treaty, but that he be excused from
coming personally to our court in the usual way.

All this we have decided to grant gladly for the sake of our   6
brotherhood with you in royalty on this condition, that he be re-

quibusque in locis aufugerint, ad nos quam primum illos remittere debeat, quemadmodum et nos fugientes nostras ad partes suos quoscumque homines reddere constituimus.

7   Quae quidem igitur omnia lubenti animo et placida voluntate concessa hoc pacto firma rataque esse decrevimus, quod et te-cumque et aliis quibusque sociis et adhaerentibus tuis simulque nobis et nostris pax, amicitia fraternalisque benivolentia esto. Cuiusce rei gratia regio nostro de more tuo coram oratore Sthoyka iuravimus pacem ipsam firmam, veram, bonam atque tranquillam absque dolo vel fraude decem per annos stabilem observare.

8   Quapropter regiae praecellentiae tuae mittimus nostrum hunc fidelem, nobilem et perstrenuum virum, Solima Begh, ut eius in conspectu serenitati tuae placeat regio tuo vestratumque religionis more fideliter recteque iurare absque ullo dolo vel fraude, quod ab hodierno die ad futurum usque decimum temporis annum bonam, stabilem tranquillamque invicem pacem nobiscum habebitis atque eam constanter inviolabiliterque observabitis.

9   Datum Hadrianupoli nostro de more XII Iunii MCCCCXLIIII.

10   Harum litterarum copiam, cum antea ab homine non satis erudito editae fuissent et illico Franciscus Drapperius noster ad socios misisset, responsa regia quae paulo meliora cecineram hisce exemplata videbis.

11   Vale et me hodie Bizantium petens una cum Georgio Salimbene me equitaturum puto. Ex Hadrianupoli, XIIII Kalendas Iulii.

12   Cetera vero a Napoleone egregio oratore vestro noveritis late. Te tuosque valere opto. Iterum vale. Finis. Τέλος. Ἀμήν. θεῷ χάρις.

quired to send us a hostage every year, and also that he be required
to send back to us, as quickly as possible, any of our people who
take refuge in any of his lands; just as we on our part agree to return any of his people who flee to our territory.

With a glad heart and untroubled will we declare all these con-   7
cessions to be firm and fixed on the condition that there be mutual
peace, friendship and fraternal good will between you and each of
your other allies and adherents and ourselves and our people.
With this end in view, in the manner befitting a king, in the presence of your emissary Stojka, we have sworn to observe for ten
years a true, good, tranquil and stable peace without guile or deceit.

Wherefore we are sending to your royal Eminence this our   8
faithful, noble and vigorous man, Suleiman-Beg, so that your Serenity may be pleased to swear in his presence in your royal manner and in that of your peoples' religion, reliably, correctly and
without any guile or deception, that from today on for ten years
you will maintain a good, stable and tranquil mutual peace with us
and that you will observe it firmly and inviolably.

Given at Adrianople on the 12th of June 1444, our style.   9

[Covering note:] An earlier translation of this letter was circulated   10
by a person of insufficient learning and sent off immediately by
Franzesco di Drapieri to his associates. You will see here a copy of
a somewhat better version of the Sultan's reply, of which I am the
author.

Farewell. I think that I will set out today by horseback for By-   11
zantium with George Salimbene. From Adrianople, 18 June.

[Postscript:] You will get the rest of the news from your distin-   12
guished representative, Napoleone. I hope that you and your family are well. Again, farewell. The end. Amen. Thanks be to God.

: 10 :

1 [...] Posteaquam per Illyricum et ipsa in Ragusio civitate, fortissime atque magnanime princeps, certis plerisque nuntiis et praecipue cardinalis optumi et angelici nominis pontificia potestate legati veris epistolis novimus quanta qualiave ad Christianum pium propagandum imperium perstrenua et insuperabili virtute tua tuique florentissimi exercitus probitate provide, constanter ma-
2 gnanimiterque gessisti; te vere insignem pietate principem stratagemiphorumque militiae ducem dignumque ac verum Christianae religiosae pientissimaeque gentis pugilem vocitandum appellandumque fore censebam; potestatem imperiumque tuum oceano, honores vero et laudes atque nomen astris te dignum terminare putavi. Quapropter animum meum omnem, fidem mentemque et affectionem ac meipsum totum inclytae virtuti et celsitudini tuae devovi dedicavique, magne τροπαιοφόρε τε ἀνήρ.
3 Cum vero deinde me ad Threiciam Hadrianopolim, regiam et, heu, barbara ditione subactam opulentissimam urbem, et elati regis Asiae praesentiam plerisque et honestis de causis contulissem, regios nuper et celsitudinis tuae Georgiique despotae egregios oratores vidimus et quanta apud ipsum elatum principem gesserint audivimus, ut omnia vobis ex relatu vestrae legationis et eiusdem Murath Beg regiis litteris nota erunt; ad quae et formanda vobis-

: 10 :

Fragment of a letter to ?John Hunyadi, 12 June 1444,
Adrianople

[...] After [we had journeyed] through Illyria, and [were staying] 1
in the city of Ragusa itself, most brave, great-hearted prince,[1] we
came to learn from many reliable sources, and in particular from
the authentic dispatches of the cardinal-legate whose excellent
nickname is "angel," a man endowed with the pontifical power,
about the magnitude and quality of your achievements—how you
strove for the expansion of the holy Christian empire with your
own vigorous and unconquerable courage and the excellent virtue
of your highly effective army, with forethought, steadfastness, and
nobility of spirit. I realized then that one must address and hail 2
you as a prince truly outstanding in loyalty, a military leader
abounding in strategies, and a worthy and true champion of the
holy and deeply dedicated Christian people. I thought you deserved to define the limits of your power and supreme command
by the ocean, your honors and glory and reputation by the stars.
For this reason I have devoted and dedicated all my heart, my loyalty, my mind and affections, indeed my whole self, to your illustrious courage and eminence, great bearer of trophies.

But when I came [from Ragusa] to Thracian Adrianople, a 3
royal and very prosperous city subject, alas, to foreign control,
and, for many honorable reasons betook myself to the presence of
the proud king of Asia, we saw that distinguished emissaries had
come from the king, from your highness, and from the despot
George, and we learned of their great achievements with the
proud prince, as will be made known to you by the report of your
representative and by the royal letter of the same Murad-Beg. To

cum foedera Solymam Beg, barbarum fidelem suum, et Graecae utique nationis homines mittit.

4 Sed omnia a vobis hac in re exorta motave optimo consilio peracta putandum est, ut e providentissimis sapientissimisque principibus ac magnarum gerendarum rerum expertissimis. Quam ob rem vobis et almae Christicolum religiosae atque excolendissimae expeditioni meliora felicioraque omnia semper successura speramus.

5 Opto bene valeatis. Ex Hadrianupoli, pridie Idus Iunii, Eugenii pontificatus anno XIIII, excolendissimae illustrissimaeque celsitudinis tuae devotus et dicatissimus Kyriacus Anconitanus.

: II :

1 Scripsimus haec ex Hadrianupoli, Christianissime princeps, in barbaros, quoad licuerat, moderate, ut barbaram nempe saevam perniciem vitaremus. Nam latius de rei conditione deque eorum coacta pace dixissem, cum et ingenti formidine territos, ut e vestris late noveritis, quotidie Teucros moenia reparare turresque propugnaculis ligno munire, militem ad fugam potius quam ad pugnam aptare cognovimus.

2 Alia vero ex parte Charamannum in Asia in ipsum Amorath motum in armis et loca oppidaque sua vastatum pessundatumque iri tyrannus hic superbus percepisset, in eum furens, relicto in Thracia Cialaby filio cum et Chalil Bassia, collega primario suo,

confirm this treaty with you, Murad is sending Suleiman-Beg, a Turk loyal to him, and men of Greek nationality as well.

Well, one must assume that all this was initiated, set in motion 4 and carried through on the best advice, since it emanates from princes of great foresight and wisdom and experience in grand enterprises. Therefore, we hope that the result of all this will turn out to be ever better and more successful for you and for the holy and religious Christian campaign, which must be kept alive.

I hope that you are well. From Adrianople, 12 June, in the 14th 5 year of the pontificate of Eugene. Cyriac of Ancona, your honorable and distinguished highness' devoted and dedicated servant.

: II :

To ?John Hunyadi, 24 June 1444, Galata/Pera[1]

Most Christian prince, I wrote the enclosed[2] from Adrianople. Its 1 tone with respect to the barbarians was as moderate as possible, to avoid a cruel and savage death.[3] For I would like to have said more about the situation there and about the peace that [the Turks] were compelled to accept, since we knew that, frightened with a mighty fear, as you will learn in detail from your [representatives], they spend every day repairing their walls, fortifying their towers with ramparts of wood, and preparing their army for retreat, rather than battle.

In fact, when this proud tyrant learned that on another front, 2 in Asia, the Karaman had moved militarily against Murad himself and was about to devastate and destroy his lands and towns, [the sultan], in a rage against him, left his son Çelebi in Thrace with his principal colleague, Halil Pasha, and chose personally to cross

suis cum plerisque cohortibus ipse Hellespontum transfretare et copias magna vi in Asiam ductitare delegerat.

3   Ut etsi vos, Christiani optumi principes, pacem hanc improbam et penitus execrandam observare coeperitis, statim conflicto fugatove aut aliqua condictione pacato Charamanno, ingenti animo, auctis in Asia copiis, Hellesponto remenso, in Thraciam iterum validiori cum exercitu remeare et Moesiam Pannoniamque tota sua cum potestate repetens, praeteritam recentemque a vobis illatam sibi cladem enixe vindicare curabit.

4   At etsi, quod magis putandum et ipsum formidare iam cernimus, vos, pace maligna penitus spreta, in eum paratas iam vestras invictas et florentes copias in Thraciam ipsam admovisse cognoverit et classe Hellespontum a nostris occupaturum perceperit, ni forte in Europa interciperetur, ipse minori ignominia maneret in Asia. Quare agite, principes optumi, et indicite dignum Christianae religionis bellum et sanctissimam gloriosamque iam felicibus auspiciis coeptam expeditionem ad exoptatum perducere finem numquam absistere velitis.

5   Ex Byζantiana Pera, eo quo ad eam venimus VIII Kalendas Iulias, fausto et praecursoris Baptistaeve sanctissimi venerandissimo die.

: 12 :

1 Ad Iduum Quintilium serenum et genii nostri sanctissimi iocundissimum diem, cum serenissimus imperator ipse una et suus Porphyrogenitos frater Theodorus, despotes inclitus, regio de more

the Hellespont with most of his divisions and to lead the great strength of his army into Asia.

Excellent Christian princes, if you undertake to observe this unsound and utterly detestable peace, as soon as [Murad] has closed with Karaman and either put him to flight or agreed on terms of peace with him, he will cross back over the Hellespont with high heart and forces augmented in Asia, and will return to Thrace with a stronger army, will make for Moesia[4] and Hungary with all his military power, and will devote all his efforts to avenging the defeat that you inflicted on him in the recent past.[5] 3

But if he learns that you have taken what we now clearly perceive to be the more reasonable course, and one that he now fears, i.e. that of repudiating utterly the disadvantageous peace, and are moving your unconquered forces into Thrace itself, forces already primed against him; and [if he] observes that the Hellespont will be occupied[6] by our fleet, he may choose the less shameful course of remaining in Asia rather than risk being cut off in Europe. Act, therefore, excellent princes, and declare a war worthy of the Christian religion and may you be willing never to shrink from bringing to its desired conclusion a most holy and glorious campaign, already begun under favorable auspices. 4

From Pera near Byzantium, on the day we arrived, 24 June, the auspicious and revered feast of the Precursor, [John] the Baptist. 5

: 12 :

To ?Andreolo, 19 July 1444, Constantinople

On the 15th of July, the clear and cheeriest day of our most holy guardian spirit, the most serene emperor himself, John Palaiologos, and his brother, Theodore Porphyrogenitos, the renowned 1

comitati splendide primis et nobilioribus suis ex Bizantio venatum ivissent, primum apud Aphamniam, Threiciam antiquam et mediterraneam urbem surgentem secus amoenissimum fontem, emptoria regis circumque nobilium sceniculas posuere, e quis equidem ipse non longe vidimus antiquam civitatis portam, magnis quoque lapidibus conditam, et vetusta undique solo diruta atque collapsa moenia.

2   Et illico ex Galathea Pera nobili vestratum colonia Boruele Grimaldus, nobilissimus praetor, plerisque suis cum egregiis civibus nec non ex urbe ipsa regia Veneti plerique nobiles una generoso cum iuvene Nicolao Superantio, Marini spectabilissimi baiuli filio, ad inclitum imperatorem ipsum et despotem illustrem praedigne ornateque convenere.

3   Qui postquam perhumane a principibus suscepti consedere, ad posterum denique faustum Iovialemque diem, primo iamque sereno albescente Phoebo, alii per dumos[1] pictas quaeritant avibus aves, alii quidem per flumina escatis sub unda hamis varigenos laqueare pisces magna animi cupiditate curabant. Nempe ipsis cum principibus primi et animi praestantiores alii ad altos per invia lustra colles orthoceros insectari cervos aprosve spumantes et fulvos utique leones aut maculoso tegmine pantheras plerisque venabulis armis canibusque percurrunt; et denique inter valles et collis declivia e silvis exeuntes, ingentes plerosque et alipedes cervos cursu campos transmittere nosque late praetervectos vidimus.

4   Et hinc ulterius procedentes alteram ad antiquam venimus Threiciam civitatem undique longa collapsam vetustate, quam Miliademam vocant, ex qua longa murorum videntur vestigia et ingentes templorum reliquiae; et ab ea tandem non longe binos saetigeros[2] apros binosque cervorum pullos praeda venatores ad

despot,[1] left Byzantium to go on a hunt, splendidly accompanied in the usual royal manner by his more high-born principal courtiers. First, they set up the king's pavilion at Aphamnia,[2] an ancient inland Thracian city, beside a beautiful rising spring, and, round about it, the tents of the nobles. From there I saw, not far away, an antique city gate built of great stones and old city walls everywhere fallen to the ground in ruins.

There [two groups] converged to meet the famous emperor and 2 the distinguished despot with appropriate pomp and circumstance: from your noble Genoese colony Galata/Pera, Boruele Grimaldi, its celebrated *podestà*,[3] with several of its distinguished citizens; and from the royal city itself a number of Venetian nobles, including Niccolò Superanzio, son of the noted consul,[4] Marino.

These were received courteously by the princes and tented 3 down. The next day, Jove's lucky day,[5] as the unclouded sun grew bright, some went falconing for colored birds among the thorn bushes, while others tried with great eagerness to catch varieties of fish in the rivers, using submerged, baited hooks. Others, the leading citizens and those superior in courage, of course, with the princes themselves, moved rapidly through pathless forests to high hills, [armed] with many hunting spears, weapons, and dogs in pursuit of straight-horned stags, foaming boars, tawny lions, or spotted panthers. Finally, we saw emerging from a wood between the valleys and slopes of the hills a large number of huge, wing-footed stags; they crossed the plains, passing us by at a distance.

Moving farther on from there, we came to another ancient 4 Thracian city that they call Myliadema, everywhere in a state of collapse because of its great age. From there one sees long traces of walls and huge remains of temples; and finally, not far from there, the hunters brought to the king's tent from their booty two bristly boars and two fawns. From these the most splendid prince made gifts, first to the distinguished *podestà* of Galata and to Paolo

tentoria regi detulerant. E quis magnificentissimus ille princeps primo Galateum eximium praetorem Paulumque Grimaldum, Andronicum Francum, Benedictum Salvaticum ceterosque Genuenses eiusdem egregios comites donatos facere nec non deinde praeclarum Venetum proconsulis natum ac Nicolaum Iustinianum, Karolum Capellum ceterosque nobiles ibidem Venetos eadem ex praeda regia sua liberalitate donavit. Et demum auceps Manuel ille Chretensis, quem me coram aera per liquidum peregrinus mactaverat falco et magnum et longipedem obtulisse argironem, ac tum[3] me laetus imperator in partem praedamque vocavit.

5   Verum etenim ego cum per fluminis διώρυχα[4] ad lacum et marittimum litus una ipso cum optimo principe cymba devectus venissem ad turrim suam Studeam, noctem quievimus; et antea quam 'chrystatus ales tepidum provocaret diem', Caliopes coniugis meae excitus sorore Thalia, plerasque inter nymphas ut natus[5] ivimus.

6   Et denique florea inter et virentia rura peregrinum hoc animal nobis Polymia ab Aegypto et ipsa Memphytica Babilona detulerat. Id enim Aegyptii ΖΩΡΑΦΑΝ vocitare consueverant. Pulcherrimum namque pecus et mirabile visu, quod informae longitudinis collo et anteriori parte sexquitertia posteriori cruribus altius imminebat; cetera vero a capite ad extremas pedum et ungularum partes dorsumque et maculosi tegminis color omnia cervis damisque similia videbantur.

7   Cuiusce quidem ferae nuper nostra hac in venatione captam imaginem hodie dignissimo imperatori nostro tuaeque beatitudini dedimus, ut eam vos non secus ac nos vivam, quoad licuerat, vidisse feram putaremus, vestris manendo laribus nec dum per vos vasto,[6] ut a nobis, menso aequore aut Aegyptico Nilo inmensa vel itineris tantarum harenarum mole.[7]

Grimaldi, Andronico Franchi, Benedetto Selvatico, and the other eminent Genoese companions of the same [*podestà*]; and out of the same booty he gave with his royal generosity to the illustrious son of the Venetian consul and to Niccolò Giustiniani, Carlo Capelli, and the other Venetian nobles there.[6] And from these the most splendid prince made gifts, first to the distinguished *podestà* of Galata. And finally, the Cretan falconer Manuel held out a large, long-footed lizard[7] that a peregrine falcon had killed before my eyes in the clear sky. Then the jovial emperor invited me to receive a portion of the prey.

To resume, I then sailed with the excellent prince himself   5
aboard a small boat down the channel of a stream[8] to a lake and the seacoast, arriving at his tower [in the monastery of] the *Prodromos tou Stoudiou*, where we rested the night. Awakened "before the crested bird roused up the languid day"[9] by Thalia, the sister of my spouse Calliope, I went among the numerous Nymphs as their son.[10]

At length, in the midst of flowering green fields, Polyhymnia   6
brought us this exotic animal from Egypt and the Memphitic Babylon. The Egyptians are wont to call it a *zoraphan*, a very handsome beast, and wondrous to look upon, which towered [above us], with a neck of disproportionate length and legs that were one and one-third times longer in the front than in the back; but in other respects, from its head to the tips of its feet and its hooves and its back, the color of its spotted skin looked very like that of stags and does.

Today we have given to the most worthy emperor, and [now] to   7
your Beatitude, a likeness of it that I made recently during our hunt, so that in our estimation, as far as possible, you have seen the living beast as we did, though you remain at your hearth and have not yet traversed the vast sea as we have in our journey, or the Egyptian Nile, or the immeasurable expanse of so much sand.[11]

8   Valere te diu bene atque iocundiorem opto, eximie et elegantissime vir. Ex Bizantio XIIII Kalendas Sextilis, Eugenii papae anno XIIII.

: 13 :

1 Ad insignem virum Andreolum Iustinianum, amicum optimum et concordem.

2   Breves pridie hac ex urbe tibi litteras dedi, karissime Andreole, et breviores hodie beatitudini tuae dabo. Nam et tantum volebam, nescius ne esses hoc ex epigrammate hac ipsa in regia civitate nuper ex me Latinis et expolitis licteris nobile in epistile comperto, P. Caninium genio sanctissimo nostro Maiaeque divae parenti aedem signaque de sua pecunia faciundum curasse:

P.CANINIVS.APOLLONIVS.VI.VIR.| AVGVST.
SIGNA.ET.AEDEM.MAIAE.| MERCVRI | D.S.P.F.C.
IDEMQ DEDICAVIT[1]

3   Valere te tuosque omnes diu feliciores opto et periocunde quam citius revisere. XII Kalendas Sextiles. Ille idem Kyriacus tuus.

I wish you long good health and increasing happiness, distinguished and most elegant sir. From Byzantium, 19 July, in the fourteenth year of the reign of Pope Eugene. 8

: 13 :

To Andreolo, 21 July [1444], Constantinople

To the eminent Andreolo Giustiniani, my excellent and agreeable 1 friend.

On the day before yesterday I sent you a short letter from this 2 city, dear Andreolo, and today I will send your Beatitude an even shorter one. For I had a great desire that you know from this inscription, which I found recently in the royal city itself, written in well-executed Latin lettering upon a noble architrave, that a Publius Caninius paid out of his own pocket to have a temple and statues erected to my most holy protective deity and to his divine mother, Maia:

> Publius Caninius Apollonius *Sevir Augustalis* had the images
> and temple of Maia and Mercury built from his own money
> and himself dedicated them.

I pray for your and your whole family's well-being and ever 3 better good fortune; and [I long] to revisit you sooner rather than later. 21 July. That same Cyriac of yours.

: DIARY I :

1 SALUBREA. Ad VIII Kalendas Augusti ex Bizantio Salubream per Ponticum venimus, Cappaneo Salubriano ducente navarcho, ubi a magnifico iuvene Thoma Georgii filio Cataguzino, pro Theodoro Porphyrogenito despote praefecto, quam honorifice suscepti, nullum fere antiquitatis suae monumentum comperimus praeter hoc secus portam vetusto in lapide Atticis litteris epigramma:

ΑΝΤΙΦΙΛΟΣ ΣΑΜΥΛΟΥ | ΑΓΩΝΟΘΕΤΗΣ ΕΡΜΑΙ[1]

2 Exinde vero concedens ipsum per Ponticum Heracleam Perinthum petens, piscatoria scapha devectus, ad isthmon qui Propronticum a Pontico mari disterminat et Bizantianum terminat Cheronesum venimus, ubi ad utrumque mare vergentem mirificum et magnis conditum lapidibus murum antiquum constituisse magnis relictis partibus et longo tractu vestigiis comperi.

3 Et inde secundis afflantibus Boreis Perinthum, antiquam et in Propontico Threiciam olim nobilem et potentissimam urbem venimus, ubi, quamquam magna ex parte collapsa moenia undique videantur, manent tamen magna nobilium murorum vestigia, et nova utique ab Heraclio principe Constantinopolitano, a quo no-

25 July 1444 to 25 February 1445
The Propontis and Northern Aegean

: DIARY I :

Travels in the Propontis, 25 July to 12 August 1444

[Constantinople to Selymbria, 25 July 1444. Heraclea Perinthus]

SELYMBRIA. On the 25th of July, guided by the ship's commander 1
Cappaneo of Selymbria, we journeyed from Byzantium by way of
the Pontic Sea to Selymbria.[1] There we were received with the utmost ceremony by Thomas Cantacouzenos, a splendid young
man, son of George, governor on behalf of the despot Theodore
Porphyrogenitos. We found nothing there to remind one of the
city's antiquity except this inscription in Attic lettering on an ancient stone by the port:

> Antiphilos son of Samylos, president of the games, to Her-
> mes.

Departing from there, we made for Heraclea Perinthus[2] 2
through the Pontic Sea aboard a fishing boat, arriving at the neck
of land that divides the Propontis from the Pontic Sea and marks
the [westernmost] boundary of the Byzantine Chersonese. There I
found, sloping down toward both seas, a marvelous ancient wall
built of large stones. Large sections of it remain [intact], with
traces of it [extending] over a considerable distance.

From there, under favorable north winds, we came to 3
Perinthus, an ancient Thracian city on the Propontis, once famous
and most powerful. Although its [ancient] defensive walls are
mostly in a state of collapse, still there remain extensive traces of
fine [building] walls. I also found numerous relatively modern

61

men civitati inditum est, moenia turresque videntur quamplures;
et Romanorum utique principum Vespasiani Domitiani Antoni-
nique Pii nobilia palatia et pleraque statuarum ingentia monumenta columnaeque bases et Latinis Graecisque litteris epigrammata nec non ex antiquissimis suis principibus plerasque reliquias
comperi.

4   Sed quod mirum est, sui tam magni et celeberrimi amphitheatri
nullum fere vestigium nostram ad diem relictum apparet nisi aliqua magna parietis pars et plerique veterrimi arcus, quos veteres
incolae eiusdem operis fuisse nobis testabantur.

5   At quae potissimum aestimanda duximus epigrammata hinc
inde diversis in lapidibus comperta hisce reponenda curavimus:

6   Perinthea magnis ex lapidibus moenia:

7   ΑΓΑΘΗΙ ΤΥΧΗΙ | ΑΥΤΟΚΡΑΤΟΡΑ ΚΑΙΣΑΡΑ ΘΕΙΟΥ
| ΤΡΑΙΑΝΟΥ ΠΑΡΘΙΚΟΥ ΥΙΟΝ ΘΕΙΟΥ | ΝΕΡΟΥΑ
ΥΙΩΝΟΝ ΤΡΑΙΑΝΟΝ | ΑΔΡΙΑΝΟΝ ΣΕΒΑΣΤΟΝ Ī
ΥΠΑΤΟΝ | ΤΟ Γ̄²

8   ΑΓΑΘΗΙ ΤΥΧΗΙ | ΥΠΕΡ ΥΓΕΙΑΣ ΚΑΙ ΝΙΚΗΣ ΤΟΥ
ΚΥΡΙ|ΟΥ ΗΜΩΝ ΑΥΤΟΚΡΑΤΟΡΟΣ ΚΑΙΩΝΙΟΥ |
ΔΙΑΜΟΝΗΣ ΛΟΥΚΙΟΥ ΣΕΠΤΙΜΙΟΥ ΣΕ|ΒΗΡΟΥ
ΠΕΡΤΙΝΑΚΟΣ ΑΡΑΒΙΚΟΥ ΑΔΙΑ|ΒΕΝΙΚΟΥ ΚΑΙ
ΜΑΡΚΟΥ ΑΥΡΗΛΙΟΥ ΑΝΤΟ|ΝΙΝΟΥ ΚΑΙΣΑΡΟΣ ΚΑΙ
ΤΟΥ ΣΥΜ|ΠΑΝΤΟΣ ΟΙΚΟΥ ΚΑΙ ΙΕΡΑΣ ΣΥΓΚΛΗ|
ΤΟΥ ΚΑΙ ΔΗΜΟΥ ΠΕΡΙΝΘΙΩΝ ΝΕΟΚΟ|ΡΩΝ
ΜΑΡΚΟΣ ΩΡΟΥ ΤΟΝ ΤΕΛΑΜΩΝΑ | ΤΩ ΒΑΚΧΕΙΩ
ΑΣΙΑΝΩΝ ΕΚ ΤΩΝ ΙΔΙ|ΩΝ ΥΠΕΡ ΤΗΣ ΕΙΣ ΑΥΤΟΝ
ΑΕΙ ΤΕΙΜΕΙΣ | ΚΑΙ ΕΥΝΟΙΑΣ ΑΝΕΘΗΚΕΝ ΗΓΕΜΟ|
ΝΕΥΟΝΤΟΣ ΣΤΑΤΕΙΛΙΟΥ ΒΑΡΒΑΡΟΥ |
ΙΕΡΟΜΝΗΜΟΝΟΥΝΤΟΣ ΠΟΜΠ[Ι]ΟΝΙ|ΟΥ
ΙΟΥΣΤΙΝΙΑΝΟΥ ΚΑΙ ΑΡΧΙΜΙΣΤΟΥΝ|ΤΟΣ ΜΑΞΙΜΟΥ
ΤΟΥ ΚΛΑΥΔΙΟΥ ΙΕΡΑ|ΤΕΥΟΝΤΟΣ ΕΥΤΥΧΟΥΣ
ΕΠΙΚΤΗΤΟΥ | ΕΥΤΥΧΕΙΤΕ³

defensive walls and towers [built] by the Byzantine emperor
Heraclius[3] after whom the city was named. Also, the noble palaces
of the Roman emperors Vespasian, Domitian, and Antoninus
Pius, numerous huge remnants of statuary, column-bases, inscriptions in Latin and Greek lettering, and numerous remains from
[the time of] the city's most ancient rulers.

Astonishingly, there appears to be almost no trace remaining to   4
our day of the large, well-known amphitheater, except for a large
stretch of wall and numerous very old arches that the old inhabitants testify had been parts of the same building.

But we did take care to record here the most important inscrip-   5
tions that we found on a variety of stones scattered here and there:

The Perinthean walls [built] of large stones:[4]   6

Good fortune. Emperor Caesar Trajan Hadrian Augustus,   7
son of the divine Trajan, victor over the Parthians, grandson
of the divine Nerva, consul for the third time.

Good fortune. For the health, victory and eternal presence of   8
our lord the emperor Lucius Septimius Severus Pertinax,
victor over Arabia and Adiabene and of Marcus Aurelius
Antoninus Caesar and the entire [imperial] house and the
holy Senate and the People of Perinthus, the temple warden,
Marcus son of Horos, dedicated this statue to the worship-
ers of Bacchus of Asia at his own expense because of the reverence and favor [shown] to him when Statilios Barbaros
was president, Pomponios Ioustinianos was in charge of the
temples, Maximos son of Klaudios was leader of the initiated, and Eutyches son of Epiktetos was priest. Be well.

9   IOVI ZBELSVRDO SACR. IMP. CAESARE
DOMITIANO AVG. GERMAN. XIIII COS. PROC. |
THRAC. Q. VETTIDIO BASSO TI. CLAVDIUS AUG.
L. ZENA TRIER. CLASSIS PERINTHIAE | CVM
CLAVDIS TI. FILIS QVIR. MAXIMO SABINO LVPO
FVTVRO FILIIS SVIS PRI | MVS CONSECRAVI

ΔΙΙ ΖΒΕΛΣΟΥΡΔΩ | ΑΥΤΟΚΡΑΤΟΡΙ ΚΑΙΣΑΡΙ
ΔΟΜΙΤΙΑ|ΝΩ ΣΕΒΑΣΤΩ ΓΕΡΜΑΝΙΚΩ ΤΟ ΙΔ |
ΥΠΑΤΩ ΕΠΙΤΡΟΠΕΥΟΝΤΟΣ ΘΡΑΚΗΣ | Κ.
ΟΥΕΤΤΙΔΙΟΥ ΒΑΣΣΟΥ ΤΙ. ΚΛΑΤ|ΔΙΟΣ ΣΕΒΑΣΤΟΣ
ΑΠΕΛΕΤΘΕΡΟΣ | ΖΗΝΑ ΤΡΙΗΡΑΡΧΟΣ ΚΛΑΣΣΗΣ
ΠΕΡΙΝ|ΘΙΑΣ ΣΤΝ ΚΛΑΤΔΙΟΙΣ ΤΙ. ΤΙΟΙΣ ΚΤΡΕΙΝΑ |
ΜΑΞΙΜΩ ΣΑΒΕΙΝΩ ΛΟΤΠΠΩ ΦΟΤ | ΤΟΤΡΩ
ΤΕΚΝΟΙΣ ΙΔΙΟΙΣ ΠΡΩΤΟΣ ΚΑΘΙΕΡΩΣΕΝ[4]

10   DIIS AVCTORIBUS AD REIPVBLICAE
AMPLIFICANDAE | GLORIAM PROCREATO PI
. . . . . NOSTRO IOVI O . . . . . | MAXIMO | TI.
NOBILISSIMO CAESARI VS . . . . . VEM PRAEF. |
PRAETOR[5]

11   Ad aliam marmoream et ornatissimam basin ad aedem Praecursoris:

ΑΓΑΘΗΙ ΤΥΧΗΙ | Η ΒΟΤΛΗ ΚΑΙ Ο ΔΗΜΟΣ
ΕΤΕΙΜΗ|ΣΑΝ ΠΟ. ΑΙΛΙΟΝ ΑΡΠΟΚΡΑΤΙΩ|ΝΑ ΤΟΝ
ΚΑΙ ΠΡΟΚΛΟΝ ΤΟΝ ΤΟ ΤΤΧΑΙΟΝ |
ΚΑΤΑΣΚΕΤΑΣΑΝΤΑ ΑΛΕΞΑΝΔΡΕΙΣ | ΟΙ
ΓΡΑΜΜΑΤΕΤΟΜΕΝΟΙ ΕΝ ΠΕΡΙΝΘΩ | ΤΟΝ
ΑΝΔΡΙΑΝΤΑ ΑΝΕΣΤΗΣΑΝ ΤΗΜΗΣ | ΧΑΡΙΝ[6]

12   Ad portum:[7]

ΜΑΚΕΔΟΝΕΣ | ΜΗΤΡΟΔΩΡΟΣ ΦΙΛΙΣΤΙΩΝΟΣ |
ΛΑΜΕΔΩΝ ΛΑΚΡΙΤΟΥ | ΛΕΟΝΤΙΣΚΟΣ ΛΕΟΝΤΟΣ |

To Zeus Zibelsourdos. Tiberios Klaudios Zena, freedman   9
of the emperor, commander of the fleet of Perinthos, together with his own sons, the Claudii, sons of Tiberius of
the tribe Quirina—Maximus, Sabinus, Lupus and
Futurus—first dedicated [this statue] to the emperor Caesar
Domitian Augustus, victor over Germany, consul for the
fourteenth time, when Caius Vettidius Bassus was proconsul
of Thrace.[5]

By the command of the gods. To our pious great Tiberius   10
most noble Caesar, born for increasing the glory of the state
[...] praetorian prefect.[6]

On another very handsome marble base at the church of the 11
Precursor:[7]

Good fortune. The Council and the People honored Poplios
Ailios Harpokration, also called Proklos who built the
shrine of Tyche; the Alexandrians who do business in
Perinthos set up the statue in his honor.

At the harbor:[8]   12

Macedonians: Metrodoros son of Philistion, Lamedon son of
    Lakritos, Leontiskos son of Leon, Apollonios son of
    Sosimenos, Herakleides son of Aischimos

ΑΠΟΛΛΩΝΙΟΣ ΣΩΣΙΜΕΝΟΥ | ΗΡΑΚΛΕΙΔΗΣ
ΑΙΣΧΙΜΟΥ ΑΚΑΡΝΑΝΕΣ | ΔΕΛΦΩΝ ΑΡΙΣΤΟΜΑΧΟΥ
| ΖΟΠΥΡΟΣ ΚΡΙΤΩΝΟΣ | ΕΤΑΝΔΡΟΣ ΑΝΔΡΩΝΟΣ |
ΣΩΤΗΡΙΔΑΣ ΣΤΡΙΣΚΟΥ | ΑΓΕΜΑΧΟΣ ΕΥΔΑΜΟΝ |
ΑΡΙΣΤΙΩΝ ΣΩΣΟΝ | ΔΙΟΚΛΗΣ ΣΩΤΗΡΜΟΥ |
ΔΙΟΝΥΣΙΟΣ ΦΙΛΩΝΟΣ | ΠΟΔΑΡΓΟΙ |
ΚΑΛΛΙΣΤΡΑΤΟΣ ΗΓΙΝΟΣ | ΑΓΑΘΟΚΛΗΣ
ΑΠΟΛΛΩΝΟΣ | ΑΡΙΣΤΟΔΗΜΟΣ ΑΡΙΣΤΑΡΧΟΣ |
ΑΓΗΣΙΛΑΟΣ ΑΠΟΛΛΟΔΩΡΟΣ | ΔΗΜΑΡΕΤΟΣ
ΖΗΝΟΔΟΤΟΣ | ΣΩΕΙΣΗΣ ΜΕΝΚΡΑΤΕΥΣ | ΣΩΣΙΣ
ΑΠΟΛΛΟΔΩΡΟΣ | ΑΜΦΙΛΟΧΟΣ ΥΠΕΡΧΙΔΗΣ |
ΚΑΛΛΙΦΩΝ ΣΩΣΙΟΣ | ΚΑΛΛΙΜΕΔΩΝ ΑΠΟΛΛΩΝΟΣ
| ΝΑΞΙΒΙΟΣ | ΤΕΛΕΥΝΤΕΣ | ΠΥΘΙΩΝ ΜΗΤΡΟΒΙΟΣ
| ΤΑΚΤΩΡ ΠΛΕΙΣΤΟΡΟΣ | ΘΕΟΔΟΤΟΣ ΒΑΤΑΔΟΣ |
ΣΙΜΟΣ ΜΗΝΟΦΩΝΤΟΣ | ΝΙΚΑΝΔΡΟΣ ΔΑΥΝΙΟΣ |
ΛΕΟΝΤΙΑΔΗΣ ΑΡΙΣΤΟΚΕΛΕΥΣ | ΙΠΠΟΛΟΧΙΔΗΣ
ΙΠΠΟΛΟΧΟΣ | ΘΕΟΝΟΜΟΣ ΑΠΟΛΛΟΦΑΝΕΥΣ
ΩΡΕΙΣ | ΑΧΕΛΩΙΟΣ ΠΥΓΟΡΕΩ | ΜΗΤΡΟΔΩΡΟΣ
ΖΩΙΛΟΣ | ΙΜΕΡΟΣ ΗΡΟΣΤΡΑΤΟΣ | ΜΙΚΙΩΝ
ΑΛΚΑΙΟΣ | ΕΚΑΤΟΔΩΡΟΣ ΜΗΤΡΟΠΥΘΟΟΣ |
ΑΛΚΙΜΑΧΟΣ ΞΕΙΝΟΘΕΜΙΟΣ ΑΙΓΙΚΟΙ |
ΕΧΕΚΡΑΤΗΣ | ΜΟΛΠΙΣ | ΡΟΔΥΣΡΟΣ | ΖΟΙΛΟΣ |
ΠΟΣΙΔΕΙΟΣ | ΑΧΕΛΩΙΟΣ | ΜΗΤΡΟΔΩΡΟΣ |
ΚΡΑΤΕΥΣ ΑΚΕΣΑΝΔΡΟΣ ΑΡΤΕΜΙΔΩΡΟΣ |
ΑΥΤΟΛΙΚΟΣ ΔΗΜΟΔΟΤΟΣ ΚΑΣΤΑΛΕΙΣ |
ΖΗΝΟΔΟΤΟΣ ΣΤΗΣΑΤΟΡΕΩ | ΤΙΜΟΘΕΟΣ
ΔΙΟΔΟΤΟΣ | ΠΑΥΣΑΝΙΑΣ ΒΑΚΧΙΟΣ | ΖΗΝΟΔΟΤΟΣ
ΑΠΟΛΛΟΘΕΜΙΟΣ | ΑΡΙΣΤΑΝΔΡΟΣ ΕΥΡΥΜΑΧΟΣ |
ΑΣΤΥΝΟΜΟΣ ΑΜΑΝΤΙΟΣ | ΒΟΣΠΟΡΙΟΣ[8]

13   Ο ΔΗΜΟΣ | ΠΟΠΛΙΟΝ ΚΟΣΙΝΙΟΝ | ΠΟΠΛΙΟΝ
ΤΙΟΝ ΚΑΠΙΤΩΝΑ | ΑΓΟΡΑΝΟΜΗΣΑΝΤΑ
ΕΠΙΜΕΛΩΣ[9]

Akarnanians: Delphon son of Aristomachos, Zopyros son of
  Kriton, Euandros son of Andron, Soteridas son of Syriskos,
  Agemachos son of Eudamos, Aristion son of Sosos, Diokles
  son of Soterios, Dionysios son of Philon
Podargoi: Kallistratos Heginos, Agathokles Apollonios,
  Aristodemos son of Aristarchos, Agesilaos Apollodoros,
  Demaretos Zenodotos, So[sikles] son of Menekrates, Sosis
  son of Apollodoros, Amphilochos son of Hypereides,
  Kalliphon son of Sosios, Kallimedon son of Apollonios,
  Naxibios
Geleuntes: Python son of Metrobios, Taktor son of Pleistor,
  Theodotos son of Batas, Simos son of Menophon,
  Nikandros son of Daunis, Leontiades son of Aristokles,
  Hippolochides son of Hippolochos, Theonomos son of
  Apollophanes
Boreis: Acheloios son of Pyathores, Metrodoros son of Zoilos,
  Himeros son of Herostratos, Mikion son of Alkaios,
  Hekatodoros son of Metropythos, Alkimachos son of
  Xeinothemis
Aigikoreis: Echekrates, Molpis, Rodysros[?], Zoilos, Posideios,
  Acheloios, Metrodoros, Krateus Akesandros, Artemidoros,
  Autolykos son of Demodotos
Kastalians: Zenodotos son of Stesagores, Timotheos son of
  Diodotos, Pausanias son of Bachios, Zenodotos son of
  Apollothemis, Aristandros son of Eurymachos, Astynomos
  son of Amantis, Bosporios

The People [honored] Poplios Kosinios Kapiton son of   13
Poplios, who carefully regulated the market

14   ΜΑΤΙΔΙΑΝ ΣΕΒΑΣΤΗΝ | Η ΒΟΥΛΗ ΚΑΙ Ο ΔΗΜΟΣ
     | Ο ΠΕΡΙΝΤΗΙΩΝ[10]

15   Apud aedem Theodori ad promontorium Perintheum:

     ΝΕΟΣ ΕΘΗΚΕΝ ΤΗΝ ΣΟΠΟΝ ΤΩ ΙΔΙΩ | ΘΡΕΨΑΝΤΙ
     ΙΟΥΒΕΝΤΙΩ ΕΡΜΗ ΜΝΕΙΑΣ ΧΑΡΙΝ | ΧΑΙΡΕ
     ΠΑΡΟΔΕΙΤΑ[11]

16   Ad Apostolorum metropolitanam aedem ad ornatum marmo-
     reum lapidem:

     ΑΥΡ. ΦΙΛΙΠΠΙΑΝΟΣ ΧΡ. ΕΠΟΙΗΣΑ ΕΜΑΥ | ΤΩ ΚΑΙ
     ΤΗ ΓΥΝΑΙΚΙ ΜΟΥ ΑΥΡ. ΔΕΚΝΙΑΝΗ | ΧΡ. ΚΑΙ ΤΩ
     ΠΑΤΡΙ ΜΟΥ ΑΥΡ. ΝΕΟΦΥΤΩ | ΧΡ. ΕΙ ΔΕ ΤΙΣ
     ΤΟΛΜΗΣΕ ΕΤΕΡΟΝ ΒΑΛΕΙΝ | ΔΩΣΕΙ ΤΙΣ
     ΑΔΕΛΦΟΙΣ Χ. Φ.[12]

17   Η ΠΟΛΙΣ | ΤΟΝ ΠΡΩΤΟΝ ΤΗΣ ΠΟΛΕΩΣ | ΚΑΙ
     ΤΩΝ ΕΛΛΗΝΩΝ Μ. ΑΥΡ. ΘΕΜΙΣ|ΤΟΚΛΕΑ
     ΙΠΠΙΚΟΝ ΓΡΑΜΜΑΤΕΑ ΜΟΝΟΝ | ΕΦΕΣΙΩΝ ΚΑΙ
     ΑΣΙᴾˣ | ΑΥΡ. ΗΡΚΛΑΣ ΤΟΝ ΕΑΥΤΟΥ | ΣΥΝΗΓΟΡΟΝ
     ΚΑΙ ΠΡΟΣΤΑΤΗΝ | Ψ. Β.[13]

18   TROPAIOPHORO FRATRE EX PROVINC.
     PANNONIA IN AMPLISSIMUM ORDINEM
     ADSVMPTO PRAEF. COH. IMBRIVCORUM EQVITES
     SINGVLAR. EIVS[14]

19   A Teucris ad mare traductus marmoreus e Vespasianis atriis la-
     pis hoc habet:

     Η ΒΟΥΛΗ ΚΑΙ Ο ΔΗΜΟΣ ΤΗΣ ΛΑΜΠΡΟ|ΤΑΤΗΣ
     ΠΕΡΙΝΘΙΩΝ ΠΟΛΕΩΣ ΣΤΑΤΕΙ|ΛΙΟΝ
     ΧΡΙΤΩΝΙΑΝΟΝ ΤΟΝ ΚΡΑΤΙΣΤΟΝ | ΕΠΙΤΡΟΠΟΝ
     ΤΟΝ ΣΕΒΑΣΤΟΥ[15]

The Council and people of Perinthus [honored] the Augusta
Matidia.

14

At the church of [St.] Theodore on the promontory of
Perinthus.

15

[...]neos built the tomb for his own foster-child Ioubentios
Hermes for his memory. Hail, passer-by

At the metropolitan church of the Apostles on an embellished
marble stone:

16

Aurelios Philippianos [the Christian] made [this tomb] for
myself and my wife Aurelia Dekniane [the Christian] and
my father Aurelios Neophytos [the Christian]. If anyone
dares to put another [body here], he shall pay 500 denarii to
the Brothers.

The city [honors] the first man of the city and of the
Greeks, M. Aur[elios] Themistokles, the knight, sole secretary, Ephesian, Asiarch; Aur[elios] Heraklas [honors] his
own advocate and patron. By decree of the Senate.

17

[with] his brother Tropaiophoros from the province of Pannonia, who has been received into the most glorious order
[the Senate], prefect of the third cohort of the Breuci, his
cavalry body guards [dedicated this]

18

A marble stone dragged down to the sea by the Turks from the
atria of Vespasian has this [inscription]:

19

The Council and People of the most illustrious city of
Perinthus [honors] Statilios Chritonianos, the most excellent procurator of the Emperor.

20 ΤΟΝ ΛΑΜΠΡΟΤΑΤΟΝ ΚΑΙ ΑΓΝΟΤΑΤΟΝ |
ΗΓΕΜΟΝΑ Μ. ΟΥΛΠΙΟΝ ΝΕΚΙΩΝΑ ΣΑ|ΤΟΥΡΝΙΝΟΝ
ΤΟΝ ΤΗΣ ΟΜΟΝΙΑΣ ΤΩΝ | ΠΟΛΕΩΝ ΠΡΟΣΤΑΤΗΝ
Η ΛΑΜΠΡΟΤΑΤΗ | ΜΗΤΡΟΠΟΛΙΣ ΤΗΣ ΑΣΙΑΣ
ΝΕΩΚΟΡΟΣ | ΚΥΖΙΚΗΝΩΝ ΠΟΛΙΣ ΔΙΑ ΤΑΣ ΠΕΡΙ
ΑΥ|ΤΗΝ ΕΥΕΡΓΕΣΙΑΣ ΕΠΙΜΕΛΗΘΕΝΤΟΣ | ΤΗΣ
ΑΝΑΣΤΑΣΕΩΣ ΤΟΥ ΑΝΔΡΙΑΝΤΟΣ | Μ. ΑΥΡ.
ΑΜΕΡΙΜΝΟΥ ΣΕΙΤΟΦΙΛΑΚΟΣ | ΤΗΣ ΠΟΛΕΩΣ[16]

21 Ad aliam marmoream basim:

ΟΚΤΩΚΑΙΔΕΚΑΤΟΥ ΜΕ ΚΑΤΕΡΧΟΜΕΝΟΝ
ΛΥΚΑΒΑΝΤΟΣ | ΑΡΤΙ ΤΕ ΡΗΤΟΡΙΚΗΣ ΕΡΓΑ
ΔΙΔΑΣΚΟΜΕΝΟΝ | ΛΕΣΒΩ ΙΝ ΕΥΔΕΝΔΡΩ
ΒΑΡΤΑΛΙΗΣ ΝΟΤΣΟΣ ΕΔΑΜΝΑ | ΚΑΙ ΟΙΚΕΤ ΕΣ
ΕΙΜΕΡΤΗΝ ΓΑΙΑΝ ΕΒΗΝ ΕΦΕΓΟΥ
ΠΛΙΡΟΚΑΣΙΓΝΗΤΟΣ ΔΕ ΚΑΜΩΝ ΜΑΛΑ ΠΟΛΛΑ
ΤΟΤΕΤΣΙΝ | ΠΕΝΘΟΣ ΕΠ ΩΚΤΑΛΟΥ ΝΗΟΣ ΕΔΩΚΕ
ΦΙΡΩΝ | ΝΑΙΩ Δ ΗΡΩΩΝ ΙΕΡΟΝ ΔΟΜΟΝ [Ο]ΥΚ
ΑΧΕΡΟΝΤΟΣ | ΤΟΙΟΝ ΓΑΡ ΒΙΟΤΟΥ ΤΕΡΜΑ
ΣΟΦΟΙΣΙΝ ΕΝΕΙ[17]

22 ΠΕΡΙΝΘΩ Ε.Α. Α[Δ]ΡΙΑ | ΕΝ ΚΥΖΙΚΩ |
ΝΕΙΚΟΜΗΔΙΕΙΑ

23 ΑΥΡ. ΚΕΝΟΣ

24 ΑΣΚΛΗΠΙΟΔΟΤΗ[18]

25 Η ΒΟΥΛΗ ΚΑΙ Ο ΔΗΜΟΣ ΤΗΣ ΛΑΜΠΡΟ|ΤΑΤΗΣ
ΠΕΡΙΝΘΙΩΝ ΠΟΛΕΩΣ ΣΤΑ|ΤΕΙΛΙΟΝ ΧΡΙΤΩΝΙΑΝΟΝ
ΤΟΝ ΚΡΑΤΙ|ΣΤΟΝ ΕΠΙΤΡΟΠΟΝ ΤΟΝ ΣΕΒΑΣΤΟΝ[19]

The most illustrious metropolis of Asia, the temple-warden   20
city of Cyzicus [honors] the most excellent and upright governor Marcus Ulpius Senecio Saturninus, patron of harmony between the cities, because of his benefactions to her;
Markos Aurelios Amerimnos, grain inspector of the city,
was in charge of erecting the statue.

On another marble base: 21

As I was leaving my eighteenth year and just beginning the
study of rhetoric, a grievous illness overcame me in well-
wooded Lesbos, and I had not yet reached the pleasant land
of Ephesus. My brother, by a great deal of work, gave this
sadness to be borne to my parents on a swift ship. I dwell in
the holy house of heroes, not in Acheron — for such is the
end of life for the wise.

[...] in Perinthus; Hadrianic [Olympian games] in Cyzicus;   22
[...] in Nicomedia[9]

Aurelios [...]kenos   23

Asklepiodote   24

The Council and People of the most illustrious city of   25
Perinthus [honors] Statilios Chritonianos the most excellent
procurator of the Emperors.

[Perinthus to Artace (Turk. Erdek) and Cyzicus,
31 July to 2 August 1444]

26 Ad pridie Kalendas Augusti ex Perintho Proconensium insulam
Cyzicumque petens Artacem venimus, antiquum Cyzicenorum vicum, ubi permulta videntur antiquitatis vestigia — columnarum
statuarumque fragmenta et colosseam hanc inter vineas dirutam
comperi marmoream perpulchram imaginem.

27   Verum et cuius ergo[20] veneram et Propontiacum superavimus
mare, cum ad mirificum et nobilissimum illud Proserpinae templum revisendum me contulissem, dum insignem[21] sui magnitudinem eximiamque fabrefactorum opem atque vivos de marmore
vultus[22] aspexissem, haud immerito Sulmoneum poetam dixisse
cognovimus, sua haec per elegia canens:[23]

Inde[24] Propontiacis haerentem Cyzicon oris
Cyzicon, Haemoniae nobile gentis opus.

28   At Plinius deinde, ille *Naturalis Historiae* conditor diligentissi-
mus, ea in parte qua ingenua et nobiliora mundi opera commemorat, quom hoc praecipuum existimasset opus, in principio inquit:
'Durat et Cyzici delubrum, in quo filum[25] aureum commissuris
omnibus politi lapidis subiecit artifex', et reliqua. Cuiusce vero po-
siti fili latitudinem et concavitatem vidimus, et eam ipsam atque
alia pleraque eiusdem eximiae aedis insignia diligenter inspecta
metitaque hisce quoad licuerat describendum atque stilo defingen-
dum curavimus.

29   Sed heu! quantum ab illo deformem revisimus, quod[26] antea bis
septem iam annis exactis perspeximus; nam tunc xxx et unam columnas erectas vidimus extare, nunc vero unam de xxx manere et
partim epistilii destitutas cognovi. Sed et quae integrae fere omnes

[Perinthus to Artace (Turk. Erdek) and Cyzicus,
31 July to 2 August 1444]

On July 31st, on our way from Perinthus to the island of Pro- 26
connesus and Cyzicus, we arrived at Artace, an ancient suburb of
Cyzicus, where many traces of antiquity are to be seen—fragments of columns and statuary; and among the vines I found this
ruined [but] very lovely colossal marble statue.[10]

The reason for my crossing the Propontic Sea and coming [to 27
Erdek] was to revisit that marvelous, highly celebrated temple of
Proserpina. After gazing at its massive size, the extraordinary
workmanship of its builders, and the lifelike marble features [of its
sculptures], I realized that the poet from Sulmo was not wrong
when he said in elegiac song,

> On this side, Cyzicus, clinging to the shore of the Propontis,
> Cyzicus, elegant creation of the Thessalian people.[11]

And then there was Pliny, that most industrious author of the 28
Natural History, who in the passage where he recalls the more famous indigenous structures of the world, expressing the opinion
that this work was exceptional, says in the beginning, "The temple
at Cyzicus also survives, in which the builder inserted a golden
thread in all the joints of the polished stone,"[12] and so forth. We
saw the width and hollowing out where the thread had been
placed; and after examining and carefully measuring numerous
other noteworthy details of the same remarkable temple we undertook to have it described as well as possible and to have a drawing
made of it.

But alas! How unsightly a structure we returned to, compared 29
to the one we inspected fourteen years ago![13] For then we saw
thirty-one surviving columns standing erect, whereas now I find
that [only] twenty-nine columns remain, some shorn of their architraves. And the famous walls, almost all of which were [then]

inclitae parietes[27] extabant, nunc a barbaris magna quidem ex parte diminutae soloque collapsae videntur. Sed enim[28] insigni suo[29] et mirabili in frontispicio eximia deum et praeclarissima illa de marmore simulacra Jove ipso optimo protectore suaeque eximiae celsitudinis patrocinio inlaesa tutantur et intacta[30] suo fere prisco splendore manent.

30   Cuiusce amplissimi templi magnitudo pro columnarum spacio constat longitudine cubitorum CCXL, latitudine vero CX; LXXque pedum[31] altitudine metiuntur altissimi parietes atque immanes[32] columnae.

31   Ad IIII[33] Nonas Augusti faustum Kyriaceumque diem Cyzicum venimus, nobilem et olim Asiae metropolim et potentissimam urbem.

32   ΙΠΠΑΡΧΟΥΝΤΟΣ ΚΛ ΕΤΙΩΝΕΩΣ | ΗΡΩΟΣ
ΣΤΡΑΤΗΓΟΥΝΤΩΝ ΔΕ ΤΗΣ | ΠΟΛΕΩΣ ΛΑΡΚΙΟΥ
ΝΟΥΜΙΚΙΟΥ | ΚΑΙΚΙΝΑ Π[Α]ΤΣΑΝΙΟΥ
ΜΟΣΤΡΑΤΙΟΥ | ΠΡΑΞΙΑΝΑΚΤΟΣ ΖΩΙΛΟΥ ΓΑΜΟΥ |
ΤΟΥ ΘΑΛΛΟΥ ΕΠΕΙΛΗΧΟΤΟΣ ΙΣΤΤΟΥ | ΣΤΡΑΤΙΟΥ
ΑΝΕΔΕΙΧΘΗ ΕΥΤΥΧΕΙ Ο ΤΟΥ | ΑΜΜΩΝΟΣ
ΣΤΕΦΑΝΟΣ ΥΠΟ ΚΕΙΜΕΝΟΥΣ | Ο ΚΑΙ ΜΟΣΧΟΥ
ΤΟΥ ΣΤΡΑΤΙΟΥ ΤΟΥ ΣΤΡΑ|ΤΗΓΟΥ ΤΗΣ ΠΟΛΕΩΣ
ΚΑΙ ΙΕΡΕΩΣ ΤΗΣ | ΣΩΤΗΡΑΣ ΚΟΡΗΣ Β. ΚΑΙ
ΕΞΗΓΗΤΟΥ | ΤΩΝ ΜΕΓΑΛΩΝ ΜΥΣΤΗΡΙΩΝ ΤΗΣ |
ΣΩΤΗΡΑΣ ΚΟΡΗΣ[34]

33   ΘΗΜΙΣ ΕΤΑΚΟΥΣ ΑΝΕΘΗΚΕΝ | ΤΗΝ ΘΥΓΑΤΕΡΑ
ΑΡΙΕΜΟΥΝ ΦΙΛΗΤΟΡΟΣ | ΗΡ[35]

34   ΣΩΣΙΓΕΝΗΣ ΕΥΚΡΑΤΟΥΣ | ΕΠΟΙΗΣΕΝ[36]

35   ΑΥΤΟΚΡΑΤΟΡΙ ΤΡΑΙΑΝΩ ΑΔΡΙΑΝΩ | ΚΑΙΣΑΡΙ
ΣΕΒΑΣΤΩ ΟΛΥΜΠΙΩ ΣΩΤΗ|ΡΙ ΚΑΙ ΚΤΙΣΤΗ[37]

36   ΣΤΡΟΘΙΣ | ΗΡΑΚΛΕΙΔΟΥ[38]

intact, now in great part lie ruined and dashed to the ground, evidently by the barbarians. On the other hand, those exceptional, glorious marble figures of the gods on [the temple's] outstanding, wondrous facade, remain unharmed in their nearly pristine glory, thanks to the protection of almighty Jove himself and the patronage of his exalted majesty.

It follows from the spacing of the columns that the size of this 30 very large temple was 240 cubits in length and 110 [cubits] in width, and the highest walls and huge columns measure seventy feet in height.

On the 2nd[14] of August, a favorable Lord's day, we came to 31 Cyzicus, a famous and once very powerful metropolitan city.

When the late Klaudios Eteones commanded the cavalry 32 and Larkios son of Noumikios, Kaininas son of Pausanias, Moschos son of Stratios, Praxianax son of Zoilos and Gamos son of Thalos were chief magistrates of the city, and Histios son of Stratios was allotted successor, the crown of Ammon was fortunately received by Klaudios Eumenes and Moschos son of Stratios, chief magistrate of the city and priest of the Saviour Kore for the second time and expounder of the mysteries of Savior Kore.

Themis, daughter of Euakes, dedicated [the monument to] 33 her daughter the late Artemous, daughter of Philetor.

Sosigenes, son of Eukrates, made this. 34

To the Emperor Trajan Hadrian Caesar Augustus, the 35 Olympian, Savior and Founder.

Strouthis, daughter of Herakleides. 36

37 ΚΤΙΣΤΑΡΧΟΙ | ΚΑΡΠΟΣ Β | ΣΗΣΤΟΣ ΦΑΤΣΤΟΣ
ΙΕΡ. | ΤΠΑΤΟΣ ΠΑΠΤΛΟΤ | ΙΕΡ. ΑΛΚΟΡΟΣ ΙΕΡ. |
ΚΛΗΜΗΣ ΤΕΛΕΣΦΟΡΟΤ ΙΕΡ. | ΜΕΙΩΝ ΤΑΛΛΟΤ
ΙΕΡ. | ΓΡΕΙΜΟΣ ΕΡΜΟΤ ΙΕΡ. | ΠΟΛΛΙΩΝ
ΑΝΤΙΟΧΟΤ ΙΕΡ. | ΦΛ. ΑΠΟΛΛΩΝΙΟΣ ΙΕΡ. ΜΤΣΤΑΙ
| ΛΟΛΛΙΟΣ ΑΤΡΗΛ. ΧΡΤΣΑΝΘΟΣ | ΠΟΤ
ΑΝΤΩΝΙΑΝ[Ο]Σ ΖΩΣΙΜΟΣ Τ. ΦΛ. ΕΤΦΤΜΟΣ |
ΒΟΤΛΚΑΚΙΟΣ ΑΛΕΞΑΝΔΡΟΣ ΧΑΡΕΑΣ ΔΙΟΓΕΝ ..... |
ΣΤΑΤΙΟΣ ΡΟΤΦΟΣ ΣΤΑΤΙΟΣ ΑΠΟΛΛ. ΠΡΟΚΛΟΣ |
ΚΛ. ΠΡΟΚΛΟΣ ΒΟΤΛΚΑΚΙΟΣ ΠΟΛΛΙΟΣ | ΛΙΚΙΝ.
ΡΟΤΦΟΣ ΚΛ. ΡΟΤΦΟΣ ΣΩΤΗΡΙΧΟΣ | ΑΝΔΡΟΚΛΟΣ
Π. ΒΗΔΙΟΣ ΜΗΤΡΩΔΩΡΟΣ | Μ. ΚΑ. ΣΕΒΗΡΟΣ ΑΤΡ.
ΦΛ. ΚΛΑΤΔΙΑΝΟΣ ΠΟΛΤΒΙΟΣ | ΛΤΣΙΑΣ ΜΟΤΣΑΙΟΤ
ΟΤΛ. ΠΛΩΤΕΙΑ ΝΕΙΚΟΣΤΡΑΤ | ΕΤΦΡΟΣΙΝΟΣ
ΤΡΟΦΙΜΟΤ ΑΘΗΝΟΔΩΡΟΣ ΕΤΦΡΟΣΤ | Τ. ΜΤΚΙΑΣ
ΚΑΡΙΤΟΤ Π. ΑΙΛΙ. ΕΡΜΗΣ | ΚΑΡΠΟΦΟΡΟΣ
ΠΟΠΛΙΟΤ Τ. ΜΤΚΙΑΣ. Ⲇ.³⁹

38 At cum civitatem undique collapsam aspexissem, et in dies a
barbaris omni ex parte pessundatum iri cognovissem, indolui; et
humani generis calamitatem inferentes ab humanis quoque principibus animadvertendum duxi, et ὦ civitatum Asiae restitutorem
divum Augustum Caesarem exclamavi. Vidimus tamen eius verendissimae vetustatis pleraque nobilia monumenta nostram ad diem
tantae magnitudinis testimonia praestare, et praecipue partem extare vidimus ex primaevis eximiis eius serpentino⁴⁰ e lapide moenibus, ingentes statuas et immania hinc inde conspersa solo marmorea et ingenue fabrefacta saxa.

39 Sed quod potissimum Cyzicenam amplitudinem testatur eximiam, extant ad quartum et ad sextum ab urbe lapidem et Artace
(vocant sub Byzantiano Imperatore habitantes) et alia quae pro-
pinquiora civitati oppida iacent inculta marmoreisque moenibus
condita, quorum pars non exigua erecta turritaque videtur.

Chiefs of the initiated: Karpos Jr., the priest Sestos Faustos, 37
the priest Optatos son of Papylos, the priest Alkoros, the
priest Klemes son of Telesphoros, the priest Menon son of
Thallos, the priest Preimos son of Hermos, the priest
Pollion son of Antiochos, the priest Fl. Apollonios.

Initiates: Lollios Aurel. Chrysanthos, Pou. Antonianos
Zosimos, T. Fl. Euphemos, Boulkakios Alexandros,
Chaireas son of Diogenes, Statios Roufos, Statios Apoll.
Proklos, Kl. Proklos, Boulkakios Pollios, Likin. Roufos, Kl.
Roufos Soterichos, Androklos, P. Bedios Metrodoros, M.
Kl. Seberos, Aur. Fl. Klaudianos Polybios, Lysias son of
Mousaios, Oul. Ploteina Nikostrate, Euphrosynos son of
Trophimos, Athenodoros son of Euphrosynos, T. Mykias
son of Charitos [?], P. Aili. Hermes, Karpophoros son of
Poplios, T. Mykias Jr.

But when I had seen the city everywhere in ruins and had rec- 38
ognized that, day by day, it had been utterly ruined by the barbarians, I grieved; and I felt that human princes must also be made
aware of those who are inflicting devastation on the human race.
And I exclaimed, "O divine Caesar Augustus, restorer of the cities
of Asia!" Even so, we did see that to our day numerous fine remnants of its venerable antiquity bear witness to its greatness; and
we saw that there survive, especially, a portion of its remarkable
prehistoric walls made of serpentine stone, as well as huge statues,
and, scattered on the ground on all sides, enormous marble blocks,
the product of local workmen.

But what most especially testifies to the remarkable importance 39
of Cyzicus, there exist at the fourth and sixth milestones from the
city, both the town of Artace—this is what the inhabitants subject
to the Byzantine emperor call it—and other towns that lie nearer
to the city, overgrown [now, but] built with marble walls, large
portions of which are seen to be upright and fortified with towers.

40   Cum vero templi huiusce mirifici magnitudinem habilius consi-
derassem metirique certius maluissem, comperimus parietes hinc
inde pro templi latere CXL pedum longitudinis, latitudinis vero pedum LXX constare; totidem altitudine parietes constant. Columnae
vero ab utroque latere XXX numero, eiusdem parietum altitudinis,
XIIII[41] pedum invicem distantes, totidem pedum ab ipsis parietibus distant; et ingenti lapidum magnitudine inter columnas et
conspicuos parietes nobile pavimentum hinc inde lata euntibus
deambulatoria praebet. Praeterea ante faciem templi, pronaonis
decore, inter quae pro lateribus extant columnae quino ordine qua-
ternae, viginti numero, extitisse videntur, ornatissimis epistiliis la-
quearibus protectae. Sed a posteriori parte delubri, praeter quas
pro lateribus extabant, quaternas trino ordine XII habuisse columnas cognovimus. Ex quo omnes ingentis templi columnae LXII numero fuisse videntur, praeter X quae intus ornatissimae minores
quino ordine hinc inde parietibus annexae permanent.

41   Cyzici ante templi frontispicium hinc inde proporticum vel pro-
naon habentes quinas hinc inde parietibus annexas et eximia arte
pampineis vitibus et uvis ornatissimas columnas:

[DRAWINGS]

42   Epigramma apud Cyzicum ad inclitum admirandissimum Proserpinae templum: Illustrissimi heroes et optimi Cyzicenorum civitatis cives maximae inferiali et coelesti dearum gloriosae nympharum a Jove productarum Proserpinae talem construxerunt
aedem.[42]

ΕΚ ΔΑΠΕΔΟ[Υ] ΜΩΡΘΩΣΕΝ ΟΛ[ΗΣ Α]ΣΙΑ[Σ]
[ΕΥΤΕΧΝΩΝ] | ΑΦΘΟΝΙΗ ΧΕΙΡΩΝ ΔΙΟΣ
ΑΡΙΣΤ[ΑΙ]Ν[Ε]ΤΟΣ[43]

When I investigated more conveniently the size of this admira- 40
ble temple,[15] and chose to measure it more accurately, we found
that the walls in each direction, in proportion to the side of the
temple, were a hundred and forty feet long and seventy feet wide;
the walls are of the same height.[16] The columns on each side are
thirty in number, of the same height as the walls, standing thirteen feet apart from each other; they stand the same number of
feet from the walls themselves; and a noble pavement with stones
of huge size, between the columns and splendid walls provides
broad ambulatories on both sides for people to walk. Moreover,
one sees that columns stood in front of the facade of the temple,
adorning the pronaos, in front of the side walls, four columns in
each of five rows, twenty in number, covered by a coffered ceiling
[resting on?] ornamental architraves. But in the back of the temple, besides the columns that stand in front of the side walls, we
noticed it had twelve columns in three rows of four. From this it is
clear that the total number of columns of the huge temple were 62,
besides the ten smaller, very elaborate interior columns that remain attached to the walls on either side in [two] rows of five.

In front of the facade of the temple of Cyzicus, on each side a 41
proporticus or pronaos having five columns connected on each
side to the walls and highly ornamented in superb style with
tendrilled vines and bunches of grapes:[17]

[DRAWINGS]

An inscription at the famous, most admirable temple of 42
Proserpina. Famous heroes and the best citizens of the city of
Cyzicus built this shrine to the greatest of the glorious goddesses
[and] nymphs of the lower world and the heavens, Jove's daughters:

> From the level earth, with the wealth of the whole of Asia,
> and with countless hands, the godlike Aristainetos erected
> me.[18]

E fundamento me erexit totius Asiae copia manuum gloriosus Aristenetus.

43 Apud Cyzicum delubrum ad marmoreum et semifractum lapidem haec vetustissimis et expolitis literis τῶν ἱερομνημόνων templi nomina comperiuntur:

ΘΕΟΙΣ | ΕΠΙ ΕΡΜΟΔΩΡΟΤ ΑΡΧΟΝΤΟΣ Ε ΚΤΖΙΚΩ |
ΙΕΡΟΜΝΗΜΟΝΕΣ | ΠΛΕΙΣΤΑΔΟΤΟΣ ΠΟΛΤΚΛΕΟΣ |
ΗΡΑΓΟΡΗΣ ΜΟΤΣΟΚΛΕΟΣ | ΑΝΘΕΜΙΣ ΕΤΑΛΚΙΔΟ |
ΑΠΟΛΛΟΔΩΡΟΣ ΑΠΟΛΛΟΝΙΟ | ΔΙΦΙΛΟΣ ΔΙΟΝΤΣΟ
| ΜΑΚΑΡΕΤΣ ΠΟΣΕΙΔΟΝΙΟ | ΑΡΤΕΜΙΔΩΡΟΣ
ΙΕΡΟΤΙΑΔΟ | ΑΓΗΣΙΛΑΣ ΚΗΡΤΚΙΔΟ | ΙΦΙΚΡΑΤΗΣ
ΜΗΤΡΙΚΕΤΕΟΣ | ΙΔΙΩΤΑΙ | ΑΠΟΛΛΟΔΩΡΟΣ
ΑΘΗΝΟ | ΔΗΜΗΤΡΙΟΣ ΑΠΟΛΛΟΔΩΡΟ | ΑΓΕΛΛΗΣ
ΜΗΝΟΔΩΡΟ | ΔΙΩΝ ΔΙΟΚΛΕΟΣ | ΑΓΑΘΙΝΟΣ
ΑΠΟΛΛΟΝΙΔΟ | ΙΠΠΩΝΑΞ ΑΚΕΣΑΙΟ |
ΜΑΝΤΙΚΛΗΣ ΞΕΝΟΘΕΜΙΟΣ | ΠΡΩΤΕΑΣ
ΑΠΟΛΛΟΔΩΡΟ⁴⁴

[Perinthus revisited, 12 August 1444]

44 ΧΡΗΣΜΟΣ ΣΙΒΤΛΛΗΣ ΕΠΑΝ Δ Ο ΒΑΚ|ΧΟΣ
ΕΤΑΣΑΣ ΠΛΗΣΤΑ ΠΟΤΞ ΑΙΜΑ | ΚΑΙ ΠΤΡ ΚΑΙ
ΚΟΝΙΣ ΜΙΓΗΣΕΤΑΙ⁴⁵

45 ΣΠΕΛΛΙΟΣ ΕΤΗΘΙ[Ο]Σ | ΑΡΧΙΒΟΤΚΟΛΟΣ |
ΗΡΑΚΛΕΙΔΟΤ ΑΛΕΞΑΝΔΡΟΤ | ΑΡΧΙΜΤΣΤΟΤΝΤΟΣ
| ΑΛΕΞΑΝΔΡΟΣ ΣΠΕΙΡΑΡΧΟΣ | ΑΡΡΙΑΝΟΣ
ΑΓΑΘΙΑ | ΗΡΟΞΕΝΟΣ ΜΑΓΝΟΤ | ΣΩΤΗΡΙΚΟΣ
ΔΑΔΑ | ΜΗΝΟΦΙΛΟΣ⁴⁶

46 Apud Perinthum Thraciae olim metropolin, quam hodie Heracleam dicunt, vetustam in Propontico civitatem, fatale et sibyllinum hoc epigramma comperimus ad ipsam metropolitanam

From its foundation, with the wealth of all Asia, with an abundance of hands, glorious Aristenetus erected me.[19]

At the temple of Cyzicus, on a partially broken marble block 43
are found these names of the temple priests [carved] in ancient, elegant script:

> To the gods. When Hermodoros was *archon* [chief magistrate] in Cyzicus Priests [*hieromnemones*]: Pleistadotos son of Polykles, Heragores son of Mousokles, Phanothemis son of Eualkidos, Apollodoros son of Apollonios, Diphylos son of Dionyso[doros], Makareus son of Poseidonios, Artemidoros son of Hieroitiados, Agesilas son of Kerykidos, Iphikrates son of Metriketes. Private individuals: Apollodoros son of Atheno[doros], Demetrios son of Apollodoros, Agelles son of Menodoros, Dion son of Diokles, Agathinos son of Apollonidos, Hipponax son of Akesaios, Mantikles son of Xenothemis, Proteas son of Apollodoros

[Perinthus revisited, 12 August 1444]

Oracle of the Sibyl: When Bacchus cries out and wanders, 44
then blood and fire and dust will be mixed.

Spellios Euethios president of the worshippers of Dionysus 45
in bull form; when Herakleides son of Alexander was leader
of the initiated; Alexander the cohort commander, Arrianos
son of Agathias, Heroxenos son of Magnos, Soterikos son of
Dada, Menophilos

At Perinthus, once the chief city of Thrace, which today they 46
call Heracleia, an ancient city state on the Propontis, we found
[the above] fateful Sibylline inscription at the metropolitan church

Beatae Virginis aedem ad dexteram arae partem in marmore Graecis litteris et eximiis consculptum.

47   Ad pridie Idus Augusti, Eugenii pontificis anno XIIII.[47]

: 14 :

1   Kyriacus Raphaeli suo salutem dicit et ὁμόνοιαν.

2   Bis iam tui gratia Perinthum venimus [...][1] et primo atque altero adventu aufugeras et nostro te aspectu subtraxisti. Equidem
vero cum primum adveneram, apud ipsum Cydonem praefectum
et oppidanos Heraclidas Perinthios olim cives exclamavi: 'quae regio Raphaelem, quis habet locus? Illius ergo venimus et magnum
Propontidis penetravimus aequor.' Illi vero te Pontum vel Bithy-
niam primum, secundo vero Zurlaeum in Thracia oppidum accer-
situm habere.

3   Ego vero, quamquam me Byzantium quam citius petere res
haud inopportunae cohercerent, te hic tamen per diem e Zurlo remeaturum duximus expectandum; et tibi quae hic nobilia veterum
monumenta comperimus quodque deinde apud Cyzicum revisimus Haemoniae nobile gentis opus, si veneris, ostentabo, dulcis-
sime Raphael, optime iuvante deo Iove.

4   Ex Perinthea Threicia, olim praeclara urbe, pridie Idus Augusti.

: DIARY I, CONTINUED :

[Perinthus: Gift of a Vespasian coin to Raffaelle Castiglione. 14 August]

48   Apud Turcummale, Perinthiae civitatis vicum, ad compertum nuper in agro lapidem:

of the Blessed Virgin to the right of the altar, carved in marble in elegant Greek script.

12 August, in the 14th year of the reign of Pope Eugene.   47

: 14 :

To Raffaele Castiglione, 12 August 1444, Perinthus

Cyriac wishes health and concord to Raffaele.[1]   1

This is now the second time I have come to Perinthus to see   2
you [...][2] and both times you fled from my approach and withdrew from my sight. The first time I came, I cried out in the presence of the governor Kydones and his townsmen, citizens of what was once Heraclea Perinthus, "What land, what place holds Raffaele? It is for his sake that I have come and crossed the great expanse of the Propontic Sea."[3] On that first visit [they told me] you had been summoned to the Black Sea and Bithynia; on this second, that you had gone to Çorlu, a town in Thrace.[4]

As for myself, although matters of no little urgency constrain me   3
go on to Byzantium rather soon, I have decided I should wait here a day for you to return from Çorlu. If you do come, my dearest Raphael, with the help of the great god, Jove, I will show you important remains of antiquity that I found here, and then an important handiwork of the Thracian people that I saw again in Cyzicus.[5]

From Perinthus in Thrace, once a splendid city, 12 August.   4

: DIARY I, CONTINUED :

[Perinthus: Gift of a Vespasian coin to Raffaelle Castiglione. 14 August]

At ?Turcummale, a village of the city of Perinthus, on a stone re-   48
cently found in a field:

Ο ΔΗΜΟΣ ΠΟΛΥΚΡΙΤΟΝ ΧΑΒΡΙ|ΟΥ ΑΝΔΡΑ
ΑΓΑΘΟΝ ΓΕΝΟΜΕΝΟΝ | ΕΝ ΤΗΙ ΠΟΛΙΤΕΙΑΙ[1]

49   Ad Vespasiani Caesaris argenteum nomisma:

IMP. CAES. VESP. AVG. CENS.

Argenteum hoc ipsum Vespasiani Caesaris nomisma hodie xix
Kalendas Septembris apud Mystreum Perinthinae civitatis vicum
Raphaeli Castillioneo amico dulcissimo nostro dedi, ut ad quem
almae Christicolum religionis nostrae amatorem cultoremque
pium et observatorem diligentissimum cognovi. Nam nil dignius
nilque nostrae amicitiae memorandae preciosius monumentum
sibi nostris antiquis de rebus dare delegimus, quam Vespasiani sa-
cratissimi capitis agalma, ut vir ipse Christiani nominis amantissi-
mus, Christi iniuriarum ultoris imaginem videre, colere atque saepius memorare possit.

:   15   :

1   Andreolo Iustiniano, viro insigni.

2   Postquam beatitudini tuae scripsimus et Paridi nostro magnifico Antonioque Bocchono litteras ad te reddendas dedimus,
hodie vi Kalendas Septembris reverendissimum patrem Leonardum, Lesbeum pontificem, ad hanc urbem adventantem magna
hylaritate revisimus et de te vestris omnibus valitudinem et felicitatem laete ab eo intelligere placitum mihi iterum atque iterum
fuit.

3   Sed te aliosque vestratum quam plures nescio qua improbae vo-
cis fama nostri interitus doluisse displicuit et te facile falsum credi-

The people [honor] Polykritos son of Chabrios who was a
good man in civic life.

On a silver coin of Vespasian Caesar: 49

Emperor Caesar Vespasian Augustus Censor.

Today, the 14th of August, at the Mystrean village of the Perin-
thian state, I bestowed this very coin of Vespasian Caesar on
Raffaele Castiglione, my very dear friend, as upon a man whom I
know to be a lover and a devout and assiduous worshiper of our
nourishing Christian faith. For I could choose from my [collection
of] antiquities no worthier keepsake to give him as a souvenir
of our friendship than the image of the most sacred head of
Vespasian, a man most devoted to the Christian name, a portrait
of the avenger of the wrongs done to Christ for him to look upon,
to reverence, and to recall again and again.[1]

: 15 :

To Andreolo, 27 August [1444], ?Constantinople

To the distinguished Andreolo Giustiniani.   1

My letter to Your Beatitude I had already entrusted to our   2
magnificent Paride and to Antonio Boccone for delivery to you,
when today, the 27th of August, the reverend Father Leonardo,
bishop of Lesbos, came to this city and I had a very joyful reunion
with him, in the course of which it pleased me and gave me joy
again and again to learn that you and all your family enjoy good
health and good fortune.

But I was displeased that you and very many other friends of   3
yours were grieved by some rumor or other, based on a mischie-

disse rumorem admirabar, qui tam laete semper Kyriacum tuum
tutelaresque suos omnes cognovisti deos deasque terra marique
potentes, et quemadmodum non magno sine numine divum flumina tanta paramus, at et tam parvam Mercurio curam esse nostri
existimare, virum peritissime, potuisti, ὃς καὶ καθάπερ Ὀδυσ-
σεῖ πρὸς Κίρκην καὶ κατὰ Κίρκης φαρμάκιον φάρμακον
πόρεν μόλυ, οὕτως καί μοι ῥίζα μέλαν καὶ γάλακτι ἴκελον
ἄνθος ἔδωκεν, ἑρμοδώρωι μοι δωρησάμενος εἰεργωτας
θεός.

4   Valere te diu felicem hylaremque desidero et magna quoque voluptate te longaevam beatamque vitam ducere peropto. Iterum
atque iterum vale.

: 16 :

1   Ad eundem Iulianum cardinalem Sancti Angeli Kyriacus Anconitanus.

2   Scripsimus ad te pridem ex Hadrianopoli et Byzantio quae digna nobis potissimum visa sunt, fortunatissime Iuliane pater. Sed
inde paucos post dies reverendissimum vicecancellarium cardinalem, optimum tuum hac sanctissima in expeditione collegam, pontificia cum beatissima classe Hellespontum Byzantiumque venisse
novisti; ex qua ita Hellespontiacum Bosporeumque fretum obser-
vatum habeto, ut ne quis Teucer hinc inde traicere possit, effectum
est.

3   At et non multum postea maior huic laetitiae accessit hilaritas
nobis et imperatori nostro fidelissimo Ιωanni. Nam cum nudius

vous source, of my demise; and I was surprised that you gave easy credence to this false report, since you know your Cyriac and all his guardian gods and goddesses, powerful over land and sea, and [you know] how I prepare for such a voyage with the emphatic approval of the gods. But [I was especially surprised] that you, cleverest of men, could have supposed that Mercury would take so little care of me; for, just as [Hermes] gave Odysseus the herb moly as a remedy against Circe and Circe's poisonous drug, so did my god give me for protection an [herb] "black at the root but its flower was like to milk," endowing me with Hermes' gift.[1]

My desire is that you are well, fortunate, and of good cheer. It   4
is my great desire that you live a long and happy life, filled with delight. Again and again, farewell.

: 16 :

To Cardinal Giuliano Cesarini,
12 and 19 September 1444, Constantinople

Cyriac of Ancona to the same Giuliano, cardinal of Sant'Angelo.[1]   1
We wrote you previously from Adrianople and Byzantium [the   2
news] that seemed particularly important, most fortunate Father Giuliano.[2] But a few days after that, as you know, the reverend Cardinal Vice-chancellor, your excellent colleague in this holy campaign, arrived at the Hellespont and Byzantium with the most blessed pontifical fleet.[3] Be assured that this fleet has the Hellespont and the Bosporus under such close observation, that, effectively, no Turk can pass from one side to the other.

Not long after that an even greater happiness was added to our   3
joy — mine and our most steadfast emperor John's. For a few days ago, on the 7th of September, when I was with him in his court,

tertius VII Idus Septembres apud eum in curia essem, angelum ab angelico te viro optimo exoptatum adventasse vidimus et litteras tuas alacres et felices regiasque et invictissimi Coniati Iani ducis ac optimorum quorumcumque principum patentes privatasque vidimus, quas equidem primum maiestati suae legimus, Graece rettulimus, et quanta ex his eum et curiam totam atque urbem et in conspectu coloniam Peram iucunditate hilaritateque repletas vidimus, hisce non facile litteris explicarem.

4   Optabam equidem magnopere omnes per orbem gentes et fidelium potissimum principes harum copiis litterarum et sanctissimi foederis et ampli apparatus et ad flumen accessus certiores fore et per navim, quae iampridem Siceliam navigavit, Alphonso regi ac aliis in Regno Ausoniave principibus exempla pleraque misimus, e quis sibi pro viribus suadere conabar, ne tam sanctissimae expeditionis eos videremus expertes.

5   Et ne his plura dicam, imperatorem hunc optimum et inclytos fratres ad rem ipsam favendam paratamque iam suam triremum classem augendam summa sua cum potestate, diligentia, solertiaque incumbere scito; ad quae non modo regiam suam urbem, sed Aegaeas utique insulas, Lemnum, Imbrum, Scyron, Scyathum, Scopulosque admiscendum curarunt.

6   Valere te quamdiu feliciorem et te sanctissima hac in expeditione revisere opto. Pridie Idus Septembres.

7   Praeterea, clusis et ad diem hunc XIII Kalendas Octobres morantibus litteris, nobiles nonnulli Genuenses viri certis ex Rhodo epistolis significarunt: Rhodios Aegyptiacae classi ingentem cladem intulisse et quos ad terram desilientes et moenia quassare calcantes convenerant, ad novem hominum milia captos caesosque fecisse,

we saw that a longed-for "angel"[4] had come from your angelic Excellency and we saw enthusiastic and cheerful dispatches, patent and private, from the king and from the invincible Prince John Hunyadi and certain excellent princes. We, for our part, first read them to His Majesty after translating them into Greek, and I could not explain easily in writing with how great a joy and gladness we saw these letters filled him, as well as his entire court and the city and the colony of Pera across the way.

For my part, I desired greatly that all the peoples of the world,   4 especially the Christian princes, be informed of your full preparation and access to the river,[5] through copies of these letters and of the most sacred treaty; and we sent numerous copies by a ship that has already started for Sicily, to King Alfonso and to other princes in the Kingdom or in Italy, from which I tried to persuade them with all my powers not to let us see them failing to participate in this most holy campaign.

Without my going into greater detail, know that this excellent   5 emperor and his famous brothers are bent on promoting the project itself and on increasing their already prepared fleet of galleys with the utmost power, industry, and skill; and they have arranged that not only [ships of] their own royal city should be included in this fleet, but also [those of] the Aegean islands of Lemnos, Imbros, Skyros, Skyathos, and Skopelos.

I wish you good health and increasing success and I hope to see   6 you again during this most holy campaign. 12 September.[6]

[Postscript:] While this letter lay sealed and waiting [for posting]   7 until today, the 19th of September, some Genoese notables sent news by reliable dispatches from Rhodes that the Rhodians had inflicted a major defeat on the Egyptian fleet, had captured or killed nine thousand men, on whom they had converged to smash as they leapt ashore and set foot in the fortified town; they had seized the barbarians' siege-engines and all their equipment; and

machinasque ac spolia barbara omnia diripuisse et inter captivos e praestantioribus admiratos sex intercepisse. Quae quidem felicissimae res, quantum Christicolis adiumenti extiterint, barbarisque profanis hostibus obfuisse sane te intelligere scimus, optime atque sapientissime pater et vere patrum insigne et immortale decus.

8   Excolendissimae reverendissimaeque paternitatis tuae dicatissimus Kyriacus Anconitanus.

: DIARY II :

[Constantinople, 20 September 1444]

1   ΑΓΑΘΗΙ ΤΥΧΗΙ. Artium, mentis, ingenii facundiaeque pater, alme Mercuri, nec non viarum itinerumve optume dux, qui tuo sanctissimo numine nostram undique mentem animumque fovisti, quique nostrum omne iucundissimum iter per Latium, Illyrriam, Graeciam, Asiam et Aegyptum terra marique tutum, rectum habileque fecisti: ita, noster inclite geni, et nunc et nostrum omne per aevum animo menti facundiaeque opitulare nostrae, nec non hodie per Propontiacum aequor Hellespontiacumque et Aegaeum ac nostrum omne deinceps per orbem iter tutum, felix, faustum atque beatum dirigere, favitare atque comitare velis.

[Departure from Constantinople, 20 September 1444.
Proconnesos, 24 September. Hellespont, 27 September.
Arrival in Imbros, 28 September]

2   ΑΓΑΘΗΙ ΤΥΧΗΙ. Ad xii Kalendas Octobris ex Byzantio Lemnum petens, et Hellespontiacam pontificiam classem petens, trire-

among their more prominent captives were six emirs. Excellent
and most wise father, truly distinguished, undying glory of our
forebears, we are quite sure you understand how helpful these
great successes will be to Christians and how prejudicial to the interests of the barbarian, infidel foe.

Cyriac of Ancona, the wholly dedicated servant of your most   8
worshipful and most reverend paternity.

: DIARY II :

Travels in the Northern Aegean
20 September 1444 to January 1445

[Constantinople, 20 September 1444]

Good Luck. Father of the arts, of mind, of wit, and of speech,   1
nurturing Mercury, best lord of ways and journeys, who by your
most holy power have everywhere blessed my mind and heart; and
who have made safe, right, and easy all my most pleasant travels
by land and sea through Latium, Illyria, Greece, Asia, and Egypt:
so, my famed *genius*, vouchsafe both now and through all my life
and in particular today, to assist my wit, mind and speech to direct, favor and accompany my journey through the Propontis, the
Hellespont and the Aegean [Sea], and then throughout the world,
[making it] fortunate, favored, and fruitful.

[Departure from Constantinople, 20 September 1444.
Proconnesos, 24 September. Hellespont, 27 September.
Arrival in Imbros, 28 September]

Good Luck. On the 20th of September, setting out from Byzan-   2
tium on course for Lemnos and [on the way] for the papal fleet

mem regiam Alexio Disypato praefecto conscendi; et ad VIII Kalendas Praeconesiam in Propontico marmorigenam insulam venimus, et ingentia marmora incisa et nostra ipsa ad littora imminentia vidimus et ingentem vivo in saxo speluncam, supra quam erat sic inscriptum:

ΙΟΤΛΙΑΝΟΣ ΓΡΑΜΜΑΤΕΤΣ[1]

3   Ad quintum Kalendas Octobris Hellespontum venimus et prope Lamsacon et contra obsidentemve Hellespontiacam Cheronesiam Calliepolim pontificiam ipsam XII navium classem comperimus, et Ludovicum Lauredanum praefectum una cum Alexio trierarcho nostro visimus; et eodem die Boreis secundantibus crebris Imbron ad insulam venimus, visis ex itineris nostri cursu Threiciis Hellespontiacisque antiquis ad Europae littora oppidis Lysimachia, Calliepoli, Sesto, Cilla Madidocrissaque, ad Asiae vero vel Phrygiae littus Abydo et Segeo, Troiae nobili promontorio, et in conspectu Tenedo insula visis et illico praetermissis.

4   Ad IIII Kalendas Octobris ex orientali Imbri littore, una viro cum docto et Imbriote nobili Hermodoro Michaele Critobulo, ad occidentalem eiusdem insulae partem ad Imbron, antiquam insignemque olim et vetustissimam civitatem, terrestri itinere equis devecti et arduos per colles et prope civitatem planiciem venimus. Ubi ad summam civitatis arcem Manuelem Asanium, virum ex Byzantio nobilem et eius insulae pro Iohanne Palaeologo Imperatore benemerentem praesidem, quem et arcem ipsam duabus iam ex partibus noviter condidisse comperimus. Ibidem vero longe antiqui et vetustate collapsi muri vestigia vidimus; et hic nonnullam e moenibus partem extare pulcherrimae suae architecturae ordine conspicuam vidimus, et ingentes ad portum antiqua ex mole lapi-

in the Hellespont, I embarked on a royal trireme captained by Alexios Disypatos; and on the 24th we arrived at the marble-producing island of Proconnesos in the Propontis [where] we saw huge blocks of marble overhanging our coastline and a huge cave in the living rock, over which was the following inscription:

Ioulianos the secretary.

On the 27th of September we arrived at the Hellespont; and near Lapsaki and, opposite it on the [Thracian] side of the Hellespont, Gallipoli, we encountered the actual papal fleet of twelve ships; and, along with our trierarch Alexios, we paid a visit to Lodovico Loredan;[1] and on the same day, with the help of frequent favoring north winds, we sailed on to the island of Imbros, sighting along the course of our voyage ancient Thracian and Hellespontic towns: on the European shore line, Lysimachia, Gallipoli, Sestos, Cilla, and Madidocrissa; and, along the coast of Asia, or rather Phrygia, sighting and immediately passing by Abydos and Segeum, the storied promontory of Troy, and, within sight of it, the island of Tenedos. 3

On the 28th of October, traveling by land on horseback with the learned and well-born Imbriot Michael[2] from the eastern shore of Imbros, over steep hills, and across a plain near the city, we came to the western portion of the same island, to the ancient and once distinguished, extremely old city of Imbros. There, at the city's highest point, we found that Manuel Asan, a well-born gentleman of Byzantium and well deserving governor of that island for [Emperor] John Palaiologos, had recently constructed the current stronghold out of two pre-existing parts. In the same place, we saw the remains of a very ancient wall that had crumbled with age; and here we also observed that a section of the [fortification] wall is extant, remarkable for its exceedingly handsome style of architecture. [We also saw] at the port huge stones from an an- 4

des et nonnulla marmorum statuarumque fragmenta, bases et vetustissimis characteribus epigrammata:

5   Ad arcem ipsam ante moenia:

ΔΙΟΔΩΡΟΣ ΦΙΛΟΦΡΟΝΟΣ | ΠΕΙΡΑΕΤΣ | ΦΙΛΟΦΡΩΝ
ΦΙΛΟΚΛΕΟΤ ΠΕΙ|ΡΑΕΤΣ[2]

6   Ad alium lapidem:

ΦΙΛΟΜΕΝΗ ΕΡΜΝΗΣΙΑΝΑΚΤΟΣ[3]

7   Ad arcem ico⟨n⟩as et magnis ex cocto latere litteris:

⳨ΠΙΚΕΡΝΗΣ Ο ΚΟΜΝΙΝΟΣ | ΚΟΙΝΤΟΣ ΣΤΕΦΑΝΟΣ[4]

: 17 :

1   ΑΓΑΘΗΙ ΤΥΧΗΙ. Kyriacus Scholario, viro Graecorum doctissimo, salutem.

2   Postquam abs te et regia Byzantio urbe concessimus, clarissime
Scholarie vir, basilea devectus trireme ad VIII Kalendas Octobris
Proeconesum, Propontiacam atque marmorigenam insulam, venimus, cum venti omnes posuissent et lento saepius in marmore
tonsae luctassent.

3   Sed inde postquam ternos per dies noctesque placidi Neptuni
liquidum sulcavimus campum, Caeceis Boreisque aspirantibus
Aeolis, Hellespontum navigavimus et prope vetustam Lampsacon
pontificiam Lauredanamve Christianissimam classem Cheronesiam in conspectu Calliepolim obsidentem comperimus; et una
nostro cum optimo Alexio Δισυπάτῳ regio trierarcho, viso salu-

94

cient, massive structure, and some fragments of marbles and statues, statue bases, and inscriptions [carved] in a very old script.

On the citadel itself, in front of the fortification walls: 5

Diodoros, son of Philophron, from Peiraeus; Philophron,
son of Philokleos, from Peiraeus.

On another stone: 6

Philoumene, daughter of Hermesianax

On the citadel, images, and large letters made of brick: 7

✠Kointos Stephanos, Cupbearer, the Comnenian

: 17 :

To George Scholarios, 29 September 1444, Imbros

Good Luck. Cyriac to Scholarios,[1] the most learned of the   1
Greeks, greetings.

After we had left you and the royal city of Byzantium, famed   2
Scholarios, sailing aboard the royal galley, we put in on the 24th
of September at Proconnesus, a marble-producing island in the
Propontis, after all the winds had fallen and the oars had struggled
too often in the sluggish surface of the sea.

Leaving there, we plowed the liquid field of peaceful Neptune   3
for three days and nights under winds that blew from the northeast and north, until we arrived at the Hellespont and came in
sight of the pontifical Christian fleet near ancient Lampsacus.
Under the command of Loredan, it was blockading Gallipoli in
the Chersonese. Along with our excellent royal captain, Alexios
Disypatos, I visited and greeted Alvise Loredan, the excellent

tatoque ac perdigne ad rem bene gerendam persuaso Ludovico
Lauredano optimo classis praefecto eodem et fausto v Kalendarum Octobrium sereno Cyriaceoque die, secundis crebrescentibus
auris, Hellespontum superavimus laeti; et hinc inde Hellespontiaca Europae atque Asiae littora triremibus nostris oportune cus-
todita conspeximus; et tandem per Aegaeum Imbron venimus insulam, oceano cadente Phoebo.

4   Ex qua cum ad posteram diem triremis expetitam ad Lemnum
navigasset, ego interim antiquam Imbron insulam et civitatem videre,

Threiciamque Samon, quae et[1] nunc Samothracia fertur,

indagare constitui, et una tuo cum amicissimo viro et Imbriotum
doctissimo, Michaele Critobulo, heri IIII Kalendas Octobres terrestri itinere scrupeos arduosque per colles Imbron ad ipsam venimus vetustam, quam Παλαιόπολιν dicunt, olim magnam atque
nobilem civitatem, ubi Manuelem Asanium novam quamvis
ἀκρόπολιν iussu regio arcem turritam condidisse et exornatam
comperimus. Ubi equidem ad primariam portam hoc breve epigramma antiquis nostro et Attico de more litteris ponendum curavimus.

5   Vale, et me ad cras exiguam per cymbam Neptuneam Samon
navigaturum habeto optimo iuvante Deo ipso, Ποσιδῶνος et Nereidum clarissima favitante placidissima Cymodocea. Ex Imbro, III
Kalendas Octobris.

captain of the fleet, and exhorted him to carry out his mission worthily. That same lucky day, the 27th of September, a bright Sunday, rejoicing in increasingly favoring winds, we passed through the Hellespont, noting that both the European and the Asiatic shores of the Hellespont are guarded strategically by our galleys. At length, as the sun was setting, we came through the Aegean to the island of Imbros.

The next day, although the galley went on to its destination, 4 Lemnos, I decided to investigate the ancient island and city of Imbros and [then go on to]

Thracian Samos, which is now called Samothrace.[2]

So, yesterday, the 28th of September, together with your good friend, the most learned of the Imbriotes, Michael Kritoboulos, I walked over rocky, steep hills to ancient Imbros itself, which they call "the Old Town," once a great and distinguished city, where we found that Manuel Asan at the emperor's orders had built and decorated on the citadel a new fortress equipped with towers. There we [composed] this short inscription following our and the Attic custom of antique lettering, and had it set up at the main gate:[3]

Farewell, and know that I shall sail in a small boat to Neptune's 5 Samos tomorrow, with the help of God and the favor of Cymodocea, the most brilliant and kindly of Poseidon's Nereids. From Imbros, the 29th of September.

: 18 :

1 [...] quem iussu regio novam inibi arcem condidisse comperimus. Ubi primum praetorianam ad aulam, bona pro nostri iucundissimi itineris ave, Caesaream hanc inscriptionem marmoreo in lapide conspexi.

2 Vale, et me ad cras Samon Threiciam, antiquam Neptuni sedem, navigaturum scito. Tu interim, vir bone, legatum optimum nostrum praedigne facito memorem, et sanctam illam Parthicam expeditionem, quam apud eum et alios iam diu tam solertissime favitare atque iuvare coepisti, ad exoptatum perducere finem die noctuque curabis. III Kalendas Octobris 1444.

: DIARY II, CONTINUED :

[Departure from Imbros, 2 October. Visit to Samothrace]

8 Ad VI Nonas Octobris ex Imbro ab Asanio praeside scapha quatuor munita remigibus largita, et Manuele Imbriote perdocto ducente nauta, Samon Threiciam venimus secundo cursu bonis faventibus Aeoliis, quam nobilem et montibus arduam in Aegaeo insulam Maro noster suo in Aenea commemorat his dictis:

Threiciamque Samon, quae nunc Samothracia fertur.

9 Equidem cum ea die ad australem insulae partem allaberemur, vidimus prope altiora illa atque nimbosa montis cacumina, quorum ab alto vertice Neptunum Graecam olim classem vento-

: 18 :

Fragment, addressee unknown, 29 September 1444, Imbros

[...] [Manuel Asan], who we found had built a new fortress there 1
at the emperor's orders. There, first of all, at the governor's palace,
as a good omen of our most joyful journey, I found this Roman
imperial inscription on a marble stone.[1]

Farewell, and know that tomorrow I shall sail to Thracian 2
Samos, ancient abode of Neptune. Meanwhile, good fellow, remember [me] suitably to our excellent legate, and strive night
and day to bring to its longed-for conclusion that holy campaign
against the Parthians, which you began long ago with him and
others to promote and assist so skillfully. The 29th of September,
1444.

: DIARY II, CONTINUED :

[Departure from Imbros, 2 October. Visit to Samothrace]

On the 2nd of October we [departed] from Imbros in a small boat 8
manned by four rowers provided by Governor Asan. Guided by
an experienced Imbriot sailor named Manuel, on a voyage made
uneventful by favoring winds, we came to Thracian Samos, a famous island in the Aegean, towering with mountains, which our
Maro recalls in his *Aeneid* in these words:

Thracian Samos, which is now called Samothrace.[1]

For our part, as we glided in towards the southern side of the 9
island that day, we observed from close at hand the taller, cloud-
enshrouded peak, from whose lofty perch, as we read in the bard

samque Ilion atque Hectoreas acies conspexisse Homerum ceci-
nisse vatem divino nempe carmine lectitavimus, quod altius hodie
culmen Ἁγίαν Σοφίαν, Sanctam Sapientiam, vocant.

10   Ad posteram vero diem ad mediterraneum novum insulae oppidum ad centum fere stadia pedites montana arduaque per loca
venimus, Manuele ipso ducente nauta, ubi primum Johannem
Lascarim pro Palamede Gatalusio praefectum comperi, qui me
postquam perhumane susceperat, ad sequentem faustum Cyria-
ceumque diem ad antiquam maritimam civitatem ipsam, quam ad
septemtrionalem insulae partem Palaeopolin vocant, me honorifice
comitatus est.

11   Ubi primum eo et ipso ductitante, vidimus antiqua et magnis
condita lapidibus moenia, quae ab alto et arduo colle longo tractu
porrecta per declivia ad mare vergentia in hodiernum aliqua ex
parte turribus portisque munita durant et diversa quidem architectorum compositione mirifica. Praeterea, quod ad eiusdem insulae
cumulum claritatis accedit, in ea Philippus adolescens adhuc
Olympiadem Alexandri illius nobilissimi regis matrem cognovit
auctore Plutarcho.

12   Vetusta Samothracum moenia:

13   Vidimus et ingentia Neptuni marmorei templi vestigia immanium columnarum fragmenta, epistyliaque et bases, atque portarum postes ornatos e coronatis boum capitibus aliisque figuris ins-
culptis arte perpulchra.

14   Et inde postquam ad novam a Palamede principe conditam arcem venimus, ad turrim ipsam pleraque vetusta arte elaborata
marmora videntur composita, ubi plerasque nympharum choreas
consculptas inspeximus; et alia complura hinc inde vetustatis
tantae urbis eximia monumenta comperimus et nobilia atque veterrima Graecis ac etiam nostratum litteris epigrammata. Epigrammata ad triangularem basim ornatam marmoreamque:

Homer's divinely-inspired song, Neptune once watched the Greek fleet and wind-swept Ilium and Hector's army, a peak that today they call "Hagia Sophia," the Holy Wisdom.

The next day, guided by Manuel himself, we walked about a hundred stadia over steep, mountainous terrain to the island's modern inland town.[2] There, I first looked up Janos Laskaris, the governor [representing] Palamede Gattilusio, who received me very kindly and did me the honor of accompanying me on the following lucky Lord's Day to the ancient city itself, which they call "the Old City," situated by the sea in the northern part of the island.

There, under his personal guidance, we first looked at the ancient walls, built of large stones. Extending from a high, steep hill over a long stretch on a decline that slopes down to the sea, they survive to our day, provided in some part with towers and gates in marvelously diverse architectural styles. Moreover, to add to the island's accumulation of celebrity, it was on it, according to Plutarch, that the young Philip came to know Olympias, the mother of that most noble king Alexander.[3]

The ancient walls of Samothrace.[4]

We saw also the vast remains of the marble temple of Neptune, fragments of immense columns, architraves and statue bases and doorways decorated with garlanded boukrania[5] and other very beautifully and artistically sculptured figures.

And after we had gone from there to the new castle built by prince Palamede, we saw at the tower itself numerous ancient, artfully elaborated, complex marbles, on which we observed numerous sculptured dancing nymphs; and we discovered on every side numerous other extraordinary remains of the antiquity of this great city and noteworthy, very old inscriptions in Greek, and even in our own countrymen's lettering. An epigram on an ornate triangular plinth made of marble:

10

11

12

13

14

[Other inscriptions from Samothrace]

15   Ad Capsulum novum ex Palamede oppidum:

ΜΗΤΡΟΦΑΝΟΤ ΧΑΙΡΕ¹

16   Ad arcem antiquae Samothraciae urbis quam hodie Παλαιόπολιν vocitant, ad antiquissimam listam marmoream insigni arte
persculptam ad turrisque parietem ornamento positam:

17   Ad aedem Demetrii Martiris:

CLAVDIO M. PERPE[R]NA COS. MENS. QVINC.
MVSTE DIEI | CL. LV[C]CEIVS M. F. LEG. P. LIVIVS
M. L. PAL. | M. LVCCEIVS M. L. ARTEMIDORVS | Q.
HORTENSIVS M. L. ARCHELAOS²

18   Ad alium lapidem:

ΘΕΟΡΟΙ ΠΑΡΑΓΕΝΟΜΕΝΟΙ | ΠΡΙΗΝΕΙΣ | ΦΙΛΙΟΣ
ΘΡΑΣΕΙΒΟΤΛΟΤ | ΒΑΣΙΛΕΙΔΗΣ ΑΠΟΛΛΟΔΩΡΟΤ |
ΤΟΤ ΠΟΣΙΔΩΝΙΟΤ | ΣΑΜΙΟΙ | ΑΠΟΛΛΟΝΙΟΣ
ΜΕΛ[Α]ΙΝΕΩΣ | ΑΡΧΕΠΟΛΙΣ ΚΑΛΛΙΣΤΡΑΤΟΤ |
ΑΡΙΣΤΙΠΠΟΣ [Φ]ΑΜΕΝΟΤ ΕΡΜΕΑΣ ΔΑΜΟΚΡΑΤΕΩΣ
| Α[Γ]ΟΡΑΝΟΜΟΤΝΤΟΣ ΑΠΟΛΛΟΔΩΡΟΤ | ΤΟΤ
ΠΤΘΑΡΑΤΟΤ³

19   Εἰς τοὺς βασιλικοὺς κήπους. Ad regios hortos prope mare:

ΔΗ[Μ]ΟΚΡΑΤ[Η]Σ ΟΤΛΙΑΔΟΤ | ΜΗΝΟΔΩΡΟΣ
ΤΕΧΝΩΝΟΣ | ΔΙΟΝΤΣΙΟΣ ΤΙΜΟ[ΚΛ]ΕΙΟΤΣ |
ΑΠΟΛΛΩΝΙΔΗΣ ΖΕΤΞΙΔΟΣ | ΠΟΛΤΧΑΡΜΟΣ
ΧΑΡΜΟΤ | ΑΛΕΞΑΝΔΡΟΣ ΑΡΤΕΜΙΔΩΡΟΤ |
ΕΠΙΓΟΝΟΣ ΜΕΝΕΣΤΡΑΤΟΤ | ΑΡΤΕΜΙΔΩΡΟΣ
ΠΤΘΕΟΤ | ΑΣΚΛΗΠΙΑΔΗΣ ΔΙΟΝΤΣΙΟΤ |
ΔΗΜΗΤΡΙΟΣ ΑΡΤΕΜΙΔΩΡΟΤ | ΑΠΟΛΛΩΝΙΟΣ
ΕΤΔΑΜΟΝΟΣ | ΣΤΡΑΤΩΝ ΕΠΙΚΡΑΤΟΤ |

[Other inscriptions from Samothrace]

At Capsulum, a new town founded by Palamede: 15

[. . . son of] Metrophanes, farewell.

On the citadel of the ancient city of Samothrace, which today   16
they call "the Old City," on a very ancient marble frieze sculptured
with extraordinary skill and positioned as a decoration on the wall
of the tower:[6]

At the church of Demetrius the Martyr: 17

Pious initiates in the month of Quinctilis [July], when
[Caius] Claudius and Marcus Perperna were consuls: Lucius
Lucceius son of Marcus, legate; Publius Livius Pal[atinus]
freedman of Marcus; Marcus Lucceius Artemidorus freed-
man of Marcus; Quintus Hortensius Archelaos freedman of
Marcus.

On another stone: 18

The envoys who were present [to consult the oracle]. From
Priene: Philios son of Thrasyboulos, Basileides son of
Apollodoros son of Poseidonios; from Samos: Apollonios
son of Melaines, Archepolis son of Kallistratos, Aristippos
son of Phamenos, Hermeas son of Damokrates. The clerk of
the market was Apollodoros son of Pytharatos.

In the royal gardens by the sea:[7]   19

Demokrates son of Ouliades, Menodoros son of Technon,
Dionysios son of Timokles, Apollonides son of Zeuxis,
Polycharmos son of Charmos, Alexandros son of Artemi-
doros, Epigonos son of Menestratos, Artemidoros son of
Pytheas, Asklepiades son of Dionysios, Demetrios son of
Artemidoros, Apollonios son of Eudaimon, Straton son of

ΑΠΟΛΛΩΝΙΟΣ ΑΠΟΛΛΩΝΙΟΤ | ΑΚΕΣΤΩΡ
ΕΤΚΤΗΜΟΝΟΣ | ΑΓΑΘΟΣ ΑΓΑΘΟΤ | ΧΑΡΙΔΗΜΟΣ
ΧΑΡΙΔΗΜΟΤ⁴

20 [ΕΠΙ] ΒΑΣΙΛΕΩΣ ΠΡΟΚΛΕΟΤΣ ΤΟΤ ΑΔΡΙΑΝΟΤ |
ΣΑΜΟΘΡΑΚΩΝ | ΑΠΟΛΛΩΝΙΟΣ ΑΠΟΛΛΟΜΕΝΟΤ |
ΑΝΔΡΟΝΙΚΟΣ ΠΟΛΤΝΙΚΟΤ | ΛΑ[Μ]ΨΑΚΗΝΩΝ |
ΑΡΤΕΜΙΔΩΡΟΣ [ΚΡ]ΑΝΤΟΡΟΣ | ΑΙΣΧΤΛΟΣ
ΑΙΣΧΡΙΩΝΟΣ | ΜΤΡΕΩΝ | ΕΤΑΓΟΡΑΣ Η[Γ]ΗΤΟΡΟΣ
| ΕΤΑΛ[Κ]ΟΣ ΟΣΕΟΤΟΤ | ΑΝΤΙΓΟΝΟΣ ΔΡΟΜΩΝΟΣ
| Ε[Φ]ΕΣΙΩΝ | ΣΩΣΙΘΕΟΣ ΗΡΑΚΛΕΙΔΟΤ |
ΑΡΤΕΜΙΔΩΡΟΣ ΞΕΝΙΟΤ | ΔΗΜΟΔΟΤΟΣ ΔΙΟΝΤΣΙΟΤ
| ΘΑΣΙΩΝ | ΑΝΤΙΦΩΝ ΣΟΦΟΚΛΕΙΟΤΣ | ΙΕ[Ρ]ΩΝ
ΑΡΙΣΤΟΦΩΝΤΟΣ | ΔΙΟΚΛΗΣ ΗΓ[Η]ΣΙΟΤ |
ΑΜΑΝΤΙΝΟΣ ΦΙΛΟΞΕΝΟΤ⁵

21 C.L.LUCC[E]I[US] C.F.EQ. | C. MISPIVS MVSTE⁶

[Imbros to Ainos, 28 October]

22 Ad v Kalendas Novembris ex Imbro insula Lemnea devectus
cymba, Aenum antiquam in Thracia 'ab Aenea profugo conditam'
civitatem venimus, ubi Palamedem Gatalusium, eiusdem urbis et
Samothracum principem, duobus cum filiis Georgeo ac Dorino invenimus, et cum his Christophorum Dentutum Genuensem clarissimum nostrum et Illyricum comitem et amicissimum revisi et
eiusdem principis optimum secretarium Franciscum Calvum, virum humanissimum diligentissimumque.

23 Qui primum principes et eximii viri me postquam perhumane
susceperant, omnia civitatis insignia mihi quam solertissime osten-
derunt; et primum extra urbem ad quinque stadia a moenibus
amotum vidimus insignem ilium Priamidae Polydori tumulum
magno terrarum aggere compositum.

Epikrates, Apollonios son of Apollonios, Akestor son of
Euktemon, Agathos son of Agathos, Charidemos son of
Charidemos.

When Prokles son of Hadrianos was chief magistrate   20
[*basileus*]. [Envoys from] Samothrace: Apollonios son of
Apollomenos, Andronikos son of Polynikes; from
Lampsacus: Artemidoros son of Krantor, Aischylos son of
Aischrion; from Myra: Euagoras son of Hegetor, Eualkos
son of Osetes, Antigonos son of Dromon; from Ephesus:
Sisitheos son of Herakleides, Artemidoros son of Xenios,
Demodotos son of Dionysios; from Thasos: Antiphon son
of Sophokles, Hieron son of Aristophon, Diokles son of
Hegesios, Amantinos son of Philoxenos.

Gaius Lucius Lucceius son of Gaius [...] | Gaius Mispius   21
initiates.

[Imbros to Ainos, 28 October]

On the 28th of October, setting out from the island of Imbros on   22
a Lemnian skiff, we came to the ancient city of Ainos,[8] founded by
the refugee Aeneas,[9] where we found Palamede Gattilusio, the
prince of this same city and also of Samothrace, along with his
sons Giorgio and Dorino. With these gentlemen I paid a return
visit to Cristoforo Dentuto, the distinguished count of Illyricum
and our very good friend, and the same prince's excellent secretary,
Francesco Calvo, a person of great kindness and diligence.

After these princes and distinguished men had received me   23
most cordially, they expertly showed me all of the city's important
sites: first, we saw outside the city, at a remove of five stadia from
the city walls, the remarkable Trojan tomb of Priam's son Polydorus, which consisted of a large mound of earth.

[Ainos, continued]

24 Ad huiusce culminis verticem una nostro cum Christoforo equis devecti conscendimus et ex Marone nostro crudele Polymnestoris Threicii regis facinus memoravimus, sacramque auri famem![7] exclamavimus.

25   Deinde vero cum urbem undique diligentius indagaremus, vidimus pleraque tantae vetustatis vestigia: ingentia marmora diversis consculpta figuris sed magna ex parte diruta, et plerasque suis cum inscriptionibus bases confractas inspeximus et principiis finibusque carentes. Quae vero integriores erant hisce inscriptae videntur et nobiliores delectae.

26   Sed primum quam apud ortum secus mare integram comperimus basim ex marmore nobilem hoc loco reponendum curavi.

27   Vidimus et prope civitatis moenia, eo ipso Francisco Calvo amicissimo ductitante nostro, plerasque manu fabrefactas vivo sub saxo cavernas, ubi Thraces ob intollerabilem hyemem vitandam inhabitare consueverant, ut nuper apud Pomponium Melam cosmographum clarum Latine perlegimus. Et nunc cavernae quae vivo in saxo videntur Bubularia dicuntur.

[Departure from Ainos, 10 November. Visit to Maroneia.]

28 Ad IIII Idus Novembris ex Aeneadum urbe Chiensi scapha et Cretensi Phantasio ducente nauta, bonis afflantibus Boreis et Caeceis, Seriphon promuntorium superantes, Maroniam venimus, antiquam in Thracia civitatem. Ubi multa ad mare sepulchra marmorea primum vidimus diruta et pro aggere ad portum coniecta et antiquitatis alia hinc inde vestigia plura, columnarum basiumque fragmenta, tripodesque et Atticis characteribus epigrammata.

29   Sed ad turritam quam noviter ediderant arcem novis Graecorum litteris epigrammata cocto de latere compositis comperi. Sed et quod magis adnotari placuit, ibidem ad fractum lapidem anti-

[Ainos, continued]

With Cristoforo we rode to the top of this mound on horseback 24
and, recalling from Vergil the cruel deed of the Thracian king
Polymnestor, we exclaimed "O accursed hunger for gold!"[10]

Then, as we explored the city everywhere more carefully, we 25
saw numerous traces of her great antiquity: huge marbles sculptured with a variety of figures, but for the most part demolished,
and we examined numerous broken statue bases with their inscriptions, whose beginnings and endings were missing. Those
that were somewhat complete and chosen as more important are
written down here:[11]

But first I made sure to record here a fine, intact marble statue 26
base that I found in a garden near the sea.

Also, under the personal guidance of our very good friend 27
Francesco Calvo, we saw near the walls of the city numerous caves
hand-carved from the living rock, where the Thracians customarily dwell to fend off the unbearable winter, as we read recently in
Pomponius Mela the illustrious geographer.[12] Nowadays, these
caverns, which are visible in the living rock, are called "Bubularia."

[Departure from Ainos, 10 November. Visit to Maroneia.]

On the 10th of November, under favoring North and Northeast 28
winds, we rounded Seriphon's promontory in a Chian skiff and,
guided by a Cretan sailor named Phantasios, arrived at Maroneia,
an ancient city in Thrace, where we saw, first off, a number of
marble sarcophagi at the port that had been demolished and
thrown together by the seaside to serve as a mole, and several
other remnants of antiquity on all sides: fragments of columns
and statue bases, tripods, and inscriptions in Attic lettering.

On the turreted citadel, a recent structure, I found inscriptions 29
in Greek letters made of brick; but what pleased me more was
to find, on a broken stone in the same place, in very old letter-

quissimis characteribus magna ex parte dirutis Democriti nobilissimi physici nomen suae coniugis gratia consculptum inveni.

ΔΗΜΟΚΡΙΤΟΥ ΓΥΝΗ[8]

[Maroneia to Thasos, 11 November]

30 Ad iii Idus Novembris ex Maronia concedentes eadem scapha
Thasium insulam nobilem petentes, antiqui Diomedis littora procul inspeximus, quem suis immanibus equis advenas ad mandendum obiectare solitum accepimus; et ob id ab Hercule oppositam
turrim et Abderam a sorore eiusdem Diomedis Abdera conditam
procul conspeximus.

31   Exinde ad ipsam venimus praeclarissimam Thasium insulam et
civitatem olim praepotentem et antiqui Stesimbroti mathematici
nobilissimam patriam.

[Thasos, continued. Dedication to Francesco Gattilusio]

32 Thasiorum nobilissimae civitatis marmorea antiqua conspicua arte
composita moenia.

33   FRANCISCO DORINI FILIO GATALVSIO, LESBEO
REGVLO MAGNIFICO AC THASIORVM OPTIMO
BENEMERENTIQVE PRINCIPI, QVI ALMAE
VIRGINIS MARIAE JOHANNISQVE SANCTISSIMI
BAPTISTAE AVSPICIIS THASIVM INSVLAM
ILLVSTREM IPSAM ET CIVITATEM PRAECLARAM
LONGI TEMPORIS LABE COLLAPSAM
PROVIDENTISSIME PIE ATQVE MAGNAMINITER
CVM OMNI CVLTV RESTITVENDAM CVRAVIT,
THASII CIVES COLONIQVE DEDERE.

ing largely effaced, the name of the famous natural philosopher Demokritos, carved for the sake of his wife:

Wife of Demokritos

[Maroneia to Thasos, 11 November]

On the 11th of November, leaving Maroneia in the same skiff and making for the famous island of Thasos, we examined from afar the shores of ancient Diomedes, who, tradition tells us, was accustomed to throw strangers to his monstrous horses for them to eat; and we spied from afar the tower that Hercules for this reason set opposite, and Abdera, founded by Diomedes' sister Abdera.[13]   30

Then we reached the glorious island of Thasos itself and its once very powerful city and the famous homeland of Stesimbrotos, the ancient mathematician.   31

[Thasos, continued. Dedication to Francesco Gattilusio]

The ancient marble walls of the famous city of Thasos, constructed with remarkable skill.   32

The citizens and inhabitants of Thasos dedicated this to Francesco Gattilusio, son of Dorino, the magnificent ruler of Lesbos and excellent, deserving prince of Thasos who, under the protection of the Virgin Mary and the most holy John the Baptist, with great foresight, loyalty, and generosity, and with all reverence saw to the restoration of the illustrious island of Thasos and its glorious city, fallen to ruins by the destructive effects of the ages.   33

[Thasos, continued]

34   Deinde vidimus antiquissima civitatis moenia ab alto collis vertice magno circuitu ad maritimum usque littus porrecta. Quae omnia candenti ex marmore magnis condita lapidibus et eximia architectorum arte conspicua, magna ex parte integra nostram ad diem turrita videntur, magnum indicium splendoris primaevae tam eximiae civitatis, familiae et praeclarissimae vetustatis.

35   Statua marmorea et eximia arte fabrefacta apud Thasii portus vestibulum nuper a Francisco Gatalusio principe erecta. Olim vero Thasiorum consilii simulacrum fuisse sua ad basim insculpta antiqua inscriptione patet.

36   Ad vetustissimum lapidem antiquissimis characteribus nomina:

ΣΑΤΤΡΟΣ ΑΝΔΡΟΓΗΘΕΟΣ | ΚΡΙΝΑΓΟΡΗΣ
ΔΕΟΝΤΟΣ | ΝΤΜΦΩΝ ΔΕΙΝΟΚΛΕΟΣ |
ΑΡΙΣΤΟΦΑΝΗΣ ΜΙΚΑΔΟΣ | ΣΟΣΤΡΑΤΟΣ ΕΤΗΡΕΟΣ
| ΔΗΜΗΣ ΜΝΗΣΙΣΤΡΑΤΟΣ | ΠΤΘΙΩΝ
ΗΓΗΣΙΠΠΙΔΕΩ | ΠΤΘΑΣ ΦΑΝΟΛΕΩ | ΔΙΚΗΚΡΑΤΗΣ
ΦΙΛΩΝΟΣ | ΗΡΑΣ ΦΙΛΩΝΟΣ | ΤΙΜΗΣΙΚΡΑΤΗΣ
ΛΕΟΦΑΝΕΟ | ΠΟΛΤΝΕΙΚΗΣ ΛΤΣΑΓΟΡΕΩ | ΦΙΛΤΗΣ
ΙΠΠΟΣΘΕΝΕΟΣ | ΦΗΤΙΩΝ ΑΝΤΙΠΑΠΠΟ[Τ][9]

37   Ad marmoream arcam extra civitatis moenia quam Karulo Grimaldo duce primum comperimus:

AELIA TVLIA QVINTIA VIVA SIBI ET MARITO SVO
DIOSCVRIDE DIOSCVRIDII | DE SVO FACTVM
CVRAVIT. HAEC ARCA HEREDEM NON
SEQVITVR.[10]

38   Ad aliud monumentum:

ΝΑΡΙΣΙΣ ΕΤΤΤΧΙΝ | ΜΟΣΧΕΙΑΣ[11]

39   ΛΕΟΓΕΝΗΣ ΚΛΕΟΔΩΡΟΤ[12]

[Thasos, continued]

Then we viewed the ancient walls of the city that extend from the   34
lofty summit of a hill in a large circuit all the way down to the seashore. All of which, constructed of large, bright, marble stones
and remarkable for its outstanding architecture, one can see in our
own day, in great part intact, towers and all, a great proof of the
grandeur of such an exceptional, youthful city, [its ruling?] family,
and its illustrious antiquity.

A marble statue fashioned with remarkable skill, erected re-   35
cently at the entrance to the port of Thasos by Prince Francesco
Gattilusio. It is clear from the ancient inscription carved on its
base that in times past it served as an [allegorical] effigy of the
Council of Thasos.[14]

On a very old stone [bearing] names in antique lettering: 36

Satyros son of Androgathes, Krinagores son of Deonys,
Nymphon son of Deinokles, Aristophanes son of Mikas,
Sostratos son of Eueres, Demes son of Mnesistratos,
Pythion son of Hegesippides, Pythas son of Phanoleos,
Dikekrates son of Philon, Heras son of Philon, Timesikrates
son of Leophanes, Polyneikes son of Lysagores, Philtes son
of Hipposthenes, Phetion[?] son of Antipappos.

On a marble sarcophagus outside the walls of the city that we   37
found first with Carlo Grimaldi as our guide:

Aelia Tullia Quinta, while she was alive, had this built at her
own expense for herself and her husband Dioscurides son of
Dioscurides. This tomb cannot be inherited.

On another monument: 38

Naris, ?Eutychin, Moscheias

Leogenes son of Kleodoros   39

40   Sunt et extra civitatis moenia innumera quidem et ornatissima ac unico ex lapide sepulchra, magnum potentissimae ac populosae urbis indicium. Sed rara sunt in quis sua epigrammata consculpta videantur, nam aliae complures arcae agraphae sunt, aliae vero deletis iam longa vetustate litteris extant.

[*Thasos, continued*]

41   Vidimus et ad marmoreum Thasii portus molum[13] unico de marmore eximia fabrefactam arte ferocem nudi hominis et leonis pugnam, ex qua superior homo, leonis collo ambobus iniectis manibus et fortiter invicem connexis, elisam enixe feram exanimare videtur.

42   At cum et ad acropolim summam civitatis arcem conscendimus, Carulo et ipso Grimaldo nobili comitante, vidimus ad medium collem per iter ingens vetusto de marmore amphitheatrum, quod et xxx integris adhuc gradibus metiebamur altitudine, et in his loca quarumcumque dignitatum sessoribus scripto deputata designatave fuisse videntur. Nam magnis et longa vetustate iam deletis litteris hoc quibusdam gradibus erat insculptum:

ΤΟΠΟΣ[14]

43   Sed postquam ipsam ad arcem praecelsam venimus, majora longe atque praeclariora vidimus marmorea magnis et condita lapidibus moenia, Iohanne Novariensi viro docto potissimum comitante, qua ex parte omnem totius urbis vastae ambitum muri vidimus, qui non multo minus xxx stadiorum circuitu civitatem ambisse videtur. Sed quod magis adnotari placuit, eximiae vetustatis indicium, hoc ad vestibulum arcis comperi vetustissimis characteribus epigramma:

Also outside the city walls there are, in fact, numerous highly 40
decorated monolithic tombs, important evidence of a very powerful and populous city. But those on which one sees inscriptions are
few, for very many of the sarcophagi are uninscribed, while the
others survive with their texts effaced by the long passage of time.

[*Thasos, continued*]

We saw, also at the marble mole of the Thasian port, [a statue] 41
fashioned with extraordinary skill from a single block of marble
[depicting] a fierce struggle between a nude man and a lion, from
which it appears that the man, gaining the advantage, with both
hands thrust around the lion's neck and forcefully joined together,
is [in the act of] strangling the broken beast to death.

But when we climbed to the top of the city's citadel, accompa- 42
nied by the high-born Carlo Grimaldi himself, we saw along the
way up, in the middle of the hill, a huge marble amphitheater,
whose height we measured by the thirty rows of seats that are still
preserved; and among these [seats] there seem to have been places
designated and reserved in writing for occupants of certain high
offices. For on certain rows, in large lettering, now effaced by the
long passage of time, was inscribed as follows:

The place [of ...].

But after we arrived at the lofty citadel itself, we saw far larger 43
and more striking marble walls constructed of large stones — the
learned John of Novara was our special companion — and from
this vantage point we saw the entire circumference of the desolate
city's wall, which surrounded the city with a circuit of no less than
thirty stades. But what pleased me more to record as evidence of
exceptional antiquity was that I found at the entrance to the
stronghold this inscription, in very ancient lettering:

44 ΕΠΙ ΘΕΟΡΩ | ΑΝΤΙΦΩΝΤΟΣ ΤΟ ΚΡΙΤΟΒΟΛΟ
ΑΘΗ|ΝΙΠΠΩ ΤΟ ΚΛΕΟ[ΛΟ]ΧΟ ΚΛΕΟ[ΛΟ]ΧΟ ΤΟ |
ΑΛΚΙΠΠΩ ΤΩΝ ΔΕΙΡΑ ΤΑ ΧΡΗΜΑΤΑ | ΤΟ
ΑΠΟΛΛΩΝΟΣ ΚΑΤΑ ΤΟΝ ΛΑΟΝ | ΤΩΝ
ΤΡΙΗΚΟΣΙΩΝ ΑΠ[Ε]ΜΑΝΤΩ ΤΟ | ΦΙΛΩΝΟΣ
ΗΡΑΣ[Τ]Α[Τ]Ο ΦΙΛΩΝΟΣ. . . . ΤΟ | ΘΕΟΓΕΙΤΟΝΟΣ
[Λ]ΤΣΙΟΣ ΤΟ ΤΙ[Μ]ΩΝΟΣ | ΔΙ[Ο]ΣΚΟΡΙΑΔΕΩ
ΝΕΟΠΟΛΙΤΕΩ | ΑΠΟΜΑΝ[Τ]Ο ΝΕΟΠΟΛΙΤΕΩ[15]

[Thasos, continued]

45 Vidimus et extra arcis moenia aliud insigne verendissimae antiquitatis vestigium quod ad summum collis verticem vivo et suapte natura saxo marmoreo insculptum videtur tabernaculum perinde ac
vetustae religionis oraculum in quo ad interiorem arcus parietem
indigenae Fauni caprigenumque pecudum genus veterrima artificis
manu persculptum atque fabrefactum est.

[Thasos, inscriptions]

46 Ad marmoream basim ante aulam principis vetustis litteris epigramma:

ΗΡΑΚΛΕΩΝ ΔΙΟΣΚΟΤΡΙΔΟΤ ΦΙΛΟ|ΚΑΙΣΑΡ ΚΑΙ
ΦΙΛΟΠΑΤΡΙΣ ΔΗΛΙΩΝ | ΦΙΛΙΠΠΟΤ ΦΙΛΟΚΑΙΣΑΡ
ΚΑΙ ΦΙΛΟΠΑ|ΤΡ[Ι]Σᵣ ΔΗΛΙΩΝ ΑΝΤΙΦΑΝΤΟΣ
ΦΙΛΟ|ΚΑΙΣΑΡ ΚΑΙ ΦΙΛΟΠΑΤΡΙΣᵣ ΠΑΝΚΡΑ|ΤΙΑΔΗΣ
ΑΠΟΛΛΟΝΙΟΤ ΦΙΛΟΚΑΙΣΑΡ | ΚΑΙ ΦΙΛΟΠΑ|ΤΡΙΣᵣ
ΦΙΛΙΠΠΟΣ ΦΙΛΙΠ|ΠΟΤ ΦΙΛΟΚΑΙΣΑΡ ΚΑΙ
ΦΙΛΟΠΑΤΡΙΣ | ΑΝΤΙΠΑΤΡΟΣ ΔΗΜΟΣΘΕΝΟΤΣ
ΦΙΛΟ|ΚΑΙΣΑΡ ΚΑΙ ΦΙΛΟΠΑΤΡΙΣ ΠΟΠΛΙΟΣ |
ΤΑΔΙΟΣ ΖΩΣΙΜΟΣ ΦΙΛΟΚΑΙΣΑΡ ΚΑΙ |
ΦΙΛΟΠΑΤΡΙΣ ΑΡΧΕΑΣ ΑΡΙΣΤΟΚΡΑ|ΤΟΤΣ

When Antiphon son of Kritoboulos, Atenippos son of   44
Kleolochos and Kleolochos son of Alkippos were magistrates [theoroi], the property of the following [became] sacred
to Apollo according to the decree of the Three Hundred:
Apemantos son of Philon, Herostratos son of Philon, [...]
son of Theogeiton, Lysios son of Timon, Dioskorides son of
Neopolites, Apemantos son of Neopolites.

[Thasos, continued]

We also saw outside the walls of the stronghold another recogniz-   45
able trace of highly revered antiquity, namely, that at the very summit of the hill, in the living, natural marble rock, one sees carved
out a shrine just like the [seat of an] oracle of the ancient religion,
in which, on the interior wall of the vault, [images of] the native
[god] Faunus and the race of beasts born of goats were carved and
fashioned by the hand of an ancient artist.

[Thasos, inscriptions]

On a marble statue base in front of the prince's hall, an inscription   46
in ancient lettering:[15]

Heracleon son of Dioskourides, Delion son of Philippos,
Delion son of Antiphon, Pankratiades son of Apollonios,
Philippos son of Philippos, Antipatros son of Demosthenes,
Poplios Tadios Zosimos, Archeas son of Aristokrates,
Philophron son of Hekataios.

ΦΙΛΟΚΑΙΣΑΡ ΚΑΙ ΦΙΛΟΠΑΤΡΙΣ | ΦΙΛΟΦΡΩΝ
ΕΚΑΤΑΙΟΥ ΦΙΛΟΚΑΙΣΑΡ | ΚΑΙ ΦΙΛΟΠΑΤΡΙΣ[16]

47   Ad ornatissimum de marmore sepulchrum alta basi praecelsum
prope torrentem et dirutum vetustate templum:

ΠΟΛΙΑΔΗ ΣΩΣΙΩΝ|ΟΣ Υ[Ι]ΟΣ ΤΗΣ ΓΕΡΟΥΣΙΑΣ |
ΚΑΙ ΑΡΧΙΕΡΕΥΣ ΧΑΙΡΕ[17]

48   Ad alium arcum:

ΚΛΑΥΔΙΟΣ ΒΑΣΙΛΙΚΟΣ | ΠΡΟΣΟΙΔΗΣ ΧΑΙΡΕ |
ΚΛΑΥΔΙΟΣ ΟΚΙΑΡΟΣ | ΧΑΙΡΕ[18]

49   AVRELIVS CASSIVS CAELIVS C. F. DICAVI
SEPVLCHRVM | DVLCISSIMAE CONIVGI FLAVIAE
ARTEMECLEAE ET FILIAE | MEAE AVRELIAE
MARCELLAE ET NATIS MEIS PVERIS DVOBVS |
AVRELIO CHRYSOGONO ET AVRELIO RVFO. IN EO
QVIDEM | NVLLVM ALIVD VOLO PONI CORPVS.
SI QVIS AVTEM AVDERIT, DABIT THASIORVM
CIVITATI POENAE NOMINE VEL PROSTIMO
AVREORVM QVINQVE MILLIA.[19]

50   Ad alium lapidem et inter vineas ante portum:

ΘΕΟΔΩΡΑ ΦΛΑΚΚΟΥ ΑΝΘΟΦΟΡΙΣΑΣΑ | ΕΤΩΝ Π.
ΠΡΟΣΦΙΛΗΣ ΜΗΔΕΝΙΣΣΟΝ | ΕΙΝΑΙ ΕΙΣ ΤΟΥΤΟ ΤΟ
ΣΟΡΕΙΟΝ ΑΠΟ ΕΤΕ|ΡΩ ΠΤΩΜΑ Η ΔΟΥΝΑΙ
ΠΡΟΣΤΕΙΜΟΥ | ΤΩ ΙΕΡΩ ΤΑΜΕΙΩ ✕. Β̄. Φ. ΚΑΙ ΤΗ
| ΠΟΛΕΙ ✕. Β̄. Φ.[20]

51   Ad alium lapidem:

[Λ]ΕΩΝ ΧΑΛΛΙΝΟΥ | ΘΥΜΑΙΟΣ ΔΙΟ[Υ] |
ΧΑΡΙΛΛΟΣ ΑΡΙΖΗΛΟΥ |ΚΑΛΑΜΙΣ ΛΕΩΔΙΚΟΥ[21]

On a highly embellished marble sarcophagus high on an ele- 47
vated base near a rushing stream and a temple ruined with age:

Farewell, Poliades son of Sosion, "Son of the Council of elders" and high priest.

On another arch: 48

Beloved Klaudios Basilikos, farewell, Klaudios Okiaros, farewell.

I, Aurelius Cassius Caelius son of Caius dedicated this tomb   49
to my sweetest wife Flavia Artemiclea and my daughter
Aurelia Marcella and my two sons Aurelius Chrysogonus
and Aurelius Rufus. I do not wish any other body to be buried in it. Anyone who dares to do so will pay the city of
Thasos a penalty or fine of 5000 gold pieces.[16]

On another stone and among vines in front of the port: 50

Beloved Theodora daughter of Flakkos, the former flower-
bearer [priestess], 80 years old. Nobody is allowed to put another body in this urn — or pay a fine of 2500 denarii to the
treasury and 2500 to the city.

On another stone: 51

Leon son of Kallinos, Thymaios son of Dios, Charillos son
of Arizelos, Kalamis son of Leodikos.

52   Ad alium lapidem:

ΠΟ. ΚΟΡΝΗΛΙΟΣ ΙΟΤΣΤΟΣ ΛΕΩΝΑΣ | ΛΕΩΝΑ
[Γ]ΛΑΤΚΙΑΣ ΦΟΡΤΟΝΑΤΟΤ Β̄. | Δ[Ι]ΟΓΕΝ[Η]Σ
ΕΤΤΡΟΠΕΙΟΤ ΕΠΕΙΚΛΗΝ | ΔΕΡΖΕΙ[Λ]ΟΤ ΤΟ Β̄.²²

53   Ad magnum et ornatissimum de marmore sepulchrum:

ΑΤΡΗΛΙΑ ΑΣΚΛΗ[ΠΙ]ΟΔΩΡΑ | ΚΑΤΕΘΕΜΗΝ
ΤΟΤΤΟ ΤΟ ΑΝΓΕΙΟΝ | ΕΜΑΤΤΗ ΚΑΙ ΤΩ ΣΤΜΒΙΩ
ΜΟΤ ΚΑΙ | ΤΟΙΣ ΤΕΚΝΟΙΣ ΜΟΤ ΕΙ ΔΕ ΤΙΣ
ΤΟΛ|ΜΗΣΕΙ ΕΤΕΡΟΝ ΑΠΟΤΕΘΗΝΑΙ ΔΩ|ΣΕΙ
ΙΕΡΩΤΑΤΩ ΤΑΜΕΙΩ ✗. Ε.²³

54   Ad aliud marmoreum monumentum:

ΙΟΤΛΙΑ ΙΟΤΛΙΑΝΗ ΦΛΑΟΤΙΑ Λ. ΠΑ|ΡΑΜΟΝΩ ΤΩ
ΓΛΤΚΤΤΑΤΩ ΣΤΜΒΙΩ | ΚΑΤΑΣΚΕΤΑΣΑΤΟ
ΑΝΓΕΙΟΝ ΚΑΤ ΕΑΤ|ΤΗ ΜΗΔΕΝΑ ΔΕ ΕΤΕΡΟΝ
ΚΑΤΑΘΕΣΘΑΙ | ΕΝ ΑΤΤΩ ΠΤΟΜΑ ΕΙ ΔΕ ΤΗΣ
ΒΟΤΛΗ|ΘΗ ΚΑΤΑΘΕΙΝΑΙ ΔΩΣΕΙ ΤΗ ΠΟΛΕΙ | ✗. Β̄.
Φ̄. | ΦΛΑΟΤΙ ΟΤΑΛΕΡΙ ΠΑΡΑΜΟΝΕ ΧΑΙΡΕ²⁴

55   Ad magnum et ornatissimum prope mare sepulchrum unico ex
marmore pedum VIII longitudine, et latitudine pedum VI, basis
vero x:

ΑΤΡ[Η]ΛΙΟΣ ΚΑΣΣ. ΚΕΛΛΙΟΣ ΓΑΙΟΤ
ΚΑ|ΤΕΣΚΕΤΑΣΑΤΟ ΣΟΡΕΙΟΝ ΤΗ ΓΛΤΚΤΤΑ|ΤΗ
ΣΤΜΒΙΩ ΜΟΤ ΦΛΑΟΤΑ ΑΡΤΕΜΕΙ|ΚΛΕΙΑ ΚΑΙ ΤΗ
ΘΤΓΑΤΡΙ ΜΟΤ ΑΤΡΗΛΙΑ | ΜΑΡΚΕΛΛΗ ΚΑΙ
ΕΓΓΟΝΟΙΣ ΜΟΤ ΠΑΙ|ΔΙΟΣ ΔΤΣΙΝ ΑΤΡΗΛΙΩ
ΧΡΤΣΟΓΟΝΩ | ΚΑΙ ΑΤΡΗΛΙΩ ΡΟΤΦΩ . . . . . ΙΣ Ο
ΟΤ|ΔΕΝΑ ΕΤΕΡΟΝ ΒΟΤΛΟΜΑΙ ΠΤΩΜΑ
ΚΑ|ΤΑΘΕΣΘΑΙ ΕΙ ΔΕ ΤΙΣ ΤΟΛΜΗΣΕΙ ΔΩ|ΣΕΙ ΤΗ
ΘΑΣΙΩΝ ΠΟΛΕΙ ΠΡΟΣΤΙΜΟΤ ✗. Ε̄.²⁵

On another stone: 52

Publius Cornelius Justus, Leonas son of Leonas, Glaukias
son of Fortunatus for the second time, Diogenes son of
Eutropeios surnamed Derzeilas for the second time.

On a large and ornamental marble sarcophagus: 53

I, Aurelia Asklepiodora laid up this sarcophagus for myself,
my husband and my children. If anyone dares to put another
[in it], he will pay the sacred treasury 5000 denarii.

On another marble monument: 54

I, Julia Juliana Flavia Valeria prepared this sarcophagus for
my dearest husband and myself. No other body may be buried in it. If anyone dares to bury [one], he will pay the city
2500 denarii. Flavius Valerius Paramonos farewell.

On a large and highly decorated sarcophagus near the sea made   55
of a single [block of] marble, eight feet long and six feet wide, with
a base of ten feet:

I, Aurelios Kassios Kellios son of Gaios built this tomb
for my sweetest wife Flavia Artemikleia and my daughter
Aurelia Markelle and my two grandchildren Aurelios
Chrysogonos and Aurelios Roufos. I do not wish any other
body to be buried in it. Anyone who dares to will pay the
city of Thasos a fine of 5000 denarii.[17]

56   Ad aliud ingens et boum capitibus exornatum sepulchrum:

ΠΑΡΑΜΩΝΟΣ ΗΒΟΑΔΟΥ ΤΟΥ ΗΒΟΑ|ΔΟΥ ΤΟΥ
ΑΡΧΙΕΩΣ ΤΟΥ ΓΥΜΝΑ|ΣΙΑΡΧΟΥ ΠΟΛΕΩΣ ΚΑΙ
ΑΡΧΙΕΡΕ|ΩΣ ΗΡΩΟΣ ΓΥΜΝΑΣΙΑΡΧΟΥ ΚΑΙ |
ΠΑΤΡΟΣ ΠΟΛΕΩΣ[26]

57   Ad alium tumulum marmoreum:

ΖΩΣΙΜΟΣ | [Ο]ΝΗΣΙΜΟΥ | ΧΑΙΡΕ | [Ο]ΝΗΣΙΜΟΣ
ΖΩΣΙΜΟΥ ΧΑΙΡΕ[27]

58   Ad Glycadeam vallem prope erutam aedem ad ingentia et prae-
celsa extra civitatem moenia ad III miliarium:

Π[ΑΡ]ΑΜΟΝΟΣ ΠΑΝΚΡΑΤΟ[Υ] | ΧΑΙΡΕ | ΘΕΟΓΕΝΙΣ
ΗΡΟΔΟΤΟΥ | ΓΥΝΗ ΔΕ ΠΑΡΑΜΟΝΟΥ ΤΟΥ
ΠΑΝΚΡΑΤΟΥ | ΧΑΙΡΕ | ΠΑΝΚΡΑΤΗΣ
ΠΑΡ[Α]ΜΟΝΟΥ ΧΑΙΡΕ[28]

[Thasos to Mount Athos, 19 November]

59 Ad XIII Kalendas Decembris ex Thaso insula apud Athon, religione sanctum insignemque et altissimum Macedoniae montem,
venimus. Est enim eiusdem Macedoniae regionis praeclarae in
eiusdem Thasi insulae conspectu nobile promuntorium, ad quod
equidem ipse ob celeberrimum eius et religiosissimum nomen me
quoque lubentissime contuli. Et cum innumera ibidem Deo sacra
heremita monasteria sint, horum clariora quoad licuerat indagare
atque visere decrevi.

[Vatopedi]

60 Vatopedion igitur primum venimus, monasterium ab Andronico
II Palaeologo principe almae Annunciatae Virgini dedicatum, ad
maritimum littus altis muris turribusque munitum. Ecclesia vero

On another huge sarcophagus adorned with boukrania;   56

Paramonos son of Herodotos the late high priest and director of the gymnasium and father of the city.

On another marble grave: 57

Zosimos son of Onesimos farewell. Onesimos son of Zosimos farewell.

At Glycadea, a valley near a ruined shrine [church?] on the   58 huge, high walls outside the city at the third milepost:

Paramonos son of Pankratos farewell. Theogenis daughter of Herodotos and wife of Paramonos son of Pankratos, farewell. Pankrates son of Paramonos farewell.

[Thasos to Mount Athos, 19 November]

On the 19th of November we journeyed from the island of Thasos   59 to Athos, a religiously sacred mountain, remarkable, the highest in Macedonia. It is, in fact, a well-known promontory of the same illustrious region of Macedonia that is visible from the same island of Thasos, to which I myself repaired most willingly because of its distinguished religious reputation; and since there are numerous eremetical monasteries consecrated to God there, I decided to investigate and visit the more famous of these, insofar as it was permitted.

[Vatopedi]

So we went first to Vatopedi, a monastery dedicated by the em-   60 peror Andronikos II Palaiologos to the gracious Virgin of the Annunciation and protected at the seashore by lofty walls and towers. The holy church is adorned by a high roof, porches, and walls of

sacra alta testudine, proporticibus et parietibus expolito de marmore, porphyritibusque et colore vario lapidibus, columnis et mirifico pavimento exornata.

61   Ubi Thomam jeromonachum monachorumque patrem, quem
Graece [...][29] vocant, hominem Aenopolitem inveni. Qui me postquam perhoneste suscepit, omnia mihi eiusdem sacresacra sacro-
rumque et gentilium librorum bibliothecam diligentissime ostenta-
rat, Macario *prohegumeno*, Arsenjo, Ignatio, Acacioque sacris et
primariis monachis comitantibus, ubi antiquissimam Homeri Iliadem Ovidiumque Graece traductum et alia quae inferius nobilia
volumina patent inspeximus.

[Pantocrator, 22 November]

62   Ad x Kalendas Decembris ex Vatopediano nobili monasterio ad
aliud eiusdem loci proximum monasterium, quod Pantochratora
vocant, venimus, David monaco paupere terrestri itinere commitante. Ubi Nicander eiusdem monasterii abbas mihi plerosque sua
ex bybliotheca libros ostendit, et potissimum Dyonisii Areopa-
gytae antiquissimum volumen, in quo omnia eiusdem excellentissimi viri opera antiquis et rectissimo ordine litteris conscripta sunt
et Maximi commentatoris optimi postillae, ex quo breve, quod in
principio habebat, alphabeti ordine vocabularium excipiendum curavimus.

[Iveron, 23 November]

63   Ad sequentem vero diem, ipso commitante abbate benignissimo
Nycandro, ad insignem et antiquissimum Hyberiae monasterium
venimus, ubi nos primum Jacobus ecclesiarches Strymonius, suavissimus et dulcissimus homo, perhumane suscepit, Hierasimo
Hibero abbate ad Theucrum oratore absente. Ipse vero ecclesiarches mihi omnia insignia monasterii ostendit et tris quas antiquas
in monitione habent ingenti magnitudine vegetes, nam quam vino

polished marble, varicolored stones streaked with purple, columns, and a wonderful pavement.

There I encountered Thomas, a monk and father of monks, 61 whom they call in Greek [...],[18] a citizen of Ainos, who, after he had received me very kindly, in the company of the prior Macarios and the holy principal monks Arsenios, Ignatios, and Acacios showed me very conscientiously all the sacred objects and a library of sacred and secular books, where we examined a very old *Iliad* of Homer, a Greek translation of Ovid, and other fine volumes listed below.

[Pantocrator, 22 November]

On the 22nd of November, [we left] the renowned monastery of 62 Vatopedi accompanied overland by the poor monk David, and arrived at another monastery of the same region, the nearest one, called the Pantocrator. There Nicander, the abbot of the same monastery, showed me numerous books from his library, and in particular a very old volume of Dionysios the Areopagite, in which are written in an ancient script and in correct order all the works of the same preeminent author, and the annotations of the great commentator Maximus, from which we took pains to copy in alphabetical order the brief vocabulary list that it had at the beginning.

[Iveron, 23 November]

On the following day, accompanied by the very gracious abbot 63 Nicander himself, we went to the outstanding and very ancient monastery of Iveron, where the sacristan Iacovos, a most agreeable and likeable man from near the river Strymon, was the first to receive me with great kindness in the absence of the Georgian abbot of Iveron, Hierasomos, who was on a diplomatic mission to the [Great] Turk. It was the sacristan himself who showed me all the

plenam primum ostendit xx pedum longitudine, latitudinem vero pedum decem diametri metiti sumus.

64 Sed et libros plerosque mihi sacrarum litterarum ostendit atque gentilium Graecos Hyberosque, et in his nobile Plutarchi volumen erat, in quo eiusdem philosophi Moralia XIIII libris conscripta sunt et alia pleraque opera, quod praeclarum equidem volumen ab eo aere pensato magna voluptate recepi, in quo ultra Plutarchi Ethicam talia potissimum habet:

65 Phalaridis tyranni Agrigentinorum epistolas CXXXVIII ad Megarenses, ad Pythagoram et alios,

Abaris ad Phalaridem epistolam I;

Pythagorae ad Hieronem regem I;

Anacharsei ad Athenienses, ad Solonem, ad Hipparchum, ad Trasilocum, ad Croesum et alios potentes principes epistolas IX;

Mitridatis ad nepotem epistolam I;

Bruti Romani ad Pergameos, Cyzicenos Rhodiosque et alias urbes et principes et ab iisdem responsivas epistolas LXX;

Chionis ad Matridem, Bionem, Clearchum et Platonem epistolas XVII;

Euripidis poetae ad Archelaum principem, ad Sophoclem poetam, ad Cephisophontem epistolas V,

Hippocratis Coi medici insignis ad Artaxersem magnum Persarum regem, et Artaxersis ad eum;

item eiusdem Hippocratis ad praesidem Hellesponti Hystanen et Abderitorum consilium, ad Dionysium et alios principes epistolas XII.

important holdings of the monastery including three ancient winecasks, huge in size, for we measured the first one that he showed us, full of wine, as twenty feet long and ten feet wide in diameter.

But he also showed me numerous books of sacred and secular 64 writings, Greek and Georgian, and among these there was a fine volume of Plutarch, in which were written the same philosopher's *Moral Essays* in fourteen books as well as numerous other works. With great pleasure I purchased this splendid volume from him.[19] It contains, besides the *Moral Essays* of Plutarch, the following items worthy of special mention:

138 letters of Phalaris, the tyrant of Agrigentum, to the 65 Megarians, to Pythagoras, and others;

One letter of Abaris to Phalaris;

One [letter] of Pythagoras to King Hiero;

Nine letters of Anacharsis to the Athenians, to Solon, to Hipparchos, to Thrasylochos, to Croesus, and to other powerful princes;

One letter of Mithridates to his nephew;

Seventy letters of the Roman Brutus to the Pergamenes, Cyzicenes, and Rhodians and other cities and princes, and replies from the same;

Seventeen letters of Chion to Matris, Bion, Clearchos, and Plato;

Five letters of the poet Euripides, to prince Archelaos, to Sophocles the poet, to Cephisophon;

[Letters of] Hippocrates, the distinguished Coan physician, to Artaxerxes, the Great King of Persia, and Artaxerxes' reply to him;

Likewise, twelve letters of the same Hippocrates to the governor of the Hellespont Hystanes and to the Council of Abderos, to Dionysios, and to other princes.

[Philotheou, 25 November][30]

66   Ad vii Kalendas Decembris ex Hiberiano Niceanae Eleusae mise-
ricordiosaeque Virginis monasterio apud altum terrestri itinere
montem Philotheanum monasterium venimus, a Philotheo hiero-
monacho olim viro sancto Beatae utique Virgini Nunciatae sacrum, ubi Hierasimon monachum pneumaticum spiritualemque
comperi, Callisto abbate eiusdem monasterii absente.

67   Sed inter eiusdem ecclesiae libros antiquum Homeri in Iliadem
commentum inveni quod talem habebat inscriptionem:

> Εὐσταθίου μαΐστωρος | τῶν ῥητόρων ἐκκλησιαστικ[ῶν]
> ἐπὶ τῶν δεήσεων τοῦ Ὁμήρου τοῦ ὕστερον
> Θεσσαλονίκης <ἀρχιεπισκόπου> παρεκβολαὶ τῆς
> Ὁμήρου Ἰλιάδος.
>
> εἰς τὸν ποιητήν. τῶν Ὁμήρου Σειρήνων καλὸν μὲν ἴσως
> εἴ τις ἀπόσχοιτο τὴν ἀρχὴν ἢ κηρῷ τὰς ἀκοὰς
> ἀλειψάμενος ἢ ἀλλ' ἑτέραν τραπόμενος ὡς ἂν
> ἀποφύγῃ τὸ θέλγητρον.

[Karakallou, 25 September. Morphinou, 25 September]

68   Exinde vero eodem et ipso die ad aliud monasterium veni, Chara-
calcum nomine et beatis Petro Pauloque apostolis sacrum, ubi
pauperes monachi David abbate e Serviana Moesia Graecam religionem servant; et inde ad posteram diem ad parvum aliud monasterium ivimus, quod beato Nicolao sacrum Morphinon dicunt,
sub magni Laureani monasterii gubernatore atque tutela.

[The Grand Lavra, 26 December]

69   Ad vi Kalendas Decembris Laureanum maius omnium et insigne
monasterium venimus, quod sub altiori Athei montis vertice non
longe a mare ad extremam acrotereamve promontorii ripam edi-

[Philotheou, 25 November]

On the 25th of November, [departing] from the monastery of 66
Iveron [dedicated to] the Nicaean Eleusa and the compassionate
Virgin, we traveled by land to the monastery of Philotheou on a
lofty mountain, consecrated by the monk Philotheos, a holy man
of the past, to the Blessed Virgin of the Annunciation, where I encountered the spiritual monk Hierasimon, Kallistos, the abbot of
the same monastery, being absent.

But among the books of the same church I found an ancient 67
commentary on the *Iliad* of Homer inscribed as follows:

A compilation of the critical remarks on the entreaties in
Homer's *Iliad* by Eustathius the master of ecclesiastical ora-
tors, later the archbishop of Thessalonica.

On the poet: Of the Sirens of Homer, it is good if a person
should shy away from them from the beginning, either by
stopping up his ears with wax or by turning to another device in order to escape their spell.

[Karakallou, 25 September. Morophinou, 26 September]

Then, on the same day, I came to another monastery, called 68
Karakallou and dedicated to the blessed apostles Peter and Paul,
where under the abbot David poor monks from Serbian Moesia
practice the Greek religion; and from there on the next day, we
came to another small monastery, which they call Morphinou,[20]
dedicated to blessed Nicholas, under the rule and protection of
the Grand Lavra.

[The Grand Lavra, 26 December]

On the 26th of December we came to the greatest monastery of 69
them all, the [Grand] Lavra, which the very devout Emperor
Phocas dedicated to the most holy monk Athanasios[21] 480 years

tum et turritis moenibus late munitum, exactis iam CCCC et LXXX
annis, Phocas religiosissimus imperator Athanasio monacho sanctissimo sacrum dicavit, ipsumque ob monachorum incolentium
amplitudinem Graeco vocabulo λαύραν ut in hodiernum vocitant, appellavit.

70   Ubi primum Danielem venerandum abbatem, quem ut monachorum omnium ducem ἡγούμενον dicunt, inveni, qui visis Pala-
medis Franciscique Gatalusiorum Aeni Thasiique principum prae-
clarorum litteris, me perbenigne suscepit, et una cum Neophyto
qui et Zacchaeo prohegumeno Dositheoque ecclesiarche omnia
mihi eiusdem loci nobiliora monstravit.

71   Et primo sacram et egregiam vidimus aedem, quae fere Vatope-
dianae amplitudinis instar et pulchritudinis et formae, columnis
proporticibus ianuis pavimentis atque parietibus expoliti marmoreis porphyreisque et iaspideis varioque colore eximia arte contex-
tis lapidibus, ampliori quantulumcumque testudine omni ex parte
conspicua conspectabatur, ubi secreta aedis in parte lapideo loculo
sepultum beati Athanasii corpus die noctuque accensis lychnariis
et lampadibus perenni lumine religiosissime colunt. Habet et ante-
porticus et frontispicia ⟨et⟩ ampliori in aula amplam et expolitam
unico de marmore urnam marmoreis circum columnis alta plum-
beaque et subter eximie depicta testudine protectam, nec non
pulcherrime elaboratis undique delicato et candenti de marmore
spondis munitam.

72   At quod libentius inspectare placuerat, amplissimam eius vidimus bibliothecam Graecarum quidem litterarum omnigenum dis-
ciplinarum voluminum multitudine refertam. Sed in his potissimum e sacris almae religionis nostrae auctoribus nomina legi, nam
Chrysostomi, Basilii, Dionysii, Gregorii, Eusebii, Cyrilli, Athanasii, Polycarpique et aliorum plura peregregia atque magnifica eo

ago. It stands at the foot of the highest peak of Mt. Athos, not far from the sea, constructed at the very farthest shore of the promontory and extensively fortified by turreted walls. Because of the abundance of monks dwelling there, he called it by the name that is still used today, the Greek word *lavra*.[22]

There the first person I encountered was the revered Abbot 70 Daniel, whom as the leader of all the monks they call the *hegoumenos*. When he saw the letters [I carried] of Palamede and Francesco Gattilusio, the illustrious princes of Ainos and Thasos, he received me with great kindness and, along with Neophytos as well as the prior Zachaios and the sacristan Dositheos, showed me all the more noteworthy holdings of the same place.

First, we saw the sacred, admirable church, which in every visi- 71 ble aspect appeared pretty much like [the church] of Vatopedi in its size and beauty, with its columns, porches and doors, its pavements and walls of polished marble, porphyry and jasper, variously colored stones put together with consummate art, and with a somewhat larger roof. There in a sequestered part of the church, where lamps and torches burn day and night with perpetual light, they venerate most devoutly the body of the blessed Athanasios, entombed in a stone coffin. The church also has porticoes in front and a facade and, in a larger hall, a capacious, polished urn made from a single piece of marble, with marble columns round about it protected by a high leaden roof painted superbly on its underside, and provided with very beautifully finished benches of elegant, bright marble on all sides.

Yet I was more pleased to examine [the monastery's] very con- 72 siderable library filled with a multitude of volumes of Greek writings on every kind of discipline. But among these I especially picked out [books by] sacred authors of our nourishing faith, for I noticed in that place numerous splendid volumes, outstanding in quality, of Chrysostom, Basil, Dionysius, Gregory, Eusebius, Cyril, Athanasius, Polycarp and others; and among the secular

loco volumina conspexi. Vidimus et inter gentiles Platonis, Aristotelis, Galeni, Hippocratisque et alia pleraque vetusta philosophorum opera, sed Herodoti historici insignis et aliorum quorumdam auctorum opera.

73   Quae magis mihi placuerant, hisce principia quaedam duximus annotanda: Εἰς τὴν τῆς ἱερᾶς Λαύρας μονῆς βιβλιοθήκην.

> Συνεσίου περὶ ἐνυπνίων. εἰ δέ εἰσιν ὕπνοι προφῆται καὶ
> τὰ ὄναρ θεάματα τοῖς ἀνθρώποις.
> Λιβανίου σοφιστοῦ ἐς τὴν ῥητορικήν. οἱ λύκοι παρὰ
> προβάτων εἰρήνης ἡσυχίαν ᾔτουν.
> Εὐσταθίου εἰς τὴν Ὁμήρου Ἰλιάδα. τῶν Ὁμήρου
> Σειρήνων καλὸν μὲν ἴσως εἴ τις ἀπόσχοιτο τὴν
> ἀρχήν.
> Ἡροδότου Ἁλικαρνασέως. Περσέων μὲν ὧν οἱ λόγοι
> Φοίνικάς φασι γενέσθαι τῆς διαφορῆς αἰτίους.

74   Νόννου ποιητοῦ Διονυσίακα·

> εἰπὲ θεὰ κρονίδαο διάκορος αἴθοπος εὐνῆς
> καὶ στεροπὴν Σεμέλης θαλαμηπόλον, εἰπὲ δὲ φύτλην
> Ζεὺς βρέφος ἡμιτέλεστον ἀμαιεύτοιο τεκούσης
> ἄρσενι γὰρ γαστρὶ λόχευσε πατὴρ καὶ πότνια μήτηρ
> ὃς πάρος ὄγκον ἄπιστον ἔχων ἐγκύμονι κόρσῃ
> ἄξατέ μοι νάρθηκα τινάξατε κύμβαλα, Μοῦσαι,
> ἀλλὰ χοροῦ ψαύοντα Φάρῳ παρὰ γείτονι νήσῳ
> ποικίλον εἶδος ἔχων, ὅτι ποικίλον ὕμνον ἀράσσων
> μέλψω θεῖον ἄεθλον, ὅπῃ κισσώδεϊ θύρσῳ

writers, the works of Plato, Aristotle, Galen, Hippocrates, and numerous other ancient works of philosophers, but also the works of Herodotus, the noted historian and of certain other authors.

The *incipits* of those that pleased me more we decided should be   73
noted down here.[23]

In the library of the holy monastery of Lavra:

Of Synesios, *Concerning Dreams*: "If dreams are prophetic and the dream is a vision for human beings . . ."[24]

Of Libanios the sophist *On Rhetoric*: "The wolves asked the sheep for the respite of peace . . ."

Of Eustathios *On the Iliad*. "Of Homer's Sirens: perhaps it would be good if one should shy away from [them] from the beginning . . ."[25]

Of Herodotus of Halicarnassos: "Of the Persians, whose accounts say the Phoenicians were the cause of the dispute . . ."

The *Dionysiaca* of the poet Nonnos:[26]   74

Tell the tale, O goddess, of Cronides' courier with fiery flame, the gasping travail which the thunderbolt brought with sparks for wedding-torches, the lightning in waiting upon Semele's nuptials; tell the naissance of Bacchos twice-born, whom Zeus lifted still moist from the fire, a baby half-complete, born without midwife; how with shrinking hands he cut the incision in his thigh and carried him in his man's-womb, father and gracious mother at once—and well he remembered another birth, when his own head conceived, when his temple was big with child, and he carried that incredible unbegotten lump, until he shot out Athena scintillating in her armor. Bring me the fennel, rattle the cymbals, ye Muses! Put in my hand the wand of Dionysos whom I

εἰ δὲ λέων φρίξειεν ἐπαυχενίην τρίχα σάων
μαζὸν ὑποκλέπτοντα λεοντοβότοιο θεαίνης
πόρδαλις αἴξη πολυδαίδαλον εἶδος ἀμείβων. [...]

[Iveron revisited, 28 November]

75 Ad iiii Kalendas Decembris iterum Hiberianum revisimus monasterium, ubi abbatem eiusdem Hierasimon, Hiberum eorum
lingua litterisque perdoctum, ex Macedonia remeantem comperimus. Et ab eo de regione sua plura didicimus, regemque suum
nomine Vactanghen iuvenem triginta annorum ferme aetate re-
giamque urbem Typhlis inhabitare percepimus, nec modo Hiberis
quin et Albanis Colchis regem ipsum intelligimus imperitare.

76 Verum et hoc unum minime praetermittendum censui, quod
postquam diligentius ipso cum ecclesiarche Jacobo pulcherrimam
illius monasterii conspeximus aedem, expolitis marmoreis porphyreisque lapidibus, columnis parietibus pavimentisque tam eximia
elaboratis arte omni ex parte conspicuam, ⟨eam⟩ et Vatopedianam
ipsam nobilem atque Laureanam quodammodo superasse cognovimus, quam Euthymus olim optimus Hiberorum princeps quin-
gentos ante annos magna almae Virginis affectione cum omni
cultu dicandam exornandamque curavit.

sing; but bring me a partner for your dance in the neighboring island of Pharos, Proteus of many turns, that he may appear in all his diversity of shapes, since I twang my harp to a diversity of songs. For if, as a serpent, he should glide along his winding trail I will sing my god's achievement, how with ivy-wreathed wand he destroyed the horrid hosts of giants serpent-haired. If as a lion he shake his bristling mane, I will cry "euoi!" to Bacchos on the arm of buxom Rheia, stealthiy draining the breast of the lion-breeding goddess. If as a leopard he shoots up into the air with a stormy leap from his pads, changing shape like a master-craftsman [...]

[Iveron revisited, 28 November]

On the 28th of November we returned again to the monastery of Iveron, where we came upon Hierasimos, its abbot, a man very learned in their Georgian language and literature, on his return from Macedonia. We learned more from him about his own region — that its king is called Vahtang, a young man of about thirty years, who dwells in the royal city of Tiflis and that he rules, not only the Georgians [a tribe south of the Caucasus], but also the Albanians of Colchis. 75

But I thought that this one fact must not be passed by, that, after we examined more diligently with Iacovos the sacristan the beautiful church of that monastery, conspicuous for its polished marble and porphyry stone, columns, walls and pavements elaborated with such extraordinary skill in every section, we realized that in some ways it surpasses both the famed [churches] of Vatopedi and of Lavra, which Euthymus, a highly regarded former superior of Iveron, five hundred years ago, out of great devotion to the fostering Virgin, had dedicated and embellished with all ceremony. 76

[*Pantocrator revisited, 29 November*]

77 Ad III Kalendas Decembris ad sacrum Pantocratoris monasterium iterum veni, Hiberiano ipso ecclesiarche Iacobo suis cum decem monachis parva scapha maritimum per iter comitante, ubi optimus abbas ille Nicander antiquum Athanasii librum mihi primum alios inter ostendit, in quo prooemium hoc in principio aureis quoque litteris inscriptum erat:

78 τοῦ ἁγίου Ἀθανασίου ἀρχιεπισκόπου Ἀλεξανδρείας πρὸς Ἀντίοχον ἄρχοντα περὶ πλείστων καὶ ἀναγκαίων ζητημάτων τῶν ἐν ταῖς θείαις γραφαῖς παρὰ πολλοῖς ἀπορουμένων καὶ παρὰ πᾶσι Χριστιανοῖς γινώσκεσθαι ὀφειλομένων ἐρωτη-
79 μάτων. πιστεύσαντες καὶ βαπτισθέντες εἰς Τριάδα ὁμοούσιον καὶ λέγοντες θεὸν εἶναι τὸν πατέρα καὶ θεὸν εἶναι τὸν υἱὸν ὡσαύτως καὶ θεὸν εἶναι τὸ πνεῦμα τὸ ἅγιον, πῶς οὐ λέγωμεν αὐτοὺς τρεῖς θεούς, ἀλλ' ἕνα καὶ μόνον θεόν; καὶ εἰ μὲν ἕνα προσκυνοῦμεν θεόν, εὔδηλον ὅτι εἰς μοναρχίαν πιστεύοντες ἰουδαίζομεν. εἰ δὲ τρεῖς πάλιν θεούς, πρόδηλον ὅτι ἑλληνίζομεν πολυθείαν εἰσάγοντες καὶ οὐκ ἕνα θεὸν εὐσεβῶς προσκυνοῦντες.

[*Thasos, 2 December 1444 to January 1445*]

80 Ad IIII Nonas Decembrium ex Vatopediano monasterio Thasion insulam civitatemque revisi, ubi adusque incarnati Verbi natalicia festa morantes, hoc in Franciscum Gatalusium principem epigramma conscripsi:

81 FELIX DIVES FAVSTVM ATQ. |
FORTVNATISSIMVM ESTO | MAGNANIME
FRANCISCE | PRINCEPS | TVVM HOC HVIVS
THASIAE | NOBILIS INSVLAE DOMINII |

[Pantocrator revisited, 29 November]

On the 29th of November I returned to the holy monastery of the   77
Pantocrator, accompanied by Iakovos, the sacristan of Iveron with
his ten monks. We traveled by sea in a small skiff. There that excellent abbot Nicander showed me, first of all among others, an
ancient book of Athanasios, in the beginning of which this pream-
ble was inscribed in golden letters:

> [A treatise] of St. Athanasios the archbishop of Alexandria,   78
> to the archon Antiochos concerning very many necessary
> inquiries by many persons about puzzling passages in the
> sacred Scriptures, questions that ought to be understood
> among all Christians:

> If we believe and were baptized into a Trinity having one sin-   79
> gle nature, and if we say that the Father is God and the Son
> is God and in like manner the Holy Spirit is God, surely we
> are not saying that they are three gods, but that there is only
> one God, and if we worship one God, it is clear that, believ-
> ing as we do in monarchy, we are imitating the Jews; but if,
> on the other hand, we believe in three gods, we are imitating
> the Greeks by introducing polytheism, and not devoutly
> worshiping one God.

[Thasos, 2 December 1444 to January 1445]

On the 2nd of December, from the monastery of Vatopedi, I re-   80
turned to the island and city of Thasos, where I lingered until the
feast of the Nativity of the Incarnate Word. During my stay there
I composed the following inscription in honor of Francesco
Gattilusio:

> Magnanimous Prince Francesco, may this beginning of your   81
> rule over this noble island of Thasos, or rather, of the con-

CONSTITVTAEQVE RESTAV|RATIONIS AC
OPTIMAE IAM | C[O]EPTAE GVBERNATIONIS |
PRINCIPIVM | SINTQ. FELICIA ET BEATA |
PRAECLARA HAEC ABS TE | HODIE TVA HAC
THASIANI | REGIA CIVITATE CELEBRATA |
RECENTISQ. ANNI RECENSI|TA DIVA ATQ.
SOLEMNIA | HUMANATI IOVIS EIVSCE | VE
INCARNATI VERBI NATA|LICIA | NEC NON ILLE A
TE TVA HAC | TVRRITA IN AVLA SERO TAM |
LAETVS AD LAREM FLAGRAN|TIBVS FOCIS
ADMOTVS IN|GENS DICATVS ET LAETITIA | DIE
LIBATVS AC PRINCIPIVM | VETVSTO DE MORE
SACER | ET MEMORABILIS TRVNCVS | VT
PERINDE AC HODIE .VIII. | KL. IANVARIAS A
EIVSDEM | INCARNATI IOVIS ANNO | MILLENO
QVATRICENTENO | QVINTO ET QVATERDENO |
MAGNIFICO LESBEO MITYLE|NEO VE PRINCIPE
DONANTE | DORINO OPTIMO | PARENTE | TVO |
THASIANAM HANC INSVLAM | PRAECLARAM
ATQ. MARMO|REAM VRBEM ET EIVSDEM |
INSVLAE OCCIDENTALE EM|PORIVM
NEOCASTRVM CALI|RACHIVM ANASTASIVM
PO|TAMIVM CHINARVM SVIS|CVMQ. OMNIB.
ADIACENTIB. | VICIS VILLISQ. ET MAGNALIB. |
AGRISQ. ET PLVRIGENVM | LINGVIS HOMINIB.
FELICITER|QVE IMPERITARE VIDEMVS ITA
ADVENTVRA EIVSCE IN|CARNATI VERBI
SOLEMNIA | AC DEINCEPS LONGAEVOS | VTIQ.
PER ANNOS OMNES PER | TRACIAM VRBES ET
OPPIDA | AGROSQ. ET HOMINES ATQ. | SACRA
QVAE DVDVM EIVSDEM | TVAE INSVLAE
DICIONIS FUE|RE BARBARICA ILLA S[A]EVA
TYRA[N]NIDE ET OPPRESSIO|NE SVBLATA TVA

firmed restoration of an excellent governance already begun,
be auspicious, prosperous, favorable, and fortunate. And
may this magnificent, solemn observation of the birth of
Jove-made-man, Jove's incarnate Word, celebrated today by
this, your royal city of Thasos and [serving as] a review of
the past year, be auspicious and happy. May that huge, sacred, memorable [Yule] log, which you lately brought home
with such joy to set your hearth ablaze, be dedicated with a
cheerful libation in this, your turreted palace according to
the ancient custom of princes. Today, the 25th of December,
in the 1445th year of the same Incarnate Jove, we see you
happily ruling this illustrious island of Thasos and its marble
city and Neokastro, the western port of the same island, and
Calirachium, Anastasium, Potamium and Chinarum, with
all their adjacent towns and villages and their mighty works,
fields, and men of many races and tongues; all this a gift of
Dorino your excellent father, the majestic prince of Lesbos
and Mytilene. In the same way, from this point on, through
the long years, may we see [restored] to your excellent and
most worthy rule the solemn celebration of the Word-made-
flesh, observed auspiciously, favorably and most laudably, and
the cities and towns, lands and men and holy places of
Thrace, that had long been under the rule of your very same
island but were stolen away by that uncivilized, cruel, tyranny and oppression. [May we see this brought about] by
the power of the excellent and great Jove and the fostering

SVB OPTI|MA ATQ. DIGNISSIMA POTES|TATE
FELICITER FAVSTE | QVAMQ. LAVDATISSIMAE |
VIDEAMVS | OPTIMI MAX.Q. IOVIS ET BEATE |
VIRGINIS ALMAE JOANNISQ. | SS. EVANGELISTAE
PROTEC|TORIS TVI AVSPICANTE NV|MINE
CAETERISQ. CAELICO|LVM IVVANTIB. DIVIS
ALMIS | FELICISSIMISQ. NVMINIBVS | IAMQ. VALE
FELIX FRANCISCE | INGENVA PALAEOLOGVM
PRO|LES ET INSIGNE GATALVSIAE | NOBILISSIME
GENTIS DECVS

*[Thasos, 1 January 1445. Poem addressed by
the isle of Lesbos to Francesco Gattilusio]*

82   Qual fato o qual destin o corso astreo,
qual ordin prisco o novo senatorio,
qual presidiale regno o qual pretorio,
qual signoril governo o qual tropheo;
        qual cantar de syrene o son phoebeo,
qual mai di humano o divin concistorio
armonia sciese d'organ meritorio,
qual nymphe thasiane, al son di Orpheo,
        che mi potesse, ne l'aevo moderno,
farmi del signor mio, Francisco, priva,
gientil Francisco, honor de Lesbo eterno?
        Ma se la signoria di Thasso diva
ti trasse a sé, col buon voler paterno,
spero d'il gran tuo honor esser gioliva.
        E per dartene oliva,
Kiriaco, tuo fidel, sen vene a Thasso,
cerchando il Vostro Honor per ogni sasso.

83   Francisco Gatalusio inclyto Tassiorum principi et Dorini Lesbei
illustrissimi ducis filio dilectissimo Kiriacus Anconitanus devotus

Virgin Mary and of the most holy John the Evangelist, your protector, and the fostering, auspicious assistance of the other heaven-dwellers. And now farewell, blessed Francesco, honorable scion of the Palaiologoi and distinguished pride of the noble family, the Gattilusi.

*[Thasos, 1 January 1445. Poem addressed by
the isle of Lesbos to Francesco Gattilusio]*

What fate, what destiny or course of stars,   82
what early government or new senatorial rule,
what kingdom ruled by garrison or by praetorian guard,
what patrician order or what meritorious dynasty;
   what Siren's song or Apollonian melody
what ever harmony of human or divine assembly
descended from a praiseworthy organ,
what Thasian nymphs at the song of Orpheus
   could possibly, in this modern age,
deprive me of my lord Francesco,
noble Francesco, eternal glory of Lesbos?
   But if the rulership of divine Thasos
drew you to itself, by appealing to your fatherly good will,
I hope to rejoice at your great honor.
   So as to give you the olive crown for it,
Cyriac your devotee to Thasos comes,
searching every stone for the honor of your name.

Cyriac of Ancona presented [this poem] to Francesco Gat-   83
tilusio, the famous prince of Thasos, beloved son of Dorino, glorious duke of Lesbos, out of devotion and dedication to their ma-

ac eorum maiestati dicatissimus dedit, anno ab humanati Iovis, antiquatae legis ritu circumcisi, milleno quatricenteno quinto et quaterdeno, Eugenii papae anno XIIII.

: 19 :

1 Ad Iωannem Pedemontanum, Francisci Thassiani principis praeceptorem. Ex Aeno.

2   Cum ad sequentem recentis anni celebratae Thassiana in aula solemnitatis noctem post dulces et invicem iteratos amplexus nos Aenum antiquam petentes scapham bonis avibus conscenderemus, sub remis fusi per dura sedilia nautae carpebant somnos, Κυριακὸν δέ σου οὐκ ἔχε νήδυμος ὕπνος.

3   Sed multum antea quam cristatus ales vigili ore tepidum provocaret diem, ἀλληλούϊα canens socios navarchum excitavi; et cum alta quievissent aequora cunctaque videremus caelo constare sereno,

    Arcturum pluviasque Hyadas geminosque Triones,

soluta e mole[1] puppe illico iucundum nostrum remis velisque tendimus iter, ac insignem placidumque Thassii portum ἱεραμουλήντε linquentes, diu felici sub Gatalusiae gentis imperio valere ciemus.

4   Aspirant aurae in noctem nec candida cursum[2]
luna negat, splendet tremulo sub lumine pontus.

    Tum placidi Neptuni liquidum sulcando campum Thassianam protinus arcem ostendimus, Thraciaeque fines legimus et saevi

jesties. [Given] on the [feast of] the Circumcision [of Christ] according to the Old Law, in the 1445th year of the incarnate Jove and the 14th year of [the reign] of Pope Eugene IV.

: 19 :

To Giovanni Pedemontano, January 1445, Ainos

To Giovanni Pedemontano,[1] tutor of Francesco, the prince of 1
Thasos,[2] from Ainos.

    On the night after the festival that celebrated the new year in 2
the court of Thasos, we embraced each other lovingly and often, then embarked with good omens on a small boat, whose destination was ancient Ainos. The sailors, sprawled on their hard benches beneath the oars, caught some sleep, but sweet sleep did not hold your Cyriac.

    For long before the cock with his wakeful voice called forth the 3
warm day, I roused the captain and his crew by singing "alleluia." When the deep sea was quiet and we saw that all things were still beneath the fair sky,

    Arcturus, the rainy Hyades and the two Wains,[3]

we release the stern from the mole and immediately start our pleasant journey with oars and sails; and as we leave the famous placid port and sacred breakwater of Thasos, we invoke long prosperity on the happy reign of the Gattilusi.

    The breezes breathe on the night, the bright moon does not 4
    deny us our course, the sea gleams beneath the trembling
       light.[4]

Then, as we plough the liquid plain of calm Neptune we expose to view the citadel of Thasos. We sail by the boundaries of Thrace

proxima Diomedis radimus littora, quem suis immanibus equis advenas ad mandendum dare solitum accepimus.

5   Quae ne talia monstra nos pii pateremur homines, neve dira littora subiremus, Mercurius ipse noster vela secundis impleverat ventis, hinc inde Nereidum iuvante serenissimo choro. Nam altera ex parte Doris, flavaque comis Doto,

et Galatea secant spumantem pectore pontum,

dextera vero ex parte Panopea Amphitriteque, et Parthenia Glauce iucundissime secundabant niveis hinc inde lacertis, natante ac alto ab aequore modulante meque interdum osculis dulciter perrorante nympharum omnium praeclarissima Cymodocea ferreamque desubter optime baiulante carinam.

6   Et tandem die noctuque placidum aequor secantes, Cyriaceum ad celebrem diem antea quam sol caeli medium conscenderet orbem, muros arcemque procul et rara domorum tecta videmus portumque et piscosa vada, quibus inclytus ille Trojanus Aeneas profugus conditor nomen indiderat, et nunc Palamedea Gatalusia ingenua proles imperat.

7   Huc plenis allabimur velis, et haud mora principes regulos, nam pater Samothracem degerat, amicosque revisi, et Arduini Franciscum, dulcem et amicissimum nobis virum, abs te salutatum feci. Praeterea enim Segestrem sociosque una ipsa cum principis rate Lesbeam Mythilenem incolumes applicuisse percepimus.

8   Pannones vero patriam ad reparandas augendasque copias remeasse, Theucrorumque regem Asiam per Hellespontum revisisse filiumque in Thracia principem reliquisse dicunt.

and skirt the nearby shores of cruel Diomedes who, we are told, used to feed strangers to his monstrous horses.[5]

To keep us from suffering such a disaster by coming to that 5 dread shore, Mercury, our guardian, filled our sails with a favoring wind and on both sides of us the bright band of nymphs gave help. For on one side Doris, yellow-haired Doto

and Galatea cleaved the foaming sea with their breasts,[6]

and on the right side Panopea and Amphitrite and Parthenian Glauke helped joyfully with their snowy-white arms here and there, while Cymodocea, the most glorious of all the nymphs, swam and made music from the depths of the sea, from time to time bedewed me sweetly with her kisses and carried the iron keel from below.

Finally, after cleaving the calm sea for a day and a night, on the 6 festal Sunday before the sun climbed to the middle of the orb of heaven, we saw at a distance walls and a citadel and thinly scattered houses and a port and waters abounding in fish, a place on which the famous Trojan exile, Aeneas, has bestowed his name as its founder.[7] Now it is ruled by the noble family of Palamede Gattilusio.

Hither we glided under full sail and without delay I revisited 7 the prince-rulers (for their father was living in Samothrace) and my friends, and I greeted Francesco Arduini, our delightful friend, for you. We learned in addition that Segestris and his companions had put in safely at Mytilene on Lesbos on the prince's ship.

They say that the Hungarians have gone back to their country 8 to restore and increase their forces and that the Turkish sultan has returned to Asia via the Hellespont and has left his son as ruler in Thrace.

: 20 :

1 Spectabili et generoso viro, Borueli Grimaldo, amico honorificentissimo.

2 Magnifice ac generose vir, tuam rogo spectabilitatem, si forte libellum, quem de navali conflictu regis Alphonsi a me editum tibi reliqui, Nicolao Ceba non reliquisti, apud Chyon Andreolo Iustiniano, amico praestantissimo nostro, dimittere velis.

3 Teque semper feliciorem valere desidero ac videre iterum iocundissime cupio. XVIIII Ianuarias MCCCCXLV, ex Aeno.

: 21 :

1 Ad Andreolum Iustinianum, virum clarissimum.

2 Ad v Kalendas Martias ex Imbro Lemnum venimus, Barneote duce nauta, ubi Theodorum Branas, praesidem pro Ioanne Paleologo imperatore insulam curante comperimus, quo iuvante omnia eiusdem loci insignia vidimus, et primum apud Ephaestiam urbem et dyrutam ad aedem Alexandri martyris antiquam basim lapideam:

Ο ΔΗΜΟΣ | Ο ΗΦΑΙΣΤΙ|ΕΩΝ
Ο ΔΗΜΟΣ | Ο ΜΤΡΕΙ|ΝΑΙΩΝ

ΟΚΤΩ ΚΑΙ ΔΕ[ΚΕ] ΤΙΝ ΜΕ ΧΤΤΗ Κ[ΟΝ]ΙΣ ΗΔΕ
ΚΑΛΤΠΤΕΙ

144

: 20 :

To Boruele Grimaldi, 19 January 1445, Ainos

To Boruele Grimaldi,[1] my distinguished, noble and most faithful 1 friend.

Magnificent and noble, sir, if by chance you did not leave be- 2 hind with Niccolò Ceba the booklet I published about the naval battle of King Alfonso,[2] which I left behind with you, would you please send it off to our most excellent friend Andreolo Giustiniani in Chios?

I wish you continual health and ever better luck and I rejoice 3 greatly in my desire to see you again. 19 January 1445, from Ainos.

: 21 :

To Andreolo, 25 February [1445], Hephaisteia, on Lemnos

To the distinguished Andreolo Giustiniani. 1

On the 25th of February we came from Imbros to Lemnos 2 under the guidance of the seaman Barneote, where we found Theodoros Branas, who governs the island for Emperor John Palaiologos. With his help we saw all the important sights of the same place and especially, in the city of Hephaisteia at a ruined church of the martyr Alexander, on an ancient stone base:

The people of Hephaisteia   The people of Myrina.

This heaped-up dust conceals me, eighteen year old Kallisto, who received my mother's name. To her, I leave extremely la- mentable sorrow in the home, and to my father Zoos bitter

ΚΑΛΛΙΣΤΩ ΜΗΤΡΟΣ ΔΕΞΑΜΕΝΗΝ ΟΝΟΜΑ
ΗΙ ΛΕΙΠΩ ΠΑΝΟΔΥΡΤΟΝ ΕΝΙ ΜΕΓΑΡΟΙΣΙΝ ΑΝΕΙΗΝ
ΠΑΤΡΙ Τ ΕΜΩ ΖΩΗ ΔΑΚΡΥΑ ΛΥΓΡΟΤΑΤΑ
ΝΑΙΩ Δ ΕΥΣΕΒΕΩΝ ΑΓΝΟΝ ΠΕΡΙΚΑΛΛΕΑ ΧΩΡΟΝ
ΣΥΝΘΡΟΝΟΣ ΗΡΩΩΝ ΕΙΝΕΚΑ ΣΩΦΡΟΣΙΝΑΣ
ΑΚΜΗΝ Δ ΟΥ ΓΕΝΕΤΗΡΕΣ ΕΜΗΝ ΟΥΚ ΕΣΘΛΟΣ
    ΟΜΑΙΜΟΣ
ΟΥ ΠΟΣΙΣ ΑΛΛ ΑΙΔΗΣ ΛΥΓΡΟΣ ΕΚΑΡΠΙΣΑΤΟ
ΤΟΙΟΣ ΤΟΙ ΘΝΗΤΩΝ ΜΟΓΕΡΟΣ ΒΙΟΣ ΩΝ ΑΤΕΛΕΣΤΟΙ
ΕΛΠΙΔΕΣ ΑΙ ΜΟΙΡΩΝ ΝΗΜΑΤ ΕΠΙΚΡΕΜΕΤΑΙ
ΑΛΛΑ ΜΟΙ Ω ΓΕΝΕΤΗΣ ΕΣΑΘΡΗΣΑΝΤΕΣ Ο ΘΝΗΤΩΝ
ΩΣ ΦΕΡΕΤΑΙ ΠΑΝΤΩΝ ΛΥΓΡΟΠΑΘΗΣ ΒΙΟΤΟΣ
ΗΔΗ ΔΥΣΤΗΝΟΥ ΚΑΤΑ ΔΩΜΑΤΑ ΛΗΓΕΤΕ ΠΕΝΘΟΥΣ
ΚΑΙ ΦΘΙΜΕΝΗ ΓΑΡ ΕΜΟΙ ΤΟΥΤΟ ΠΟΘΕΙΝΟΤΑΤΟΝ

ΚΑΛΛΙΣΤΩ ΖΩΟΥ ΕΛΕΥΣΕΙΝΙΟΥ ΘΥΓΑΤΗΡ | Η
ΦΙΛΟΣΤΟΡΓΟΣ ΠΡΟΣ ΓΟΝΕΙΣ ΑΓΝΗ ΠΕΡΙ| ΓΑΜΟΝ
ΗΕ ΚΑΙ ΚΑΛΗ ΚΑΙ ΑΓΑΘΗ ΑΡΕΤΗ ΔΙ|ΑΦΕΡΟΥΣΑ

    Ο ΔΗΜΟΣ | Ο ΙΜΒΡΙ|ΩΝ
    Ο ΔΗΜΟΣ | Ο ΤΕΝΕΔΙ|ΩΝ[1]

tears. I dwell in the beautiful, holy land of the blest, sharing the throne the heroes because of my moderation. Not my parents, nor my fine brother, nor my husband, but miserable Hades enjoys my prime of life. Such is the wretched life of mortals, who have unfulfilled hopes that hang on the thread of the Fates. But, my parents, as you consider what the mournfully suffering life of all mortals brings, cease your unhappy sorrow at home, for that is very desirable for me, even among the dead.

Kallisto daughter of Zoos of Eleusis, who was loving to her parents and pure in her marriage, beautiful and good, excelling in virtue.

The people of Imbros   The people of Tenedos

1   Spectatissimo et praeclarissimo viro, Andreolo Iustiniano, amico optimo.

2   Heri postero quo a te concesseram die, bonis faventibus Boreis, Miconum venimus, insulam Delo sacrae proximam, iuvante Deo, ubi Franciscum Namny, virum generosum pro Venetis praesidem, comperimus et qui me perhumane susceperat et omnia quae ibidem et in aliis quibusque adiacentibus insulis, eo iuvante, videre atque perscrutare curabo.

3   Interea hanc epistolam, quam ad cardinalem Nicaenum scripsi, Athanasio monacho chaloyrove apud ecclesiam sancti Francisci comoranti dare velis, qui in navi Grimalda Italiam navigaturus est.

4   Valere te quidem semper feliciorem opto. Ex Micono, postero quo ad eam venimus, pridie Nonas Aprilis MCCCCXLV.

5   At et pro bona nostri iocundissimi itineris ave hoc ex Delo advecta in marmorea basi in divum Trayanum principem et nostri portus providentissimum conditorem epygramma comperimus:

ΑΥΤΟΚΡΑΤΟΡΑ ΝΕΡΟΥΑΝ ΤΡΑ|ΙΑΝΟΝ ΚΑΙΣΑΡΑ
ΣΕΒΑΣ|ΤΟΝ. ΓΕΡΜΑΝΙΚΟΝ ΔΑΚΙ|ΚΟΝ Η ΠΟΛΙΣ
ΕΠΙΜΕΛΗΘΕΝ|ΤΟΣ ΤΗΣ ΑΝΑΣΤΑΣΕΩΣ ΤΙΤΟΥ |
ΦΛΑΟΥΙΟΥ ΔΗΜΗΤΡΙΟΥ[1]

6   Vale diu felix atque iterum vale, mi Andreole iocundissime.

April to December 1445
The Cyclades and Crete

: 22 :

To Andreolo, 4 April 1445, Mykonos

Most notable and excellent sir, my good friend, Andreolo 1
Giustiniani.

Yesterday, the day after I left you,[1] we came with God's help 2
under a favoring north wind to Mykonos, the island nearest to sacred Delos, where we found Francesco Namny, the noble Venetian
governor, who received me cordially. With his help I shall make a
point of seeing and investigating everything there and in each of
the other neighboring islands.

Meanwhile, please give the enclosed letter, which I wrote to the 3
Cardinal of Nicaea,[2] to the monk Athanasius, who is staying in
the church of St. Francis. He is about to sail to Italy in a Grimaldi
ship.

I wish you continued good health and good luck. From 4
Mykonos, the day after our arrival, 4 April 1445.

[Postscript:] As a good omen of a happy journey, I found this in- 5
scription on a marble base brought here from Delos. It honors the
divine prince Trajan, the provident founder of our port.[3]

The city [honors] the Emperor Nerva Trajan Caesar Augustus, Victor over Germany and Dacia. Titus Flavius
Demetrius was in charge of erecting [the statue].

Fare well and fortunately and again farewell, my delightful 6
Andreolo.

: DIARY III :

Cycladum Nobilia Monumenta
ex Kyriaco Picenicollensi Anconitano

[Mykonos]

1 ΣΤΝΤΤΧΗ ΚΑΡΠΟΤ | ΧΡΗΣΤΕ ΧΑΙΡΕ ΖΗ |
ΛΕΤΚΙΟΣ | [Ο]ΦΕΛΛΙΕ | ΖΩΣΑ | ΧΡΗΣΤΕ ΧΑΙΡΕ[1]

[DRAWING]

2 Apud Miconum ad sacram sanctissimi Baptistae praecursoris
aedem bona pro nostri iucundissimi itineris ave hoc ad marmoream magnam et ornatissimam basim epigramma nostrum in divum principem Traianum atticis doricisve litteris inveni:

ΑΤΤΟΚΡΑΤΟΡΑ ΝΕΡΟΤΑΝ ΤΡΑΙΑΝΟΝ | ΚΑΙΣΑΡΑ
ΣΕΒΑΣΤΟΝ [ΠΑΡΘΙΚΟΝ?] ΓΕΡΜΑΝΙΚΟΝ |
ΔΑΚΙΚΟΝ | .Η.ΠΟΛΙΣ | ΕΠΙΜΕΛΗΘΕΝΤΟΣ ΤΗΣ
ΑΝΑΣΤΑΣΕΩ|Σ ΤΙΤΟΤ ΦΛΑΤΙΟΤ ΔΗΜΗΤΡΙΟΤ[2]

Imperatorem Nervam Traianum Caesarem Augustum Ger-
manicum Dacicum civitas Delia curante erigendae statuae
Tito Flavio Demetrio.

3 Ad Miconum oppidum maritumum ad portam ex Delo advecta
statuarum fragmenta candido de marmore et eximia arte pers-
culpta:

ΧΡΤΣΟΓΟΝΗ.ΤΟΤ.ΕΡΜΟΔΟ[Ρ]ΟΤ[3]

ΑΡΤΕΜΙΔΟΡΑ.ΔΙΟΔΟΤΟΤ.ΓΤΝΗ | ΧΡΗΣΤΕ.ΧΑΙΡΕ[4]

[DRAWINGS]

: DIARY III :

Notable Documents of the Cyclades
from [the Journals of] Cyriac de'Pizzicolli of Ancona

[Mykonos]

Hail, good Syntyche, daughter of Karpos; she is living. Hail,   1
good Lucius Ofellius; he is living.

[DRAWING]

In Mykonos, at the church of the most holy Precursor, [St.   2
John] the Baptist, I found this inscription in honor of the divine
Emperor Trajan, on a large, ornate marble statue base in Attic/
Doric lettering. It was a good omen that our journey will be most
agreeable:

The city [honors] the Emperor Nerva Trajan Caesar Augustus, Victor over Parthia, Germany, and Dacia. Titus Flavius
Demetrius was in charge of erecting [the statue].[1]

At the seaside town of Mykonos, at the gate, [I saw] fragments   3
of bright marble statues, brought there from Delos, carved with
extraordinary skill:

Chrysogone, daughter of Hermodoros

Farewell, good Artemidora, wife of Diodotos.

[DRAWINGS]

[Delos]

4   Ex Micono Delon venimus, sacram et nobilissimam Cicladum insulam, comperimus et primum ad magnam rotundam prope theatrum et marmoream basym epigramma:

ΒΑΣΙΛΕΩΣ.ΜΙΘΡΑΔΑΤΟΥ | ΕΥΠΑΤΟΡΟΣ.[Κ]ΑΙ ΤΟΥ
ΑΔΕΛΦΟΥ | ΑΥΤΟΥ ΜΥΘΡΑΔΑΤΟΥ. ΧΡ[Η]Σ[Τ]ΟΥ |
Δ[Ι]ΟΝΤΣΙΟΣ ΝΕΩΝΙΟΣ ΑΘΗΝΑΙΟΣ |
Γ[Υ]ΜΝΑΣΙΑΡΧΗΣΑΣ. ΑΝΕΘΗΚΕΝ⁵

[DRAWING OF THE BASE]

5   Ad summam Deliae civitatis arcem prope vetusta moenia in marmoreo capulo:

ΑΡ[ΕΙ]ΟΣ ΧΡΥΣΙΠΠΟΥ.ΜΑΡΑΘΩΝΙΟΣ | ΤΗΣ
ΔΗΛΟΥ⁶

6   Ad aliam basim marmoream:

[ΦΙΛΟΣΤΡΑΤΟΝ ΦΙΛΟΣΤΡΑΤΟΥ] ΑΣ[Κ]Α[Λ]ΩΝΙΤΗΝ
| ΤΡΑ[Π]Ε[Ζ]ΕΙΤΕΥΟΝΤΑ | ΔΙΟΔΟΤΟΣ ΑΝΤΙΠΑΤΡΟΥ
| ΑΣΚΑΛΟΝΙΤΗΣ ΤΟΝ ΕΑΥΤΟΥ.ΘΕΙΟΝ.ΚΑΙ.ΤΡΟΦΕΑ
| ΚΑΙ ΣΩΤΗΡΑ.ΚΑΙ ΕΤΕΡΓΕΤΗΝ | ΚΑΙ [ΔΙΙ]
ΚΥΝ[ΘΙ]Ω ΚΑΙ ΑΘΗΝΑΙ ΚΥΝ[ΘΙΑΙ]⁷

7   Ad rotundam dimidii stadii naumachiam:

ΒΑΣΙΛΕ[Ω]Σ ΜΙΘΡΑΔΑΤΟΥ ΕΤΕΡΓΕΤΟΥ |
ΣΕΛΕΥΚΟΣ.ΜΑΡΑΘΩΝΙΟΣ | ΓΥΜΝΑΣΙΑΡΧΩΝ⁸

[DRAWINGS]

8   Ad expolitam nigerrimo⁹ de lapide basim aliquantulum dirutam in foro:

[Delos]

From Mykonos we journeyed to Delos, the famous sacred island 4
of the Cyclades, and the first thing we found was an inscription on
a large, round marble statue base near a theater:

> Dionysios son of Neon, the Athenian, ex-gymnasiarch, dedi-
> cated [the statue] of King Mithradates Eupator and his
> brother Mithradates Chrestos.

[DRAWING OF THE BASE]

On top of the Delian city's citadel near some old walls, on a 5
marble sarcophagus:

> Areios, son of Chrysippos, the Marathonian from Delos.

On another marble base: 6

> Diodotos, son of Antipatros, from Ascalon, dedicated [the
> statue of] Philostratos, son of Philostratos, of Ascalon, the
> banker [in Delos], his own uncle, foster-father, savior and
> benefactor, to Zeus Kynthios and Athena Kynthia.

At a round *naumachia* half a stade [in diameter?]:[2] 7

> Seleukos the Marathonian, the gymnasiarch [dedicated the
> statue] of King Mithradates the Benefactor.

[DRAWINGS]

In the forum, on a well-finished statue base made of a very dark 8
stone, slightly damaged:

ΒΑΣΙΛΕΥΣ ΜΑ[Κ]ΕΔΟΝΩΝ ΦΙ[Λ]ΙΠΠΟΣ | ΒΑΣΙΛΕΩΣ
ΔΗΜΗΤΡΙΟΥ | ΑΠΟ ΤΩΝ ΚΑΤΑ ΓΗΝ ΑΓ[ΩΝΩΝ]
ΑΠΟΛΛΩΝΙ[10]

[DRAWING]

9   Apollinis collosei candido de marmore simulacrum XXIIII cubitorum altum:

10 Marmorea Apollinis collosei simulacri marmorei basis latitudinis pedum XII, longitudinis vero XVI:

ΝΑΞΙΟΙ ΑΠΟΛΛΩΝΙ[11]

11 Delii Apollinis templi vestigium et ingentes ruinarum candido
de marmore reliquiae:

[DRAWING]

12 Ad aliam basim marmoream:

ΚΑΛΛΙΔΙΚΟΝ ΔΙΟΔΟΤΟΥ | Ο ΔΗΜΟΣ[12]

13 Ad marmoream agonae et ornatissimam portam adhuc tribus
integris lapidibus adhuc integro ordine morantem hoc magnis et
fere deletis antiquitate litteris comperimus epygramma:

ΔΙΟΤΙΜΟΣ ΚΑΙ ΕΡΜΟΝΑΞ ΟΙ ΠΑΜΜΕΝΟΥ |
ΑΘΗΝΑΙΟΙ ΥΠΕΡ | ΤΟΥ ΔΗΜΟΥ ΤΟΥ ΑΘΗΝΑΙΩΝ
ΑΠΟΛΛΩΝΙ ΤΩΙ ΔΗΛΕΙΩΙ | ΕΠΙΜΕΛΗΘΕΝΤΩΝ[13]

[DRAWINGS]

14 ΑΣΤΥ[Χ]ΩΡΟΣ ΤΡΙΦΩΝΙΟΥ | ΑΘΗΝΑΙΩΝ ΚΑΙ |
ΑΠΟΛΛΩΝΙ |[14]

[DRAWINGS]

Philip, King of Macedon, son of King Demetrios, to Apollo, from [the spoils] of his land battles.

[DRAWING]

A colossal statue of Apollo twenty-four cubits tall made of 9
bright marble:[3]

The marble base, twelve feet wide and sixteen feet long:[4] of the 10
colossal marble statue of Apollo, [is inscribed]:

The people of Naxos to Apollo.

The traces and substantial, white marble remains of the ruined 11
temple of Delian Apollo:

[DRAWING]

On another marble base:[5]   12

The people [honors] Kallidikos, son of Diodotos.

On the ornate marble gate of a gymnasium, remaining with its 13
three undamaged [epistyle?] blocks still in their proper position,
we found this inscription in large letters almost obliterated by the
passage of time:[6]

Diotimos and Hermonax the Athenians, sons of Pammenes,
to the Delian Apollo for the people of Athens [...] were in
charge.

[DRAWINGS]

Astychoros son of Tryphonios [for the people of] Athens   14
and to Apollo.

[DRAWINGS]

15   ΛΑΩ[ΝΙΔ]ΙΣ ΚΑΙ ΑΘΗΝΑΓΟΡΑΣ | ΑΘΗΝ[Α]ΙΟΙ
ΤΠΕΡ ΤΟΤ ΔΗΜΟΤ | ΤΟΤ ΑΘΗΝΑΙΩΝ.ΑΠΟΛΛΩΝΙ |
ΤΩ ΔΗΛΕΙΩΙ ΕΠΙΜΕΛΗΘΕΝΤΩΝ | ΔΙΟΝΤΣΙΟΤ[15]

16   ΑΠΟ ΤΩΝ ΚΑΤΑ ΓΗΝ ΑΓ[Ω]ΝΩΝ ΕΝ ΔΗΛΩΙ |
ΔΙ[Ο]Ν[Τ]ΣΙΟΣ ΙΕΡΑΣΙΜΟΤ ΑΘΗΝΑΙΟΣ ΙΕΡΕΤΣ
ΓΕΝΟΜΕΝΟΣ[16]

17   Vidimus et prope mare iuxta Apollinis templum ingens et marmoreum theatrum, xxv graduum altitudinis, amplitudinis vero ad
cubitorum LX fuisse videtur:

[DRAWING]

18   Videntur et balnearum vestigia ante nobile ipsum theatrum.

[DRAWING]

19   Antiqua arcis Deliae civitatis moenia serpentinis et magnis lapidibus condita:

[DRAWING]

20   Vidimus autem non longe Apollinis a delubro ingentis Deliae
Dianae templi vestigium et magnas de marmore reliquias:

[DRAWING]

21   Ad naumachiam dimidii stadii amplitudine circularem aquarum adhuc plenitudine[17] constantem et murorum aggere munitam
et columnarum ornamentis compositam, ad marmoream basim:[18]

[DRAWING]

[Π]Ο[Π]ΛΙΟΣ ΣΑΤΡΙΚΑΝΙΟΣ | [Π]Ο[Π]ΛΙΟΤ.ΤΙΟΣ |
ΜΑΑΡΚΟΣ ΑΤΔΙΟΣ ΜΑΑΡΚΟΤ ΣΑΤΡΙΑΣ |
ΔΕΚ[Ι]ΜΟΣ ΣΤΕΡΤΙΝΙΟΣ .ΣΠΟΡΙΟΤ. ΤΙΟΣ |
ΣΑΡΑΠΙΟΝ ΑΛΕΞΑΝΔΡΟΤ ΤΙΟΣ ΝΕΑΠΟΛΕΙΤΙΣ |
ΣΙΜΑΛΟΣ. ΤΙΜΑΡΧΟΤ. ΤΙΟΣ. ΤΑΡΑΝΤΙΝΟΣ |

Leonides and Athenagoras, Athenians, to the Delian Apollo   15
for the people of Athens. Dionysios [and ...] were in charge.

[...] from the spoils of battles on land [...] Dionysios son of   16
Ierasimos, the Athenian, who had become a priest in Delos.

Also by the sea, near the temple of Apollo, we saw a huge   17
marble theater twenty-five rows high [and] about sixty cubits in
width:

[DRAWING]

One sees also, in front of the imposing theater itself, the re-   18
mains of a bath:⁷

[DRAWING]

The ancient walls of the Delian city's citadel, built of large, ser-   19
pentine blocks:⁸

[DRAWING]

Not far from the temple of Apollo we saw the traces and large   20
marble remains of a huge temple of Delian Diana:⁹

[DRAWING]

At a circular *naumachia* half a stade in width, still standing filled   21
with water and provided with an embankment of walls complete
with ornamental columns, [there is the following inscription] on a
marble statue base:¹⁰

[DRAWING]

Poplios Satrikanius son of Poplios, Markos Audios Saurias
son of Markos, Dekimos Stertinios son of Sporios, Sarapion
of Neapolis son of Alexander, Simalos of Tarentum son
of Timarchos, Gnaios Lokretios son of Leukios, Publios
Kastrikios son of Poplios, Dekimos Stertinios Damas son of

ΓΝΑΙΟΣ. [Λ]ΟΚΡΗΤΙΟΣ ΛΕΤΚΙΟΤ ΤΙΟΣ ΠΟΠΛΙΟΣ
ΚΑΣΤΡΙΚΙΟΣ ΠΟΠΛΙΟΤ | ΔΕΚ[Ι]ΜΟΣ ΣΤΕΡΤΙΝΙΟΣ
.ΔΕΚ[Ι]ΜΟΤ.ΔΑΜΑΣ | ΜΑΡΚΟΣ. ΑΡΕΛΙΟΣ.
ΚΟΙΝΤΟΤ | ΓΑΙΟΣ Σ[Α]ΤΦ[Ε]ΙΟΣ.
ΑΤΛΟΤ.ΖΗΝΟΔΩΡΟΣ | ΤΙΤΟΣ.ΝΟ[Τ]ΙΟΣ. ΑΤΛΟΤ
ΤΡΤΦΩΝ | ΕΡΜΑΙΗΙ. ΚΑΙ. ΑΠΠΟΛΛΩΝΙ [ΑΣΤΑΙ][19]

22   Ad aliam agonalem marmoreis innumerisque columnis ornatissimam aulam in marmoreis pro lateribus scalis latinis expolitisque
litteris epigrammata:

BRAVNDVTIVS L. [F?]. ARISTIPPVS | DE SVO
FECIT[20]

23   Ad alium subinde inscriptio:

M. AVRELIVS M. F. SCAVRVS [Q].[21]

24   Ad aulam prope Deliam civitatis arcem antiquissimis atticisque
litteris inscriptio lata in tabula expolito de marmore:

ΛΕΩΝΙΔΗΝ. ΑΘΗΝΑΓΟΡΟΤ | ΑΘΗΝΑΙΟΝ |
ΑΘΗΝΑΓΟΡΑΣ ΚΑΙ [Ζ]ΗΝΩΝ | ΚΑΙ ΔΗΜ[Η]ΤΡΙΑ
ΤΟΝ [Α]ΔΕΛΦΟΝ | [Θ]ΕΟΙΣ | ΕΠΙ ΕΠΙΜΕΛΗΤΟΤ
ΤΗΣ. Ν[Α]ΣΟΤ ΔΡΑ[Κ]ΟΝΤΟΣ. ΤΟΤ ΟΦΕΛΟΤ
ΒΑΘΕΝ ΚΑΙ ΤΩΝ. ΕΠΙΤΡΟΠΩΝ | ΑΡΚΕΤΟΤ
ΚΤΔΑ[Θ]ΗΝΑΙΕΩΣ. ΚΑΙ. ΕΣΤΙΑΙΟΝ | ΕΠΙ ΙΕΡΕΩΣ.
ΣΕΛΕΤΚΟ[Τ] ΤΟΤ ΑΝΔΡΟΝΙΚΟ[Τ] [Ρ]ΑΜΝΟΤΣΙΟΤ[22]

25   Solinus de insula Deli:[23]

Meminisse hoc loco par est quod primum [post] diluvium
Ogigi, *secundum fuit diluvium in Achaia Iacob patriarchae et Ogigi*
temporibus. [Notandum] cum IX et amplius mensibus diem
continua nox inumbrasset, Delon ante omnes [terras] radiis
solis illuminata. Sortitum ex eo nomen quod primum

Dekimos, Markos Arelios son of Kointos, Gaios Saufeios Zenodoros son of Aulos, Titos Novios Tryphon son of Aulos, worshippers of Hermes and Apollo [...]

At another contest-hall elaborately adorned with numerous 22 marble columns, at a marble stairway in a prominent position on the side [of the building], in smoothly executed Latin lettering, [is the following] inscription:

Braundutius Aristippus, son? of Lucius, made this from his own funds.

Inscription on another [stone] immediately below: 23

Marcus Aurelius Scaurus son of Marcus, q[uaestor?]

At a hall near the city's Delian citadel, a long inscription in an- 24 cient Attic lettering, on a slab of finished marble:

Athenagoras and Zenon and Demetreia [dedicated the statue of] Leonidas of Athens son of Athenagoras, their brother, to the gods, when Drakon son of Ophelas, of Bate, was administrator of the Island and Arketos of Kyda- thenaion and Hestiaios [of Halai] were in charge of the tem- ple, and when Seleukos son of Andronikos, of Rhamnous, was priest.

Solinus on the island of Delos:[11] 25

It is apropos to mention in this context that after the first flood [in the time] of Ogyges, there was a second flood in Achaea, in the time of Jacob the patriarch and Ogyges. It is to be noted that, when continual night had overshadowed the day for nine months and more, Delos was illuminated by the rays of the sun before any other land. It therefore got its name because it was the first place restored to sight.[12] The

reddita foret visibus. [Inter] Ogigum sane et Deucalionem medium aevum DC annos datur.

26 ΑΠΟΛΛΟΝΙΟΣ. ΣΕΛΕΤΚΟΤ | ΑΠΟΛΛΩΝΙΑ. ΑΝΤΙΟΧΙΑ | ΓΤΝΗ. ΧΡΗΣΤΕ. ΧΑΙΡΕ²⁴

[DRAWING]

[Interlude: Prayer to Mercury]²⁵

27 ΑΓΑΘΗΙ ΤΤΧΗΙ. Artium, mentis, ingenii facundiaeque pater, alme Mercuri, viarum itinerumque optime dux, qui tuo sanctissimo numine nostram iamdiu mentem animumque fovisti, quique nostrum iucundissimum iter undique per Latium, Illiriam, Graeciam, Asiam et Aegiptum terra marique tutum habileque fecisti; ita, noster inclyte geni, nunc et nostrum omne per aevum ingenio, menti facundiaeque opitulare nostrae, nec non hodie III Iduum Aprilis fausto felice Kyriaceoque iucundissimo die e sacra olim et phoebigena Delo per Aegeum ad ipsam in conspectu Miconem Tinonque, una generoso cum viro Francisco Nanni has nobiles Cycladum insulas pro Venetis quaestoria potestate curante et praetoria sua bis septem munita remigibus navi honorifice, altoque aequore nympharum nereidumque choro amante, hoc nostrum omne deinceps per orbem iter tutum, felix, faustum atque beatum dirigere, favitare atque comitare velis.

[DRAWING OF HERMES/MERCURY]

[Naxos]

28 Ex Micono Naxon, 'bacchatam iugis insulam,' *venitur.²⁶* In scopulo ante ipsam civitatem ingentes Liberi patris marmorei templi reliquiae *visuntur.* Eiusce eximiae parietes magna ex parte suo ordine

era between Ogyges and Deucalion, of course, is given as 600 years.

Apollonios son of Seleukos, Apollonia wife of Antiochos[?], 26
good one, farewell.

[DRAWING]

[Interlude: Prayer to Mercury]

Good Luck. Nurturing Mercury, father of the arts, of mind, of 27
wit, and of speech, best lord of ways and journeys, who by your
most holy power have long blessed our mind and heart, just as you
have made safe and easy our most pleasant travels by land and sea
through Italy, Illyria, Greece, Asia, and Egypt: so, our bright
spirit, be pleased to assist our wit, mind, and speech both now and
through all my life and on this happy favorable, fortunate, most
pleasant Day of the Lord *[i.e. Sunday]*, the third day before the
Ides of April *[i.e., 13 April]*, as I depart from once-sacred Delos,
birthplace of Phoebus, through the Aegean for Mykonos, which is
within view, and for Tenos, accompanied by the noble Francesco
Nanni, who has charge of these famous Cycladic islands for Venice as their financial officer, aboard the governor's flagship, which
is equipped with fourteen rowers. [We pray also, that you be
pleased] to direct, favor, and accompany this our journey after that
through the whole world. [Bless us] with a favoring sea and a chorus of nymphs and nereids and, in your kindness, make [our voy-
age] a blessed and happy one.

[DRAWING OF HERMES/MERCURY][13]

[Naxos]

From Mykonos one comes to Naxos "on whose hills Bacchic revel- 28
ries are held."[14] On a projecting rock in front of the city [of
Naxea] one views the substantial remains of a marble temple to

adhuc integrae manent et ingens ex quattuor magnis lapidibus porta:

[DRAWING]

29　Apud antiquam Naxei ducis domum antiqua in marmorea basi ibidem aliunde ornamento adducta:

ΤΙΒΕΡΙΩΙ. Κ[ΛΑ]ΤΔΙΩΙ. | ΚΤΡΕΙΝΑ. Τ. ΓΕΜΕ[ΛΛ]Ω.| Τ[Η]Ν ΣΤΗ[Λ]ΗΝ[27]

[DRAWING]

30　Ex Naxea urbe ad Carram amoenissimam villam *venitur*, nobilem olim et glebis uberem Naxeae regiae civitatis vicum, ubi ad sacram beatae[28] Virginis aedem, quam χαριοτίσαν in hodiernum appellant, hoc antiquis Doricisque litteris epigramma expolito in marmore *comperitur*:

[DRAWING]

ΑΠΟΛΛΟΔΩΡΟΤ. ΙΕΡΕΩΣ.| ΤΩΝ. ΧΑΡΙ[Τ]ΩΝ. ΔΙΑ ΒΙΟΤ| ΛΕΤΚΙΟΤ. ΠΟΠΙΛΛΙΟΤ | ΑΤΛΟΤ. ΤΙΟΤ[29]

31　Ad aedem annunciatae Virginis extra Naxeam urbem:

ΑΝΤΙΟΧΟΤ.ΗΡΑΚΛΕΙ|ΔΟΤ ΑΘΗΝΑΙΟΤ.[30]

32　Ad alium lapidem prope Naxeam urbem:

ΤΕΡΤΙΑ ΙΑΣΩΝΟΣ.| ΒΡΕΝΤΕΣΙΝΗ. ΧΡΗΣΤΕ.| ΧΑΙΡΕ.[31]

33　Ex Naxea arce ad septemtrionem insulae partem Apollineum ad collem *venitur*, ubi non longe a littore stom[a],[32] quem et hodie Apollineum a numine Ἀπόλλωνος πόταμον dicunt, Deliae insulae in conspectu ad arduum montem ipsum Apollinis marmo-

Father Liber. Its splendid walls still remain mostly intact in their original arrangement, as does the huge door made of four large blocks:[15]

[DRAWING]

At the antique dwelling of the duke of Naxos, on an antique   29
marble statue base brought from elsewhere to adorn the building:

[...] [dedicated] the monument to Tiberios Klaudios Gemel-
los [of the tribe] Quirina.

[DRAWING]

From the city of Naxea one comes to the charming village of   30
Carra, once a celebrated and fertile country seat of the royal
Naxean city, where, at the church of the Blessed Virgin, which
they call Chariotissa today, one finds this inscription on a smooth
marble block in antique Doric lettering:

[DRAWING]

Of Leukios Popillios Apollodoros son of Aulos, priest for
life of the Graces.

At the church of the Virgin's Annunciation outside the city of   31
Naxea:

Of Antiochos Herakleides the Athenian.

On another stone near the city of Naxea: 32

Tertia Brentesine daughter of Jason; good one, farewell.

From the citadel of Naxea one comes to the northern part of   33
the island, to the hill called Apollo's, where, not far from the
shore, is the mouth of a river that they call "Apollo's River" after
the god. One climbs this steep marble height of Apollo, which is
important for its ancient religious associations, with its view of the

reum et antiqua religione insignem *ascenditur*. Ubi ad summum verticem et marmoreum vivo de saxo parietem et suapte natura expolitam in orientem solem nitido candore spectantem hoc vetustis et magnis caracteribus epigramma *comperitur*:

ΟΡΟΣ | [ΧΩ]ΡΙΟ[Τ] | ΙΕΡΟΤ | ΑΠΟΛΛΩΝΙΟΣ[33]

34 Ex Solino de insula Naxos:[34]

Naxon a Delo ΙΙ die ΧΙΙ milia passuum separant, in qua [Stragile][35] oppidum, sed Naxos Dyonisias quam Naxos [prius] dicta [vel] quod hospita Libero patri vel quod fertilitate vitium meteris [vincat ceteras]. Sunt praeterea Cyclades plurimae, sed in supra dictis praecipuum est quod memoriae debe[a]tur.[36]

35 Virgilius de Naxo hos:

Linquimus Ortigiae portum[37] pelagoque volamus
bacchatamque iugis Naxon viridemque Don[us]am
Olearon niveamque Paron sparsasque per aequor
Cycladas, et crebris legimus freta con[c]ita terris.

36 Ovidius:

'Naxon', ait Liber, 'cursus advertite vestros!
Illa mihi domus est, vobis erit hospita tellus.'

37 Apud Delon, insulam in Aegaeo Cycladas inter insignem, Apollinis Collosei simulacri pedes ΙΙΙΙ pedum longtudinis *invenitur*, quorum ad propriam Pario eodem de marmore basim conditorum operis nomen Doricis quoque litteris sic erat inscriptum:

ΝΑΞΙΟΙ ΑΠΟΛΛΩΝΙ[38]

island of Delos. There, at its highest point, a naturally smooth marble wall of living rock that looks toward the rising sun with a brilliant white reflection, one finds this inscription in large, ancient characters:

Boundary of the village [belonging to] the temple of Apollo.

From Solinus, on the island of Naxos:[16]   34

Twelve miles separate Naxos from Delos, in which is the town of Stragile. But Naxos was previously called Dionysias rather than Naxos, either because it was host to father Liber or because [it surpasses the other islands] in the fertility of its vines. There are, besides, numerous [other] Cyclades, but those mentioned above are the principal ones to be recalled.

Vergil [wrote] these [verses] about Naxos:[17]   35

We leave the port of Ortygia and fly over the sea and past Naxos, that holds the rites of Bacchus on its heights, and green Donysa, Olearos, and snowy-white Paros, Cycladic islands strewn over the sea, and thread our way through waters made rough by congested lands.

Ovid on the island of Naxos:[18]   36

"Steer your course toward Naxos," says Liber. "That is my home and it will be for you a welcoming land."

On Delos, the island in the Aegean among the Cyclades that is   37
especially significant, one finds the feet of a colossal statue of Apollo, four feet long. On the same Parian marble base that belongs to them was inscribed in Doric letters the identity of the statue's donors:

The people of Naxos to Apollo.

Scilicet ex Naxea insula cives vel accolae Naxei Apollini Delio opus illud insigne dicarunt.

38   Ad argenteum et antiquissimum Rhodiorum nomisma, ubi primo in latere collosei Apollinis caput radiis solis coronatum *videtur*, et ex altero, punicei pomi Rhodium ipsum ad florem, Athanodori[39] Rhodiorum antiquissimi principis nomen talibus antiquis litteris inscriptum habet: A[Θ]ANOΔΩΡOΣ[40]

[Paros][41]

39   Ad XIII[42] Kalendas Maias ex Naxea insula et civitate praeclara niveam Paron venimus, clariorem[43] et marmorigenam illam vatum memorem et celeberrimam insulam; et primum ad maritimam Pariaepolitanae civitatis coloniam, quam Ἀγουταν dicunt, Cursinum Summaripa, optimum loci principem et veterem nobis amicum, obviam occurrentem vidi. Qui tum me postquam magna hillaritate suscepit, ad posteram diem eo comite ad antiquam ipsam et memorabilem venimus Pariae civitatis sedem, ubi tam ingentia et nobilia reverendissimave aeternitatis monumenta videntur, ut non exiguum esset opus omnia litteris explicare.

40   Vidimus namque suis candente marmore amplissimis et conspicuis moenibus adhuc suo ordine partem quoque turritam extare. Sed quisnam diceret eximia illa ornatissima olim tantae urbis aedificia undique solo collapsa immensis vel convulsa ruinis, maximasque templorum reliquias, statuas innumeras et miro ordine arte perspicuas, tametsi magna ex parte longinqua vetustate et cultorum ignavia hominum defectas soloque obrutas inspectaremus?[44] Quis et innumera illa memoraret[45] eximia de marmore sepulchra epistiliaque[46] et immanium columnarum fragmenta, bases et nobilibus litteris epigrammata, nec non divorum[47] Caesarumque principum nostrorum trophealaia ingentia pleraque candente de marmore ornamenta?

That is, the citizens of the island of Naxos—the Naxian people—
dedicated this remarkable work to Delian Apollo.

On an ancient silver Rhodian coin, on one side of which one 38
sees the head of the colossal Apollo crowned with the rays of the
sun; and on the other, at the Rhodian blossom itself, the pome-
granate, is inscribed the name of A[th]anodorus, the ancient ruler
of Rhodes, in antique lettering, as follows: Athanadoros.

[Paros]

On 22 April [1445][19] we journeyed from the splendid island and 39
city of Naxos to snow-white Paros, a [still] more luminous island,
also marble-producing, mindful of its poets and great in its
fame;[20] and the first person I saw, at the seaside settlement of the
Parian state they call ?Naousa,[21] was Crusino Sommaripa, the excellent prince of the island and an old friend of ours, coming to
meet us. He received me with good cheer, and the next day we accompanied him to the ancient and memorable seat of the Parian
state, where such large, noble, and venerable remnants of antiquity
are seen that it would be no slight task to explain it all in writing.

For we saw that a turreted section of it survives, with its exten- 40
sive, striking walls of shining marble. But who could describe
those distinctive, richly adorned buildings of a once-great city
fallen to the ground in every direction, an enormous confusion of
ruins: the extensive remains of temples, numerous statues extraordinary for their marvelous symmetry and artistic quality? —
though we observed that in great part they were diminished and
fallen to the ground in ruins by the long passage of time and the
lazy neglect of human beings. Who could describe those tombs,[22]
too many to recall, made of finest marble, the architraves, the fragments of giant columns, the statue bases and grandly lettered inscriptions, and the numerous, huge triumphal monuments of our
divine princes, the Caesars, ornaments in gleaming white marble?

41 Quorum ad marmoream niveamque a posteris et vetustis operibus reconditam Pariaepolitanam arcem ad magnam et ornatissimam listam hoc in divum Augustum atticis litteris epygramma
comperimus:

ΑΥΤΟΚΡΑΤΟ[Ρ]Ι. ΚΑΙΣΑΡΙ | ΘΕΩΙ ΣΕΒΑΣΤΩΙ ΘΕΟΥ
ΥΙΩΙ[48]

42 Quod in eiusdem arcis ornamentum ad portam ipsam regiam
divi Augusti gratia restituendum latineque traducendum curavimus talibus litteris subscriptis:[49]

IMP. CAESARI | DIVO AVGVSTO DIVI FILIO.
CVRSINVS S.R. PARIVS ANDRIVSQ.|
B.M.PRINCEPS.| PARIAE.POLITANAE ARCI
RESTITVIT | KYRIACO ANCO. CURANTE[50]

Egei Pelagi Monumenta Fragmentaque
Reperta Kiriaci Anconitani Opera[51]

43 Vidimus et ad praeclaram marmoream arcem ad magnam statuarum basim antiquissimis litteris epygramma, quod ob praeclara
Nardi Isocratisque nomina Leonardo Iustiniano, Veneto patricio
nobili et amplissimo hieromnenonum ordine nostro transmittendum curavimus:

ΝΑΡΔΟΥ ΚΑΙ ΙΣΟΚΡΑΤΟΥ ΚΑΙ ΠΟΛΛ[Υ]ΦΑΝΟΥ
ΜΕ[ΣΣΙΟΥ] ΜΝΗΣΙΘΕΟΥ | ΚΑΙ | ΠΟΛΥΚΛΕΟΥΣ |
ΚΑΙ | ΦΙΛΟΝΙΚΟΥ[52]

44 Exinde ad occiduam abditamque et eminentiorem civitatis partem non longe a littore magnas et insignes vidimus Aesculapii
templi reliquias et parietis marmoreae partis colosseique insigne

Among these monuments, on the city of Paros's snow-white 41
marble citadel, which later inhabitants constructed out of ancient
building parts, on a large, decorated architrave, we found this inscription to the divine Augustus in Attic lettering:

To the divine Emperor Caesar Augustus, son of the god.

Out of reverence for the divine Augustus we had this inscrip- 42
tion restored and translated into Latin for the adornment of the
same citadel at the palace gate, with the following addition:

To the divine Emperor Augustus Caesar, son of the god.
Crusino S[omma]r[ipa], the deserving prince of Paros and
Andros, restored [this inscription] for the citadel of the city
of Paros through the offices of Cyriac of Ancona.

Monuments and Fragments of the Aegean Sea
Found by Cyriac of Ancona's Efforts

Also on the brilliant marble citadel, we saw an inscription in an- 43
tique lettering on a large statue base.[23] Because of the famous
names of Nardus and Isocrates we caused a copy of it to be sent to
Leonardo Giustiniani, a noble patrician of Venice and a distinguished prelate:

Of Nardos and Isokrates and Pollyphanes. Of Messios
Mnesitheos and Polykles and Philonikos.

Then, on the western, hidden, and more elevated part of the 44
city not far from the seashore, we saw large, important remains of
a temple of Asclepius, parts of a marble wall, and a significant

dei fragmentum simulacri, cuius amplum pectus ad quinque pedum latitudinis constat; et suam ad maximam basim magnis et vetustis litteris comperimus epygramma:

ΤΟΝ. ΣΩΤΗΡΑ. ΑΣΚΛ[ΗΠ]ΙΟΝ. | ΚΛΑΥ[ΔΙΟΣ]
Α[Γ]ΗΣΙΛΟΧΟΣ | ΤΗΙ ΠΑΡΙΩΝ. ΠΟΛΕΙ[53]

45   Vidimus et ibidem pleraque eiusdem ad honorem dei simulachra, diversorum bases solo magna ex parte suffossas et e nobis non sine labore ab ipsa matre revulsas et in lucem deductas, et ad integriores harum talibus imaginibus epigrammata comperimus:[54]

[Ζ]ΩΣΙΜΟΣ ΟΝΗΣΙΦΩΝΤΟΣ | ΚΑΙ ΤΡΕΙΤΩΝΙΣ.
ΥΠΕΡ ΤΟΥ. [ΥΙ]ΟΥ | ΟΝΗΣΙΦΩΝΤΟΣ ΑΣΚΛΗΠΙΩΙ
ΚΑΙ ΥΓΙΕΙΑΙ[55]

46   Ad alias eiusdem imaginis bases:

ΠΑΥΣΑΝΙΑΣ ΑΘ[Η]ΝΟΚ[Λ]ΕΟΥΣ | ΚΑΙ ΕΙΑ
ΔΕΞΙΚΡΑΤΟΥΣ ΥΠΕΡ | ΤΟΥ ΥΙΟΥ ΠΑΥΣΑΝΙΟΥ |
ΑΣΚΛΗΠΙΩΙ ΚΑΙ ΥΓΙΕΙΑΙ.[56]

[DRAWINGS]

47   ΑΓΕΛΛΙΩΝ ΚΑΙ ΠΑΜΦΥΛΑ ΥΠΕΡ | ΤΟΥ ΥΙΟΥ
ΑΝΤΙΦΑΝΟΥ ΤΟΥ ΘΡΑΣΩΝΙ | ΑΣΚΛΗΠΙΩΙ ΚΑΙ
ΥΓΙΕΙΑΙ[57]

48   ΚΤΗΣΩΝ.ΑΡΙΣΤΟΦΑΝΤΟΣ ΚΑΙ ΦΡΥ|ΝΙΣΑ
ΚΛΕΟΔΑΜΑΝΤΟΣ ΥΠΕΡ ΤΟΥ | ΥΙΟΥ
ΚΛΕΟΔΑΜΑΝΤΟΣ [Α]ΣΚ[Λ]ΗΠΙΩΙ ΚΑΙ | ΥΓΙΕΙΑΙ[58]

49   ΛΟΙΚΙΟΣ. ΜΑΙΟΣ. ΒΥΒ[Λ]Ο[Σ] ΚΑΙ ΠΟΛΛΑ ΑΡΕΛΛΟΥ
ΥΠΕΡ ΤΟΥ ΥΙΟΥ ΠΕΙΟΥ ΑΣΚΛΗΠΙΩΙ ΚΑΙ ΥΓΙΕΙΑΙ[59]

50   ΕΠ[Α]ΦΡΟΔΙΤΟΣ ΣΕ[Λ]ΕΥ|ΚΛΕΟΣ ΥΠΕΡ ΤΟΥ | ΥΙΟΥ.
ΕΠΙΓΟΝΟΥ ΑΣΚΛΗΠΙΩΙ ΚΑΙ ΥΓΙΕΙΑΙ[60]

fragment of a colossal statue of the god, whose large chest is five feet broad, and on its very large base we found this inscription in large, ancient lettering:

Klaudios Agesilochos [dedicates the statue of] the savior Asklepios to the city of the Parians.

In the same place we saw several statues in honor of the same god, the bases of different statues largely sunken into the ground. We extracted them from mother [earth] not without effort and brought them to light. On the more complete ones we found inscriptions along with representations like this: 45

Zosimos son of Onesiphon and Trionis to Asklepios and Hygieia for their son Onesiphon.

On other bases of the same [type of] image: 46

Pausanias son of Athenokles and Eia daughter of Dexikrates to Asklepios and Hygieia for their son Pausanias.

[DRAWINGS]

Agellion and Pamphyla to Asklepios and Hygieia for their adopted son Antiphanes son of Thrasonides. 47

Kteson son of Aristophon and Phrynis daughter of Kleodamas to Asklepios and Hygieia for their son Kleodamas. 48

Loikios Maios Byblos and Polla daughter of Archelaos to Asklepios and Hygieia for their son Peios. 49

Epaphroditos son of Seleukos to Asklepios and Hygieia for his son Epigonos. 50

51 ΛΕΥΚΙΟΣ. ΒΑΒΥΛΛΙΟΣ ΕΡΩΣ. | ΚΑΙ ΒΑΒΥΛΛΑ
ΣΕΚΟΝΔΑ ΥΠΕΡ | ΤΟΥ ΥΙΟΥ ΚΑΙ ΛΕΥΚΙΟΣ
ΒΑΒΥΛΛΙΟΣ | ΕΠΑΦΡΟΔΙΟΤΟΣ. ΥΠΕΡ | ΤΟΥ
ΘΡΕΠΤΟΥ ΑΥΛΟΥ ΒΑΒΥΛΛΙΟΥ | ΚΡΙΣΣΦΟΥ⁶¹

52 Η ΒΟΥΛΗ | ΚΑΙ Ο ΔΗΜΟΣ | ΛΕΥΚΙΟΝ | ΑΥΩΝΙΟΝ |
ΠΡΙΣΚΟΝ⁶²

53 Η ΒΟΥΛΗ | ΚΑΙ Ο ΔΗΜΟΣ | ΠΟΛΛΑΝ ΜΝΑΣΕΤΑ
ΑΡΕΤΗΣ ΕΝΕ|ΚΕΝ ΚΑΙ ΣΩΦΡΟΣΥΝΗΣ⁶³

54 ΑΦΡΟΔΙΣΙΑ | ΠΑΡΜΕΝΙΩΝΟΣ | ΕΛΠΙΣ | ΘΕΟΤΕΙΜΗΣ⁶⁴

55 ΑΣΚΛΗΠΙΩΙ ΚΑΙ ΥΓΙΕΙΑΙ⁶⁵

[DRAWING]

56 Η ΒΟΥΛΗ ΚΑΙ | Ο ΔΗΜΟΣ | ΣΤΕΦΑΝ[Ω]Ι
ΧΡΥΣ[Ε]Ω | ΠΡΑΣΙΚΛΕΑ ΣΤΕΦΑΝΩ |
ΠΡΑ[Ξ]ΙΚΛΕΟΥ ΥΙΟΝ | ΤΟΝ ΦΙΛΟΠΑΤΡΙ ΚΑΙ |
ΤΟΝ ΠΑΝΤΑ [Τ]ΡΟΠΟΝ | ΠΟΛΕΙΤΟΥ|ΟΜΕΝΟΝ⁶⁶

[DRAWING]

57 Ad mag⟨n⟩um aliud sepulchrum:

ΜΑΡ|ΚΟΥ| ΚΟΣΣ|ΟΥΤΙΟΥ⁶⁷

[DRAWING]

58 [Ζ]ΟΣΙΜΗ. ΚΛΕΟΜΒΡΟ|ΤΟΥ ΧΡΗΣΤΕ ΧΑΙΡΕ⁶⁸

59 Ad posterum⁶⁹ vero et ix Kalendas Maiarum faustum Iovialem
atque iucundissimum diem, eo ipso Cursino ductitante principe,
ad quinquaginta ab urbe stadia marmoreos ad montes venimus,
ubi tris ingentes et mirificas vidimus, ne dicam λατομίας λι-
θουργίαςve aut marmifodinas, quin et humanae potentiae por-
tentuosum et inexplicabile ac omnium quippe humani ingenii la-

Leukios Babyllios Eros and Babylla Sekonda for their son,   51
and Leukios Babyllios Epaphroditos for his foster-son Aulos
Babyllios Krispos.

The Council and People [honor] Leukios Auonios Priskos.   52

The Council and People [honor] Polla daughter of Mnaseas   53
for her virtue and moderation.

Aphrodisia [daughter or husband] of Parmenion; Elpis   54
daughter of Theotime.

To Asklepios and Hygieia.   55

[DRAWING]

The Council and People crown with a golden crown   56
Praxicles son of Praxicles, the lover of his country, who per-
forms his civic duties in every way.

[DRAWING]

On another large tomb: 57

Markos Kossotios

[DRAWING]

Zosime daughter of Kleombrotos, good one, farewell.   58

On the next day, the 23rd of April, Jupiter's favorite, joyful day,   59
accompanied by the governor Crusino himself, we came to the
marble mountains fifty stades from the city. There we saw three
huge and marvelous — I would call them, not so much stone quarries (in Greek *latomias* or *lithourgias*), as an achievement of human capability, ominous and inexpressible because more worthy of
wonder than all the products of human ingenuity. For after I had
chosen to look inside the first [of these quarries], there came into

borum admirabilius opus. Nam posteaquam primam[70] interius conspectare malueram, tam vasto hiatu immanes fabrefactae manu videntur cavernae, ut non facile litteris explicarem. At et cum ad eius vastae altitudinis baratra per immania montis viscera Cursino ipso comite accensis lampadibus penetravimus, missis denique in accessus ad intima famulis, ad pleraque stadia excisa ferro atque manibus antra in abruptum[71] patuisse percepimus. Sic et utique[72] non minori amplitudine quin et altiores binas alias non longe ab ea perscrutavimus latomias, tametsi plures huiuscemodi magnitudinis eadem in insula speluncae marmifodinae esse dicuntur. Quod et tam inmensum humani generis opus a C. Plinio, dum labirintha commemoraret, praetermissum esse miror, quin et ea tam mirifica opera et inter pyramidum barbara ut Memphis miracula memoratu haud indigniora videntur. At etsi forte antiquioribus ab auctoribus memorata extiterint, longi temporis labe abolita, non intercedentibus commentariis, ad nostram non usque aetatem pervenerint.

60   Equidem ad harum primariam ad fauces et ipsum ante vestibulum Herculis, Nympharum Faunumque symulachra solida in rupe mira et vetusta manu fabresculpta videntur, et sub eis tale doctis et vetustissimis characteribus epygramma compertum est:[73]

ΑΔΑΜΑΣ | ΟΔΡΥΣΗΣ | ΝΥΜΦΑΙΣ[74]

[DRAWINGS, ONE INSCRIBED:][75]

61   ΚΑΤΑΓΡΑΦΟΣ | ΝΙΚΙΟΥ[76]

62   ΠΡΕΙΜΕ ΧΑΙΡΕ[77]

[DRAWING: GRAVE STELE, INSCRIBED:]

63   ΙΟΥΛΙΑ | ΕΥΓΕΝΙΑ | ΧΡΗΣΤΕ | ΧΑΙΡΕ[78]

[DRAWING, INSCRIBED:]

view vast, widely-gaping, hand-wrought caverns, not easy for me to describe in writing. And when, with Crusino as our companion, we penetrated with lit torches through the vast heart of the mountain to shafts of immeasurable height [and] we sent the servants to approach the inmost parts, we learned that the caves, carved out by hand with iron tools, extended for several stades to a precipice. In the same way we examined the other two quarries not far away from it, no less wide, but higher, although it is said that there are several more marble-quarrying caves of this size on the island. I am surprised that Gaius Pliny passed over this tremendous human achievement when he listed the labyrinths.[24] Indeed, such remarkable works as these seem no less worthy of mention than the foreign marvel of the pyramids at Memphis. But even if perchance they were mentioned by older authors, their memory would have been effaced by the long passage of time, and they would not have survived to our own age without commentaries in the intervening time.

At the most important of these [quarries], at the mouth, in 60 front of the entrance itself, representations of Herakles, the nymphs and fauns are seen in the living rock, sculptured by a marvelous ancient hand. And below them one discovered the following inscription in expert, ancient characters:[25]

Adamas Odryses to the Nymphs.

[DRAWINGS, ONE INSCRIBED:]

Image of Nikias. 61

Preimos, farewell. 62

[DRAWING: GRAVE STELE, INSCRIBED:]

Julia Eugenia, good one, farewell. 63

[DRAWING, INSCRIBED:]

64   ΕΙΚΟΝΑ [ΣΟΥ] ΠΟΛΥῚΚ[Λ]ΕΙΣ ΑΝΑ [Π]ΑΣΤΑΔΑ
        ΤΑΝΔΕ ΠΟΛΙΤΑΙ
        ΘΗΚΑΝ Ο ΜΥΡΙΕΤ[Η]Σ ΜΑΡΑΝΕΙΣΕ ΧΡΟΝΟΣ
        ΕΝ [ΒΟΥΛΑΙΣ ΜΕΝ] ΑΡΙ|ΣΤΟΝ ΑΓΩ[Σ]Ι ΔΕ ΤΟΙΣ ΠΕΡΙ
           ΠΑΤΡΑΣ
        ΑΛΚΙΜΟΝ ΕΝ ΔΕ ΒΙΩΙ ΣΩΦΡΟΝΑ ΔΕΡΚΟΜΕΝΟΙ[79]

[DRAWINGS, INSCRIBED:]

65   Η ΒΟΥΛΗ | ΚΑΙ Δ[Η]ΜΟΣ | ΛΕΥΚΙΟΝ | ΑΥΩΝΙΟΝ |
        ΠΡΙΣΚΟΝ[80]

66   Η ΒΟΥΛΗ | ΚΑΙ Ο ΔΗΜΟΣ | ΠΟΛΛΗΝ ΜΝΑΣΕ
        |ΤΑ ΑΡΕΤΗΣ ΕΝΕ|ΚΕΝ ΚΑΙ [Σ]Ω|ΦΡΟΣΥΝΗΣ[81]

[DRAWINGS, ONE OF THEM INSCRIBED AS FOLLOWS:]

67   ΘΡΑΣΥΞΕΝΟΣ ΘΡΑΣΩΝΟΣ ΙΔΡΥΣΑΤΟ | ΤΥΧ[Η]Σ
        ΑΓΑΘΗΣ[82]

68   ΗΡΠΑΧΘΗ ΜΕΓΑΡΟΝ ΜΑΡΚΟΥ [Δ]ΑΜΑΡ ΟΥΔΕ
           ΠΡΟΣΕΙΠΕΝ
        ΚΟΥ[Ρ]ΙΔΙΟΝ ΓΑΜΕΤΗΝ ΠΩΛΛΑ ΦΙΛΟΝ
           ΦΘΑΜΕΝΗΙ
        ΗΡΠΑΧΗΘΙ ΔΑΙΜΩΝ ΔΕ ΠΙΚΡΥΣ ΟΥ ΛΗΘΕΤΟ
           ΜΟΙΡΗΣ
        ΑΜΑ ΚΑΙ ΕΝ ΜΑΓΑΡΟ|ΙΣ [Υ]ΙΕΑ ΛΙΠΟΜΕΝΟΝ |
        ΕΛ[Ε]ΕΙΝΟΥΣ | ΚΗΔΕΣΙ ΚΑΙ ΓΟΕΡΗ ΠΑΣ ΕΔΑΚΡΥΣΕ |
           ΠΟΛΙΣ
        ΑΛΛΑ ΤΥΧΗΣ ΟΥ ΕΣΤΙ ΦΥΓΕΙΝ ΑΜΕΤΡΟΠΑ
           Δ[Ω]ΡΑ
        ΜΑΡΚΕ ΤΗΣ | ΑΠΛΗΣ ΤΟΥ ΠΕΝΘΕΩΣ ΩΦΕΛΙΗΙ
           ΤΕΤΛΑΘΙ
        ΚΑΙ ΓΑΡ ΑΝΑΚΤΕΣ ΑΝ ΜΗΔΗΤΩ | ΠΟΤΕ | ΠΕΝΘΕΙ |
        ΚΥΡΣΑΝΤΕΣ ΤΟΙΗΣ ΑΛΓΟΣ ΕΧΟΥΣ ΟΔΥΝΗΣ[83]

Your fellow citizens, Polykleis, have dedicated the image in   64
the colonnade, so that time with its many years may not ex-
tinguish [your memory]; they regard you as best in counsel,
brave in contests for your country and moderate in life.

[= §52].   65
[= §53].   66

[DRAWINGS, ONE OF THEM INSCRIBED AS FOLLOWS:]

Thrasyxenos son of Thrason dedicated [the altar of] Good   67
fortune.

[DRAWING]

Marcus' wife has been taken away from his palace; Polla can   68
no longer address her dear wedded husband; she has been
taken away; the god did not forget bitter fate, but suddenly
took away her son Rufus who was left in the palace; he dark-
ened the pitiful house with cares; the entire mournful city
wept. But it is not possible to flee the unalterable gifts of
Fate. Marcus; what use is insatiable grief? Endure; even
kings who met with gloomy grief have the pain of such
suffering.

[UNINSCRIBED AND INSCRIBED DRAWINGS:]

69   Pisce super curvo vectus cantabat Arion[84]

70   ΖΕΥ ΒΑΣΙΛΕΥ ΙΛΑΘΙ

: 23 :

1   Nicolao A. filio Zancarolo, Cydonio sagittifero viro praestanti atque optimo arciferum victori, qui perstrenua virtute et probitate sua hodie, III Nonas Quintilium, Deliae pharetrigerae Dianae fausto sereno atque celeberrimo die, hac ipsa in Cydonea, nobilissima olim marittimas inter Cretensium urbes, nunc vero Caneae nominis praeclara Venetum colonia, P. Balduo viro praeclaro nobile pro Venetis praeside et agonothete dignissimo suiscumque claris consulari potestate collegis, Luca Mudacio et Daniele Barbadico egregiisque spectantibus accolis civibus et colonis, constituto[1] ante urbis moenia ad arenas athletum agone, et singulari praeposito vincenti volucri sagitta, decertantium praemio, non modo insignes illos pharetrigeros Parthos Scythosque et Hyrcanos ceterosve peregrinos sagittiferos superavit, quin et ipsis expertissimis arcu Cydonibus praecellentior, valido diversis incurvato lacertis arcu, ab auribus impulsam nervo transverberatum per aera sagittam, medio expetito abmotoque stadii longa intercapedine signo, praefixit, Kyriacus palaeophilos Anconitanus Apollinis Pythii, pharetrati arci-

178

[UNINSCRIBED AND INSCRIBED DRAWINGS:]

Arion sang as he rode on the curved fish.   69

King Zeus, be gracious.   70

⁚ 23 ⁚

To Niccolò Zancarolo, 5 July 1445, Cydonia, Crete

[Dedication of a coin]

To Niccolò Zancarolo,¹ son of A., the outstanding Cydonian ar- 1
cher and excellent victor over bowmen. Today, the fifth of July, the
favorable, fair and celebrated day of quiver-bearing Delian Diana,
he defeated, by his vigorous courage and worth, not only the outstanding Parthian, Scythian and Hyrcanian archers as well as others from foreign parts, but also proved superior to the expert
Cydonian bowmen in an athletic contest held on the sand before
the city walls, here in Cydonia, once the noblest of the Cretan
coastal cities, now the illustrious Venetian colony of Khania. [The
contest was held] under the worthy presidency of the noble and illustrious Venetian governor, P. Balduo, together with his eminent
colleagues in consular power, Luca Mudacio and Daniele Barbadico, [and took place] under the gaze of the distinguished citizens and colonists. A unique prize was proposed for the contes-
tant who would be victorious with the flying arrow. Bending the
mighty bow with his arms set apart, propelling the arrow through
the pierced air from the string drawn to his ear, he aimed at the
center of the target, which was the long distance of a stade away,
and struck it. To him Cyriac of Ancona, lover of antiquity, gave a
silver coin engraved with the image of the sacred head of Pythian

ferentisque divi, argenteam sacri capitis ymaginem Rhodio et
Anthaeo principe nomismate insignitam dedit memoriae atque
honoris gratia.

2   NICOLAO A. filio Zancarolo ἀπολλοδώρῳ τῷ κυδονίῳ τοξο-
φόρῳ ἀνδρὶ παναρίστῳ καὶ τῶν ἐν τῇ Κυδονία πόλει
ἀγωνισάντων τοξονικήσαντι· Κυριακὸς ἑρμόφιλος ὁ καὶ
παναριστόφιλος τὸ τοῦ ἑκατηβόλου Ἀπόλλωνος ἀργύριον
ἱερᾶς κεφαλῆς νόμισμα ἔδωκεν· μνείας φιλοξενίας τε καὶ
φιλοτιμίας χάριν.

[Testimonia about Crete]

3   Isidorus de Creta:

Creta, quae primum a temperie coeli dicta est, a suo
indigena modo sic dicitur. Est enim ingens Graeciae pars
quae quondam a centum suis urbibus dixere quaeque omnibus studiis claruit et potissimum remis et sagittis.

Idem de sagittis:

Sagicta a sagaci iactu dicta est, idest veloci ictu his primum
Cretenses usi sunt, quibus et pennea ob velocitatem
aptantur.

4   ὁ Πίνδαρος

Ἰὼ Κράτας τοξοφόρον νάει ἔνοπλον κάτοχον γένος.

5   Lucanus:

Iam dilecta Iovi centenis venit in arma
Creta vetus populis Gnosiisque agitare pharetris[2]
Docta nec Eois peior Cydona[3] sagittis.

Apollo, the quiver-and-bow-bearing god [on one side] and the Rhodian prince Anthaeus [on the other]. He did this to commemorate and honor him.

To Niccolò Zancarolo, son of A., gifted by Apollo, excellent 2 Cydonian archer and victor over those engaged in the archery contest in the city of Cydonia, Cyriac, lover of Hermes and of excellence, gave a silver coin of far-shooting Apollo [bearing Apollo's] sacred head. He did this as a remembrance of hospitality and generosity.

[Testimonia about Crete]

Isidore, on Crete:[2] 3

> Crete, which was first named after the mildness of its climate, is now called what it is after its own native manner. For it is a huge part of Greece which at one time they named after its hundred cities and which was distinguished for all its skills, especially in rowing and archery.

The same [author], on arrows:[3]

> The [word] sagitta is derived from [the expression] "sagax iactus," that is, from the fact that the Cretans, who fitted feathers on them for speed, first used them, because of their swift stroke.

Pindar:[4] 4

> Ah, the bow-bearing, enduring people of Crete dwell armed.

Lucan:[5] 5

> Next ancient Crete of the hundred cities, beloved of Jove, comes to battle, skilled in the use of Cnossian quivers, and Cydonia not inferior in archery to the orientals.

6   Virgilius:

Non secus ac nervo per nubem impulsa sagicta
Armatam saevi Parthus quam felle veneni
Parthus sive Cydon telum imedicabile torsit
tridens et celeres incognita transfolat auras.

7   Ovidius:

Armaque equosque habitusque Cydoneasque pharetras

8   Apulegius:

Cretes sagittiferi Dictaeam vocant Dianam.

9   Kyriacus idem hermophylos Anconitanus in Cydonum Chreten-
siumve omnium sagictiferum probitatis argumentum antiqua[4]
haec omnia praeclara auctorum poetarumve inclita dicta his rescri-
benda delegit hodie, Nonis Iuliis, praeclaro geniique nostri Mercurii venerandissimo die, Eugenii papae anno xv, ab urbe Venetum
condita MXXIIII.

10   Actius haec cernens arcum intendebat Apollo
Desuper; omnis eo terrore Aegyptus et Indi,
Omnis Arabs, omnes vertebant terga Sabaei

[DRAWING]

: 24 :

1   Ad III Idus Iulii e Cydonia urbe, ut ad Leucos montes altas
quoque cupressus inspicerem una venerando cum patre Luca Gri-

Vergil:[6]   6

Even as an arrow, shot from string through a cloud, which,
armed with gall of fell poison, a Parthian — a Parthian or a
Cydonian — has launched, a shaft beyond all cure; whizzing,
it leaps through the swift shadows, known of none.

Ovid:[7]   7

[...] their arms, their horses, their dress, their Cretan quiv-
ers.

Apuleius:[8]   8

The arrow-bearing Cretans call upon Dictaean Diana.

Cyriac of Ancona, lover of Hermes, chose all these brilliant and   9
famous sayings of the ancient writers and poets to record here as a
proof of the ancient worth of all the Cydonian and Cretan archers.
Done this day, the seventh of July, the glorious and venerable day
of my protecting deity, Mercury, in the fifteenth year of the reign
of Pope Eugene, one thousand and twenty-four years after the
foundation of Venice.[9]

Actian Apollo saw the sight, and from above   10
was bending his bow; at that terror all Egypt and India,
all Arabians, all Sabaeans, turned to flee.[10]

[DRAWING][11]

:   24   :

To ?Andreolo, 15 July 1445, Cydonia

On the 13th of July we left the city of Cydonia to inspect the tall   1
cypresses on the White Mountains. With the reverend Father

mano, Hagiensi optimo Cydonum pontifice, Hagienses suos ad agros venimus et antiquam in his primum Hagiensem ipsam et cathedralem suam ecclesiam Beatae Virgini sacram veneramur; quam et longa vetustate collapsam et ab eo ipso antistite optimo reparatam cum percepissem, haec Latina Graecaque epygramata ipsa in aede positura condidimus:

2 DEO. EXCELSO. SACRAM |LVCAS. D. F. GRIMANVS. HAGIENSIVM | CYDONVMQ. OPT. PONT. HAGIENSEM | CATHEDRALEMQ. HANC ALMAE VIRGINIS | AEDEM HAGIENSI IN CYDONIAE CIVITATIS | AGRO. L. T. LABE GRAECAQ. VETERVM | INCVRIA SACERDOTVM. MAGNA EX PARTE COLLAPSAM RESTITVIT

3 ΛΟΤΚΑΣ ΓΡ.Ο.ΑΙΔΗΣΙΜΟΣ ΕΠΙΣΚΟΠΟΣ.ΤΗΝ | ΑΓΙΑΝ.ΤΗΣ ΑΓΙΟΤΑΤΗΣ. ΑΓΝΩΤΑΤΗΣ ΤΕ | ΠΑΡΘΕΝΟΤ.ΜΑΡΙΑΣ ΘΕΟΤ ΜΗΤΡΟΣ.ΕΚ| ΚΛΗΣΙΑΝ. ΧΡΟΝΩΙ ΦΘΑΡΗΣΑΝ.ΕΝ | ΠΑΓΚΟΣΜΙΟΤΗΤΙ ΝΕΟΡΓΙΣΕΝ

4 Eodem vero III Iduum Quintilium die, secus Leuci montis radices ad Misceam, ipsam pontificam suam consedimus villam [...].[1]

5 [...] his redeuntes ad villam, in ripis antiquam alteram vidimus et veneramur arboreis ubribus clausam Beatae Virginis aediculam.

6 Sed et cuius ergo venimus et tantum coeptavimus iter, ⟨ut⟩ montanas illas nobiles ciparisseas arbores videremus et vetusta quaedam oppidum monumenta, quae adhuc alto in vertice montis extare audieram, vestigarem, ad sequentem faustum Iovialemque diem una optimo cum pontifice plerisque agrestis comitati et venatoribus accolis, scrupeos arduosque per colles ad ipsos Leucos montes ascendimus; ubi primum, turritis disiectisque veterrimi cuiusdam oppidi moenibus inspectis, situ denique permenso, Po-

Luca Grimani, his excellency the bishop of Cydonea, we came to his territory of Ayia, and first of all we paid our respects to his ancient cathedral church in Ayia, dedicated to the Blessed Virgin. When we learned that this church, which had collapsed from great age, had been restored by that excellent bishop himself, we composed these Latin and Greek inscriptions for placement on the building itself:

> His Excellency Luca Grimani, son of D., bishop of Ayia and   2
> Cydonea, restored this church of the Blessed Virgin, the ca-
> thedral of Ayia, sacred to God on high, in the territory of
> the city of Cydonea, which lay mostly in ruins, owing to the
> long passage of time and Greek neglect of past priests.

> Luca Grimani, the venerable bishop, restored with complete   3
> propriety the holy church of the most holy and most pure
> Virgin Mary, Mother of God, which had fallen into ruins in
> the course of time.[1]

On the same 13 July we settled down in the bishop's country   4
house near Miscea, at the foot of White Mountain [...].[2]

[...] returning to the country house, we saw on the banks and   5
reverenced another small, old church of the Blessed Virgin enclosed by trees laden with fruit.

But, to see what we came to see and for which we undertook so   6
long a journey — those famous mountain-cypress trees — and to inspect certain antique remnants of towns[3] that I had heard still exist on the high summit of the mountain, on the next day, Jove's lucky day,[4] along with his excellency the bishop and accompanied by a number of rustics and huntsmen from the neighborhood, we climbed through rocky, steep hills to the White Mountains themselves. There we first inspected the towered, scattered walls of a certain very old town and finally, after going over the site from end to end, we determined that these were the remains of the Cretan

lyreniae Cretae civitatis vestigia novimus et campos ubi urbs illa vetustissima fuit.

7　　Ibi enim cum ad inspectandum magnis composita lapidibus moenia sacram et Deo laudem persolvendam pontifex morarier maluisset, equidem uno ex accolis comitatus Basilio ad altiores ne-morososque montium vertices arduum quippe et raro suetum per iter pedibus et Hyrcano quoque tegmine tal⟨a⟩ratis conscendi, nostro et ipso alipede ductitante Mercurio, ubi demum expetitas plerasque vidimus altas coniferas redolentes coelumque comis mi-nantes perpetuoque virentes, insigne decus nemorum cupressus.

8　　Ad alteram cuius ardui montis partem ad australe litus Paulum Apostolum, ab Agrippa appellatum ad Caesarem, Caesarea e Pa-laestina Romam navigantem, applicuisse dicunt; ubi et aedem illi sacram ad nostram diem Cretes religiose colunt eosque montes a nautis Sancti Pauli nomine saepe vocitarier audivimus.

9　　Vale et iterum vale.

: DIARY IV :

1　　IMP CAESARI DIVI NERVAE.F.NERVAE | TRAIANO
OPTIMO AVG.GERMANICO | DACICO.PONT.MAX.
TR.POT.XVIIII.IMP.IX | COS. VI. P. P.
PROVIDENTISSIMO. PRINCIPI.| SENATVS. P.Q.R.
QVOD ACCESSVM | ITALIAE. HOC. ETIAM.
ADDITO. EX. PECVNIA. SVA | PORTV. TUTIOREM.
NAVIGANTIBVS. REDDIDERIT

city of Polyrrhenia and this, the plain where that ancient city had been.

There the bishop chose to linger, to study the walls, which were   7
composed of huge stones, and to render to God due glory; whereas I, accompanied by a local, Basil, climbed to higher, wooded summits of the mountains, a steep, unfamiliar trail, my feet clad in sandals of Hyrcanian hide; and, under the personal guidance of our wing-footed Mercury, we saw at last the object of our quest, numerous cypresses, tall, fragrant conifers menacing the sky with their foliage, ever green, the distinguished glory of the forests.

On the other side of this steep mountain, on the southern   8
shore, they say Paul the Apostle put in after his appeal from Agrippa to Caesar and while he was on his voyage to Rome from Caesarea in Palestine. There until our own day the Cretans keep a chapel sacred to him and, we heard that sailors often refer to those mountains as "St. Paul's."

Farewell and again farewell.   9

: DIARY IV :

Travels in Crete, July to October 1445

The Senate and People of Rome [dedicated this] to Emperor   I
Caesar Nerva Trajan, son of the divine Nerva, Victor over Germany and Dacia, High Priest, with the power of tribune for the eighteenth time, saluted *imperator* nine times, Consul for the sixth time, Father of the Country, the most provident sovereign, because by creating this port also from his own funds he made the approach to Italy safer for sailors.

[Left side:] PLOTINAE CONIVGI.AVG.

[Right side:] DIVAE AVG MARCIANAE AVG SORORI.
AVG.[1]

2   Apud Cretam, insularum insignem, plerisque suis in antiquis et
iam collapsis urbibus epigrammata nuper ex Kyriaco Picenicolleo
Anconitano comperta.

3   Apud Lytton, antiquam et mediterraneam urbem magna ex
parte deletam, prope villam quam Pediadam dicunt:

ΑΥΤΟΚΡΑΤΟΡΙ ΚΑΙΣ ΘΕΟΥ ΝΕΡΟΥΑ ΤΙΩ ΝΕΡΟΥΑ
ΤΡΑΙΑΝΩ ΣΕΒΑΣΤΩ ΓΕΡΜΑ|ΝΙΚΩ ΔΑΚΙΚΩ
ΑΡΧΙΕΡΕΙ ΜΕΓΙΣΤΩ | ΔΗΜΑΡΧΙΚΗΣ ΕΞΟΥΣΙΑΣ
ΤΟ ΙΖ | ΥΠΑΤΩ ΤΟ Γ. ΠΑΤΡΙ ΠΑΤΡΙΔΟΣ | ΤΩ ΤΗΣ
ΟΙΚΟΥΜΕΝΗΣ ΚΤΙΣΤΗ ΛΥΤΤΙΩΝ Η ΠΟΛΙΣ ΔΙΑ
ΠΡΩΤΟ | ΚΟΣΜΟΥ Μ. ΠΟΜΠΗΙΟΥ ΚΛΕΥΜΕΝΙΔΑ[2]

4   Ad antiquam aliam Cretae urbem, olim Lampeam, mediterraneas inter praeclaras, quam prope Rhithymnam hodie Polin dicunt:

ΛΑΠΠΑΙΩΝ | Η ΠΟΛΙΣ ΜΑΡΚΟΝ ΑΥΡΗ|ΛΙΟΝ
ΚΛΗΣΙΠΠΟΝ | ΤΕΙΜΗΣ ΚΑΙ ΜΝΗΜΗΣ | ΧΑΡΙΝ[3]

5   Apud Hierapetram ad australe littus amplissimam olim Cretensium urbem, ubi alia inter suae magnitudinis monumenta duorum
amphitheatrum naumachia⟨e⟩que spectaculi reliquias et vestigia
vidimus, inter quae binas Caesareas statuas basesque hisce suis
cum inscriptionibus Atticis et eximiis quoque litteris comperi:

6   Ad primam Caesaream basim:

ΑΥΤΟΚΡΑΤΟΡΑ ΚΑΙΣ | ΜΑΡΚΟΝ ΑΥΡΗΛΙΟΝ |
ΑΝΤΩΝΕΙΝΟΝ ΣΕΒΑΣΤΟΝ ΤΟΝ .ΚΥΡΙΟΝ | ΤΗΣ
ΟΙΚΟΥΜΕΝΗΣ Λ. ΦΛ. ΣΟΥΛΠΙΚΙΑΝΟΣ | ΔΩΡΙΩΝ[4]

[*Left side:*] To Plotina wife of the Augustus

[*Right side:*] To the divine Marciana Augusta, sister of the Augustus.[1]

On the exceptional island of Crete Cyriac de'Pizzecolli of Ancona found [the following] inscriptions in several of its ancient, now ruined cities. 2

At Lyttos, an ancient inland city mostly in ruins, near a country estate called Pediada:[2] 3

> Through [the agency of] Markos Pompeios Kleomenidas, the chief magistrate, the city of Lyttos [dedicated this altar] to Emperor Caesar Nerva Trajan, son of the divine Nerva, Victor over Germany and Dacia, High Priest, holding tribunician power for the seventeenth time, being Consul for the sixth time, Father of his Country, [and] the Restorer of the World.

At another ancient city of Crete, once named Lampea,[3] famous among the inland cities, near Rethymnon, which today they call [simply] "The City":[4] 4

> The city of Lappa [dedicated this statue of] Markos Aurelios Ktesippos for his honor and memory.

At Hierapetra,[5] once a very prosperous city of ancient Crete on the southern coast, where we saw, among other reminders of its greatness, the remains and traces of two amphitheaters for the performance of [mock] naval battles as spectacles, among which I found two statues of the Caesars and their bases with the following elegantly lettered Attic inscriptions on them: 5

On the first Caesar's statue base: 6

> Leukios Flaouios Soulpikianos Dorion [dedicated this statue of] Emperor Marcus Aurelius Antoninus, Lord of the World.

7   Ad aliam basim:

ΑΥΤΟΚΡΑΤΟΡΑ ΚΑΙΣΑΡΑ | ΛΟΥΚΙΟΝ ΑΥΡΗΛΙΟΝ
ΒΗΡΟΝ | ΣΕΒΑΣΤΟΝ ΑΡΜΕΝΙΑΚΟΝ | ΤΟΝ ΚΥΡΙΟΝ
ΤΗΣ ΟΙΚΟΤΜΕΝΗΣ | Λ. ΦΛ. ΣΟΥΛΠΙΚΙΑΝΟΣ |
ΔΩΡΙΩΝ⁵

8   Εἰς Ἱεραπέτραν, ad sacram et olim eximiam divae illius Hie-
rapetreae Cereris et Persephonis aedem:

ΤΑΝ ΔΑΜΑΤΡΑ | ΚΑΙ ΤΑΝ ΚΩΡΑΝ | ΑΡΧΕΔΙΚΑ
ΖΗΝΟΦΙ|ΛΩ ΜΕΤΑ ΤΑΝ ΠΕΡΙ|ΣΤΑΣΙΝ ΥΠΕΡ ΤΑΣ |
ΠΟΛΕΟΣ ΕΚ ΤΩΝ ΙΔΙΩΝ | ΙΔΡΥΣΑΤΟ⁶

*[Verses in honor of Cyriac by Leonardo Dati and
Antonio Beccadelli, "il Panormita"]*

9   In Italia apud urbem Romam <scripsit> Leonardus Dathus Flo-
rentinus in Kyriacum Anconitanum epigramma:

Vidisti Latias urbes ubi fortia facta,
      Vidisti Argivas barbaricasque simul,
Vidisti insculptos divos et Martia bella
      Quae gessere etiam Belerophontis equum,
Vidisti veterum septem spectacula rerum,
      Vidisti toto quicquid in orbe fuit,

καὶ τὰ λοιπά.

10   A. Panormita:

Kyriace, altiloquos inter celeberrime vates,
      Cuncta vetustatis qui monumenta tenes,
Lustrasti longos terrae pelagique recessus,
      Legisti veterum nomina pyramidum.
Ancon Kyriaco tamen gaudebat alumno
      Doctiloquo quantum Mantua Virgilio.

The other base:　　　　　　　　　　　　　　　　　　　　　　7

Leukios Flaouios Soulpikianos Dorion [dedicated this statue of] Emperor Lucius Aurelius Verus, Victor over Armenia, Lord of the World.

At Hieropetra, at the sacred, once-distinguished temple of　8
Hieropetra's goddesses, Ceres and Persephone:

Archedika daughter of Zenophilos [dedicated these statues] of Demeter and Kore for the city from her own funds, after the crisis.

*[Verses in honor of Cyriac by Leonardo Dati and
Antonio Beccadelli, "il Panormita"]*[6]

In Italy, in the city of Rome, Leonardo Dati of Florence [wrote]　9
this epigram in honor of Cyriac of Ancona:

You have seen the cities of Latium, where brave deeds were done; you have seen the cities of the Greeks and the barbarians as well; you have seen sculptured gods and the martial wars they waged, and even the horse of Bellerophon; you have seen the seven wonders of the ancient world; you have seen whatever there was in the entire world,

and so forth.
Antonio Panormita:　　　　　　　　　　　　　　　　　　　　10

Cyriac, highly regarded among poets of lofty eloquence, you who preserve all mementos of antiquity, you have traversed far-distant recesses of land and sea, you have scanned the names of ancient pyramids. Still, Ancona kept rejoicing in her son Cyriac as much as did Mantua in her learnedly eloquent Vergil.

11   Antonius Panormita in Kyriaci Anconitani matris Masiellae
ἐπιτάφιον:

> Anconis splendor iacet hoc Masiella sepulchro
> Una vetustatis Kyriacique parens.

: 25 :

1   Salve, mi suavissime Bandine et Picenarum Rhodiarumque Musarum cultor, haud indignae decorisque nostrae spes altera patriae
tellurisve Picenae.

2   Quom hac hora pridie Iduum Sextilium augusto fausto Iovia-
lique celeberimo die ex Idaeo, Creteo inclito Iovis monte, ad
Ampelusium, hoc olim Gnosiae antiquissimae civitatis emporium,
Candidas nunc et praeclaram Venetum coloniam alacer remeas-
sem, Bonacursius, eiusce publicae rei scriba, bene nobis occurrens
praedulcem illam mihi tuam et officio plenam epistulam dedit; ex
qua suis undique partibus collectis, almae primum telluri nostrae
congratulabar Picenae, quae iam tot talesque suum ad extollendum
nomen aevo quoque nostro viros edidisse conspicitur.

3   Et quamvis Rhodianae insulae monumenta pluries indagasse
sim memor, et Camirae, Lideae Ieliseaeque civitatum vestigia et relicta nobis aetative nostrae mirifica opera nobiliaque veterum epigrammata nostris quoque per Asiam commentariis adiecissem, tui
tamen gratia, ut et tibi quoque tam digno et humanissimo desiderio morem gererem, eam iterum revisere quoad liceat operam
dabo. Sed interim ob exoptabilem in Teucros Pannoniae gentis
motum Bisantium remeare cardinalemque legatum revisere cogor.

Antonio Panormita, an epitaph for Masiella, mother of Cyriac 11
of Ancona:

Masiella lies in this tomb, the glory of Ancona, mother of
both antiquity and Cyriac.

: 25 :

To (?Melchiore) Bandino, 12 August 1445, Candia, Crete

Hail, my very dear Bandino,[1] devotee of the Muses of Picenum 1
and Rhodes, other hope of our worthy, glorious homeland,
Picenum.

Just this moment, on the 12th of August, Jove's lucky, most 2
festive day,[2] I returned eagerly from Ida, Jove's famous Cretan
mountain, to Ampelusium, once the mart of the very old city of
Cnossos and now the illustrious Venetian colony of Candia. Here
Buonaccorso, secretary of that municipality, met us hospitably and
gave me that charming, most courteous letter of yours. After
studying all its parts from every angle, I first congratulated our
bountiful land of Picenum, which is seen to have produced even in
our own age so many men of such high quality to praise her name.

And although I recall having searched out the monuments of 3
the island of Rhodes several times, and had entered into my Asian
journal the ruins of the cities of Kamiros, Lindos, and Ialyssos,
wonderful structures left behind for us and for our age, and noteworthy inscriptions of the ancients, still, for your sake, to indulge
you also and your most humane request, I shall make an effort to
visit there again[3] as time permits. But meanwhile, I am con-
strained to return to Byzantium and to revisit the Cardinal Legate
in connection with the most welcome rising of the Hungarian nation against the Turks.

4   Nec minus interea ut quid mei tuique dignum habeas hoc ex
me monumentum honestum vel pignus amoris, Rhodium argenteum hoc ex me compertum collosei Apollinis Rhodii capite insignitum nomisma, quo olim aere Rhodii Artemone principe ute-
bantur, hysce tibi hylari animo transmittendum delegi. Tu quidem
contra si aliquid nostri dignum vetustae rei signum inveneris, 'vivos' vel, ut aiunt, 'de marmore vultus', meo nomine habendum curabis; nec non si forte lapides, inter quos vetustos quandoque effodiunt, epigramma comperis, rescribere velis.

5   Et ut de compertis ex me nuper magna hac in insula aliquid
nostri nostraeque et utique dignum patriae videas, Graecam hanc
apud Litton[1] egregiam olim mediterraneas inter Cretensium urbem inscriptionem ex me pridie compertam nostrum in Caesa-
reum et optimum nostrae exornatorem patriae Traianum principem ac utique in parte reponendam curavi, optime vel aliter
Picenorum decus.

6   Rhodium argenteum numisma: ΑΡΤΕΜΩΝ. Latine, Artemon,
Rhodiorum princeps. Habet florem punici pomi quem Graeci *rhodion* dicunt ex Rhodia insula dicta.

7   Artium mentis ingenii facundiaeque pater alme Mercuri, qui
tuo sanctissimo numine nostram iam diu mentem animumque fovisti, quique [...].

8   ΑΥΤΟ[Κ]ΡΑΤΟΡΙ ΚΑΙΣΑΡΙ [Θ]ΕΟΥ | ΝΕΟΥ ΝΕΡΟΥΑ
ΥΙΩ ΝΕΡΟΥΑ | ΤΡΑΙΑ[Ν]Ω ΣΕΒΑΣΤΩ ΓΕΡΜΑΝΙΚΩ
| ΔΑΚΙΚΩ ΑΡΧΙΕΡΕΙ ΜΕΓΙΣΤΩ | ΔΗΜΑΡΧΙΚΗΣ
ΕΞΟΥΣΙΑΣ | ΤΟ $\overline{ΙΖ}$ ΥΠΑΤΩ ΤΟ $\overline{Γ}$. ΠΑΤΡΙ |
ΠΑΤΡΙΔΟΣ ΤΟ.ΤΗΣ.ΟΙΚΟ|ΥΜΕΝ[Η]Σ.| ΚΤΙΣΤΗ |
ΑΥΤΤΙΩΝ.Η ΠΟΛΙΣ | [Δ]ΙΑ ΤΟΥ
ΠΡΩΤΟΚΟΣΜΟΝΙΔΑ[2]

And meanwhile, that you may have from me a reminder worthy 4
of me and a handsome pledge of our mutual love, I have chosen,
with a light heart, to send you this Rhodian silver coin, here enclosed, that I found, engraved with the head of the colossal Apollo
of Rhodes, that the people of Rhodes used as money long ago in
the reign of prince Artemon. For your part, if you find any antique
sculpture worth my attention, living faces fashioned from marble
as they say,[4] see that it is acquired in my name; and if, among the
ancient stones that they dig up from time to time, you come upon
an inscription, please copy it.[5]

And, O excellency, also on other grounds the glory of Picenum, 5
that you may see something appropriate to us and to our homeland from among my recent finds on this great island, I have taken
the trouble to have restored, in part to be sure, this Greek inscription [below, §8] that I found yesterday in Lyttos, once distinguished among the inland cities of Crete. It is dedicated to our imperial prince Trajan, who best adorned our homeland.

The Rhodian silver coin [is inscribed] ΑΡΤΕΜΩΝ, in Latin 6
Artemon, a prince of the Rhodians. It has the flower of the pome-
granate [on it], which the Greeks call rhodion, after the island of
Rhodes.

Nurturing father of the arts, of mind, wit, and speech, Mer- 7
cury, who by thy most holy divine power have long blest my mind
and heart, and who [...]

The city of Lyttos [dedicates this] through the magistrate 8
[M. Pompeios Kleumenidas] to Emperor Caesar, son of the
divine Nerva, Nerva Trajan Augustus, Victor over Germany
and Dacia, Pontifex Maximus, having the power of tribune
for the 17th time, consul for the third time, Father of the
country, Founder of the world.

Latine: Imperatori Caesari divi Nervi filio Nervae Traiano Augusto Germanico Dachico pontifici maximo tribunicia potestate XVII consul III [...].

9   Kyriacus Anconitanus tuus salutem tibi et hilaritarem dicit.

:   26   :

1   ΕΥΤΥΧΗΣ | ΔΙΟΣΚΟΥΤΡΙΔΟΥ | ΑΙΓΕΛΙΟΣ ΕΠΟΙ|ΕΙ

2   Ad M. Laepomagnum ex Kyriaci Anconitani litterarum particula de Alexandri Macedonis in cristallino sigillo comperta nuper imagine praescripta cum inscriptione.

3   [...] Praeterea ut insigne admodum aliquid tibi referam, cum mihi Ioannes Delphin, ille Ναύαρχος diligens καὶ φιλοπονώτατος, apud eum per noctem praetoria sua in puppi moranti pleraque nomismata preciosasque gemmas ostentasset, alia inter eiusdem generis supellectilia nobile mihi de cristallo sigillum ostendit, quod policiaris digiti magnitudine galeati Alexandri Macedonis imagine pectore tenus miraque Eutychetis artificis ope alta corpo-
4   ris concavitate insignitum erat; et expolitae galeae ornamento bina in fronte arietum capita, certa Ammonii Iovis insignia parentis, tortis cornibus impressa, ac summo a vertice thyara cursu veloces hinc inde Λαγονικοὺς Molosos gerere videtur eximia artis pul-

196

In Latin:

To the Emperor, Caesar, the son of the divine Nerva, Nerva
Trajan Augustus Germanicus, the conqueror of the Dacians,
Pontifex Maximus, with the power of a tribune for the sev-
enteenth time, consul for the third time [...].[6]

Your Cyriac of Ancona wishes you health and happiness.　　9

: 26 :

Fragment of a Letter to M. Lepomagno, ?October 1445, Candia

Eutyches, son of Dioskourides of Aigae, made it.　　1

Fragment of a letter from Cyriac of Ancona to M. Lepomagno　　2
concerning the recently discovered image of Alexander of Macedon engraved on a crystalline intaglio seal.[1]

[...] Moreover, to tell you something very special, when Gio-　　3
vanni Delfino, that diligent and most industrious fleet commander, had displayed numerous coins and precious gems to me as I
lingered by night with him on his flagship, he showed me, among
other items of the same sort, a splendid crystalline signet seal the
size of a thumb that is engraved in deep relief with a bust of hel-
meted Alexander of Macedon, the marvelous workmanship of the
artisan Eutyches;[2] and adorning the polished helmet, imprinted　　4
on its front, were two rams' heads with twisted horns, unmistak-
able attributes of his father, Jupiter Ammon; and at the top of
his headpiece, a tiara is seen to bear on either side swift-running,
hare-mastering, Molossian hounds of extraordinary artistic
beauty; and beneath the helmet the prince, very tiny strands of

197

chritudine, et sub galea tenuissimis[1] hinc inde capillamentis princeps, suctili velamine et peregrino habitu elaboratis a summitate
listis amictus, dexteram et nudam cubitenus manum, veste summo
a pectore honeste pertentantem, videtur admovisse, et gestu mirifico facies regioque aspectu acie obtuitum perferens, vivos nempe
de lapide nitidissimo vultus et heroicam quoque suam videtur magnitudinem ostentare.

5   Cum et ad lucem solidam gemmae partem obiectares, ubi cubica corporalitate intus sublucida et vitrea transparenti umbra
mira pulchritudine membra quoque spirantia enitescere conspectantur, et tam conspicuae rei opificem suprascriptis inibi consculptis litteris Graecis atque vetustissimis intelligimus.

⋮ DIARY IV, CONTINUED ⋮

12   Ad x Kalendas Novembres ex Agauusia Modatia villa proxima[1]
deletam penitus longa vetustate urbem in Creta mediterraneam ad
mirificum Dictaeae Dianae fontem venimus, quem ad ipsas Dictaei montis occidua ex parte radices per centum ferme stadia a
Hierapytna non longe ab aquilonare Phanuriano littore situm
comperimus, eumque sub arduo scrupeoque et alto a vertice scisso
suapte ruina saxo a summo montis cacumine excataruentem[2] et
angustae[3] scissurae anfractibus sonoro ruente latice profundo repleto lacu naturali rotunditate urna et xxx fere cubitum latitudine
complexu exuberantibus undis vidimus defluentem.

13   Sed quod potissimum belle mireque dignum spectatione compexeram, vivo in ipso et ferro intractabile saxo, natura ipsa opifice

hair showing beneath his helmet on either side, dressed in a fine robe and foreign garment, its borders decorated along the top, seems to have moved his right arm, bare to the elbow, which is holding his vesture honorably at the top; and his countenance, with wondrous attitude and regal appearance, directing his gaze straight ahead, seems truly to manifest living features made from gleaming stone as well as his own heroic greatness.

When one holds the solid part of the gem to the light (where, 5 because of its three-dimensional corporeality with a barely lit, glass-like, translucent shadow within, breathing limbs are seen to gleam with wondrous beauty) we learn [the name of] this superb object's artificer from the very ancient Greek characters inscribed on it.[3]

: DIARY IV, CONTINUED :

On the 23rd of October, we journeyed from Agauousia Modatia, a 12 rural village close by, [to] an inland city in Crete that had been utterly ravaged by the passage of time, [and] to the marvelous spring of Diktaian Diana, which we found situated at the very foot of Mt. Dikte, on the western side, about a hundred stadia from Ierapytna, not far from the northern Phanourian coast. We watched it as it flowed down from the from the top of the mountain, rushing down from beneath a steep, jagged, lofty rock that had been torn from its crest by its own downward thrust, its waters plunging with a loud roar through the winding course of a narrow cleft to fill a deep pool, a naturally round basin about thirty cubits in width, with its abundant waves.

But what I attended to especially as suitably and marvelously 13 worth inspection [was this]: in the living rock and unmanageable by tools, its artisan being Nature herself and its architect the Cre-

et ipso demogorgone architecto, spondalem ipsam circum et expolitam urnae parietem venarum semipedalibus ingenitis suapte natura listis, velut artifici manu variis purpureis, croceis, caeruleis glaucisque nitentem coloribus convexa insinuatione depictam, ipsam polycromatem sub nubibus in solem mille vibrantem coloribus arcum Iunioniam Iridem aemularier inspectares.

14   Quo mirandissimo in fonte sunt ex accolis circumstantes per vicos et ᾿Αγανούσια in villa Graeca quoque religione sacerdotes, qui nostra aetate Dianam ipsam suis cumque candentibus nymphis, albis depositis vestibus, nudas abluentes quandoque vitreo ipso sub gurgite demergere vidisse testantur.

15   VE[NE]TIARVM.DVCALE.INCLITVM | ARISTOCRA-TICA.LIBERTATE | DOMINIVM Leonidei Marci evangelistae sanctissimi fausto auspicantae numine Francisco Foscaro serenissimo duce, navistatium νεώριον.ve hoc .V̄. iam ab annis incendio consumptum, Candidae Creteae, neometropolitanae praeclarae coloniae suae, ad pristinam sui faciem splendoremque restituit curantibus Andrea Donato, Caesareo equite claro, viro praeclaro et bene merente duca, suiscunque claris praefectorio consulari ordine collegis, Fantino Viario, M. Legio et Pandulfo Contareno, patriciis egregiis atque nobilibus viris Christi humanati Iovis adventus anno 1446. XVII. Kalendas Februarias.

[At this point Cyriac attached the following ancient epistolary texts to his manuscript]

16   Βροῦτος τῶι Δαμᾷ Περγαμένοις

᾿Ακούω ὑμᾶς Δολοβέλλᾳ δεδωκέναι χρήματα, ἃ εἰ μὲν ἑκόντες ἔδοτε, ὁμολογεῖτε ἀδικεῖν με· εἰ δὲ ἄκοντες, ἀποδείξατε τῷ ἐμοὶ ἑκόντες δοῦναι.

ator,[1] around the enclosing, smooth [inner] wall of the basin[2] on a completely natural frieze half a foot wide, as if painted by an artist's hand, that glistened with various colors—purples, yellows, blues and grays—in a rounded curve, one could watch a many-colored rainbow vie with Juno's Iris herself, as it shimmered with a thousand colors in the sunlight beneath the clouds.

In connection with this most wondrous spring, there are among   14 the inhabitants in surrounding villages, and particularly in Agauousia, priests of the Greek religion who testify that, even in our own day, they have sometimes seen Diana herself with her dazzling nymphs, their white robes cast aside, nude bathers submerged in the translucent waters.

The ducal Signoria of Venice, famed for its aristocratic free-   15 dom, under the favoring protective power of the most holy, leonine evangelist Mark, when Francesco Foscari was reigning most serenely as doge, restored to its pristine appearance and splendor this harbor/shipyard, destroyed by fire five years previously, of Candia in Crete, the newly-designated metropolitan city of her illustrious colony, under the supervision of Andrea Donat, imperial knight, the brilliant and well-deserving duke [of Crete], along with his illustrous colleagues in the consular prefecture, Fantino Viario, M. Legio, and Pandolfo Contarini, outstanding aristocrats and noblemen. [Given on] the 16th of January in the 1446th year of the coming of Christ, the incarnate Jove.[3]

[At this point Cyriac attached the following ancient epistolary texts to his manuscript]

Brutus to Damas of Pergamon:[4]   16

I hear that you gave money to Dolobella. If you gave it willingly, admit that your did me an injustice; if unwillingly, demonstrate it by giving willingly to me.

Brutus Damae Pergamenis.

Intelligo vos Dolobellae pecunias dedisse, quas si quidem volentes dedistis me iniuria lacessisse proferemini; si forte invite, ostendite his mihi lubentes optitulari.

17 Βροῦτος τῷ Δαμᾷ.

ὅπλων καὶ χρημάτων χρεία: ἢ πέμπε ἢ ἀποφαίνου

Brutus Damae.

Armis pecuniisque summe indigemus; vel mitte vel denega

18 Δαμᾶς τῶι Βρούτωι.

Εὐπορούντων ἔργων τὸ πέμψαι, πενομένων τὸ ἀποφαινώθαι

Opulentium opus est mittere, indigentium autem denegare

19 Χίων Μάριδι χαίρειν.

ὁ ἀποδιδούς σοι τὸ γράμμα Ἀρχέπολις ὁ Λήμνιος ἐμπορευόμενος εἰς τὸν Πόντον ἐδεήθη μου ὅπως αὐτὸν συστήσαιμι σοι. ἐγὼ δὲ ἄσμενος ἐδεξάμην. καὶ γὰρ οὐδὲ φίλος μοι ὢν ἐτύγχανε. κέρδος οὖν μέγα ᾠήθην ἀφορμὴν λαβεῖν τοῦ ποιῆσαι τινὰ φίλον μὴ ὄντα πρότερον, εἰς ὃ κέρδος συλλήψῃ μοι. καὶ σὺ φιλαν[θρώπ]ως αὐτὸν εἰσδεξάμενος. πείθομαι καὶ μέτριον ἔμπορον αὐτὸν εἶναι, καὶ γὰρ φιλοσοφήσας πρότερον εἶτα ἐμπορεύεται: χαίρειν.

Chio Matridi in L⟨itteris⟩

Archepolis Lemnius qui has nostras tibi litteras reddet, mercemonii causa transmeaturus in Pontum, rogavit me ut eum ipsum tibi summopere comendarem. Ego vero ipse quam laeto animo suscepi. Tan[...][4]

Brutus to Damas:[5]   17

We need weapons and money; either send them or say why [not].

Damas to Brutus[6]   18

It is the part of those who are well off to send them; it is the part of those who are poor to say why [not].

Chion to Matris, greetings.[7]   19

The person who delivers this letter to you, Archepolis of Lemnos, a traveling merchant on his way to Pontus, asked me to introduce him to you. I was happy to honor his request, for in fact, although he does not happen to be a friend of mine, I thought that taking the occasion to make someone a friend who was not one before [would prove to be] greatly advantageous, an advantage in which you, too, will share with me if you receive him kindly. I believe that he is also a virtuous merchant because, before he took to commerce, he devoted himself to the study of philosophy.

20 MCCCCXLV.⁵ *Candida.*

21 ἀγαθῇ τύχῃ quae Cheronemiae Cretea per aequora nimphae nobis ad Samonium, orientale insulae promuntorium, navigantibus,
postquam Graece cecinerant, Latine atque nostro Italo idiomate
subdidere:

> Koiriacus Anconitanus Picenicoleus
> O decus Anconitum, qui puppim flectis amice
> Auribus, ut nostros possis agnoscere⁶ cantus —
> Nam nemo hoc unquam transvectus caerula cursu
> Quin prius astiterit vocum dulcedine captus —
> Posteaquam variis avido sacratus pectore Musis
> Doctior ad patrias lapsus perveneris oras,
> Nunc grave certamen belli clademque canemus,
> Pannona quam Teucris divino numine vexit
> Omnibusque elatis regnum vestigia terris.

22 Inclitam deinde Creteam in laudem Ideumque Iovialem in
montem versae, altius attollens a gurgite capita, lepidissime talia
ambroseo ab ore subdidere Sirenae:

> Inclito hospitio del gran Lion sancto,
> Creta grande, saturn⟨i⟩o aureo regno,
> cuna al gran Iove et habitar sí degno
> che cento alme cità te fe' già manto.
>   Insula in mezo el mare, honor e vanto
> de Europa e d'arte dedala e d'ingegno,
> d'alta tua nobil[i]tà mostrando el segno
> Teucro, Minos, Eacho e Radamantho.
>   Tua d'archo e de sagitte disciplina,
> la tua Dictea Diana al tuo corbello,
> monstrò in Cydona, in Gnoscia et in Gortina
>   vincendo Greci, Hircani et Parti in bello.
> Sed tua que gaza et que regna uberina

After the "Good luck" that the Thracian nymphs sang to us in   21
Greek as we sailed through Cretan waters toward Samonium, the
island's eastern promontory, they added in Latin and our own
Latin tongue:[9]

> Cyriac of Ancona de' Pizzecolli: O pride of Ancona, who
> turn your ship about in friendly manner so you can hear and
> recognize our song—for no one has ever sailed through the
> blue waters on this course without first having stopped, en-
> tranced by the sweetness [of our singing]—once you, wiser
> because consecrated with hungry heart to the multifarious
> Muses, have arrived effortlessly at your native shores, we
> shall sing of the intense struggle and carnage of war that, by
> God's will, the Pannonian inflicted on the Turks, and of the
> rule and example [he has laid down] for all proud lands.

Then, turning to the praise of storied Crete and of Juppiter's   22
Mount Ida, the Sirens raised their heads higher from the waters
and with utmost charm added [this] from their immortal lips:

> Illustrious home of the great and saintly Lion,
> Crete, golden kingdom of the famed Saturnian age,
> cradle of mighty Jove and so worthy a dwelling place
> that hundreds of kindly cities once called you protector.
>   Island in the midst of the sea, honor and pride
> of Europe and of Daedalos's skill and genius;
> your exalted lineage was shown and demonstrated by
> Teucer, Minos, Aiakos and Rhadamanthos.
>   Your discipline in the art of bow and arrow,
> your Diana of Dikte demonstrated, at your quiver,
> in Cydonia, in Cnossos and in Gortyn,
>   defeating in combat Greeks, Hircanians and Parthians.
> But the worthy Quintus Metellus, in Rome showed

mostrò in Roma el bon Quinto Metello;
e nel celico hostello
tua gloria spande el tuo bon Iove eterno,
Neptuno in mare e Pheton per l'inferno.

23 MAGNIFICO . ET . GENEROSO . VIRO |BERTVTIO
DELPHINO . VENETVM ALEXANDREAE .
FOELI|CISSIMAE . CLASSIS | PRAEFECTO |.
KYRIACVS . ANCONITANVS . ex Candida praeclarissima
Venetum colonia |DEDIT |eo quo et portu bonis auspiciis solverat
pridie Kalendas Novembrium, sereno, fausto Kyriaceoque felicissimo
die | EVGENII PONTIFICIS ANNO XV |et Venetum
serenissima ab urbe condita anno MXXIIII.

24 Ad cristallinam Alexandri capitis ymaginem haec antiquis
Graecis litteris descriptio consculpta videtur:

ΕΥΤ[Υ]ΧΗΣ [Δ]ΙΟΣΚΟΥΡΙ[Δ]ΟΥ ΑΙΓΕΛΙΟΣ ΕΠΟΙΕΙ

Quod latine sonant:

EVTICHES / DIOSCVRIDIS / AEGELIVS FE/CIT

: 27 :

1 Praestantissimo viro Andreolo Iustiniano, amico optimo.
2 Binas tibi sedes ciparisseas mitto, karissime Andreole, vel or-
chestralia sedilia, quas tibi redderet, imposui Phylippo Pangioti,
Eurupontino huius naviculae navarcho. Et ex iis unam, si placet,
Paridi nostro magnifico viro dabis.
3 Et me ad vos quam citius remeaturum scias. Valere te felicem
tua cum omni ex domo familia natosque primum et praeclaram
Clarentiam, coniugem opto.

the qualities of your riches and your fertile kingdoms;
  and in the heavenly abode your mighty,
kindly Jove spreads wide your glory; so too, does
Neptune through the seas and Phaeton in the lower world.

To a grand and noble gentleman, Bertutio Dolfin, captain   23
of Venice's highly successful Alexandrian fleet, Cyriac of
Ancona made this presentation from the port of Candia,
Venice's most glorious colony. [Given] on the day when he
set sail from this port on the 31st of October, a day of good
omen, a cloudless, propitious, and very favorable day of the
Lord, in the fifteenth year of [the reign of] Pope Eugene and
1,024 years after the foundation of the most serene city of
Venice:[10]

This inscription in ancient Greek letters is seen on the crystal-   24
line image of the head of Alexander.[11]

Eutyches Aigelios son of Dioskourides made [this].[12]

: 27 :

To Andreolo, 7 November 1445, Candia

To the very distinguished Andreolo Giustiniani, my best friend.   1
  Dearest Andreolo, I am sending you two chairs made of cypress   2
wood, seats for the theater, which I have charged Philippos Pangiotis, the Eurupontine[1] captain of this little ship, to deliver to
you. Please give one of them to our magnificent friend, Paride.
  And know that I shall return to you as quickly as possible. I   3
hope you and your whole household and your children and your
glorious wife, Carenza, are well and happy.

4   Ex Candida, Cretensi colonia Venetum, VII Idus Novembris, Kyriacus Anconitanus tuus.

5   Scripsimus per alias ad te latius; nunc vero tam breviter, vela dare Nothis properante navigio.

: 28 :

1   Claro et elegantissimo viro Andreolo Iustiniano, amico optimo et iocundissimo.

2   Posteaquam ex Naxo beatitudini tuae ultimas ad te litteras dedimus, iocundissime Andreole, 'niveam Paron' iterum revisere placuerat. Nam et praeclara sua atque nobilia almae suae veternitatis monumenta 'non semel vidisse satis est, sed iuvat usque morari'. At et cum una suo cum principe Cursino pleraque prius comperta laeto quidem animo revisissem, non nullos quoque 'vivos de marmore vultus' vivaque et peregrinis armis ornata de lapide nitissimo corpora nuper, Cursino ipso curiosissimo curante principe, defossa perquam iocunde[1] conspexi, et potissime laetatus sum Trasyxeni ingentis olim delubri statuarumque et nobilium plurigenum operum conditoris nomine comperto, nec equidem ingratius vidi ipso in Pario portu onustam iam navim expolitis plerisque Pario ipso de lapide listis, Chyensi praeclarae coloniae vestrae insigni decore et ornamento futuris.

3   Et cum his dictis te iam valere finemque epistolae imponere voluissem, ipso in portu magna hylaritate Nereydes cana vitreo de

From Candia, a Cretan colony of the Venetians, 7 November,   4
your Cyriac of Ancona.

[*Postscript:*] I have written to you more extensively in other letters;   5
I am so brief now in this one because the ship is in haste to set sail
before a southerly wind.

: 28 :

To Andreolo, December [1445], Paros

To the distinguished, cultivated Andreolo Giustiniani, my good   1
and most delightful friend.

    After I wrote your Beatitude last from Naxos,[1] most delightful   2
Andreolo, I decided to revisit "snow-white Paros,"[2] for "it is not
enough to have seen only once" the radiant, noteworthy monuments of its nurturing past, and "it is a delight to tarry there."[3]
And when, accompanied by the Duke of Paros, Crusino,[4] I had
the pleasure of revisiting my numerous previous finds, I was absolutely delighted to gaze on "life-like faces made of marble"[5] and
life-like bodies adorned in alien armor [carved] from dazzling
stone recently excavated under the very careful supervision of
Duke Crusino. I was especially delighted by the discovery of the
name of Thrasyxenos, the founder of a once huge temple and of
statues and of many kinds of notable works, and I personally
found it not uncongenial to see in the port of Paros itself a ship already loaded with numerous finished friezes in Parian marble des-
tined to embellish and adorn in signal manner your illustrious colony of Chios.

    When, having said this, I was about to bid you farewell and   3
end this letter, the Nereid Sirens of Paros in this very port, raising

gurgite capita altiora tollentes talia lepide idiomate nostro Pariae cecinere Sirenae.

4   Et tu utique claro Paridi Clarentiaeque sanctissimae coniugi natisque et ceteris tua de domo tuis ex me salutem dabis. Kyriacus Anconitanus tuus.

5   Nivea Paros, di marmor candente,
      Cycladum decus equoris Egei,
      honor delli heroi magni et delli dei,
      sicch, 'l mondo di te si fa splendente.
          Ornasti Apollo in cielo eùllo Oriente
      per Cyro et per Alcide, Indi et Thebei;
      Minerva Athene, et Iove e' champi alphei;
      Alexandro, Austro et Cesar l'Occidente.
          Di Phydia et Polycleto il gran valore
      mostró qual fussi da natur ornata;
      da te Lysippo e gl'altri ebbor splendore
          et da Minos, Mynoa dicta et guidata;
      ma Cursino Sommaripa, hor ch'ei minore,
      ti regge, et te, tra l'altre piú beata,
          hor[a] con sua penna grata
      l'Anchonitan ti ciercha; et per lo mondo
      rinnoverá il tuo nome almo et iocondo.

6   Ex eadem clara Pario, VIII Kalendas Ianuarii, fausto, sereno et humanati Iovis natalicio solempni et celeberrimo die. Recipe a portitore, A. Galaphato, caput unum marmoreum unumque crus et bina de cypresso scriniola pannis involuta hoc sub signo K+A.

their foam-capped heads with great joy from the glassy deep, sang
the appended charming song in our native language.

Give my greetings to the noble Paride, to your most devout wife   4
Carenza, to your children, and to the other members of your
household. Your Cyriac of Ancona.

> Snow-white Paros, of shining marble,   5
> glory of the Cyclades in the Aegean sea,
> honor of the great heroes and of the gods,
> so that the world is made radiant by you.
>   You added luster to Apollo in heaven and to the East,
> through Cyrus and Heracles, to Indians and Thebans;
> to Minerva in Athens and to Jove the plains of the Alphaeus;
> to Alexander the East and to Caesar the West.
>   The great prowess of Pheidias and Polykleitos
> showed how adorned you were by nature;
> from you, Lysippos and the others drew their splendor;
>   and governed by Minos, Minoa were you called;
> but now Crusino Sommaripa, younger than they,
> rules you, and for you, most blessed among the others,
>   the one from Ancona now searches;
> and with his kindly pen, throughout the world,
> will renew your fame so great and joyful.

From the same bright Paros, the 25th of December, the favor-   6
able, bright, solemn and greatly celebrated birthday of Jove Incarnate.[6] Receive from the carrier, A. Galaphatos, one marble head,
one leg, and two little cypress wood boxes wrapped in cloth with
this seal: K+A.[7]

1   ἀγαθῇ τύχῃ. Cum et postquam tuae claritati ex nivea Paro insula
scripserim, Andron, Andri Apollinis filii nomine claram, videre
placuisset, ex ea denique una viro cum docto Manuele Cretensi,
venerando Praedicatorum religione monaco, Chyon praeclaram insulam et coloniam vestram petentes, ad pridie Idus Ianuarias, faustum Mercurii nostri diem, ad australe insulae promuntorium allabimur, bonis Aeolis et Nereydum omnibus secundantibus
nymphis.

2   Ad quod illico honestis[1] nonnullis de causis videndique loci
gratia desilientes et ad proximam ἐπαινετὰν et masticum feracitate laudatissimam villam per noctem morantes et inde Chyon
oppidum teque et ceteros revisere amicissimos desiderantes, ad
sequentem serenum Iovialemque iocundissimum diem, nonnullis
ductantibus accolis, mediterraneum per iter emionibus devecti,
per virentia et egregia illa atque preciosa masticum nemora laeto
quidem animo transeuntes, illos demum, e quis tam eximium pre-
tiosumque emanare succum audieram, perspicere arbusculos flagitantes, ad terram descendimus; et cum denique, accola indicante,
lacrimosos inter et hylares truncos masticeas guttas quam plures
hinc inde propius elucescere conspectarem, et nonnullas manu legere placuisset, singulare loci fatalisque virgae munus et venerabile
omniparentis naturae donum admirans, et quod unicha Chyos insula sit in orbe, quae ceterum omnem suo liquore orbem aromati-

13 January to 8 April 1446
Chios, Miletus, Lesbos, Foglia Nuova

: 29 :

To Andreolo, after 13 January [1446], Chios

Good Luck. After I wrote to your distinguished[1] self from the snow-white island of Paros,[2] I was delighted to see bright Andros, named for Apollo's son, Andros. From there, in the company of the learned Manuel of Crete, revered monk of the Order of Preachers,[3] we made for Chios, your illustrious island and colony, where, with the help of favoring winds and the assistance of all the Nymphs, daughters of Nereus,[4] we put in at the island's southern promontory[5] on the 12th of January, our Mercury's lucky day.

For a number of good reasons, including a desire to see the place, we disembarked at this peninsula and stayed overnight in the nearest village, which is praised and highly commended for the fertility of its mastic trees. The next day, a clear, pleasant Thursday, we set out from there by mule on an inland journey, guided by some of the locals. Our intention was to revisit the town of Chios and you and other very good friends, but as we passed light-heartedly through those remarkably green, precious groves of mastic, we dismounted, eager to get a close look at those famous little trees, from which I had heard the extraordinarily precious substance seeps. When, as a local resident pointed them out, I finally saw drops of glittering mastic in large numbers rather nearby on every side among the tearful[6] but joyous trunks and had the pleasure of gathering some in my hand, I marveled at the singular gift of the place and its fated bough, the revered benefaction of all-begetting nature, and at the fact that Chios is the only island in the world that makes the whole world redolent with its liquid, and

zet, eam insularum omnium insignem et singulari laude celebran-
dam extollendamque fore censebam.

3   Nam et memoriae repetens me pluries Chyensi vestro in lato
et placidissimo portu scrinia pluria huius preciosissimi gummi
conferta magnis imponi[2] navibus conspexisse, late hac ex insula
mundum salubri hoc liquore donatum redolere cognoveram, cum
et perhemni tempore suo peregrinoque intercedente navigio aro-
mata haec alia per Hellespontum et Bosphorum in Thraciam et
orientalem Europam ducuntur; altera vero per Pontum et Maeotidem ad Tanaym, ut gelido sub axe Sarmathas, Scythas et Hyrcanos confoveret; aut alia ex parte per Asiam, Colchos, Albanos et
Hyberos, Cappadoces et Cilicas ac deinde Persas, Parthos Ara-
basque et Bactra atque Medos Babilonosque demulcerent; alia
quoque inmensum per Ionium atque Libicum aequor ad Aegyptum et Syriam, ut inde ad Aethyopas atque Garamanthas et Indos
transveherentur; altera vero per Illyricum ad Italiam nec non alia
omni[3] Mediterraneo aequore permenso, ad occeanum tandem et
occiduas partes, ut Gades, Gallos Germanosque et Hyspanos,
Brytannos, Hybernos atque Scotas et ultimam usque Thylem re-
focillarent, transvecta percepimus.

4   Quae cum omnia et insignia alia pleraque ad eximiam praeclarae huius insulae laudem spectantia efficacius animo considerare
cepissem, illico e nemore atque sacratissimo luco frondosos inter
et virides ramos e pulcherrimo Oreadum choro magna hylaritate
nymphae sanctissimo ab ore cecinere Chyenses:

5   Chyos, insignis es masticum, una
insula electa nel nostro hemispero,
Ionum flos et del gran vate Homero
sepulchro degno et oppinata cuna.
    Te Iove, te natura et te fortuna
dotar d'onore et don[o] tanto sincero,

I thought that I should acclaim and extol it with special praise as eminent among all the islands.

For I recalled that I had often seen numerous boxes filled with this highly esteemed gum being loaded onto the great ships in your broad and tranquil port of Chios and I knew that the world was being filled with the scent of this island's gift, this wholesome exhalation, since in the course of the years, through the agency of Genoese and foreign ships, these fragrances are carried, some through the Dardanelles and the Bosporus to Thrace and eastern Europe, others through the Black Sea and the Sea of Azov to the River Don, to comfort the Sarmatians, Scythians, and Hyrcanians beneath their cold sky; or elsewhere through Asia, to allure the Colchians, the Albanians, the Georgians, Cappadocians, and Cilicians, and thence the Persians, Parthians and Arabs and Bactrians and Medes and Babylonians. Others are carried over the immense Ionian and Libyan Seas to Egypt and Syria, thence to be transported to the Ethiopians, Garamantians, and Indians. And we know that others are brought via Illyria to Italy, while still others have been transported across the entire Mediterranean Sea, to Ocean and the western lands, to revivify Cadiz, the Gauls, Germans, Spaniards, Britons, Irish and Scotch, and far-off Thule.

When I had begun to consider in my mind all these and other remarkable facts with a view to expressing more effectively a distinguished encomium of this illustrious island, immediately from the wood and the most sacred grove amid the leafy, green branches [came] Chian nymphs, of the lovely chorus of Oreads, [who] sang joyfully with their heavenly voices:

> Chios, you are distinguished for mastic, only
> island of our hemisphere thus selected,
> flower of the Ionians and of the great poet Homer
> worthy tomb and supposed cradle.
> You, endowed by Jove, by nature and by fortune

che quale isola sia degna d'impero,
singular sempre se' sopra ciaschuna.

Herodoto, Tucydide et Solino
con piú Greci et Latin[i] giá di te hystoria
scrissono e[t] Homero al suo hymno divino.

[et] L'Anconitan tra' marmi tua memoria
rinnuova, et cho' Andromache et Quirino,
Augusto in campo Elyso anchor sen gloria.

Hor palma di victoria,
nobil[e] colonia se' de' Genovesi,
al buon ghoverno de' tuoi Maonesi.

: 30 :

1   Viro spectatissimo ac omni laude dignissimo, Andreolo Iustiniano,
    Kyriacus Anconitanus salutem plurimam dicit.

2   Cum ad IIII Kalendas Februarias, faustum, serenum Saturna-
    lemque diem, Iunoniam Samon Ephesumque Arthemisiam et an-
    tiqua Milesium palatia petens, te Chyonque relinquendo navim
    ante diluculum bonis nempe avibus conscendi, Valentino Pantheo
    solertissimo ducente nauta, illico exeuntes e portu, lenis aspiranti-
    bus auris, talia divis aequoreisque numinibus diva Caliope coniunx
    sanctissimo ab ore cecinerat:[1]

3   Nymphe Chyenses, Nereydum sancte,
        Amphytrite alma, et tu, Cymodocea,
        Doris, Doto, Glauce et Panopea,
        Thetis coll'altre per Egeo natante,
            et Nereo, padre anticho, et tu, flagrante

216

with this honor and this gift so pure,
that whatever island there be worthy of an empire,
you ever are unique and supreme over all others.

Herodotus, Thucydides and Solinus
with many Greeks and Latins of the past, histories
of you did write and Homer in his divine hymn.[7]

He of Ancona your memory renews among the marbles,
and with Andromache and Quirinus,
Augustus in the Elysian field still takes pride in it.

Now you, the palm of victory,
are a noble colony of Genoa,
under the kindly government of the guild of Maona.

: 30 :

To Andreolo, after 1 February 1446, ?Miletus

Cyriac of Ancona wishes the best of health to the highly esteemed   1
and praiseworthy Andreolo Giustiniani.

On the 29th of January, Saturn's favorable, cloudless day, as I   2
was departing from you and from Chios under favoring auspices,
on a ship captained by the highly capable seaman, Valentino
Pantheo, on my way to Juno's Samos, Artemis's Ephesus, and the
ancient palaces of Miletus, and had embarked before dawn, just as
we were leaving port under gentle winds, my spouse, Calliope,
sang with holy voice this song to the gods and divinities of the sea:

Nymphs of Chios, holy among the Nereids,   3
beloved Amphitrite and you, Cymodocea,
Doris, Doto, Glauce and Panopea,
Thetis along with the others who swim in the Aegean;
and Nereus, ancient father; and you, raging

Eolo re, col tuo sereno Borea
et con sua guida sancta argiphontea,
et tu, Neptuno, in mar sempre regnante,
    favete coeptis, iam conflata vela,
del fedel vostro Anconitan[o] giocondo,
che 'l nobil mondo anticho al nuovo exvela
    et che lustrar l'intende a tondo a tondo,
navicando hor, perch' a•llui non si^2 cela
Samo et l'Epheso, spectacul[o] del mondo.
    In lui adunque, secondo
pandete il vento e 'l mar, tanta con gratia,
che ne sian liete Chyo, Piceno et Latia.

[Samos]

4 Crebrescunt optatae aurae nosque proinde, tumescentibus velis, pelago iam volamus et tandem, una Phoebi nostroque simul expleto ad Samon cursu, omnibus gratulantibus nymphis, vetusto in ipso Pythagoreo portu consedimus.

[Miletus]

5 Sed inde ad quartam noctis vigiliam solventes, ad surgentem, faustum Kyriaceumque celeberrimum diem, antea quam sol coeli medium orbem conscenderet, Milesiis allabimur quondam nobilibus oris; et quamquam insignia illa veterum relicta nobis monumenta sua me iam adolescente sim memor, iterum atque iterum revisere haud ingratum fuerat; statimque una solerti nauta comitatus Pantheo, ilico quod ad triginta stadiorum iter a litore antiquissimae civitatis vestigia separat propriis pedibus superavimus.

6   Et primum, quod e magnis et nobilioribus veternitatis suae reliquiis nostramque ad diem fere integrum, maximum illud suum de marmore tyburnoque lapide theatrum placuit revisisse; cuiusce amplitudinis fastigia effecerant, ut accolae et omne ferme per

King Aeolus with your cloudless North Wind,
together with his guide, the holy slayer of Argos;
and you, Neptune, ever ruling in the sea,
    favor the enterprise, having already filled the sail
of your servant, the blithe one from Ancona,
who unveils the noble ancient world to the new
    and who now intends to explore it all about
by navigating it, so that to him be not concealed
Samos and Ephesus, the wonder of the world.
    To his ship, therefore, with your great grace,
bestow a following wind and favorable sea
that Chios, Picenum and Latium may rejoice.

[Samos]

The longed-for breezes grew in intensity, our sails swelled, and we   4
flew over the sea, finishing the sun's and our journey to Samos at
the same time, and, to the rejoicing of all the nymphs, we put in at
the Pythagorean port itself.[1]

[Miletus]

But we left there at the fourth watch of the night, at the dawning   5
of a favorable, festive Lord's Day; and before the sun had climbed
to mid-sky we were gliding toward the once noble Milesian shores;
and, although I remember having seen as a youth the signal monuments of its antiquity that remain for us, it has been far from un-
pleasant to visit them over and over again; so, accompanied by the
skilled seaman, Pantheo, we walked the distance of thirty stades
that stands between the coast and the ruins of the ancient city.
    The primary reason was my decision to revisit one of the great   6
and more notable remains of [the city's] antiquity, almost intact
even to our own day: its famous, great theater of marble and trav-
ertine stone. Its towering bulk caused the inhabitants and almost

Graeciam vulgus, Mylesiae quondam nobilissimae civitatis totius
Ioniae metropolis nec minus sapientissimi Thaletis gratia memorandae antiquo tam et celebri abolito nomine, palatia tantum voci-
tent, et urbis locum et utique vestigium omne tantum vetustas et
nostri temporis ignavia gentis mutare valent.

7   Eiusdem vero ampli theatri longitudo ab anteriori facie cubitorum CC, et a solo ad summum culmen LX constat altitudo et conspicua in medio intersecante lista, duabus amplis et ornatissimis
portis ab una et altera parte decoratis atque comodatis parietibus,
et in angulo Graecis posteriorum manu litteris epygramma comperimus harum characterarum insculptum:

Α Ε Η Ι Ο Υ Ω ΑΓΙΕ ΦΤΛΑΞΟΝ ΠΟΛΙΝ |
ΜΙΛΗΣΙΩΝ ΚΑΙ ΠΑΝΤΑΣ ΤΟΥΣ ΚΑΤΟΙΚΟΥΝ|ΤΑΣ³

Quod Latine sonat: Tu, sancte, custodi civitatem Milesium et omnes habitantes.

8   Vidimus praeterea hinc inde per antiquissimae urbis loca pleraque suae nobilitatis vestigia, sed exiguam e moenibus partem extare. At enim vero multa de marmore columnarum statuarumque
fragmenta leonumque et variarum ferarum imagines, quae et cetera inibi relicta veterum monumenta, una ingenuis cum adoles-
centibus Nicolao Mulazana et Iacobo Carmeno, qui Genuenses cives tum forte cum palatinis Milesiis negociabantur, inspeximus.

9   Est et secus urbem Milesiam lacus, qui ad CCC stadiorum circuitu paucis ab altera parte collibus complexus, e planitie exur-
gens, multorum atque varigenum piscium ferax, et ex eo exiguo
quoque cursu flumen haud exiguum in Meandrum nobilissimum
amnem immixtum ad mare defluit, ex quo permixtus latex fere sal-
sus et minus potabilis est.

10   Sed quod ibidem et prope theatrum epygrama comperimus,
hisce reponendum delegimus:

all the common people of Greece to forget the ancient and celebrated name of the noble city of Miletus, the metropolis of all
Ionia, which should be remembered no less because of the great
sage Thales, and call it simply, "the palaces," so great is the power
of the long passage of time and the laziness of the people of our
own era to alter the location, and indeed every trace, of a city.

The length of the same sizeable theater is two hundred cubits 7
along the front and its height from the ground to the highest point
is sixty. A clearly visible strip intersects [the auditorium] in the
middle and there are two large and highly ornate doors on either
side with suitably decorated walls. In a corner, done by later people in Greek letters, we found the following inscription, carved
with these characters:

A.E.$\overline{\text{E}}$.I.O.U.$\overline{\text{O}}$.[2] Saint, protect the city of Miletus and all
its inhabitants.[3]

We saw, besides, here and there throughout the site of the an- 8
cient city that numerous traces of its celebrity, but [only] a small
section of its walls, survive; but we also inspected many fragments
of marble columns and statues and representations of lions and
various [other] wild animals along with other abandoned memori-
als of the ancients there. My companions were the noble youths,
Niccolò Mulazana and Iacopo Carmeno, Genoese citizens who
chanced at that time to be doing business with the Milesian "Pala-
tines."[4]

Also, near the city of Miletus, there is a lake, three hundred 9
stades in circumference, bordered by low hills on the other side,
that rises up from the plain, abounding in many and varied kinds
of fish. Out of this slim course flows a far from slim stream that
joins the storied Meander river, and flows into the sea. Because of
this mixture its water is somewhat salty and less potable.

I have chosen to record here an inscription that I found in the 10
same place near the theater:

ΙΟΥΛΙΑΝ ΑΝΤΙΠΑΤΡΟΥ ΘΥΓΑΤΕ|ΡΑ ΑΡΤΕΜΩΙ ΤΗΝ
ΥΔΡΟΦΟΡΟΝ | ΤΗΣ ΠΥΘΙΗΣ ΑΡΤΕΜΙΔΟΣ ΚΑΙ
ΠΕΡΕΙ|ΑΝ ΔΙΑ ΒΙΟΥ ΤΗΣ ΒΟΥΛΕΑΣ ΑΡΤΕ|ΜΙΔΟΣ
ΚΑΙ ΛΟΥΤΡΟΦΟΡΟΝ ΜΕΓΑΛΩ|Ν ΘΕΩΝ [Κ]ΑΒΕΙ-
ΡΩΝ ΤΕΙΜΗΘΗΣΑΝ | ΥΠΟ ΤΗΣ ΒΟΥΛΗΣ ΚΑΙ ΤΟΥ
ΔΗΜΟΥ | ΣΕΞ. ΚΑΙΛΙΟΣ ΕΡΜΟΚ[Λ]ΗΣ ΚΑΙ ΣΕ. |
ΚΑΙΛΙΟΣ ΑΝΤΙΠΑΤΡΟΣ ΕΑΥΤΩΝ ΜΗΤΕΡΑ⁴

Quod Latine sonat:

Iuliani Antipatri filiam Artemo, aquigeram Pythiae Dianae
et sacerdotem, dum vixerat, Buleae Dianae et balneis prae-
fectam magnorum deorum Labirorum, honore donatam a
consilio et populo, Sextus Caecilius Hermocles et Sextus
Caelius Antipatros, eorum matrem.

11   Ad aliam basem prope barbaram et marmoream sedem:⁵

ΤΩΝ ΓΗΣ ΚΑΙ ΘΑΛΑΣΣΗΣ ΚΑΙ ΠΑΝ|ΤΟΣ
ΑΝΘΡΩΠΩΝ ΕΘΝΟΥΣ ΔΕΣ|ΠΟΤΗΝ ΦΛ. ΚΛΑΥΔΙΟΝ
ΙΟΥΛΙΑ|ΝΟΝ ΑΥΤΟΚΡΑΤΟΡΑ ΤΟΝ ΠΑΣΗΣ
ΟΙ|ΚΟΥΜΕΝΗΣ ΔΕΣΠΟΤΗΝ Η ΛΑΜΠΡΑ ΤΩΝ
ΜΙΛΗΣΙΩΝ ΜΗΤΡΟΠΟΛΙΣ ΚΑΙ | ΤΡΟΦΟΣ ΤΟΥ
ΔΙΔΥΜΕΟΥ ΑΠΟΛΛΩ|ΝΟΣ ΕΥΤΥΧΩΣ⁶

Quod Latine sonat:

Terrae marisque et totius hominum gentis dominum,
Flavium Claudium Iulianum, imperatorem et totius orbis
principem, splendida Milesiorum metropolis et alumna
Didymei Apollinis fortunate.

[Didyma]

12   Deinde vero post biduum extra Mylesiam urbem ad centum ferme
⟨stadia⟩ in australem et marittimam Ioniae partem venimus ad lo-

Sextos Kailios Hermokles and Sextos Kailios Antipatros [honored] their mother Julia Artemo daughter of Antipatros, water-carrier [priestess] of Pythian Artemis, priestess for life of Artemis Boulaia and carrier of water from the baths of the Great gods, the Kabeiroi; she was honored by the Council and the People.

In translation it runs:

Sextus Caecilius Hermocles and Sextus Caelius Antipatros [honor] their mother Artemo, daughter of Julianus Antipatros: while she lived she was water-carrier and priestess of Pythian Diana and mistress of the baths for the Great Gods, the Labiri. She was honored by the Council and the People.

On another statue base near a marble Turkish dwelling: 11

The illustrious metropolis of Miletus, nourisher of Didymean Apollo [honors] the lord of land and sea and the entire human race, the emperor Flavius Claudius Julianus, lord of the whole world. Good luck.

Which means in Latin:

The glorious metropolis of the Milesians and fortunate daughter of Apollo of Didyma [honor] the Lord of land and sea and of the whole human race, Flavius Claudius Julianus, emperor and first citizen of the entire world. Good luck.

[Didyma]

Then after two days, about a hundred [stades] outside the city of   12
Miletus, to the south, along the coast of Ionia, we came to a place

cum qui olim a priscis Didymus dictus constat, nunc aut⟨em⟩ ob
ingentia marmorei aedificii fastigia, veluti antiquiora Milesium
moenia, Γέροντα,[7] scilicet antiqua palatia, vocant; at equidem
maximum et vetustissimum Apollinis in Didymo sacrum a Milesiis fuisse delubrum, et eiusdem imaginem formae, parietes colum-
nasque marmoreas nobiles et immanes et quod amplissima in basi,
veterrimis Ionicis et exactissimis litteris, e Seleuco et Anthioco,
nobilissimis Asiae regibus, epygramma comperimus, manifestum
ostentari cognovimus.

13   Verum et eximium hoc templum, exemptis deorum imaginibus
insculpturisque plurimis folearum et auratis lapidum commissuris,
haud inferius opus nobilissimi Ciziceni delubri videtur extitisse, ut
eius figuram suo cum epygrammate propriis hisce caractheribus
designabo.

14   Nobile epygramma ad insigne et marmoreum Didymei Appol-
linis templum:

ΕΠΙ ΣΤΕΦΑΝΗΦΟΡΟΥ ΠΟΣΕΙΔΙΠ|ΠΟΥ
ΤΑΜΙΤΕΥΟΝΤΩΝ ΤΩΝ ΙΕΡΩΝ | ΧΡΗΜΑΤΩΝ
ΤΙΜΕΑ ΤΟΥ ΦΥΡΣΩ|ΝΟΣ ΑΡΙΣΤΑΓΟΡΑ ΤΟΥ
ΦΙΛΗΜΟΝΟΣ | ΚΛΕΟΜΗΔΟΙΣ ΤΟΥ ΚΡΕΣΩΝΟΣ |
ΦΙΛΙΠΠΟΥ ΣΩΣΙΣ|ΤΡΑΤΟΥ ΑΛΕΞΑΝΔΡΟΥ ΤΟΥ
ΛΟΧΗ|ΓΟΥ ΠΟΛΥΞΕΝΟΥ ΤΟΥ ΒΑΒΩΝΟΣ| ΤΑΔΕ
ΑΝΕΘΗΚΑΝ ΒΑΣΙΛΕΙΣ ΣΕ|ΛΕΥΚΟΣ ΚΑΙ ΤΟΥ
ΑΝΤΙΟΧΟΣ ΤΑ ΕΝ ΤΗΙ | ΕΠΙΣΤΟΛΗΙ
ΓΕΓΡΑΜΜΕΝΑ | ΒΑΣΙΛΕΥΣ ΣΕΛΕΥΚΟΣ ΜΙΛΗΣΙ|ΩΝ
ΤΗΙ ΒΟΥΛΗΙ ΚΑΙ ΤΩ ΔΗΜΩΙ | ΧΑΙΡΕΙΝ
ΑΦΕΣΤΑΛΚΑΜΕΝΕΙΣ ΤΟ ΙΕ|ΡΟΝ ΤΟΥ ΑΠΟΛΛΩΝΟΣ
ΤΟΥ ΕΝ ΔΙ|ΔΙΜΩΙ ΤΗΝ ΤΕ ΛΥΧΝΙΑΝ ΤΗΝ
ΜΕ|ΓΑΛΗΝ ΚΑΙ ΠΟΤΗΡΑ ΧΡΥΣΑ ΚΑΙ | ΑΡΓΥΡΑ
ΕΙΣ ΑΝΑΘΕΣΙΝ ΤΟΙΣ ΘΕΟΙΣ | ΤΟΙΣ ΣΩΤΗΡΣΙ
ΚΟΜΙΖΟΝΤΑ ΠΟ|ΛΙΑΝΘΗΣ ΕΠΙΓΡΑΦΑΣ ΕΧΟΝΤΑ |
ΥΜΕΙΣ ΟΥΝ ΟΤΑΝ ΠΑΡΑΓΕΝΗΤΑΙ | ΛΑΒΟΝΤΕΣ

that the ancients once called Didyma. Now, however, because of its huge, towering marble edifice, as in the case of the rather antique walls of Miletus, they call it *Geronta*, i.e., "Ancient Palace." But for our part, both the impressive, huge marble walls and columns, a specimen of the same style [of architecture] as that of the temple in Miletus, and the fact that we found on a very large base, in very ancient and precise Ionic lettering, an inscription from Seleucus and Antiochus, the renowned kings of Asia, have convinced us as clearly established that it was the very large and very old temple of Apollo in Didyma, dedicated by the Milesians.

This remarkable temple seems to have been a structure in no   13
way inferior to that of the famous shrine of Cyzicus, apart from [the latter's] statues of the gods, abundant sculptured foliage, and the gilded joins of its blocks, as I shall illustrate by my drawing of it,[5] along with its inscription in its own proper lettering, as follows.

The noble inscription on the distinguished marble temple of   14
Apollo at Didyma:

> When Poseidippos was crown-wearer [magistrate] and the treasurers of the sacred funds were Timeas son of Phryson, Aristagoras son of Philemon, Kleomedes son of Kreson, Philippos son of Sosistratos, Alexandros son of Lochegos, and Polyxenos son of Babon, kings Seleucus and Antiochus made the dedications described in this letter: "King Seleucus to the Council and People of Miletus, greetings. We have sent to the temple of Apollo in Didyma the large lampstand and gold and silver cups bearing inscriptions, as offerings to the Savior Gods. Polyanthes is escorting them. When they arrive, accept them, with good fortune, and hand them over

ΑΤΤΑ ΤΥΧΗΙ ΑΓΑΘΗΙ | ΑΠΟΔΟΤΕ ΕΙΣ ΤΟ ΙΕΡΟΝ
ΙΝΑ ΕΧΗ|ΡΕΣ ΠΕΝΤΕ ΚΑΙ ΧΡΑΣΘΑΙ ΤΠΟ |
ΑΙΝΟΝΤΩΝ ΗΜΩΝ ΩΝ ΚΑΙ ΕΥΤΥ|ΧΕΣΤΑΤΩΝ ΚΑΙ
ΤΗΣ ΠΟΛΕΩΣ | ΔΙΑΜΕΝΟΥΣΗΣ ΩΣΕΙΣ[8]

15   Quae Latine sonant fere huiusce intellectus:

Sub coronato, scilicet Apollinis pontifice, Posydippo,
sacrarum pecuniarum aerariis Timeo Phyrsonis, Arystaghora
Phylemonis, Cleomede Cresonis, Phylippo Sosysthrati,
Alexandro Lochegi, Polixeno Babonis, haec autem
obtulerunt oblaveruntque reges Seleucus et Anthiocus, quae
in epistola scripta sunt talia: Rex Seleucus Mylesiorum
consilio et populo salutem. Destinavimus ad sacrum Apollinis in Didymo candelabrum magnum et calices aureos et
argenteos in oblationem diis salutaribus, portitorum
habentem inscriptiones multi intellectus. Vos igitur ea, cum
aderint, accipientes optima cum fortuna, reddite in sacrum,
ut in sacrificiis et libamine uterentur nostram in laudem et
optimam nostri felicitatem civitatisque tutelam.

: 31 :

Ad elegantem et eruditissimum virum, Bonaccursium Grimanum
optimum ac bene merentem Cretensium secretarium.[1]

1   Andreolus Iustinianus Bonaccurso viro eleganti et bene merenti
Cretensium secretario salutem plurimam dicit.

to the shrine, so that you have them for libations and [other] uses, for our health and fortune and for the safety of the city."

The approximate sense of it is as follows:[6]   15

Under the garlanded [i.e. priest of Apollo] Posidippus, when the treasurers of the sacred funds were Timaeus, son of Phryson, Aristagoras, son of Philemon, Cleomedes, son of Creson, Philippos, son of Sosistratos, Alexander, son of Lochegos, and Polyxenos, son of Babon, the kings Seleucus and Antiochus made these offerings which are described in the following letter: "King Seleucus to the Council and People of the Milesians, greetings: We have sent a carrier of great intelligence to the shrine of Apollo in Didyma with a large candelabrum and inscribed golden and silver cups as an offering to the Savior Gods. When they arrive, accept them both with good luck and hand them over to the shrine, so that they may be used in sacrifices and libations to our praise and our good fortune and for the safety of the state."[7]

: 31 :

From Andreolo to Buonaccorso Grimani,
12 February [1446], Chios

To the elegant and most learned Bonaccorso Grimani, the excellent and well deserving secretary of the Cretans.

Andreolo Giustiniani wishes the best of health to Bonaccorso, the   1
elegant and highly deserving Secretary of the Cretans.[1]

2   Cum pridie Kyriacus ille noster ex Creta Chyon remeasset, tuam mihi praedulcem et quam brevem epistolam detulit. Et quamquam satis e tuis paucis dictis tuae probitatis affectum et erga me benivolentiam cognovissem, ipse tuus amicissimus mihi latius et de virtute et singulari humanitate tua perbellissime declaravit. Ex quo quantum mihi gratum fuerat, non his paucis litteris explicandum censui, sed cum forte oportunum quidem amicitiae nostrae declarandae inciderit, re gratius ostendere placitum fore. Nam et eo quo tuam cognoveram amicitiam fausto equidem die, ipsum 'meliore lapillo' numerandum duxi.

3   Vale ex Chio, pridie Idus Februarias.

: 32 :

1   Ad Andreolum Iustinianum, virum insignem et amicum optimum et incomparabilem.

2   Cum ad III Kalendas Martiarum, laetum, faustum Kyriaceumque celeberrimum diem, Lesbeam Mytilenem petentes, Chyon praeclaram coloniam vestram teque et celebranda Chyensium nympharum agonalia intuitus, quin et solerti accersitus navarcho ἀθυμότατος reliquissem, optume Andreole, una nostro cum Chreteo venerando et perdocto monacho, Manuele Ceteyam, et onerariam navim Aloysio Buondenario praefecto ante diem conscendimus.

3   Et protinus, solertissimo festinante navarcho, invitis Chieis omnibus divis et ornatissimis nymphis, suis quibusque palaeis et iocundissimis choreis expletis, invita Clio et alma Caliope, nostra sorore diva flocci pensa Therpsicore, nec non Aeolo invito rege,

When our Cyriac returned to Chios from Crete yesterday, he 2
brought me your most welcome, if quite brief, letter. And though I
am sufficiently aware from these few words of your honor's affection and good will toward me, he, your very good friend, spoke to
me at greater length, and most charmingly, about your good character and remarkable cordiality. Accordingly, I thought I should
explain how pleased I was, not in this brief note, but I decided it
would be more gracious to show it when the opportunity presents
itself to do so in person. For I felt that the lucky day on which I
came to know of your friendship should be marked with the
"better stone."[2]

Farewell from Chios, 12 February.   3

: 32 :

To Andreolo, 2 March 1446, Khardamyla, Chios

To the distinguished Andreolo Giustiniani, my good, incompara- 1
ble friend.

On the 27th of February, a joyful, lucky, festive Lord's day, after 2
witnessing the fabled festival of the Chian nymphs, we were summoned by the skillful ship's captain, and, accompanied by our revered and learned Cretan monk, Manuel Ceteyam, departed most
reluctantly from you, good Andreolo, and from your illustrious
colony of Chios, boarding before daylight a cargo ship bound for
Lesbian Mytilene, whose master was Lodisio Bondenari.

Suddenly, as the highly skilled captain hurried, against the will 3
of all the gods and the most honored nymphs of Chios, whose ancient, joyful dances were finished, and of Clio and fostering Calliope, of our sister Terpsichore, who thought little of the idea, and
of King Aeolus, at whose command all the winds stopped and

quin et eius imperio pausatis omnibus et residentibus auris, demum puppi ab alta Cyriaceo Clavario solertissimo sibilante nau-
clero, nautae iussi, carbasa solventes vacua, nullo vel suspenso
flatu, ante diluculum aeri opaco dedere.

[Kardhamyla, Chios]

4 Et dum per liquidum aequor vestrae inclitae in conspectu coloniae
modico cursu laborantes subveheremur, tandem surgente Phoebo,
Lesbeis hinc trahentibus nymphis et repugnantibus inde Chyeis
obliquo persaepe sinu, die noctuque maria sulcantes, iussus cum
forte audacior die postero Boreas, velis denique retropulsis, pup-
5 pim in Lesbon atque rostra Chyon advertere cohercuerat, evadere
Chyenses Nereae sanctissimae nymphae compotes voti sui, suo
nos Cardamileo lato et placidissimo in portu duxere, ubi postquam nautae navim anchora fundarunt, mihi magna hylaritate
Nereydes gratularier insurgere. Quam et ob rem hunc nos adventare sinum impulerint, detexere et quam tu mihi ναόν, vir diligentissime, dudum iam et pridie saepius recensebas, propinquiorem
esse et sororia illa nostra Πολύμνια et Cardamileae Driades
Oryadesque cecinere deae.

6 Et protinus πρόθυμος ἐγώ. Sequentem ad Martialem et sup-
premam pinguium saturnalium diem, dum nautae alii per colles
pingues quaeritant cum matribus agnos, alii per densa ferarum
tecta silvas et semina flammae rapiunt, Lodovico Borlasca lepido
intercedente scriba et Michaele Lesbeo ductitante ποδότα, aquilo-
narem ad insulae partem per arduos atque scrupeos secus littora
colles ad xxx stadiorum iter pedibus superantes ad ipsas prope li-
7 tus vetustissimi templi reliquias venimus; quarum ingentia et olim

died down, Cyriac de Chavaro, the skillful mate,[1] whistled from the high poop, the sailors were given their orders, and, slackening the limp sails (no breeze caught them), gave them to the dark air before dawn.[2]

[Kardhamyla, Chios]

And as we labored our way at a moderate speed through the liquid 4 deep within sight of your famous colony, finally at sunrise there was a struggle between the nymphs of Lesbos, who pulled us on, and those of Chios, who fought back, breasting the waves against them. Through the day and night we plowed the sea when, on the next day[3] the north wind, becoming bolder on orders, drove back the sails and forced our stern to turn towards Lesbos and our prow toward Chios. The holy Nereid nymphs of Chios ended up 5 getting what they wanted and they brought us into the wide and sheltered port of Kardhamyla, where, after the sailors anchored the ship, the Nereids rose to felicitate me with great joy. They revealed why they had driven us into this gulf, and my sister Polymnia and the dryads and oreads of Kardhamyla sang that the temple which you, diligent sir, often in the past and even the other day, told me about, was nearby.

Immediately I was enthusiastic. On the following day, Tuesday, 6 the last day of carnival,[4] while some of the sailors roamed the hills seeking "plump lambs and their mothers," and others plundered "the forests, thick homes of wild beasts," and [sought] "the seeds of flame," we, through the good offices of the amusing secretary, Lodovico Borlasca,[5] and guided by Michael, the *podestà* of Lesbos, completed a journey along the shore of some thirty stades, on foot over steep and rocky hills, to the northern part of the island, to the actual remains of a very old temple near the shore. Its many 7 huge stone blocks, once squared up by the hands of artisans, and [now lying] dislodged in one location, on this side and on that, are

artificum manu quadrata uno et loco convulsa pleraque hinc inde saxa, non ut putaras ad futurum quodcumque opus condendum parata congestave esse, quin et dirutae antiquissimae aedis collapsas, vel nunc longi temporis labe relictas moles, et nexae aere lapides perforataeque lapidum commissurae adhuc rubigine tinctae declarant.

8   Templum vero olim cuiusque deorum fuisse et forma lapidum et Graecum ab indigenis servatum nomen ostendit. Nam et ab eo litus et vicinum omne locum hodie ναόν appellant; quoi vero e diis deabusve sacrum fuisse, Neptuno Apollinive, Homero vel vati divo aut alteri cuipiam numini, nullis intercedentibus litteris, anceps quippe nobis opinio est. Sed[1] potius Phoebeum fuisse putarim, quod inibi inter lapides magni trypodis vestigium comperimus, ingentis ut bipedum amplitudine marmorei leonini pedis imaginem causabat.

9   Sed inde remenso itinere, Iride tua comitante Iunonia humentibus roscida totum per aera pennis, nobilem Bondenariam navim sociosque revisimus. Et denique postquam una nostro magnifico cum praefecto tota et iocundissima cum cohorte, Iohanne[2] Fridiman potissimum iubilante Germanico, splendide oppipareque in symposio suscepti, explendo saturnalia dapibus epulamur opimis, Cardamileae placidissimae nymphae nos placide usque suo in portu bona spe repletos consistere iussere tutos, donec tumidas iratasque sibi Lesbeas aquilonaresve Nereydum sorores, Aeolo iubente rege ac optimo maximoque annuente Neptuno placidis et honestissimis rationibus, Iove optimo iuvante, placent.

10   Tu interim vir iocundissime, vale et optimo regioque praetori nostro Paridique magnifico sororio tuo clarissimaeque sanctis-

not, as you supposed, blocks made ready and piled up for the construction of some future building, but the fallen, massive remains, of a ruined, very old temple, even now abandoned to the deterioration of great age, as is proved by the fact that the stones are bound together with bronze clamps and the holes in the joints of the blocks are stained with rust.

Both the nature of the stone-work and the Greek name preserved by the locals indicate that this was once a temple of one of the gods, for today they call the shore and the whole neighboring area *naos*; but to which of the gods or goddesses it was dedicated—Neptune or Apollo or the divine poet Homer or some other divinity—remains for us a moot question in the absence of written evidence. Still, I rather think it was [a temple of] Phoebus, because in it we found among the blocks the trace of a huge tripod, as if something the size of a large biped had caused the imprint of a marble lion's foot. 8

From there we retraced our steps, accompanied by Juno's messenger, your Iris, dewy with damp wings over the whole sky, and we returned to Bondenari's familiar ship and our companions. At length, after we were welcomed brilliantly and sumptuously with a drinking party, and had feasted on a rich meal to round off carnival together with our magnificent captain and his whole, most delightful company—Johann Fridiman, the German, was especially ecstatic—the very tranquil nymphs of Kardhamyla bade us continue to stay tranquilly in their port, sated with high hopes and safe, until, at the command of King Aeolus and with the permission of Neptune, the best and greatest, they should pacify their northern sister Nereids from Lesbos, who were swollen with wrath at them, with calming, respectable arguments and the help of goodly Jove. 9

Meanwhile farewell, most joyous sir, and to our excellent, princely *podestà*,[6] to your sister's magnificent husband Paride, to your most brilliant, deeply devout wife and your excellent, upright 10

simae coniugi tuae et optimis atque ingenuis natis ex me et venerando Manuele nostro salutem plurimam hylaritatemque dabis. Ex
Cardamileo eodem tuto et placidissimo portu, VI Nonarum Martiarum, religioso, fausto, ventoso et Mercuri genii felicissimi nostri
sanctissimo die, MCCCCXLVI.

II Francisco Drapperio praeter ex me salutem memorem me sibi
remque meam facere velis, et sic oblicterari non dubitem, siquando
tuam viderit memorab⟨il⟩em cedulam.

∴ 33 ∴

1 Viro praestantissimo atque rerum omnigenum peritissimo,
Andreolo Iustiniano amicissimo suo.

2 Scripsimus ad te pridie, praestans et elegantissime Andreole,
quae nostra de navigatione ad Cardamileum usque portum succes-
serat. Verum et deinde postquam centenas ferme horas Lesbeae
Nereydes, ira et aquilonaribus concitae flatibus, nos eodem tuto in
portu, tumescentibus undis, ab extra frementes atque immaniter
minantes obsiderant, tandem iussu regis Borea Threicio vasto in
carcere vinclis frenato, cum alta quievissent aequora, nos iterum
Lesbon καλονιαῖον τε κόλπον innare summopere flagitantes
ad pridie Nonarum Martiarum celebrem serenum Kyriacemque
diem, pulchra ex Caliope nostra Cardamileis nymphis ac caeruleis
ceteris ponti numinibus oratione habita, cum exoptatis crebrescen-
3 tibus Euris surgente sole portum relinquentes vela daremus, tam
felici cursu transiecimus aequor, ut antea nostrum quam Phoebi
cursum expletum cognoverimus, Chyeis Lesbeisque secundantibus

234

children please convey my best wishes and those of our revered Manuel for their health and happiness. From Kardhamyla, the same safe and most peaceful port, on the 2nd of March, the sacred, favoring, windy and holy day of Mercury, our most propitious patron, 1446.

[Postscript:] In addition to greeting Franzesco di Drapieri for me, 11 please remind him of me and my enterprise. I don't think he will forget if he sees your memorandum.

: 33 :

To Andreolo, 6 March [1446], Kalloni, Lesbos

To Andreolo Giustiniani, most distinguished polymath and my 1 very best friend

I wrote you the other day,[1] Andreolo, peerless in matters of 2 good taste, about what happened on our journey to the port of Kardhamyla. To go on from there, the Nereids of Lesbos, roused by their anger and by the north winds, had blockaded us with swelling waves for about a hundred hours in that safe port, roaring from outside and threatening fiercely, when finally, by order of his king,[2] the north wind Boreas was enchained in his immense Thracian prison and the deep sea grew quiet. Since we still had a strong desire to sail to Lesbos and the Gulf of Kalloni, our beautiful Calliope interceded with the nymphs of Kardhamyla and the other blue-green gods of the sea, the southeast wind we had hoped for increased in intensity, and on the 6th of March, a festive, bright Lord's Day, we set sail from the port at sunrise. So happy 3 was our crossing of the sea, that, with the help and guidance of all the nymphs of Chios and Lesbos, we finished our course before

omnibus atque modulantibus nymphis. Et dum expetito Kalonieo ipso in sinu angustum per os et arduas inter cautes, amoenissimo secundante flatu, subveheremur, tam laete placideque nos nymphae complexere Lesbeae, ut harum pictae variaeque et assuetae ripis volucres atque aequoris alveo aethera mulcerent cantu lucoque volarent.

4   Vale et scias nobis exeuntibus e portu Cardamileo Chyenses laetae et secundantes nymphae tuas in medio obtulisse Syrenas, quibus et haec brevia reddidere Lesbeae. Ex Kalonieo sinu eo quo ad eum venimus pridie Nonarum Martiarum et, ut supra scripsimus, Kyriaceo felici et serenissimo die. Iterum atque iterum vale.

: 34 :

1   Ad praeclarissimum virum Andreolum Iustinianum, amicum suum incomparabilem.

2   Postea quam ex Calonieo portu ultimas ad te litteras dedimus, optume Andreole, Mitylenem VIII Idus Martias veni et, Dorino reviso principe, quas abs te sibi litteras et salutem dedi, hilari vultu animoque suscepit. Vidimus et alios veteres inter amicos Christianum Spinolam et cum ab eo de his quae mihi memoria recensebas sciscitaremur, eum et principem de porphyreo lapide conscripto ac alios omnes de ceteris dignis quibusque rebus, Lethaeo non adhuc amne tranato eius vero securos bibisse latices habeto. Et quod aliquid de rebus a te iam visis extet aut norant et *che S.Q.S.I.P. nol crediate.* De capitibus vero marmoreis unum ad te Spinola mittere dixit, alterum mihi in muro collatum ostendit, ineptum satis et

Phoebus completed his. And as we sailed with a very pleasant following wind through a narrow opening between steep cliffs into the Gulf of Lesbos, our destination, the nymphs of Lesbos embraced us so joyfully and gently that their multicolored birds, accustomed to the banks and the channel of the stream, soothed the air with song and flitted in the grove.[3]

Farewell, and know that, as we left the port of Kardhamyla, the joyful and helpful Chian nymphs placed your Sirens at our disposal, by means of whom the nymphs of Lesbos returned this brief loan. From the Gulf of Kalloni on the day we arrived, the 6th of March and, as I wrote above, a favorable, clear Lord's Day. Again and again, farewell. 4

: 34 :

To Andreolo, 13 March [1446], Mytilene, Lesbos

To my incomparable friend, the illustrious Andreolo Giustiniani. 1

After I wrote you my last letter from the port of Kalloni, good 2 Andreolo, I went to Mytilene on 8 March, revisited prince Dorino,[1] and gave him your letter and greetings, which he received with joy on his face and in his heart. Among other old friends, I saw Cristiano Spinola, and when I inquired of him about the matters you brought to my attention, know that he and the prince, regarding the inscribed porphyry stone, and all the others, regarding each of the other appropriate matters, though they have not yet crossed the river Lethe, have certainly drunk its "waters of unconcern;" and because something may survive of the objects you once saw, they even know it and *che S.Q.S.I.P. nol crediate*,[2] but concerning the marble heads, Spinola said he is sending you one; and the other he showed me set in a wall, quite unsuitable and largely de-

magna ex parte defectum, verum et tibi dicendum erit de quovis-
cumque duorum hac *L.D.I.C.A.E.V.C.C.*

3   Vale et scias me Lesbeam omnem insulam digniori ex parte in-
dagaturum, iuvante principe, et hic usque nunc digna aliqua com-
peruisse. Ex Mitylene, III Idus Martias. Et ex principe Dorino et
Leonardo et nostro Emanuele plurimum salutaris. Et tu vestris
omnibus ex me salutem de more dabis et ex beato optumo Gatalusio. Kyriacus Anconitanus tuus.

4   Et haec ubi dicta, venerat ad principem vester missus a vobis Cosmas, a quo vos omnes bene valere novisse laetatus sum. Et ut latius vos a principe noveritis, Theucrorum in Lesbon motus vox
rumorque cessere. Et quod ut levius iter per Asiam ad Bizantium
superarem, per eundem Cosmam nostram ad tuos lares linceam
vestem remitto. Iterum vale.

: 35 :

1   *Ad Andreolum Iustinianum, virum praestantissimum et amicum incompa-*
rabilem suum.

2   Kyriacus Andreolo suo salutem dicit et iocunditatem.

3   Ut ex P. Rocea, publico rei vestrae scriba, te novisse non dubito,
vir praestans et amicissime, ex Mytilene me pridie Phocas ad Franciscum Drapperium contuli, Lesbeis veterum monumentis digniori ex parte visis et, quoad licuerat, adnotatis. At et cognito
Francisci nostri apud Phocas adventu, ad eum me conferre delegi,
ut expetitas illas ex Theucro litteras ad meum undique per Asiam
iter tutandum certius haberemus. Postridie vero apud Lydam Ma-

fective. But I must tell you concerning each of these two [sculptures], *L.D.I.C.A.E.V.C.C.*[3]

Farewell, and know that, with the help of the prince, I shall investigate the more worthwhile part of the whole island of Lesbos, and have already found some things worth my while.[4] From Mytilene, March 13th. Both Prince Dorino and Leonardo and our Emanuel send you their warmest greetings. Please convey my good wishes to all your household, as usual, and include those of the noble Gattilusio. Your Cyriac of Ancona.

[*Postscript:*] After I had written this, your Cosmas came to the prince on a mission from you. I was glad to learn from him that you are all well. And, that you may have more news from the prince, the rumors of a Turkish move against Lesbos have abated. Also, to lighten my journey through Asia to Byzantium, I am sending my linen garment back to your house with our friend Cosmas.

⁖ 35 ⁖

To Andreolo, 8 April 1446, Foglia Nuova

To the eminent Andreolo Giustiniani, his incomparable friend.[1]

Cyriac wishes health and happiness to his Andreolo.

My eminent, best friend, as I am sure you know from P. Rocea, secretary of your commonwealth, I went yesterday from Mytilene to Foglia to see Franzesco di Drapieri. I had seen the more important of the ancient monuments of Lesbos and recorded them as well as I could, and when I learned that our Franzesco had arrived in Foglia, I decided to go to him, to be more certain of getting from the Turk[2] the letter I requested to safeguard my travel everywhere in Asia. Know, moreover, that tomorrow I will set out

gnesiam una ipso cum claro praetore Francisco ad superbum Asiae regnatorem me profecturum habeto et deinde Bizantium una et ipso optimo comitante Drapperio, revisere curabimus, bono iuvante Iove et optimo genio nostro favitante atque feliciter ductitante Mercurio.

4   Praeterea cum exactis diebus, nescio unde quo vel pacto, apud Lesbeam ipsam Mytilenem de Anconitanae patriae civitatis nostrae Venetis deditione vulgaris quispiam rumor exortus esset et in tam furiosum crevisset inmane monstrum, ut civitatem egregiam illam et tam diu sub pontificia Deique vicaria protectione unicam inter insignes in Latio primaevas urbes alma et politiarum optima democratica libertate florentem signis legibusque Venetum et magistratibus commissam esse ferebant; et ut facinori causam adderent, id factum aiebant ob Ausonici potentissimi regis imminentem in Piceno potestatem oppresionemque vitandam.

5   Quod equidem infandum quippe facinus minime atque nullatenus credens cum flocci penderem, ad te in primis karissimum et quem semper civitatis nostrae libertatisque suae honoris, decoris et eximiae dignitatis amatorem, cultorem exornatoremque et nostrum veluti concivem dilectu cognovimus, nil penitus, ut nosti, tanta de re scribendum censui, perinde ac eadem tu mente mihi, ut sane opinor, ea de re minime significandum censueras.

6   Nam et inter Mytileneis negociantes vestrae nationis homines gravioribus et caris nonnullis amicis invisum id mihi novum efficaciter nuntiantibus equidem rem deridens tuo statim apophtemate illo respondi, ut neque id verum esse neque *che S.Q.S.I.P. nol crediate*. Nam diu iam ego nostratum moribus expertus Anconitum

with the celebrated *podestà* Franzesco himself for the proud monarch of Asia in Lydian Magnesia, and after that I shall undertake to return to Byzantium, together with the excellent Drapieri himself, with the help of good Jove and the favor and fortunate guidance of Mercury, our excellent patron.

Another matter. A few days ago — I do not know where or how   4
it started — a persistent rumor cropped up in Lesbian Mytilene that my native city, Ancona, had surrendered to the Venetians. This story grew to such wild, monstrous proportions that they were saying that this preeminent city, so long under the protection of the pope, the vicar of God, the only one among the outstanding, youthful cities of Latium flourishing in democratic freedom, the nourishing, best form of government, had been handed over to the standards, laws and magistracies of Venice. To account for the outrage, they were saying that it was done to check the threatening power and pressure in Picenum of the very powerful king of Naples.

Since I did not at all believe that this unspeakable outrage had   5
occurred, and I considered [the rumor] of no importance especially to you, my dearest friend, whom I know to have always been, as it were, a fellow citizen by choice, a lover, cultivator, and embellisher of our city and its freedom, honor, glory and extraordinary worth, I decided, as you are aware, that I should write absolutely nothing to you on such a matter, just as it was the same line of thinking, I suppose, that lay behind your decision that you should in no way to comment about it to me.

For among the men of your country who were doing business   6
with some rather important men of Mytilene, including some dear friends who reported the hateful news to me effectively, I for my part scoffed at the story and replied immediately with that famous saying of yours, that you should neither believe it was true nor *che S.Q.S.I.P. nol crediate*.[3] For because I am long experienced in the ways of our men, I have a broad knowledge of the minds and

late civium mentem animumque cognovi. Noveram et eorum al-
mam erga et pulcherrimam libertatem amorem, diligentiam, affectionem ac unanimem et perennem atque ineluctabilem volunta-
tem.

7 At et postquam Phocas adveneram, vir nobilis Baptista Grimaldus, inibi negociator vel comertiarum comes et antique nobis nostra ipsa in patria notus et amicissimus, post dulces de more amplexus id ipsum mihi execrandum facinus ut et nostrae utique
amator patriae aegro animo ferens quin et mihi condolens recense-
bat. Idque multis e partibus sibi notificatum affirmabat. Cui et ego
utique de more subridens id ipsum sibi nostro de praedicato Simone facetum reddideram. Verum et foedus aliquod honestum
Anconitanos inter et Venetos, amicos et patres honorificos nostros, initum esse facilius crederem. Ad quod ipse quam grate res-
pondit: 'Tuis utinam dictis atque votis deum cuncta et Anconitanae rei numina faveant et aspirent.'

8 Ast enim vero hodie, VI Iduum, fausto nostraeque patriae tu-
telaris deae mensis Venerei Venereo laeto et iocundissimo die,
amicissimus ipse Baptista mihi magna hylaritate obviam occurrit.
Bonum mihi atque exoptabile novum se illico nuntiaturum pollicebatur, sed antea a me eiusdem rei praemium exposcebat, quod
cum laeto hylarique sibi vultu et animo lateque promitterem, mox
perosum illud et pernitiosum novum mendax et vanum habere,
quin et oppinatum a me foedus verum esse, litteris ex Rhodo habi-
tis, me certiorem fecerat et laetiorem.

9 Ex quo sibi praemium et ἀντίδωρον tale Calyopes nostra Ura-
niaque sanctissimo ab ore canentes quam grate persolvendum ius-
serant. Itaque praeceptis earum parere volens ita coepi:

hearts of the citizens of Ancona. I know as well their [attitude] toward bountiful, glorious freedom: their love of it, their hard work, their passion for it, and their harmonious, enduring and indestructible will [to defend it].

After I got to Foglia, a noble gentleman, Battista Grimaldi, a 7 business man there, i.e., a partner in commercial enterprises, and known to me from of old as a very good friend in my native city itself, embraced me warmly as usual and recounted to me the [rumor about] the accursed outrage, taking it badly as a lover of my native land, of course, but also because he grieved for me. He affirmed that he had the story from a number of sources. I smiled at him in my usual way and replied that this was a jest originating in our vaunted Simon, though I could more easily believe that an honorable treaty had been entered into between the Anconitans and the Venetians, who are our friends, and our respectable patricians. To this he graciously replied, "May all the gods that watch over the state of Ancona breathe favor upon the prayer you expressed."

Now it so happens that today, the 8th, the lucky, joyful and 8 happy day and month of Venus,[4] our native city's tutelary goddess, I encountered my good friend Battista, who was in a very happy state. He promised that he would presently give me good news that I longed to hear, but asked me first to reward him for it. When with a smile on my face and joyful heart I made a generous promise, he informed me that he had had a letter from Rhodes, and that the hateful and baleful rumor was false and groundless, that the treaty which I had conjectured was in fact a reality.[5] I was overjoyed.

Thereupon our Calliope and Urania, singing with most sacred 9 voices, bade me pay with pleasure the reward which I had promised, and so, willing to obey their instructions, I began:

Più che propheta, martyre et Baptista,
più ch'altro al mondo nato melato et granne;
celo, terra, abysso, el nome de Iohanne
illustrò sopra ogn'altra humana vista.

Quale angelo o potenza d'acto mixta
discese in terra a usar tal vivanne,
che per le selve fesse parer ghianne
d'ape exquisite a ogni alma sophista?

Questo è quel grande prode homo et patriarcha,
voce exclamante per lo gran diserto,
a·ppreparar la via del gran monarcha
che nel Giordan cognobbe et col dito erto
disse: "Ecco quello Agnel che 'l mondo scharcha
di colpa et falli il cielo mite e aperto."

Nel cui splendido merto
Batista de Grimalda con sua prole
spera et rimira come aquila il sole.

10   Vale, et tuis omnibus et Clarentiae, praeclarae coniugi, salutem
plurima ex me de more dabis. Et extra lares optimo regio praetori
vestro et Paridi magnifico, cui ut Anconitanae patriae nostrae amicissimo litteras ostentabis, Boccono intercurante suo, et fratri B.
reverendo patri et seraphici ordinis ministro, quam ad eum hisce
epistolam mitto, postquam eam perlegeris, reddendam curabis. Ex
eodem novo Phocarum emporio, eo quo supra diximus, vi[1] Iduum
Aprilis, Eugenii papae anno xvi. Iterum atque iterum vale.

More than prophet, martyr and Baptizer,
greater than any mortal man with honeyed eloquence;
Heaven, Earth, Abyss, to the name of John
gave eminence, above all other humans' fame.
    What angel or what spirit with intent endowed,
descended on earth to enjoy such viands,
which throughout the wilds he transformed into combs
of bees, exquisite food for any wise soul?
    This is that great heroic man and patriarch,
the voice crying out in the vast desert
to prepare the way for the mighty monarch
    whom he recognized in the Jordan and with finger raised
said: "Behold that Lamb who takes away sin from the world
and opens the way to Heaven and to its mercy."
    For on his glorious merit
Batista de Grimalda and his descendants base their hopes
and fix their gaze, as an eagle does to the sun.

Farewell. Give my best, as usual, to all your people and to your   10
admirable wife, Carenza, and in addition to your family, to your
excellent, princely *podestà* and to the magnificent Paride. Please
show him this letter as to a great friend of my native city of
Ancona through the kind offices of Boccone. Also, please see to it
that the enclosed letter, which I am sending to Brother B., father
and minister of the Seraphic order, is delivered to him after you
have read it From the same new trading center of Foglia, on the
day I mentioned above, April 8th, in the 16th year of Pope Eugene.
Again and again, farewell.

1   Ad Andreolum Iustinianum, virum elegantissimum et amicum suum primarium.

2   Cum heri vester et Phocarum scriba Stephanus Magnesiam adventasset, diligentissime Andreole, tuas mihi praedulces licteras detulit et in hiis ad nostra illa quam brevia Lesbea ex Calliope carmina officiosam, dignam, elegantem atque bene merentem responsionem; quam cum ob sui considerationem, tum quia tecum esse invicemque simul tanta de re affari videbar, bis terque quaterque perlegi.

3   Equidem vero praeterea vellem, si quas primum ex Mitelene nostrum per Cosmam Cicadam et postea ex Phoca ad te de patriae novitate vulgata litteras misimus excepisti, abs te me fieri certiorem, et quam alligatam tuae ad venerandum patrem ministrum transmiseram habuistis, utique intelligere cupiebam.

4   At enim interea, quam pridie hic nostri gratia Calliope ad seraphycum Franciscum pro Francisci Drapperii nostri salute orationem habuerat, lectitabis et deinde ut B. ipse optimus eiusdem seraphycae religionis minister videat, opera dabis. Quam et ut caelum tetigisse percipias, habeto quod ad celebrem resurgentis magni Redemptoris diem magnus ille Asiae regnator, regia patente porta, non, ut mos et solitus est quascumque externas vel sui generis legationes suscipere, solitum se patens in atrium contulit, quin ad domesticam suam interiorem et secretam aulam, ubi nulli fas esset externo tantum insistere limen, Franciscum nostrum ad se iusserat introire et alia pleraque ipse magnus princeps satrapesque sui

20 April to August 1446
Manisa, Foglia Nuova, Galata/Pera

: 36 :

To Andreolo, 20 April 1446, Manisa

To a man of supremely good taste and his principal friend, 1
Andreolo Giustiniani.

Yesterday, my very industrious Andreolo, when Stefano, your 2
and Foglia's secretary, arrived in Magnesia, he brought me your
most welcome letter, with your dutiful, worthy, tasteful, and well-
deserving response to that very short Lesbian poem by Calliope. I
read it two, three, four times, both because of its intrinsic worth
and because in doing so I felt I was with you and conversing with
you on this important matter.

In addition, I would like to know[1] if you received the letters I 3
sent you, first from Mytilene by the hand of Cosimo Cicada, and
later from Foglia, concerning the rumored turn of events in my
native city. I am also eager to learn whether you got my letter to
the reverend priest-minister that was attached to yours.

But meanwhile, please read the enclosed prayer to the seraphic 4
Francis for the safety of our Franzesco di Drapieri that Calliope
declaimed the other day on my behalf. Then I would like you to
make sure that B., that excellent minister of the same seraphic order, reads it. To convince you that it reached heaven, be informed
that, on the solemn day of our great Redeemer's resurrection,[2]
that great ruler of Asia, opening the royal portals, did not betake
himself to the open courtyard where he customarily receives foreign and domestic delegations, but he invited our Franzesco to en-
ter a separate, private, inner chamber, where no outsider may so
much as step on the threshold. The great prince himself and his

eximiae erga eum benivolentiae insignia declararunt. Quae omnia laetus conspexi cum sui tu et utique gratia vestri, quod et non modo sibi ipsi, quin et vestrae quoque rei comodum accedere late putabam.

5   Vale et tuis omnibus de more salutem dabis nec non ceteris claris et praedignis amicis et in primis regio praetori vestro. Ex Magnesia, xii Kalendas Maias mccccxlvi.

[*Enclosure:*]

6   Calliopes, Musarum clarissimae, ad beatum et seraphycum Franciscum oratio pro Francisci Drapperii, viri praeclari, salute et sui suorumque perpetua felicitate, apud Lydam Magnesiam ad xvii Kalendas Maiarum, Venereum Sanctum et venerandum humanati Iovis Redemptoris nostri supplicio diem, Kyriaco Anconitano amicissimo suo curante atque magna cum caritate intercedente:

7   Qual sancto in terra mai, qual seraphino
del vulnerato pecto, palme et piante
del nostro Redemptor[e] fu meditante,
quanto in sul terren[o] latino?
    Tu, d'umiltate exemplo et don[o] divino,
ornasti il mondo et di tante opre sancte,
che 'n parte et quasi il più del mondo errante
dal tuo stil si dirizza al buon[o] chamino.
    Degnati adunque ornar[e] della tua gratia
Francesco, tuo fedel, delli Drapperi,
pregio et honor de' merchanti di Latia;
    et che or sia accepto et visto volentieri
dal grande re de Lydia, Phrygia et Thratia,
sì ch' el mandi ad effetto i buon[i] pensieri.
ΧΑΙΡΕ ΧΡΗΣΤΕ ΦΡΑΓΚΙΣΚΕ

satraps also showed him many other signs of extraordinary good will. I was glad to see all this, both for his sake and for yours, because I felt that this was very profitable, not only for him personally, but for your republic as well.

Farewell, and greet all your peoples as usual as well as our other 5 illustrious and worthy friends, and especially your royal *podestà*. From Magnesia, the 20th of April, 1446.

[Enclosure:]

The prayer of Calliope, most distinguished of the Muses, to the 6 blessed seraphic Francis for the safety of the eminent Franzesco di Drapieri and for his and his family's lasting good fortune. Done at Magnesia in Lydia on the 15th of April, Holy Friday, the day revered for the suffering of our Redeemer, the incarnate Jove, Cyriac of Ancona, his close friend, acting, with great affection, as editor and intermediary:

> What saint on Earth, what Seraph, 7
> the wounded breast, palms and feet
> of our Redeemer contemplated in meditation,
> as did Francis, on Latin soil?
>   You, both example and divine gift, with your humility
> and with your many saintly deeds embellished the world,
> so that the greater part of erring humanity
> through your example directs itself along the right path.
>   Deign, therefore, to adorn with your grace
> your faithful servant, Franzesco delli Drapperi,
> pride and honor of the merchants of Latium;
>   and deign that he may now be held dear and welcomed
> by the great king of Lydia, Phrygia and Thracia
> so that he puts into effect your fine thoughts.
>   Farewell, good one, Franzesco!

1   Viro praestantissimo Andreolo Iustiniano amico concordi et honorifico suo.

2   Scripsi beatitudini tuae ex Lydia, iocundissime vir, et tuis quibusque suavissimis litteris, quoad licuit, responsum dedi. Exinde
cum ad III Nonas Maias Theucrorum princeps Threiciam Ha-
drianupolim repetens ex Magnesia recessisset, per triduum Franciscus noster ad Pergamon usque et Phrygiam Agiasmatem honorifice comitatus est et denique, nonnullis cum eo rebus exactis,
hodie V Idus Maii Phocas iterum revisimus, ubi paucos per dies
expeditis rebus ad Thraciam iter nostrum maturare curabimus,
optimo iuvante Iove.

3   Ipse vero Theucer et magnus Theucrum dux a quatuor hominum milibus comitatus, ut a Cyalabi filio magnopere accitus,
suum ad Thraciam iter haud segniter agit. Equidem vero ab eo ad
meum undique sua quaeque per loca iter tutandum litteras plenas
habui, nostro ipso amicissimo Francisco curante, quas potissimum
ut nostri desiderio magno desiderabam. Et illius ergo optimam
Francisci societatem delegi et tantum superavimus iter et Her-
meum et ceteros tranavimus amnes.

4   Praeterea cum Phocas adventaremus, ex litteris nati tui dilectissimi Nicolai percepimus te Chyeis saluberrimis thermis contulisse,
ubi postquam sancto flumine ablueris, haud equidem dubito te
tuam instaurare, conservare atque feliciter augere optimam valitudinem, optima iuvante Doto Clothoque et Panopea nec non Nereydum nympharum omnium pulcherrima Cymodocea.

: 37 :

To Andreolo, 11 May [1446], Foglia Nuova

To the distinguished Andreolo Giustiniani, my agreeable and hon-   1
orable friend.

I wrote to your excellency from Lydia, delightful friend, and re-   2
plied as well as I could to each of your most welcome letters.¹ After that, when, on the 5th of May, the leader of the Turks departed from Magnesia on his way to Thracian Adrianople, our
Franzesco had the honor of accompanying him for three days as
far as Pergamon and Phrygian Ayasmend.² Finally, after transacting some business with him, we returned today, the 11th of May, to
Foglia, where after finishing our business here, we shall make sure
to hasten our journey to Thrace, with the help of goodly Jove.

The Turk himself and great leader of the Turks, accompanied   3
by four thousand men, is on a vigorous march to Thrace as
though summoned urgently by his son Çelebi.³ But I, for my part,
did receive from him, thanks to the good offices of our very dear
friend Franzesco, a written plenary authorization to insure my safe
travel everywhere in every one of his territories. This was the principal object of my profound desire and it was for this that I chose
the excellent company of Franzesco and completed a journey of
such magnitude that involved our crossing the Hermus and other
rivers.

On another topic, when we arrived in Foglia, we learned from a   4
letter of your beloved son Niccolò that you have gone to the
healthful Chian baths, where I am sure that, having now bathed in
the sacred waters, you are restoring, preserving, and improving
your excellent good health with the assistance of Doto, Clotho,
Panopea, and Cymodocea, the most beautiful of all the Nereid
nymphs.

5   Χαῖρε καὶ ἔρρωσω, ἀνδρῶν κύδιστε, Andreole. Ex novo
Phocarum emporio, eo quo ad ipsum venimus V Iduum Maii,
fausto et genii nostri Mercurii felicissimo die.

6   Quae mihi Nicolaus ipse vester dilectus nostra de patria scripsit ex
Landino percepta lubenter vidi et meliora omnia successura speramus, ad quae Anconitanae rei numina faveant et aspirent.

7   Insuper Stephanus, Phocarum scriba tibi semper deditissimus,
suis se verbis saepe numero per commissum facit. Et ut eum Francisco quandoque tuis litteris saepius memorem et per commissum
facies optat. Et facere velis equidem ego sui gratia rogo.

8   Vale et vale. Vale atque iterum vale diu felix.

: 38 :

1   Francisco Drapperio viro claro, Kiriacus Anconitanus salutem dicit et hilaritatem.

2   Cum ad XVIII Kalendas Septembres, faustum et serenum luciferae Dianae diem, qui hodie Augustalis Caesarei mensis in medio
beatae et Dei parentis Mariae Virginis almae ad coelum ascensione clarus tua hac praeclara in colonia Bizantiana Pera ad sacram
seraphici Francisci aedem tam divinarum quam humanarum plurigenum rerum pompa fuerat solemniter celebratus, et primum regia
ipsa in urbe Constantinopolitana ad insigne illud almae Sapientiae
delubrum, Gregorio optumo celebrante patriarcha, solemnibus visis, et inde perenteream per cymbam Peram ipsam coloniam ad

Hail and farewell, noblest of men, Andreolo. From the new 5
mart of Foglia on the day of our arrival, the 11th of May, the favorable and most fortunate day of our patron Mercury.[4]

[*Postscript:*] I read with pleasure what your beloved Niccolò wrote 6
to me about my native city, [news] received from Landino, and I
hope that everything will turn out for the better. May the gods of
the Anconitan state favor and inspire this outcome.

Another thing. Stefano, the secretary of Foglia, always greatly 7
devoted to you, often places himself by what he says completely in
your trust; and he hopes that rather often from time to time in
your letters you will remind Franzesco of him and of his trust. I,
too, ask you, please, to do this for his sake.

Farewell and fare well. Farewell and again fare well. May you be 8
lastingly happy.

: 38 :

To Franzesco di Drapieri, 15 August [1446], Galata/Pera

Cyriac of Ancona wishes health and happiness to the illustrious 1
Franzesco di Drapieri.

On the 15th of August, the lucky, bright day of the light-bearer, 2
Diana,[1] the middle of the month of Augustus Caesar, a day
marked by the Assumption into heaven of the blessed mother of
God, the Virgin Mary, a day solemnized at the sacred church
of the seraphic Francis in this famous colony of Byzantine Pera
with many different sorts of religious and civil celebrations, I first
witnessed the solemn ceremonies in the distinguished church of
bountiful Wisdom in the royal city of Constantinople, presided
over by his excellency, the patriarch Gregory; then I took a ferry-
boat across to the colony of Pera itself, for the great spectacle.

tantum me spectaculum contulissem, primum praeclaras inter Ga-
latheas illas celebres et auricomas nymphas decoram illam tuam
et dilectissimam natam, Helisabet Mariam, auro et caelico colore
clamide insignem vidimus feliciter incedentem, 'qualis' olim diva
Diana 'in Eurotae ripis ⟨aut⟩ per iuga Cinthi' suos exercere 'choros'
splendidissima conspectabatur, quamque

> mille secutae
> hinc atque hinc glomerantur Oreades; illa pharetram
> fert humero gradiensque deas supereminet omnes.

3   Quam ob rem dignissima tua de hac excolendissima filia tam de
te digna claro optumoque parente et tam dignis abs te nuper do-
nata muneribus et quaeque clariora sua merita diligentius cogi-
tans, cum et eam propinquius hodie suos inter necessarios et
consanguineos nobiles et affines in laribus Iacobi Umbriaci honesto in συμποσίῳ venusta hilaritate loquentem mihique dignissime respondentem audissem, felicem denique atque perbeatum
dixi iuvenem illum nobilem et generosum, Thomam Spinolam,
quem tantae iuvenis coniugio di compotem et fortunatissimum fecerant. Nam et generosos non modo et praeclarissimos cives, quin
et principes magnos et potentissimum Asiae regnatorem tam clarum exoptasse connubium late percepimus.

4   Opto etenim eam ingenuo suo cum coniuge et tecumque diu
optimo cum parente bene atque felicissimam valere.

First, among those distinguished and celebrated golden-haired nymphs of Galata, I beheld your lovely daughter, Elisabetta Maria, whom you love dearly. I saw her striding happily, conspicuous in gold and a cloak the color of the heavens, just as once the goddess Diana was seen gloriously leading her band "on the banks of Eurotas [or] over the ridge of Cynthus,"

> followed by a thousand
> Oreades grouped here and there; Diana carried a quiver
> on her shoulder and as she walked was taller than the other
> goddesses.[2]

In particular, regarding this most worthy, highly cultivated 3 daughter of yours, so deserving of you, her distinguished and excellent father, and recently endowed by you with such fitting gifts, I thought harder about each of her brilliant qualities; and when, closer at hand today, at a respectable symposium, I heard her speaking with gracious joy and replying to me most becomingly among her friends and noble relatives and in-laws at the house of Iacopo Umbriaci, I declared that the noble and high-born youth, Tomasso Spinola, was indeed fortunate and blessed because the gods had made him the lucky possessor in marriage of such a fine young woman. For I was aware that not only noble and distinguished citizens, but even great princes and the most powerful ruler of Asia favored such a brilliant marriage.

I wish that she, together with her noble husband, and you, her 4 best of fathers, may long enjoy the best of health.

: 39 :

1 Balthasari Maruffo, Genuensi viro praestanti atque Galataeae Bizantianae Perae aequissimo et honorifico praetori, Kyriacus Anconitanus salutem plurimam dicit.

2   Quom et a teneris annis summus ille mihi visendi orbis amor innatus esset, praetor clarissime Balthasare, et inclitae huius coloniae vestrae nomen, undique iam terris deditum, magna cum laude vestrae praeclarae gentis egregie celebratum intelligerem, eam ipsam non modo diligere, quin et amare perpetuo coram et videre ac nostro utique de more litteris ornare et egregia eius ornamenta undique celebrare constitui.

3   Atque cum eam primum Anconitana navi devectus adissem situmque optimum suum et incomparabilem inspectare coepissem, summe laudandum admirandumque censebam eximium illud vestratum civium ingenium et providentiam atque animi magnitudinem, quod et illius tam magnae et imperiosae urbis in conspectu, non plus fere stadii disiuncta intercapedine freti, suam tam praeclaram condere coloniam providentissime ea in parte delegisset, qua olim qui totum orbem imperitabant, magni et sapientissimi Romani cives, Flavio Constantino principe, Itala et antiqua Romana inclyta illa sua magna et ornatissima urbe posthabita, Threicio demum in Bosphoro, Byzantiis moenibus ampliatis, suam et orbis imperi sedem imponere delegere et eam civitatem insignem, antiquo antiquato nomine, eorum antiquae urbis principisque nominibus insigniri dignati sunt, simulque Romam Novam Constantinopolimque dixere.

: 39 :

To Baldassarre Maruffo, after 21 August 1446, ?Galata/Pera

To Baldassarre Maruffo, eminent Genoese, and just and honorable   1
podestà of Pera at Byzantium, Cyriac of Ancona sends his best
wishes.[1]

Since from my earliest years I have experienced an inordinate,   2
inborn craving to see the world, illustrious *podestà* Baldassarre, and
I realized that the name of your famous colony, which one hears
everywhere, to the great praise of your distinguished people, is un-
commonly renowned, I determined, not only to value it highly, but
also to love it constantly, to see it in person, and to enhance it in
my usual way, in writing, and to celebrate everywhere its extraordinary adornments.

When I first arrived there aboard an Anconitan ship and began   3
to study its incomparably fine location, I thought your fellow citizens worthy of the highest praise and admiration for their extraordinary cleverness, foresight, and vision in choosing, very providen-
tially, to build their distinguished colony within sight of such a
great and dominant city, a distance of roughly no more than a
stade across the channel, in that location where once, in the time
of Emperor Flavius Constantine, the great and very wise citizens
of Rome, who ruled the whole world, treating as less important
that ancient, famous, great, and magnificent city of Rome, chose
at length to locate the seat of their empire—and that of the
world—on the Thracian Bosporus, extending the walls of Byzantium; and, because they thought this important city should be distinguished by the names of both their former city and their emperor, they discarded the outmoded name of Byzantium and
called it both "New Rome" and "Constantinople."

4   Ast enim vero deinde vestri optumi patres Genuenses, magna-
nimi et providentissimi cives, ad suam iisdem in partibus navigationem tam egregii situs comoditatem existimantes, dum et temporis oportunitatem cognoverant, octingentos ferme post annos,
eadem ipsa in parte caute et ingenti aere ab Andronico imperatore
solo mercato, suam hanc praeclaram et ornatam coloniam posuere.
Quam illico cum et primum Bosporeae Nereides nymphae cons-
pexissent et tam oportuna navigationi sua undique litora exornari
cognovissent, gratularier invicem erectis e gurgite capitibus insurgere, dignas deinde Genuensium laudes cecinere, et magna hilaritate Nereidum illa cana et praeclara Galathea statim suo de divo
nomine Galateam coloniam appellavit. Et mox ut una simul regia
cum urbe magna ut et gemino et ipsa nomine exornaretur, dum
saepius regii cives Galateam Galateique regia litora frequentius pe-
rentereas per cymbas, ut et nunc faciunt, transfretare consuevissent,[1] Graeco quotidie vocabulo Πέραν[2] Galateam ipsam coloniam vocitarunt.

5   Quam et ego cum pluries nostris Anconitanis navibus atque
vestris tam mercaturae causa quam et visendi orbis studio revisissem, in dies eam clariorem et conspicuis ornamentis auctam io-
cunda cum animi alacritate conspexi. Etenim exacto iam anno, Boruele Grimaldo praetore, arduo quoque Teucrum expugnationis
tempore, turrim pro moenibus Michaeli archangelo patrono
conditam atque dicatam vidimus. Et itaque cum nuper et exactis
Idibus Iunii te, virum, Maruffa, egregia de gente praeclarum, praeclaram ipsam coloniam praetoria potestate curantem invenissem[3]
tua potissimum cura atque diligentia, maritima parte a navistatio
ad[4] Christeam usque turrim moenibus ampliatis et priscae altitu-

But then, some eight hundred years later,[2] your excellent 4
Genoese ancestors, citizens of great vision and foresight, judging
that this remarkable site was perfectly suited to their shipping in
this region, recognized the opportune moment in time and, cau-
tiously and at great expense, bought land in this very location
from the emperor Andronicus and founded this distinguished and
beautiful colony of theirs. As soon as the Nereid nymphs of the
Bosporus saw it and recognized that their shore, so favorably sited
for shipping, was everywhere being readied, they raised their
heads upright from the waters to congratulate each other and then
sang a fitting eulogy of the Genoese; and with great joy the foam-
capped, bright daughter of Nereus, Galatea, immediately called
the colony Galata, after her divine name. And soon, that she
might be graced with a second name just as the great royal city is,
because the royal citizens were in the habit of crossing rather frequently to Galata, and those of Galata to the royal shores, by
means of ferries [*perentereae cymbae*] to the other side, as they do
today, they began referring to their colony of Galata in everyday
parlance as "Pera."

On my frequent return visits to Galata aboard our Anconitan 5
and your [Genoese] ships, both on business and out of a craving
to go and look at the world, I have watched her with joyful, enthusiastic attention as she has grown day by day in fame and striking ornamentation. For instance, just a year ago, when Boruele
Grimaldi was *podestà*, in the difficult time of the Turkish siege,[3] we
saw a tower under the patronage of the archangel Michael had
been erected and dedicated to bolster the fortification walls. And
in the same vein, when recently, on the 14th of June, I found that
you, Maruffo, the distinguished scion of a prominent family, are
looking after this distinguished colony in the office of *podestà* with
particular concern and industry, I notice that, through your
efforts, by extending the sea wall from the harbor to the Tower of

dinis duplo collatis, in dies tutiorem eam per vos amplioremque et
pulchriorem attollere video.

6   Quam equidem ob rem dignam, ut vestrae rei verus et perennis
amator, honoris[5] et memoriae gratia, μνείας ἤγουν καὶ φιλοτιμίας χάριν hisdem moenibus in marmore breve hoc Latinis
quoque litteris atque Graecis epigrama[6] componendum edidimus:

ΑΓΑΘΗΙ ΤΥΧΗΙ | BALTASARI B. F. MARVFO
GALATEAE | HVIVS BIZANTIANAE PERAE
THREICIO | IN BOSPHORO CL. GENVENSIVM
COLO|NIAE B. M. PRAETORI | QVI MAGISTRATVM
QVEM SVSCEPERAT | DIGNE GERENDO
SVBVRBANIS MARITIMA | HAC IN PARTE
MOENIBVS AMPLIATIS ET AD | CHRISTEAM
TVRRIM ANAVISTATIO PRISCAE | ALTITVDINIS
DVPLO COLLATIS COL. IPSAM | TVTIOREM
EXIMIEQVE PROPAGATAM EXOR|NATAMQ. FORE
CVRAVIT | GENVENSES AC SVBVRBANI |
GALATEI CIVES COLONIQ. | DEDERE.[7]

7   At enimvero praeterea ut et periocunda et alacriora aliqua
huiusce conspicuae coloniae vestrae ornamenta pertingam, nuper-
rime quippe ad XVIII Kalendarum Septembrium, faustum sere-
numque castae et luciferae Dianae diem, qui hodie Augustalis
Caesarei mensis in medio beatae et Dei parentis Mariae Virginis
almae ad caelum ascensione clarus et tua hac ipsa in colonia, te peritissimo curante praetore, ad sacram seraphici Francisci aedem
tam divinarum quam et humanarum plurigenum rerum pompa
fuerat solemniter celebratus, antea equidem regia illa in urbe
Constantinopoli ad insigne illud almae Sapientiae Dei templum,
Gregorio optimo celebrante patriarcha, sacris solemnibus visis,
cum me deinde Peram perenteream per cymbam ad tantum conspectare spectaculum contulissem, primum praeclaras inter Gala-
teas illas celebres auricomas nymphas decoram illam speciosam et

Christ and bringing it to double its original height, you are raising
the city daily to greater safety, size and beauty.

For this worthy achievement, to honor and memorialize it,[4] I,   6
for my part, as a true and constant admirer of your enterprise,
have composed this brief inscription in Latin and Greek to be [in-
scribed] on marble.[and] attached to these very walls.

> Good luck. To Baldassarre Maruffo, son of Baldassarre, well-
> deserving *podestà* of this illustrious Genoese colony, Galata/
> Pera at Byzantium on the Thracian Bosporus, who by carry-
> ing out worthily the magistracy that he had taken up by ex-
> tending the sea walls close to the city along the sea at this
> point and by doubling their original height from the harbor
> to the Tower of Christ, saw to it that the colony itself should
> be safer, considerably enlarged and adorned, the Genoese
> and the citizens and colonists of Galata who live in the out-
> skirts of the city dedicated [this].

But to touch on some joyful, more lively features of this re-   7
markable colony of yours, quite recently, the 15th of August, the
chaste light-bearer Diana's favorable, clear day, the mid-point of
Augustus Caesar's month, made bright in our time by the Assumption into heaven of the blessed mother of God, the Virgin
Mary, was celebrated solemnly in this very colony of yours under
your expert supervision as *podestà*, at the church of the seraphic
St. Francis with numerous religious and civil celebrations. For
my part, I witnessed the solemn ceremonies at the distinguished
church of the bountiful Wisdom of God in the royal city of Con-   [PLATE III]
stantinople, presided over by the eminent patriarch Gregory, before then taking the ferry to Pera to behold that great celebration.
First of all, among the distinguished, celebrated golden-haired
nymphs of Galata I saw the comely, beautiful, beloved daughter of

perdilectam Francisci Drapperii agoranomi per Thraciam atque
Asiam praeclarissimi natam, Isabeth Mariam, auro et caelico colore clamide insignem vidimus incedentem, qualis olim diva illa
pharetrigera Diana sive in Eurotae Laconicis virentibus ripis aut
Ortygia per iuga Cynthi suos exercere choros splendidissima conspectabatur.

8   Verum et cum eadem die propinquius eam suos inter necessarios consanguineosque nobiles et affines in laribus Iacobi Umbriaci
paternis ambroseis ipsis et aureis indutam muneribus honesto in
symposio venusta hilaritate loquentem mihique dignissime respondentem audissem, felicem denique et perbeatum dixi iuvenem illum nobilem et generosum, Thomam Spinolam, quem tantae iuvenis connubio Deus compotem et fortunatissimum fecerat. Nam
et generosos non modo et praeclarissimos cives, quin et principes
quoque magnos et potentissimum Asiae regnatorem tam dignum
exoptasse coniugium sane percepimus.

9   Atqui deinde cum ad XII Kalendas Septembres felicem Kyriaceumque diem ad sublimem coloniae huius arcem conscenderem,
ad perlautam Benedicti Salvatici domum convivas inter nobiles
et egregios utique cives et colonos matronasque simul et nuptas
atque innuptas puellas, Hieronimo Franco iuvene lepidissimo ducente, perveni; ubi dum tanto in coetu harum iuvenum eximiam
naturae formam et splendorem ornatus admirans, illico e caelo de-
lapsas video tris e Pieridum choro divas et praeclarissimas nymphas, quae cum se statim coetui lucido fulgore nitentes inmiscuis-
sent, quaeque suam e coetu delegere puellam et divae divina sua et
mirifica arte humana puellarum forma habituque induere, sed nomen suaeque divinitatis splendorem nitentibus oculis oreque roseo
detexere.

10   Et primum Polymnia in Lysabellam Selvaticam viduam hones-
tam pudicam atque venustissimam versa, caeruleo induta paluda-

Franzesco di Drapieri, the elegant market inspector for Thrace and Asia, Elisabetta Maria, conspicuous in gold and a cloak the color of the sky, walking just as once the chaste, quiver-bearing goddess Diana was seen gloriously leading her band on the verdant, Spartan banks of Eurotas or over the Ortygian ridge of Cynthus.[5]

When on the same day, closer at hand, I heard her among her friends, well-born relatives and in-laws at the house of Iacopo Umbriaci, clothed in her father's divine, golden gifts, speaking with gracious joy during a decent drinking party and replying to me most becomingly, I pronounced that noble, high-born youth Tomasso Spinola indeed fortunate and most blessed, whom God had made the extremely lucky husband of such a fine young lady. For I was aware that not only noble and very distinguished citizens, but also great princes and the most powerful ruler of Asia had in fact longed for so suitable a union.

But then, on the 21st of August, a fortunate Lord's Day, when, guided by Gerolimo Franchi, a charming youth, I climbed up to the lofty summit of this colony, I arrived among noble fellow-guests, especially eminent citizens, and colonists and their wives, as well as their married and unmarried daughters, at the elegant house of Benedetto Selvatico. There, while I was marveling at the extraordinary physical beauty and splendid attire of the young women in this grand assemblage, suddenly I saw descending from heaven three divine, radiant nymphs of the band of the Pierides, who, when they had mingled with the crowd, shining with a bright effulgence, each chose one maiden from the group and, through her marvelously divine skill, put on the girls' human appearance and dress. But their shining eyes and rosy lips betrayed their identity and their dazzling divinity.

First Poly[hy]mnia, who had changed into Lisabella Selvatico, an upright, modest, and most charming widow dressed in a dark-blue cloak and wearing a snowy-white veil on her head, began with

8

9

10

mento et a capite niveo amicta velamine, mihi iam sui fulgoris at-
tonito talia speciosissimo ab ore coepit: 'Kyriace, quem certe
παλαιόφιλον Dorica lingua antiqua in Latio civitas Genuensibus
amicissima genuit Ancona, et qui tam avide res inclytas generosissimae Genuae gentis meditare velis et tanto studio novam hanc ab
his paulo ante conditam Galateam coloniam laudare exornareque
conaris, aspice iamque inclitam illam nobiles intra veteres nobilium et antiquarum rerum imagines insigne atque praeclarum
agalma.

11   'Italam illam Ligustico in litore nobilem imperiosamque urbem
Genuam vides, quae posteaquam magnam illam in Latio atque rerum maximam urbem Romam senio iam confectam foreque deletam cognoverat, ut eius eximia facta, quoad licuerat, imitari velle
videretur; quanta in Latio et extra per Lybiam atque undique fere
per orbem terra marique et ingenti potissimum atque innumera
classe gesserit, reticeam quidem ego et sua ipsa suis de rebus lo-
quantur annalia. Civitatis vero originis primaevae fama est obscu-
rior annis, verum et noviora retexere minus oportunum video.

12   'Sed quia te colonias pertentasse novimus et Galateam nostram
hanc perbelle quidem dictis atque litteris exornasti, dicamne de
illa equidem gelido sub axe Capha, quam ad Chimerinum alium
Bosphorum Maeotidem prope paludem barbaras inter et ferocissi-
mas gentes Taurica in Chersoneso magna populosaque et opulen-
tissima magnanimiter ab his condita insigni colonia ac ea in parte
nobile illud Sultanei nominis oppidum portuosumque Cymba-
leum arduum et inexpugnabile ripis?

13   'Quid de Pamphylea nobilissima Amiso dicam, Amazonum
olim antiquissima urbe et Mithrydatis potentissimi regis regia,

attractive voice to speak to me, spellbound as I was by her radiance: "Cyriac, to whom Ancona, that ancient city in Latium, a city most friendly to the Genoese, surely gave birth as a *palaiophilon*,[6] to use the Doric language, you desire eagerly to reflect on the glorious achievements of the most noble people of Genoa and you seek to praise and honor with great enthusiasm this new colony of Galata, founded by them [only] a little while ago. Behold her already famous, a distinguished and brilliant image among the celebrated old representations of noble, ancient cities.[7]

"You see that famed, masterful Italian city of Genoa on the 11 Ligurian coast, which, after she realized that Rome, although a great Latin city, the greatest in the world, was already in its dotage and about to perish, was clearly determined to imitate as far as possible Rome's extraordinary accomplishments. Let me be silent about Genoa's great achievements in Latium and beyond — in Libya and almost everywhere else in the world, on land and sea, above all with her huge fleet of countless ships, and let her very annals speak out about her deeds. The traditions about the city's earliest origins are somewhat obscured by the passage of time, and I feel that now is not the opportune moment to recount her more recent history.

"But, since I know that you explored Genoa's colonies and have 12 adorned this our Galata beautifully in your speeches and your writing, might not I, for my part, speak about Kaffa under its cold sky, close by the other, Cimmerian, Bosporus, near Lake Maiotis, in the midst of fierce and barbarous people, on the Tauric Chersonese, a colony remarkable for the size of its population and its wealth, founded by these adventurous Genoese; and in that region, the famous town of Soldajal; and, rich in harbors, Cembalo, sitting high and impregnable on its cliffs?

"What shall I say about noble Pamphylian Amisos, once the 13 most ancient city of the Amazons and the royal seat of mighty King Mithridates, continuing in existence, of course, as your dis-

vestra utique praeclara in colonia deducta? Memoremne deinde regiam illam Cypriam Amacostam ob iniuriam ab rege Cyprio in-
digne sibi illatam dignissime vindicandam, perstrenue armis suae
utique dicioni subactam? Praetereo Ponticam illam praeclaram et
ornatissimam Amastron, nostrorum quoque Caesarum principum
adhuc insigne monumentum, atque propinquiorem in Aegaeo no-
tam et olim super alias insulas potentissimam Lesbon eiusque metropolim nobilem Mytilenem, egregium Gatalusiae gentis decus
Phocensiumque olim tam nobilium Graecorum emporia oppidaque barbaras inter gentes, vetustum scilicet atque novum; ac
Thracia in parte Aenon antiquam Threiciamque Samon et Pariam
utique nobilem et manduliferam Thason.[8]

14   'Sed et quisnam praeteriret insulam Ionicam illam praeclaram
et opum adhuc ditissimam clarissimorumque civium et colonum
ornatissimam Chion, quae et masticum feracitate singulari Iovis et
omniparentis naturae dono et Homeri utique tam excellentissimi
vatis tumulo ceteras antecellere insulas Ionicas et Aegaeas et antiquis ab[9] auctoribus memoriae commendatum et vobis utique manifestum et exploratissimum est καὶ ἐκφανέστατον πάντῃ?'

15   Et haec ubi dicta ⟨dedit⟩, cum illico Urania surgens nutu sibi si-
lentium imposuisset, Moysettae Cataniae iuvenis modestissimae
vultum habitumque gerens, cana ipsa induta Fide et religiosissima
Vesta, vestibus emicuit albis Sydonioque labore perlautis et continuo diva divo et ambroseo ab ore subdiderat: 'Brevia quam paucis,
Polymnia soror, antiqua de Genuensium magnitudine pertentare
maluisti, verum et longum esset hoc loco recensere fortia atque inclyta patrum facta et longissimam rerum seriem tot per viros duc-
tam et ab antiquae gentis origine. Ast enim vero multa sua ipsa

tinguished colony? Should I recall next that royal Cypriote city of Famagusta, compelled by force of arms to submit to their [Genoese] authority in greatly justified revenge for the wrong unjustly inflicted on them by the King of Cyprus? I pass over Amastris on the Black Sea, splendid and richly adorned, still a noteworthy remnant of our princes, the Caesars; and closer by in the Aegean, famous Lesbos, once supreme over other islands; and her celebrated capital, Mytilene, outstanding glory of the Gattilusio family; and the trading marts of the once famed Phocaeans, such noble Greeks, and [now] towns, both an old one and a new one, in the midst of a barbarian folk; and ancient Ainos in the Thracian region; and Thracian Samos; and Paros' colony, famed almond-bearing Thasos.[8]

"But who would pass over that distinguished Ionic island, 14 Chios, still very rich in resources and richly graced with most illustrious citizens and colonists, which excels the other Ionic and Aegean islands in the abundance of the mastic it produces, an extraordinary gift of Jove and of Nature, the parent of all things, and also because of the tomb of the greatest of poets, Homer, both as recorded by ancient authors and as made manifest and thoroughly investigated and made absolutely clear to you in every way?"

When she had finished speaking, Urania rose immediately and 15 imposed silence with a nod. She looked and dressed like the deeply modest maiden Moisetta Catania. Cloaked in age-old Honor and most sacred Vesta, she was radiant in her luxurious white garments, splendid products of the Sidonian skill. Immediately the goddess subjoined with her divine, immortal voice: "My sister, Polyhymnia, how briefly you chose to touch on Genoa's ancient greatness; yet it would take too long to survey here the brave and glorious deeds of their ancestors and the very long succession of achievements led by so many men from the beginning of this ancient people. Indeed, many weapons are seen in their distinguished city on the doors of their churches; and captured chariots

praeclara in urbe sacrarum *in* aedium postibus arma videntur captivique pendent currus et portarum ingentia claustra, spicula hastaeque et clipei nec non innumera a barbaris erepta carinis rostra.

16 'Sed quid? Ut antiquiora praeteream, memorem splendidissimum illum atque nobilissimum pretiosissimo[10] de smaragdo cratera, quem olim et plus terna et XL annorum centena, cum e Syria Caesarea ex urbe victores[11] alia inter gaza cepissent, pro insigni quodam et mirifico suae civitatis spectaculo veluti religione sacrum in sacris praedigne magna cum veneratione cultuque omne per aevum servandum colendumque decrevere et itaque quot annis annua pro et panegyrica solemnitate populis affluentibus manifestum ostentant, quemque et ipsum hunc amicissimum Anconitanum nostrum bissenis iam annis exactis, alia inter eximia Genuensium ornamenta, Filippo Insubro intercedente duce nec non Francisco Spinola et Benedicto Nigrono et Iohanne Grillo nobilibus et egregiis curantibus amicis civibus singulari civitatis gratia extra ordinem conspexisse suisque per Ligustiam comentariis quam grate adiecisse cognovimus?

17 'Multaque praeterea iidem optumi Genuenses viri sacra inter relicta mundo monumenta divum, eorum virtute patrum undique per orbem quaesita, sua eadem in urbe praeclara magna cum diligentia servant veneranturque et religiosissime colunt, sed inter potiora pretiosioraque magni illius Baptistae divi prodromi praecursorisve salutis humanae Iohannis totius corporis almi sacrum praeter caput, quod urbs Romana colit,[12] sacrosanctissimum cinerem, cuius divinae et excolendae praesentiae mira et inexplicabilis virtus praeclara alia inter prodigia suo saepius amplo et opulentissimo in portu Neptuni Aeolique pernitiosam et formidabilem procellarum et tempestatum vim impetumque sedarat.

18 'Nimirum quod ad suae religionis almae et eximiae dignitatis cumulum accedit et hac in parte digne commemorandum et per-

are suspended, and the huge bolts of gates, javelins and spears and shields, as well as numerous beaks torn from the ships of the barbarians.

"But what about this? To pass over older items, let me recall 16 that magnificent, famous bowl of very precious green stone that the victorious Genoese carried off more than 340 years ago among other spoils from the city of Caesarea in Syria and decided it should be preserved with great veneration and reverence for all time, almost as if it were a cult object, their city's extraordinary marvel, to put on display; and so every year, they expose it to the thronging public at an annual solemn festival of praise. We know that twelve years ago this very close friend of ours from Ancona saw it among the extraordinary treasures of the Genoese — outside the usual time, an exceptional favor bestowed by the city through the intervention of Filippo, the Duke of Milan, and with the help of Francesco Spinola, Benedetto Nigrone, and Giovanni Grillo, his noble and eminent friends; and he was pleased to make a note of it in his Ligurian travel diary.

"In addition, there are many objects among the sacred relics of 17 the saints left to humanity and sought out everywhere in the world by their valiant forebears that these same excellent Genoese preserve with great care, and venerate and cultivate most devoutly in that same illustrious city of theirs; but among the more important and more precious of these are the most holy remains of the great forerunner of mankind's salvation, St. John the Baptist — the entire life-giving body except for the sacred head, which the city of Rome reveres. Among other marvels, the marvelous and mysteriously magnificent power of its godlike and worshipful presence in the large and prosperous port of Genoa has more than once calmed the destructive and fearful force and onslaught of the storms and tempests of Neptune and Aeolus.

"I thought, of course, that it would be fitting and quite appro- 18 priate to recall in this part [of my speech] something that puts the

bellissime nobis visum est, quod inter tot praeclaras et insignes
Italas urbes una haec Genua civitas maximi illius humanati Iovis
humanique generis piissimi Redemptoris divique sui et tropaeo-
phori martyris Georgii veneranda atque victricia et trophealia si-
gna terra marique gerenda colendaque delegerat; quorum optumis
auspiciis tot insignibus victoriis et marittimarum potissimum rerum gloria sui quoque praestantes et solertissimi cives[13] potiti
fuere tamque late per orbem magnae suae dicionis[14] imperium
propagavere.

19   'Videres deinde haud indignius, care palaeophile, quin potius
dicam vidistin Genuensium politicam illam modestiam et gravi-
tatem, moralitatem, solertiam, liberalitatem, diligentiam, curam
atque perspicacem et assiduam gerendarum rerum omnigenum[15]
vigilantiam? Sed et quisnam crederet politicam ipsam virtutem ni-
mia quadam et heroica civium ipsorum virtute et animi magnitudine lacessitam saepius esse minusque quiescere posse? Nam et
optumi plerique cives, sua ipsa de re publica bene meriti, regno se
haud indignos intelligentes, priorem non ferre possunt, nempe
animi praestantiores alii regnare vel ita cupidi, ut neque parem in
urbe quempiam videre queant. Verum et hoc potissimum dignum
admiratione existimandum puto, quod haec ipsa civium ambitio et
pernitiosa rei publicae pestis Romanam potentissimam urbem ad
ultimam sui calamitatem brevi deduxerat, haec vero Genua civitas
tam diu eodem morbo laborans insignes inter Italas civitates in
hunc usque diem praeclarissima manet.'

20   Et haec ubi[16] roseo fulgore coruscans, perinde ac indignata
vultu, paulo altiora cecinerat, in Helisabet Mariam conversa Caliope, Phoebeo afflata numine et e paterno Ioviali munere auro et
ambrosio caelesti colore clamide amicta, auritricum cum erigens

finishing touch on Genoa's fostering religiosity and extraordinary worth: the fact that, among so many distinguished and remarkable Italian cities, this state of Genoa alone chose the revered and victorious emblem of omnipotent Jove incarnate, most holy Redeemer of the human race, and of his trophy-bearing martyr, St. George, to honor and carry by land and by sea. It is under their excellent protection that her distinguished and highly skilled citizens have gained so many outstanding victories, especially the glory of their exploits at sea, and have expanded their grand imperial dominion so widely.

"Dear lover of antiquity, might you see, not unworthily — or 19 shall I say rather, have you seen — the political moderation and seriousness, moral purpose, skill, generosity, industry, carefulness and attentive and unremitting vigilance of the Genoese in conducting every kind of enterprise? But who would believe that this very political excellence has too often been challenged and could have its peace disturbed by an excessively heroic excellence and highmindedness on the part of the citizens themselves? For many of the best citizens, who deserved well of their country, realizing they are not unqualified to rule, cannot endure anyone being ahead of them; indeed, some persons of outstanding spirit are so desirous of ruling that they cannot tolerate even an equal in the city. But I think it should be deemed especially worthy of admiration that, while this very ambition of the citizens, this pestilence destructive of the state, brought the all-powerful city of Rome to its final destruction in a short time, this city of Genoa, on the other hand, so long afflicted by the same disease, remains until today the most distinguished among the significant cities of Italy."

When [Urania] flashing with a reddish gleam, with a look as 20 though of displeasure, had ended her song on a slightly higher pitch, Calliope, transformed into Elisabetta Maria, under the inspiration of Phoebus and clad in gold and in an immortal cloak the color of the sky, her father Jove's gift, raised her gold-tressed

caput, talia facundissimo ab ore coepit: 'Aliqua, diva et Olympia soror, de Genuensium probitate brevi intelligo pertentata spatio, sed plura vacare et nos labentia sydera repetentes *finem* vehementer *imponere* iubent. Pauca sed et ego nostra de hac Galatea colonia addere cogor, ne noster hic Anconites, errore fortasse aliquo deceptus, abierit et heu! quantum ab spe ceciderit! Intelligat et rei motus potissimam causam. Nam et primum e caelo vocem sibi dicentem audivimus, "heu! fuge Thracum ignaviam terrae, fuge litus avarum et cives, non Ienuenses adhuc sed degeneres, linque barbariem inter et plurigenem asperne colonos [...]."[17]

head and began the following eloquent speech: "Divine, Olympian sister, on the subject of Genoese honor, I realize that this subject has been explored to some extent in a brief space of time. But more remains to be said, though the setting stars bid us firmly to put an end to our recollections. Still, I am compelled to add a few remarks about this, our colony of Galata, lest perchance this Anconitan of ours leave here under a false impression. Alas, how great would be his disillusionment! Let him understand the most powerful cause that sets things in motion. For, first of all, I heard a voice from heaven saying to him, "Alas, flee the weakness of the Thracians' land. Flee this rapacious shore and its citizens, no longer Genoese, but degenerates, leave them behind, colonists in a barbarous, motley land [...]."

1 Andreolo Iustiniano, viro praeclarissimo et amico competundissimo suo, Kyriacus Anconitanus salutem plurimam dicit.

2   Cum ex Pontica navigatione Delphina trireme devectus et delphynum tumidi maris ornamento per Bosphorum iocundissimo comitante choro sexto Yduum Decembrium die regiam Bizantion remearemur et haud mora Peram Galateam, illam praeclaram vestratum coloniam, revisissem, primum et primarios inter omnes amicos ad Baltasarem Marufum, virum praestantem et praeteritum eiusdem coloniae praetorem honorificum, me quam avidissime contuli. Qui vir sane humanissimus ἀληθὲς καὶ φιλάνθρωπος quanta me hylaritate susceperit, hisce paucis non facile poterim explicare. At enim vero post dulces de more amplexus, ubi primum avido sibi nostro de praeclaro itinere quicquid dignum fuerit detexissem, et meum denique te visendi desiderium cognovisset, ac ille mihi se iam inde ceteam imperialem per puppim ad te et ad patriam remeaturum abitum adornarier alacriori vultu declarasset, me sibi, viro magno magna quoque navi et honorifica stipato cohorte vecturo, qua digne comitem addere cupiens, magna quippe invicem pro voluptate delegimus.

3   Et tandem cum ad claram beati et facundissimi Pauli diem, expectatis iamdiu Bosphoreas ad columnas Boreis aspirantibus validis, Hylarione nobili et solertissimo iubente navarcho, nautae felicia vela dedissent, non adhuc equidem integre nostris ex Bizantio

: 40 :

To Andreolo, 13 February [1447], Foglia Nuova

Cyriac of Ancona sends his best wishes to his distinguished and   1
highly qualified friend, Andreolo Giustiniani.

On the 8th of December we returned to royal Byzantium after   2
a voyage through the Black Sea aboard a galley of Delfino's and accompanied through the Bosporus by a joyous school of dolphins
that adorned the swelling sea. Without delay I revisited Galata
Pera, that distinguished colony of your compatriots, and eagerly
went to see, among all my principal friends, Baldassarre Maruffo,
an outstanding person and the former honorable *podestà* of the
same colony. With what joy this truly cultivated man received me
I could not easily describe in this short account. After our usual
pleasant embraces, I first satisfied his eager curiosity by telling him
what was noteworthy about our magnificent journey. Finally, when
he learned of my desire to visit you, and told me with a cheerful
expression that he was just then preparing his departure on an imperial cargo ship to return to you and to his native city, I desired
to join myself as a fitting companion to this great man who was
about to sail on a great and honorable ship with a considerable retinue, and with great pleasure we chose each other [as compan-
ions].

But when at length on the clear feast-day of the blessed and el-   3
oquent Paul,[1] after a long wait at the mouth of the Bosporus for
strongly blowing north winds, at the command of the noble and
skilled helmsman Hilarion, the sailors hoisted the lucky sails, my
business in Byzantium was not yet entirely finished, since I had to

rebus exactis, Strabonis nostri Graeco a librario excipiendi potissimum causa detentus, ad posteram denique diem, Pulseveriano intercedente navigio, postquam Propontiacum aequor, divo crebres-
cente Aeolo, superavimus, ad Hellespontiacham in Cheronneso
Challiepolim imperialem exoptatam illam eximiam et honorificam
navim anchora fundatam comperimus.

4   Sed validissimo turbante flatu, aestuantibus undis, dum ad eam
me non facile conferre quivissem, ad posterum et IIII Kalendas Fe-
bruariarum, faustum Kyriaceumque diem, ad veterem ipsam Challiepolim descendi, Luca Catanio amico suavissimo comitante nostro, et inibi ad litora primum Iacobos Pogium Catrinellumque,
vestrae nationis homines, ac Bartolomeum ex Ancone Foroflavi-
nianum, qui tum forte Calliepolitanis barbaris cum colonis nego-
tiabantur, nobis obviam occurrentes vidimus. Et cum post hones-
tos de more amplexus iuvenis ille noster nostra me de patria
nostrorumque salute certiorem fecisset, eo et Lodovico Farmacopolo Latio duce, ut aliquid ibidem e veneranda antiquissimi oppidi
vetustate ex me compertum videas et nostri quoque dignum, hoc
ad marmoream barbarae illius superstitionis aram Graecis quidem
litteris sed Latini nominis epygramma comperimus:

Ο ΔΗΜΟΣ | ΛΟΥΚΙΟΝ ΦΛΑΟΤΙΟΝ ΒΑΛΩΝΙ|ΟΝ
ΠΟΛΛΙΩΝΑ ΤΟΝ ΠΡΩΤΟΝ | ΤΗΣ ΠΟΛΕΩΣ
ΕΤΕΡΓΕΤΗΝ | ΠΑΤΡΙΔΟΣ ΔΙΑ ΒΙΟΤ ΚΑΙ ΠΟΛ|ΔΗΝ
ΚΑΙ ΜΕΓΑΛΩΝ ΑΓΑ|ΘΩΝ ΑΙΕΙ ΓΕΓΟΝΟΤΑ[1]

Videsne, optume Andreole, antiqua hac brevi inscriptione nota-
tum Latini nominis hominem, Lucium Flavium Pollionem, quondam a populo Calliepolitano ob eius erga patriam liberalitatem et
beneficentiam statua ex aere vel marmore honoris causa donatum?

5   Nunc equidem contra vidimus barbaros longo ordine praeda,
nostrae quoque religionis homines et potissimum Graia ex natione

wait, mainly to receive my copy of Strabo from the Greek scribe. The next day, finally, on a ship provided by Pulseveriano, we crossed the Propontic Sea, divine Aeolus growing strong, and found that excellent, honorable imperial ship, the object of our quest, which we desired [to catch up with], lying at anchor at Gallipoli on the European side of the Hellespont.

But since a strong wind was agitating the sea and causing heavy waves and I could not easily get to the ship, I disembarked at old Gallipoli itself on the next day, which was the 29th of January, the favorable day of the Lord,[2] in the company of our dear friend, Luca Catanio. There on the shore, the first persons we saw coming toward us were the two Iacopos, Poggio and Catrinelli, men of your nationality, and Bartolomeo Foroflaviniano of Ancona, who happened at that time to be conducting business with the barbarian settlers of Gallipoli. We embraced each other becomingly, as usual, and that youth [Foroflaviniano] brought me up to date on our native city and on the welfare of our friends. With the Latin Lodovico Farmacopolo as my guide, I found this inscription on a marble altar of the barbarian superstition, [which I include here] that you might see a sample of the venerable antiquities of this ancient town, something discovered by me and worthy of my efforts. Although written in Greek, it deals with a Latin name:

> The People [honor] Loukios Phlaouios Vallonios Pollion, the First of the City, benefactor for life of his country, and the source of many great good things

Do you observe, good Andreolo, that this brief ancient inscription designates a man with a Latin name, Lucius Flavius Pollio, who was given a statue of bronze or marble by the people of Gallipoli to honor him for his generosity and benefactions toward their native city?

Now by way of contrast we saw long lines of barbarians laden with booty and men of our own religion, too, and especially cap-

captivos miserandum in modum ferreis sub catenis ad eiusdem civitatis emporium atque litora per Hellespontum in Asiam transvecturos. Quorum et a miseris nonnullis pientissimo ab ore certius intelligimus Murath Begh, superbum Theucrorum principem, Peloponensiacum Isthmon, ingentibus admotis copiis, hostiliter Idibus Decembribus invasisse, turritis ibidem paulo ante moenibus a Constantino Spartano rege curiosissime restitutis armato tandem milite superatis et magna ex parte machinarum vi disiectis et solo convulsis, ac inde sparto milite regionem late populatum esse.

6   Quibus flebilibus auditis vocibus, scis, vir clarissime, quantum non aegre molesteve ferre non potui audire trucem et pernitiosum illum Christianae religionis hostem, quem hac tempestate vel vix anno peracto, nostratum armis religioso vel milite superatum fugatumque et penitus e Thracum Macedonumque regnis simul et tota vel e Graecia pulsum et tergiversatum in Asyam atque Lidiam putabamus, nunc vero ignava quadam nostratum incuria principum, nostris et Pannonum paulisper abmotis et retractis viribus, tantum eum fortuna elatum atque audentem fecisse ac sibi Peloponensiacum, tam nobile et olim potentissimum Graeciae regnum, invadere licuisse. Proh scelus et heu prisca nostrorum generosissimae gentis nobilitas! Nam et illatam huic genti miserabilem a barbaris cladem, tametsi Graecos in homines et poenas quodammodo dare merentes, non sine gravi tamen nostrae religionis iactura et magna Latini nominis indignitate tam lachrymalem Christicolum calamitatem existimandum puto.

7   Sed ut de hoc alias. Postquam urbem omnem iterum eodem Bartolomaeo comite revisere placuerat, eam plerisque auctam ornamentis vidimus: aedibus scilicet barbara superstitione sacris ac

tives from the Greek nation, miserable in their iron chains, in the market of the same city and on its shores, ready to be transported across the Hellespont to Asia. From the patriotic lips of some of these wretches we learned that Murad Beg, the proud prince of the Turks, had invaded the Isthmus of the Peloponnesus with a huge force on the 13th of December. The turreted walls, which had been restored with great care a short time ago by the Spartan king Constantine, had been surmounted by armed soldiery and had been knocked down for the most part and ripped from the ground by powerful machines; the Greek army had scattered and the area had been devastated.

You can imagine, illustrious sir, that when I heard their tearful   6
tale, I could not but take it ill to learn that that cruel and destructive enemy of the Christian religion, who just about this time last year, we thought, had been beaten by the arms of our devout soldiers and had been put to flight and utterly expelled from the realms of Thrace and Macedonia and out of all Greece and had had to turn back to Asia and Lydia, now, owing to the slothful neglect of our princes, and to the fact that our forces and those of the Hungarians were withdrawn and removed for a little while, has been made so exalted and daring by fortune and has been permitted by her to invade the Peloponnesus, such a noble and once powerful Grecian realm. What an enormity! Alas for the ancient nobility of our superior race! For I think that the pitiable disaster inflicted on this people by the barbarians — even if they are Greeks and in a sense deserve punishment — that this lamentable downfall of Christians must be thought of as a serious setback for our religion and a great humiliation of the Latin name.[3]

But of that on another occasion. Having agreed to visit the en-   7
tire city again with Bartolomeo as my companion, I saw that it had been improved with numerous [architectural] embellishments. I mean, of course, sacred buildings for the rites of the barbarous religious cult; and, in particular, numerous hot baths here

innumeris potissimum hinc inde per vicos balnearum thermis quam amplis et niveo crustatoque de marmore lautis negociariaque bexestanea scena, alta atque bisbina protecta testudine, ubi innumerae Persarum Phoenicumque Cydonum barbarumque omnigenum peregrinis opibus confertae cellae videntur, quae, si nondum pietas religiove aut gloriae cupiditas potuere, praeda demum avidi nostri militis mentem non denique vehementer acuisse mirabar.

8   Verum et his tandem omnibus inspectis, cum ad Kalendas Februarias ex ea tam barbara et opum referctissima urbe per cymbam Bartolomeo Nigro scriba Urbanoque Dernixio adolescente ingenuo comitatus imperialem insignem ipsam puppim conscendissem, magnificum praefectum patronumque nobilem sociosque magna cum animi iocunditate revisimus. Et illico, ut et mea magis compleretur voluptas, alios inter egregios eadem in praetoria navi navigantes novimus venerandum illum religione virum, Thoma Umbrum, et theologum ex Ugubia civitate clarum et Picenae nostrae vicinum provinciae, qui nuper et exactis diebus Praedicatorum ordinis per orientalem Europam atque Asyam vicarius bene merens religionis gratia ex Ponto et gelida Taurica colonia vestra Chapha ad pontificem in Urbem remeaturus adventaret; quo cum peritissimo viro pluria conserebamus verba vicissim honestissimis nostris periocunda curis.

9   At enim vero cum inde nostrum ad iter vela daremus, Tenedon prope venimus cadente Phoebo, ubi cum ventis resedentibus sisteremus, ad sequentem et Veneream quoque diem Tenedeam ad ipsam descendimus insulam, Alberto Bulla, viro iureconsulto egregio ac praetoriano collega, Francisco Turturino, affini honorifico vestro, Barnabaque Marrufo ac aliis non nullis comitantibus delectis amicis; ubi alii quidem escatis sub unda hamis varigenos la-

and there along the streets, quite large and luxurious with a snowy-white marble veneer; and a commercial, twelve-columned stoa, tall and covered by a four-sided roof, where one sees numerous stalls crammed with the exotic produce of Persians, Phoenicians, Cydonians and all kinds of barbarians. I marveled that, if religious motivation or the desire for glory were not yet able to do so, the prospect of this booty did not whet strongly the appetite of our greedy soldiery.

On the first of February, after having finally seen all this, I left 8 that city, so foreign and so absolutely packed with wealth, on a small tender and, accompanied by Bartolomeo Nigro, a secretary, and Urbano Dernixio, a well-born youth, boarded the distinctive imperial ship, where I had the great pleasure of seeing again its magnificent captain and celebrated owner and crew; and straightway, to complete my pleasure, I recognized, among other prominent men sailing in the same flagship, Tomasso Umbro, a man respected for his religious profession, a distinguished theologian from the city of Gubbio and neighbor of our province of Picenum. As well-deserving vicar of the Order of Preachers for eastern Europe and Asia on matters of religious import, he had just returned a few days before from the Black Sea and your cold Crimean colony of Kaffa, and was on his way back to the pope in Rome. With this accomplished man I had a long, delightful conversation about our common, very genuine concerns.

But to go on, having set sail from there on our voyage, we came 9 at sunset hard by Tenedos, where the winds subsided and we stopped. Next day, a Friday, I disembarked onto the island of Tenedos itself accompanied by Alberto Bulla, the eminent lawyer and colleague of the *podestà*, Francesco Turturino, your respected relative by marriage, and Barnaba Marruffo, and some other chosen friends. There some indulged their pleasure by catching various kinds of fish with baited hooks, while others scurried over green fields and high hills through the pathless haunts of animals

queare pisces sua pro voluptate curabant, alii vero virentes late per campos et altos per invia lustra colles feras et fugaces insectari conilios telis balistisque et plerisque venabulis armis canibusque percurrunt. At enim expleta cum venatione die, vicarius alacer ille Albertus atque lepidus Barnabas, quos binos quidem primum baculo percussit conilios ad navim Baltassarri praetori dignissimo dono detulerant. Sed tuus ille Turturinus, vir iocundus atque comis nec non piscatoriae rei diligens et peritus, quos ad scopulum et ad marmoreum portus molum tenuis calamellis aduncisque deceperat hamis, plus semipedum bissenos sarace⟨n⟩os ac vario colore pisces praefecto ipsi navarchoque magna cum liberalitate donarat. Sed ultimo equidem Kyriacus ille vester, postea quam primum notissimam fama insulam per virides et diu desertos cultore campos, si quid e verendissima vetustate sua reliquum extaret, indagasse placuerat, et nil denique dignum annotatione comperiens, quas demum ad litus spumantia inter et asperrima saxa plerasque lapigenum concas legerat et coclidas, obtulit in medium.

10   Et cum illico alacres illi praesides hilari vultu et animo nos nostraque laeta dona susceperint, Austris denique pausantibus et Iapice perflante secundo, nos inde solventes, cum Phocas petentes haud mora vela daremus, die noctuque placidi Neptunni liquidum sulcando campum, tandem Secrion occiduum Lesbeae notissimae insulae promuntorium superantes, hodie Idibus quoque Februariis novum ad expetitum ipsum Phocarum emporium applicuimus, divis Nereydum nimirum omnibus comitantibus nymphis.

11   Vale, et me fortasse ante epistolam vidisses, ni primum Ephesum videre delegissem. Ex eodem novo Phocarum emporio, eo quo ad ipsum venimus supra iam dicto felici et luciferae Dianae die. Et vestris salutem ex me de more plurima dicito.

in pursuit of wild and fugitive rabbits with javelins and missiles and hounds and many hunting spears for weapons. Then, as the day and the hunt came to an end, first, that vivacious vice-regent Alberto and charming Barnaba brought two rabbits that he had first bludgeoned to the ship as a gift for the worthy *podestà* Baldassarre. Whereas that Turturino of yours, a joyous and friendly fellow as well as an industrious and skilled fisherman, very generously presented the commander himself and the captain with twelve ?Saracen fish of varied colors, each over six inches long, which he had caught with his thin reeds and bent hooks off a ledge of rock, and from the marble mole of the harbor. Finally it was the turn of your Cyriac. He had entertained himself at first by investigating the far-famed island's green fields, long uninhabited, to see if anything of its revered ancient past remained; but finally, finding nothing worthy of note, he made his offering a number of ?petrified conches and snail shells that he had gathered by the foaming shore among the jagged rocks.

The vivacious presiding officers immediately accepted us and our joyful gifts with cheerful countenance and heart. Finally, the south wind stopped and a favoring breeze came up from the west-northwest, so we weighed anchor and set sail without delay, making for Foglia. By day and night we ploughed the liquid field of peaceful Neptune, at length passing Sigrion,[4] the western promontory of the famous island of Lesbos, until we put in today, the 13th of February, at the new trading-post of Foglia, our destination, accompanied by all the divine Nereid nymphs.   10

Farewell. You would perhaps have seen me before my letter, had I not chosen to visit Ephesus first. From the same new trading-post of Foglia, on the day we arrived, as already mentioned, the lucky day of light-bearing Diana. Please convey my best wishes to your household as always.   11

1 Andreolo Iustiniano, viro praestantissimo et amico incomparabili suo.

2   Cum nudius octavus Phocas adventaremus, karissime Andreole, ad te quam primum nostram ex Bizantio navigationem deteximus et alios inter eodem hylari eximioque nostro navigio navigantes Thomam Ugubinum, θεολόγον dignum et Praedicatorum ordinis per orientem vicarium bene merentem, ad pontificem[1] in Italiam remeaturum ex Ponto significandum censuimus. Praeterea vero cum ipse, suis nonnullis suadentibus sua pro religione rebus, ante nos Chyon revisere delegisset, non equidem ego eum ad te meis absque litteris venire delegi. Cum et sua veneranda virtus religionisque et officii sui dignitas tum et patriae suae vicinae nostrae civitati affectio eum tibi, viro praedigno, notum amicumque facere digne me suadebant. Vellem igitur eum praedignum et venerabilem hominem, non secus ac si Kyriacum tuum videres, amice digneris suscipere et dulciter amplexum iri.

3   Vale, et vestris omnibus ex me salutem dabis et ante omnes praeclarae Clarentiae coniugi atque sanctissimae tuae. Kyriacus Anconitanus tuus. Ex eodem Phocensi optimo vestratum emporio, x Kalendas Martias. Iterum atque iterum vale.

: 41 :

To Andreolo, 20 February [1447], Foglia Nuova

To the distinguished Andreolo Giustiniani, my incomparable 1
friend.

When we arrived at Foglia eight days ago, we reported to you 2
as quickly as possible about our voyage from Byzantium and
we thought it worth mentioning that, among the others aboard
this same select, joyful ship of ours was the worthy theologian,
Tomasso of Gubbio, the well-deserving vicar of the Order of
Preachers for the east, who is returning from the Black Sea to the
pope[1] in Italy. Under pressure of some religious business he has
chosen to go to Chios ahead of us and I did not want him to come
to you without a letter from me. Because of his personal excellence, which demands respect, and the importance of his religious
office on the one hand and his fondness for our city, which is a
neighbor of his homeland, on the other, I was persuaded that it
would be suitable to introduce him to a man of your high status as
a friend. Please deign to receive this very worthy and reverend
gentleman as amicably as if you were looking upon your Cyriac,
and embrace him fondly.

Farewell. Greet all your people from me and especially your dis- 3
tinguished and virtuous wife, Carenza. Your Cyriac of Ancona.
From the same excellent trading post of the Genoese, Foglia, the
20th of February. Again and again, farewell.

1 Praeclaro et facundissimo viro, Andreolo Iustiniano, amico honorifico atque incomparabili suo.

2 Claritati tuae iam binas dedimus epistolas posteaquam Phocas
revisimus, optume Andreole, at et cum Turturinus, noster iocundus et suavissimus comes, ante nos ad te advolare constituit, ter-
tiam dare haud equidem immeritam cogor.

3 Ille enim ubi Phocarum olim tam celeberrimae gentis auricomas inter nymphas atque vestratum coloniarum plurigenum cons-
picuas inter et praeclaras domnas atque decoras iuvenes et puellas
pedibus plausere choreas, carminibus demulcentibus divis citharis
fidibusque, et omnigenum aere adorna sonante aula, et Adorno
splendido[1] Marchione Gregorio, adornisque ex praeclaro Chyo
Lesbeaque serenissima Mitylene adventantibus nymphis, ador-
naque Musarum illa nostra praeclarissima canente regina Calliope,
adorno spectante utique civium et colonum coetu, et in primis et
ante alios omnes Baltasare Marufo honorifica sua cum cohorte
magnifico praesidente praefecto, nec non hylari sua tota navali cum
et praecipua delectaque iuventute imperiali spectante Hylarione
navarcho, admiranti mihi noster ipse Turturinus non secus Adornum marchionem ipsum adornas inter et venustissimas nymphas
chorum exercentem ostendit, quam olim adornum et crinitum
Apollinem per hybernam Lyciam aut per iuga Cinthi suos agitare
choros splendidissimum ad inspectandum fuisse putamus.

4 Verum et de hoc et Brancae Spinolae Chastellionea in domo
symposio claro ore latius explicandum censui simul et de nostro

: 42 :

To Andreolo, 22 February [1447], Foglia Nuova

To the distinguished and eloquent Andreolo Giustiniani, his hon- 1
orable friend beyond compare.

I have already written two letters to your excellency since re- 2
turning to Foglia; but since our cheerful and pleasant companion
Tortorino has decided to fly to you ahead of me, I feel compelled
to write a third, which, of course, you deserve.

To carry on my account, [in a recent celebration here, those 3
present] applauded the dancing of the golden-haired nymphs of
the once famous people of Foglia, and the striking and distinguished wives and beautiful young women and girls of your manifold [Genoese] colonies. [They danced] to the inspired, soothing
music of lute and lyre to which the hall, adorned at the expense of
numerous individuals, echoed. The magnificent Marquis Gregorio
Adorno[1] was present, as were "adorned" nymphs, who came over
from beautiful Chios and bright Lesbian Mytilene. The "adorned"
queen of the Muses, our distinguished Calliope, sang; and an
"adorned" company of citizens and settlers looked on. First and
foremost beyond all the others, the magnificent master of the revels, Baldassarre Maruffo, with his honorable retinue, and the "hilarious" sea-captain, Hilarion, with his whole crew of chosen imperial youth, looked on. As I marveled at the sight, your Tortorino
pointed out to me the Marquis Adorno, who was dancing among
the "adorned" and graceful nymphs; just as, we imagine, an
"adorned" and long-haired Apollo in wintry Lycia or on the slopes
of Cynthus led his band of dancers, a sight most glorious to look
upon.

I thought I also had to expand clearly and at greater length 4
upon this party held in the home of the Castiglioni by Branca

Turturino, qui statim expletis saturnalibus, bisquinis, pulsandum aequora tonsis ad te properans naviculam actare fecerat. Nam etsi cum Georgio parente conciliatam tui gratia[2] mihi apud Cypriam Amacosten amicitiam claram et pergratam habui, longe filii cariorem, meritis pluribus suadentibus, existimandum[3] duxi.

5   Vale, et ipse utique de me et primum nostro de Baltasare praetore multa atque plura dignissima poterit declarare et nostrum potissime quantum te revisendi desiderium urgeat. Praeterea vester hic Antonius de Bancha ⟨Georgius⟩que[4] pater bene se habent et vobis salutem plurimam dare nostris utique litteris imposuere.

6   Ex Phoceis, VIII Kalendas Martias, religioso Mercuri nostri atque excolendo Christicolis die. Vale iterum.

⁝ 43 ⁝

1   Ad Andreolum Iustinianum, virum omni laude dignissimum et amicum incomparabilem, Kyriacus Anconitanus.

2   Ad XVII Kalendas Maias, faustum Saturnalemque diem, ex Chyensium emporio Homeri antiqua monumenta et nobilia sepulchri vestigia vestigare petentes, Ioanne Mulasiano et Laurentio Taurico iocundis amicis Ienuensibus viris comitatus, arduos difficilesque per colles ac arida et inculta ferme per loca ad villam quam LXXXX fere stadiis a civitate distantem Homericam vocitant nemorosa inter pineis arboribus iuga consedimus, primum turrita

Spinola, and about our Tortorino who, as soon as the revels were over, hastened to you, causing a small, ten-oared ship to be launched and stroke the seas. For even though, thanks to you, I have had a well-known and quite pleasant friendship with his father Giorgio at Famagusta on Cyprus, I considered my friendship with his son far more precious, persuaded by his more numerous good qualities.

Farewell. [Tortorino] himself will be able tell you the most 5 noteworthy news, and in greater detail, first about me and about our *podestà*, Baldassare, but most of all about how strong our yearning is to see you again. In addition, your Antonio de Bancha here and his father Giorgio are well and require me to include in my letter their warmest greetings to you.

From Foglia, the 22nd of February, the sacred day of our Mer- 6 cury and a day of special observance for Christians.² Again, farewell.

⁚ 43 ⁚

To Andreolo, 16 April 1447, from the traditional site of Homer's tomb on Chios

To Andreolo Giustiniani, most worthy of all praise, my incompa- 1 rable friend, from Cyriac of Ancona.

On the 15th of May, Saturn's lucky day, accompanied by 2 Giovanni Mulasanio and Lorenzo Taurico, cheerful Genoese friends, [we departed] from the trading center of Chios in search of an ancient monument, the reputed remains of Homer's tomb. [Our journey took us] over steep, demanding hills and a dry, virtually uncultivated terrain toward a village called "Homerica," almost ninety stadia from the city [of Chios] that lay between ridges wooded with pine trees. Our first stop was at the stronghold of Poseidonia that we saw en route: fortified with towers by later

Possidonea arce a posteris Graecis, ut se a marittimis incursionibus tutarent, ad xxx stadia a litore submota alto in collis vertice condita ex itinere visa.

3 Ad ipsam vero Homeri nomine fortunatissimam villam Angelum, dilectum Andreoli natum ab eodem parente, viro nempe diligentissimo nostrique amantissimo, antea ut nos ad rem favitaret praemissum, venantem invenimus.

4 Et ad sequentem felicem, serenum Kyriaceumque diem ad ipsa Homerica loca monumentorum venimus, longaevis plerisque indicantibus indigenis accolis, et in quadem valle vivum prope et amoenissimum fontem secus antiquissimum murum in declivo quodam viridario, cuius in conspectu a posteris beati Iohannis Apostoli sacellum dicatum est, denique ad cuiusdam ficei vetustissimi arboris radices, ubi locum tumuli esse fama per villam et longaevos inter agrestes indigenas vulgatum erat, cum aliquantum effodere fecissem, nil penitus aliud praeter terram solidam lapidumve congeriem annotatione dignum comperimus.

5 Sed summa hylaritate placuerat inspectasse loca, quae maximus ille vatum et rerum omnigenum peritissimus[1] homo altae suae meditationi digna peridoneaque διαπρεπέστατα τε delegerat in insula scilicet singulari, loca ab omni hominum frequentia late secta atque penitus abdita, et temperie aeris aestivo hybernoque tempore vitae comodatissima, recentibus aquarum fontibus et silvis redolentibus undique conferta,[2] ut usque nostram[3] ad diem μακρόβιοι longaevique coloni vitam ibidem absque ulla pestium tabe validam et robore[4] plenissimam ducere videantur.

6 Nimirum quod ille virtutis integerrimae et sobrietatis amator, Phoebo et diva Calliope ceterisque suis comitatus Musis, Faunum, Oreadum Dryadumque nympharum societate contentus et utique summa hylaritate laetus, terram quam sibi actam et accomodatam dilexit,[5] Χίον παιπαλοέσσαν scilicet aridam, placuit appellare,

Greeks to protect themselves from attacks by sea, [it stands] at a remove of thirty stades from the shore, constructed at the top of a high hill.

At the village that has the great good fortune of being named 3 after Homer we found Angelo, beloved son of Andreolo, whom that same father, our most fond and devoted friend, had sent ahead to support us in this enterprise. He was hunting.

The next day, a lucky, cloudless day of the Lord, we went to the 4 actual site of Homer's tomb. A number of elderly native residents pointed it out to us in a certain valley, near a gorgeous fresh water spring, beside a very old wall, in a sloping plantation of trees, within sight of which later inhabitants had dedicated a chapel of St. John the Apostle. At length, at the roots of a certain very old fig tree, [we came to the place] where, according to a village tradition among the elderly rustic natives, the tomb [of Homer] was said to be. I made a little excavation, but found absolutely nothing worth reporting except solid earth and a pile of stones.

But it was still a supreme joy and pleasure to gaze upon the 5 place that the greatest of poets, a man highly skilled in matters of every kind, chose as the locale worthy of and most appropriate[1] to his profound vision: on a remarkable island, cut off and completely hidden from all human concourse, and most suited to living because of the temperate character of the climate in summer and winter, filled with fresh springs of water and fragrant forests everywhere, such that, even to our own day the *makrobioi*, i.e.the long-lived settlers, clearly lead a healthy life there, free from the ravages of plague and brimming with physical well being.

No wonder that lover of perfect goodness and moderation, 6 accompanied by Phoebus and divine Calliope and their other Muses, content with the society of fauns and mountain-nymphs and wood-nymphs, and rejoicing in complete and utter enjoyment, was pleased to call this land, which he loved as made for him and

ut in suo ad Apolinem hymno his carminibus videtur conscriptum:

τυφλὸς ἀνήρ, οἰκεῖ δὲ Χίωι ἔνι παιπαλοέσσῃ.[6]
caecus homo Chyon colit hic Homerus arentem.

7   Ex Chyensium praefata Homerica villa, XVI Kalendas Maias
MCCCCXLVII.

⁑ 44 ⁑

1   Viro perfecto et sapientissimo domino Kyriaco Anconitano Dominicus Grimanus salutem.

2   Etsi licteras tuas ad me factas nunquam legerim, vir humanissime atque doctissime, aliquorum tamen utrique nostrum amicissimorum relatu comonefactus intelligo tuam in me sinceram caritatem saepe ac saepius sciscitare qualiter valeam et quamplures salutationes committere. Quo hercle animadverto te, virum excellentis prudentiae arduisque facinoribus deditum, non mea ob merita, sed tua quadam eximia probitate me amare atque diligere.

3   Indignum quippe, imo iniustissimum arbitror, si tantae tuae in me dilectioni et intimae amicitiae non reddam debitum et, si quando facultas affuerit, ipsi debito faenus adiungere. Infinitas igitur Deo et fortunae meae gratias offero, quod tanti ac talis[1] viri animum ad hoc induxerint ut me inutilem et imbeccillem pror-

suited to him, *Chion Paipaloessan,* i.e., "rugged Chios," as one sees written in these verses of his Hymn to Apollo:

Tuphlos aner oikei de Chioi eni paipaloessi.
Here the blind man Homer dwells, in parched Chios.[2]

From the above-mentioned village of Homerica on Chios, 16   7
April 1447.

∷ 44 ∷

To Cyriac in Chios from Domenico Grimani,
20 May 1447, Rhodes

Domenico Grimani sends greetings to the complete, eminently ju-   1
dicious master Cyriac of Ancona.

Most humane and learned sir, though I have never received a   2
letter from you, still, some of our mutual, very close friends have impressed on me in conversation an awareness of your genuine esteem for me. [They tell me] that, time and again, you inquire about my health and quite frequently convey your greetings. Because of this I am aware that you, a man of extraordinary circumspection, by Hercules, and given to doughty deeds, have a special regard and liking for me, not because I deserve it, but because of your uncommon goodness.

Indeed, I think it would be inappropriate, indeed most unjust,   3
if I were not to repay my debt to your great fondness and intimate friendship for me and, should the opportunity present itself, add the interest to my debt. Therefore I express my unbounded gratitude to God and to my good fortune that they have put it into the heart of such a distinguished man to deign to summon me, useless and weak though I am, and utterly unknown, to the very highest kind of friendship, the kind that binds the universe together in a

susque ignotissimum ad illud excellentissimum amicitiae genus, quod rerum omnium seriem ligat, revocare dignatus sit. Neque edepol dedignor de tam singulari eximiaque amicitia acquisita, sed me obligatissimum iudico ad conservandam fovendamque et incrementis debitis, quam diu fuero, nutriendam. Si qua enim experimenta de hac mea oblatione facere volueris, videbis certe ipso effectu quanto sit maior mea in te dilectio quam praesentium licterarum descriptio. Exerce itaque Dominicum tuum ut iusseris: tuis etenim obtemperare praeceptis ubique promptum invenies.

4   Sed de his satis. Invenies praesentibus annexas quasdam litteras quas dominus meus, dominus cancellarius Cretae, ad te dirigit. Ipsas namque instantissime mihi comendavit, ut qua possim cura et sollicitudine illas Chii transmittam et fido nuntio recommittam, quo infallanter tuis in manibus pervenire possint. Utrisque itaque susceptis, rogo ut, quam celerrime tabellarii facultas affuerit, respondere digneris, primo quidem de tua optima et integerrima sospitate et felicissima convalentia, deinde si quae tibi fuerint grata ut faciam. Scias enim nil mihi iocundius quam cum quippiam fecero quod karitati tuae gratum iri contigerit.

5   Vale, vir humanissime et amice integerrime, et me remotum atque ignotum[2] non secus ac praesentem et cognitum amare, ut coepisti, persevera.

6   Ex Rhodo, xiii Kalendas Iunias 1447.

: 45 :

1 Andreolo Iustiniano viro clarissimo ac praestantissimo.

2 Cum nuper et v Kalendas Iuniarum die Squarciaficica navis ex Genua Chyon adventasset, karissime Andreole, G. nepos,[1] Hyero-

continuous unit. Nor, by Pollux, do I disdain the acquisition of so
unique and extraordinary a friendship, but I judge myself obli-
gated in the highest degree to preserve and cherish and nourish it
as long as I live with increasing indebtedness. And if you should
wish to make trial of this my offering, you will surely see by the
very outcome how much greater is my esteem for you than can be
expressed in this letter. So use your Domenico as you are bid to:
you will find him ready to obey your every command.

But enough of that. You will find attached to this letter another   4
one that my lord, the lord chancellor of Crete, directs to you. He
entrusted it to me with the urgent entreaty that I pass it on [to
you] in Chios with the greatest possible care and responsibility by
a reliable messenger, so that it can end up in your hands without
fail. I beg that, as soon as you have received both letters, you do
me the favor of replying as quickly as the courier can bring it back;
first, indeed, about your welfare — excellent, I hope, and quite un-
diminished — and [that you are] in the best of health; then as to
whether there is any favor you would like me to do [for you]. For
know that nothing could make me happier than doing something
that will please your dear self.

Farewell, most humane and irreproachable friend, and as you   5
have begun to like me, who am far away and unknown, may you
continue to do so as though I were present and known.

From Rhodes, the 20th of May, 1447.   6

: 45 :

To Andreolo, 28 May [1447], Chios

To the most distinguished and excellent Andreolo Giustiniani.   1

When recently, on the 28th of May,[1] the ship of Squarciafico   2
arrived in Chios from Genoa, dearest Andreolo, among the many

nimus R.B. noster, intra quas nobis e nostris litteras plerasque detulerat, tuam mihi praeclaram et elegantem epistolam dedisset, eam quam grate suscepi atque lubentius lectitavi. Ex ea namque plerisque modis meum solare animum maluisti, nec solum erga me parentemque pientissimam tuam, nostram et excolendam sororem diligentiae et pietatis officium perbelle absolvendum duxisti, quin et te bonarum artium peritia ac egregiis de humanitate studiis haud expertem ostendisti. Placuit enim rerum digne memorandarum plena sententiarum dicta ornatamque et disertam ordinis compositionem vidisse.

3   Verum et venerandae D. interitum pari tecum aequanimitate tollerandum duxi, cum humana conditione conspecta tum quia² diu bene vixerit optime atque perbeate, mortali honorifice suam inter ingenuam prolem corpore relicto; ad meliora incolere loca, vita vel perhemni perfruenda migrasse sperandum.

4   Praeterea quae brevia de Britannicis Gallicisque et Italis principibus pertentare coepisti, vellem lubentius eos et praeclaras ceteras Christicolum nationes et egregias urbes, pacatis eorundem quibusque vel Italis rebus, adversus truces barbaros in Thracas et Macedonas arma transferre conspirasse intelligere, et ut pluries maiores nostri praeclarissime fecerunt, insignes ex his triumphos ducere laudatissime quandoque curasse.

5   Valere te quidem bene desidero et te Georgium F. nostrum ac praeclarum Paridem affinem grate digneque vidisse placet. Hic vero Clarentiam coniugem Angelumque natum et ceteros nostros tuo nomine salutatos fecimus, qui et tibi pergrate centuplas reddendas dixere salutes. Vale et iterum vale.

letters from our friends that G's grandson, our Geronimo R.B., brought us, I received with great pleasure the one that he gave me from you—a splendid, elegant letter!—and I read it gladly, over and over again. Through it you chose to console my heart in manifold ways; and not only did you consider that you should acquit yourself very nicely of your duty to be careful and conscientious towards me and toward your deeply devout mother and our honorable sister, but you also showed that you do not lack a share of expertise in the liberal arts and in the superior study of mankind. For I was pleased to see that your remarks are full of memorable maxims and that the composition is [both] richly adorned and skillfully organized.

But I felt that the death of the revered D. must be borne as you 3 are bearing it, with long-suffering, considering, on the one hand, the human condition, and on the other, how long she lived the good life, excellently and joyfully, leaving her mortal body amid her noble offspring; one must hope that she has gone to dwell in a better place, to enjoy eternal life.

On another subject. As to the tentative explorations you have 4 begun with regard to the rulers of Britain, Gaul, and Italy, I would be happier to learn that they and the other distinguished Christian nations and chief cities had settled their individual disputes, especially the Italians, and had united to shift their forces to Thrace and Macedonia [to use them] against the cruel barbarians and, as our ancestors often did most gloriously, had taken care that some day, to the highest praise, they would celebrate memorable triumphs over them.

I wish you good health and I am pleased that you graciously 5 and fittingly saw our George F. and Paride, a distinguished in-law. Here on Chios I have greeted in your name your wife Clarenza, your son Angelo and our other friends. They said to return to you their gracious salutations a hundredfold. Farewell and again, farewell.

[Leondari to Mistra]

1 ἀγαθῇ τύχῃ. Ad III Kalendas Augusti ex Laconica Leontinaria arce illustris Thomae Palaeologi despotis comitatus famulis Spartanos Taygeti montis ad colles venimus, ubi secus antiquam et olim nobilem Lacedaemonum urbem fere xxx stadiis distantem, arduis in ripis situm est inexpugnabile oppidum quod hodie Σπαρτοβούνην Μυσιστράτηντε dicunt.

2 Ubi Constantinum cognomento Dragas ex Regia Palaeologum prosapia despotem inclytum regnantem invenimus. Et apud eum insignem illum virum et nostro quidem aevo Graecorum doctissimum et vita moribusque et doctrina Platonicos inter philosophum quoque clarum et potissimum, ut ita loquar, cuius ergo venimus, revisi. Et utique regia ipsa in aula mihi obviam occurrentem vidi iuvenem ingenuum Nicolaum Χαλκοκανδήλην Atheniensem, Georgi amicissimi nostri et viri doctissimi filium nequidem degenerem, quin et egregie Latinis atque Graecis litteris eruditum.

3 Quos postquam magna hilaritate revisi, cum me primum inclytus ipse princeps et viri dignissimi perhumane atque benignissime suscepissent, multa mihi atque insignia praeclarissimae suae in me benivolentiae declarunt. Et alias ut obmittam.

30 July 1447 to October 1448
The Peloponnesus, Epirus

: DIARY V :

Travels in the Peloponnesus, 30 July 1447 to 17 April 1448

[Leondari to Mistra]

Good luck! On the 30th of July [1447], from the Laconian strong- 1
hold of Leondari, accompanied by servants of the illustrious despot, Thomas Palaeologus,[1] we came to the Spartan foothills of
Mount Taygetus. There near the ancient and once famous city of
the Lacedaemonians, about 30 stadia away on a steep river bluff, is
located the impregnable town they today call "Spartoboune" or
Mysistrate.

There we found Constantine Dragaš, of the royal family of the 2
Palaeologi, the gloriously reigning despot,[2] and—the reason for
my return visit—his guest, that eminent personage, the most
learned of the Greeks in our time, and, if I may say so, [a man
who] in his life, character and teaching [is] a brilliant and highly
influential philosopher in the Platonic tradition.[3] Also, I saw rushing to meet me in the palace itself the gifted young Athenian,
Laonikos Chalkokondyles, the son of my good friend, the learned
George, in no way unworthy of his father, and furthermore, remarkably learned in both Latin and Greek literature.

After I had expressed my great joy in seeing them again, [and] 3
when, first, the famous prince himself, then these most worthy
gentlemen had received me most kindly and benevolently, they
showed many special signs of their magnificent good will toward
me. Otherwise, nothing to report.

[Sparta]

4 Ad IIII Nonarum Augustarum clarum atque faustum Mercuri Geni sanctissimi nostri diem, una comitatus dilectissimo Atheniense iuvene praefato Chalcocandele, ad antiqua et cele⟨be⟩rrima illa Spartanae civitatis monumenta revisenda venimus, cum 'nec' equidem 'vidisse semel satis' fuerat, 'iuvabat sed usque morari'.

5   Et primum antiquum et insigne illud suum et memorabile gymnasium revisi, solido de marmore fabraefactum et mira olim architectorum ope conspicuum, quamquam hodie longi temporis labe ac [...] ignava posterum accolarum hominum incuria magna ex parte collapsum atque dirutum comperimus. Sed non longe plerasque vidimus nobilium quorundam gymnasiorum principum et praefectorum insignes et marmoreas statuarum bases, quarum eximia quae adexstant Graecis et exactissimis litteris epigrammata hisce reponendum curamus:[1]

ΗΠΟΛΙΣ | Μ. Α[ΙΛ]ΙΟΝ ΛΕΟΝΤΑΝ ΓΥΜΝΑ |
ΣΙΑΡΧΟΝΤΑ ΤΕ ΑΛΛΑ | ΚΑΛΩΣ ΠΟΛΙΤΕΥΣΑΜΕ|
ΝΟΝ ΚΑΙ ΜΑΛΙΣΤΑ ΤΗΝ | ΓΥΜΝΑΣΙΑΡΧΙΑΝ
ΦΙΛΟΤΕΙΜΩΣ | ΚΑΙ ΜΕΓΑΛΟΠΡΕΠΩΣ ΕΚΤΕΛΟΥ|
ΝΤΑ ΚΑΙ ΤΗΣ ΑΛΛΗΣ ΑΡΕΤΗΣ | ΧΑΡΙΝ
ΠΡΟΣΔΗΞΑΜΕΝΟΥ | ΤΟ ΑΝΑΛΩΜΑ ΠΟΠΛΙΟΥ |
ΑΙΛΙΟΥ ΔΑΜΟΚΡΑΤΙΔΑ ΤΟΥ Α|ΛΚΑΝΔΡΙΔΑ
ΑΡΧΙΕΡΕΩΣ ΤΟΥ | ΣΕΒΑΣΤΟΥ ΚΑΙ ΤΩΝ ΘΕΙΩΝ
ΠΡ|ΟΓΟΝΩΝ ΑΥΤΟΥ ΦΙΛΟΚΑΙΣΑΡΟΣ | ΚΑΙ
ΦΙΛΟΠΑΤΡΙΔΟΣ ΚΑΙ ΑΙΩΝΙΟΥ | ΑΓΟΡΑΝΟΜΟΥ
ΠΛΕΙΣΤΟΝΙΚΟΥ | ΠΑΡΑΔΟΞΟΥ ΚΑΙ ΑΡΙΣΤΟΥ
ΕΛΛΗ|ΝΩΝ ΠΡΕΣΒΕΩΣ ΝΟΜΟΦΥΛΑ|ΚΩΝ[2]

6   Item ad alteram prope Spartanorum nobile gymnasium marmoream basim:[3]

Η ΠΟΛΙΣ | Μ. ΑΥΡΗΛΙΟΝ ΑΡΙΣΤΟΚΡΑΤ[Η] |
ΔΑ|ΜΑΙΝΕΤΟΥ ΙΕΡΕΑ ΚΑΤΑ ΓΕΝΟΣ ΑΠΟ

[*Sparta*]

On the 2nd of August, the bright and auspicious day of my most   4
sacred patron, Mercury, escorted by the dearly beloved Athenian
youth Chalkokondyles mentioned above, we went back to see
again the ancient and highly celebrated remnants of the city of
Sparta, which "it was not enough to have seen only once";⁴ rather,
"it gave me pleasure to linger [there]."⁵

First I went back to see Sparta's ancient gymnasium, notewor-   5
thy and memorable, fashioned of massive marble, once striking for
the wondrous work of its architects; although today we found it in
great part fallen and pulled down by the ravages of time and the
lazy neglect of later inhabitants. But not far away we saw a great
number of remarkable marble bases for statues of certain noted di-
rectors and officials of certain gymnasiums. We preserve here in
their very precise Greek scripts the most interesting of these extant inscriptions: [PLATE IV]

> The city [honors] M. Ailios Leontas ex-gymnasiarch, who
> fulfilled that and all his civic duties well, and especially ad-
> ministered the gymnasium generously and magnificently, and
> for his other distinctions. Poplios Ailios Damokratidas, son
> of Akandridas, high priest of the emperor and his divine an-
> cestors, lover of the emperor and of his country and perpet-
> ual director of the market, an outstanding victor in many
> games and excellent ambassador of the Greeks, undertook
> the expense while he was guardian of the laws.

Likewise on another marble base near the famous gymnasium   6
of the Spartans:

> The city [honors] M. Aurelios Aristokrates, son of
> Damainetos, priest for his family, 48th from Heracles, 44th

ΗΡΑΚΛΕΟΥΣ ΜΗ. ΑΠΟ ΔΙΟΣ|ΚΟΥΡΩΝ ΜΔ.
ΑΙΩΝΙΩΝ ΓΥΜΝΑ|ΣΙΑΡΧΟΝ ΜΕΤΑ ΔΙΟΝΥΣΙΟΥ
ΚΑΙ | ΑΡΙΣΤΟΤΕΛΟΥΣ ΚΑΙ ΠΟΛΙΤΗΝ ΚΑΙ
ΓΥΜΝΑΣΙΑΡΧΟΝ ΑΣΥΝΚΡΙΤΟΝ |
ΠΡΟΣΔΕΞΑΜΕΝΩΝ ΤΟ ΑΝΑΛΩ|ΜΑ ΤΩΝ
ΠΡΟΣΤΑΝΤΩΝ ΕΝ ΤΩ | ΓΥΜΝΑΣΙΩ ΦΙΛΩΝ
ΜΕΜΜΙΟΥ | ΕΥΤΥΧΟΥ Β. Μ. ΑΥΡΗΛΙΟΥ
ΑΡΕ|ΤΩΝΟΣ ΤΟΥ Β ΑΒΙΔΙΟΥ ΣΑΤΥ|[Ρ]ΟΥ ΤΟΥ
ΕΥΤΥΧΑ[4]

7   Η ΠΟΛΙΣ | ΓΑ ΠΟΜΠΩ ΑΓΙΝ ΑΛΚΑΣΤΟΥ ΤΑ ΤΕ |
ΑΛΛΑ ΚΑΛΩΣ ΠΕΠΟΛΙΤΕΥΜΕΝΟΝ ΚΑΙ |
ΓΥΜΝΑΣΙΑΡΧΟΥΝΤΑ ΛΑΜΠΡΩΣ
ΠΡΟ|ΣΔΕΞΑΜΕΝΟΥ ΤΟ ΑΝΑΛΩΜΑ ΓΑ | ΠΟΜΠΟΝ.
ΑΛΚΑΣΤΟΥ ΤΟΥ ΑΔΕΛΦΙΔΟΥ[5]

8   Ad aliam marmoream basim:

Η ΠΟΛΙΣ | Π. ΑΥΡΗΛΙΟΝ ΧΡΥΣΟΓΟΝΟΝ ΤΟΝ
ΙΕΡΕΑ ΤΗΣ | ΤΗΣ ΤΕ ΚΑΤΑ ΤΗΝ
ΓΥΜΝΑΣΙΑΡΧΙΑΝ ΛΑΜ|ΠΡΩΣΗΤΟΣ ΚΑΙ ΤΗΣ ΤΩΝ
ΛΥΚΟΥΡΓΕΙΩΝ [ΗΘ]ΩΝ[6] ΠΡΟΣΤΑΣΙΑΣ ΤΗΣ ΤΕ
ΑΛΛΗΣ ΣΥΜΠΑΣΗΣ | ΑΡΕΤΗΣ ΕΝΕΚΕΝ
ΔΕΞΑΜΕΝΩΝ ΤΟ ΑΝΑΛΩΜΑ ΤΩΝ ΤΕΚΝΩΝ
ΑΥΤΟΥ ΣΩΦΡΟΣΥ|ΝΑ ΚΑΙ ΣΩΤΗΡΙΔΑ[7]

9   Ad aliam basim:

Η ΠΟΛΙΣ | ΞΕΝΑΡΧΙΔΑΝ ΔΑΜΙΠΠΟΥ
ΓΥΜΝΑΣΙ|ΑΡΧΟΥΝΤΑ ΑΞΙΩΣ ΤΗΣ ΠΟΛΕΩΣ
ΕΥΝΟΙΑΣ | ΧΑΡΙΝ | ΟΙ ΣΥΝΑΡΧΟΝΤΕΣ ΤΗΣ
ΠΑΤΡΟΝΟΜ[ΙΑΣ] | ΠΡΟΣΔΕΞΑΝΤΟ ΤΟ ΑΝΑΛΩΜΑ[8]

from the Dioskouroi, permanent gymnasiarch with Diony-
sios and Aristoteles, incomparable citizen and gymnasiarch.
His friends and supporters in the gymnasium, Memmios
Eutyches Jr., Markos Aurelios Areton Jr. and Avidios
Satyros son of Eutychas undertook the expense.

The city [honors] Gaios Pomponios Agis son of Alkastos   7
who fulfilled all his civic duties well, and held the office
of gymnasiarch splendidly. His nephew Gaios Pomponios
Alkastos undertook the expense.

On another marble base: 8

The city [honors] the priest Poplios Aurelios Chrysogonos
for his munificence in the office of gymnasiarch, his care for
the institutions of Lycurgus, and for all his other virtues.
His sons Sophrosynas and Soteridas took the expense upon
themselves.

On another base: 9

The city [honors] Xenarchidas son of Damippos, who worthily held the office of gymnasiarch, for his benevolence toward the city. His fellow members of the Council undertook
the expense.

10   Item inibi ad aliam basim:

Α ΠΟΛΙΣ | Π. ΜΕΜΜΙΟΝ ΣΠΑΡΤΙΑΚΟΝ ΕΚΓΟΝΟΝ
ΗΡΑΚΛΕ|ΟΤΣ ΚΑΙ ΡΑΔΑΜΑΝΘΤΟΣ M ΑΠΟ
ΔΙΟΣΚΟΤ|ΡΩΝ ΠΟΛΙΤΕΤΟΜΕΝΟΝ ΚΑΛΩΣ[9]

11   Ad aliam basim:

Η ΠΟΛΙΣ | ΓΑ ΡΟΤΒΡΙΟΝ ΒΙΩΝΟΡΑ ΣΟΡΑ
ΑΛΕΙΠΤΗΝ | ΤΗΣ ΤΕ ΠΕΡΙ ΤΟ ΛΑΚΩΝΙΚΟΝ ΗΘΟΣ
ΣΕ|ΜΝΟΤΗΤΟΣ ΚΑΙ ΤΗΣ ΕΝ ΤΟΙΣ ΓΤΜΝΑΣΙΟΙΣ |
ΑΡΕΤΗΣ ΧΑΡΙΝ[10]

[Ithome in Messenia]

12   Extant et alia pleraque amplissimae civitatis monumenta et inter
nobiliora ingentia tria theatra conspeximus, quorum maximum
pluribus inter sedilia scalis intermunitum, ne adeuntes exeuntesve
spectaculo consessoribus impedimento essent, nec minori utique
ornamento pulchro marmoreum columnarum ordine circumsec-
tum fuisse, plurimae adhuc suo loco erectae columnae ipsae declarant. Alterum pulcherrima muri parietumque compositione munitum stadieae longitudinis hippodrom nobile quondam extitisse
videtur.

13   Vidimus et egregias plerasque domorum et sacrarum aedium
reliquias, columnarum dirutarum congeries basesque et ornata
figuris epistilia, nec non statuarum fragmenta basesque et nobilibus antiquisque litteris epigrammata, quorum quae clariora inte-
griorave comperimus hisce reponendum curavimus.

14   Antiquum Ithomeae civitatis epigramma ad marmoreum epistile:[11]

ΕΠΙ ΙΕΡΕΟΣ ΚΡΕΣΦΟΝΙΟΤ ΕΤΟΤΣ ΠΝΖ |
ΑΓΩΝΟΘΕΤΗΣ } ΤΙΒ. ΚΛΑΤΔΙΟΣ ΚΡΙΣΠΙΑΝΟΤ
ΤΙΟΣ ΑΡΙΣΤΟΜΕΝΗΣ | ΙΕΡΟΘΤΤΑΙ |

Likewise on another base in that location: 10

The city [honors] Poplios Memmios Spartiakos, the descendant of Heracles and Rhadamanthys, sprung from the Dioskouroi, who performed his civic duties well.

On another base: 11

The city [honors] Gaios Rubrios the trainer for his reverence for the Laconian customs and for his distinction in the gymnasia.

[Ithome in Messenia][6]

There survive other remnants, quite numerous, of a very large   12
city; and among the more noteworthy we noticed three huge theaters. The numerous columns that still stand in place show us that the largest of these was built with several stairways among the seats, to prevent those entering and leaving the performance from blocking the view of those who are seated, and that the marble [auditorium] was divided all around by a handsome row of columns, to serve as a no less handsome ornament. A second, built with a very attractive arrangement of outer and inner walls, seems once to have been a fine racetrack, a stade in length.

We also saw numerous excellent remains of houses and sacred   13
temples, heaps of ruined columns, and bases and architraves adorned with images, as well as fragments and bases of statues, and inscriptions in fine, antique lettering. We have preserved here the clearer and more intact of those that we found.

An ancient inscription of the city of Ithome on a marble archi-   14
trave:

In the year 157, when Tiberios Klaudios Aristomenes, son of Kresphontios, was president of the games, the sacrificing priests Aristoboulos son of Aristoboulos and Nobios

ΑΡΙΣΤΟΒΟΤΛΟΣ ΑΡΙΣΤΟΒΟΤΛΟΤ ΝΟΒΙΟΣ |
ΑΙΛΙΑΝΟΣ ΓΡΑΜΜΑΤΕΤΣ ΣΟΦΟΣ |
ΧΑΛΕΙΔΟΦΟΡΟΣ ΚΛΑΤΔΙΟΣ ΤΡΩΙΛΟΣ[12]

15 Ad alium lapidem antiquum ea[n]dem in Ithomea civitate epigramma:

ΤΙΒ. ΚΛ. ΣΑΙΘΙΔΟΣ ΚΑΙΛΛΙΑΝΟΣ | ΑΡΧΙΕΡΕΤΣ
ΤΩΝ ΣΕΒΑΣΤΩΝ | ΔΙΑ ΒΙΟΤ ΚΑΙ ΕΛΛΑΔΑΡΧΗΣ
ΑΠΟ | ΤΟΤ ΚΟΙΝΟΤ ΤΩΝ ΑΧΑΙΩΝ ΔΙΑ | ΒΙΟΤ
ΠΑΤΗΡ ΚΛΑΤΔΙΟΤ ΦΡΟΝΤΕΙΝ|ΟΤ ΚΑΙ ΠΑΠΠΟΣ
ΚΛΑΤΔΙΩΝ ΣΑΙΘΙΔΑ | ΚΑΙ ΝΕΙΚΗΡΑΤΟΤ ΤΙΟΣ ΔΕ
ΚΛΑΤΔΙΩΝ | ΤΟΤ ΚΛΑΤΔΙΟΤ ΟΣΤΕΙΛΙΟΤ ΚΑΙ[13]

Reliqua deleta sunt.

[Messene]

16 Ad iiii Nonas Octobris ex Ithomea Andrusa, Thomae despotis Messaniacae regionis villa, Coroneum ad oppidum Francum venimus, Messanae antiquissimae urbis paucis extantibus nempe reliquiis ex itinere visis. Modicum vero nostram ad diem tantae civitatis vestigium apparet.

17 Sed eo in Franco oppido Χριstophorum, strategeum amicum laepidissimum nostrum perquam iucundum, revisimus et eo ductitante non nulla per agros et virentia rura amoenosque et frondosis arboribus placidissimos ortos Messaneae civitatis monumenta conspeximus.

[Corone]

18 Deinde[14] equidem Nonis Octobribus ad ipsam Coroneam venimus antiquam Messaneo in sinu civitatem, quam et unam e vii urbibus, quas nobilem Graecorum ducem Agamemnonem Achilli in dotem spopondisse ferunt πήδασον ἀμπελοέσσαν Peda-

306

Ailianos, the secretary Sophos, the cupbearer Klaudios
Troilos [...]

On another ancient stone in the same city of Ithome, at the   15
end:

Tiberios Klaudios Saithidas Kailianos, high priest of the
emperors for life and Helladarch [chosen] by the Achaean
League for life, father of Klaudios Phronteinos, grandfather
of Klaudios Saithidas and Klaudios Neikeratos, and son of
Klaudios Hostilios [son of Klaudios and Klaudia] [...]

The rest of the text has been wiped out.

[Messene]

On the 4th of October, from Ithomean Androusa, an estate   16
of Thomas, despot of the Messenian region, we journeyed to a
Frankish town in the ambit of Corone, having inspected along
the way the few extant remains of the extremely ancient city of
Messene; but only a slight trace of such a great city survives to our
day.

But in that Frankish town we revisited our very witty officer   17
friend, Christophoros, an extremely delightful person; and with
him as our guide we inspected some remnants of the city of
Messene [scattered] throughout fields and verdant countryside
and charming, most peaceful gardens, with trees abounding in foliage.

[Corone]

Then, on the 7th of October we came to Corone itself, an ancient   18
city on the gulf of Messene, one of the seven cities they say Agamemnon, the noted Greek general, pledged to Achilles as a dowry,
called by Homer at that time *Pedasos ampeloessa*, i.e., "Pedasos,

sumve vinealem tunc ab Homero dictam, nunc vero praedigne in
Venetum coloniam deductam. Eam Mapheum Bolanum, virum
praeclarum, nobilem pro Venetis praetoria potestate curantem invenimus una suis cum consularibus collegis, Marco Quirino et
Bartholomeo Phalerio.

19 Qui me postquam perhumane susceperant, his et Marco Calergio viro ex Creta generoso atque docto indicantibus, nonnulla antiquae civitatis insignia comperimus et potissimum ad Cheronen-
sum, quem ante urbem secus mare Lebadea insulam vocant,
pleraque eiusdem antiquitatis monumenta vidimus et vetustarum
potissime aedium ac omnis fere soli pavimentum, eximiae artis
hinc inde pulcherrima compositione depictum. Et itaque marmoreos inter lapides et antiquarum basium fragmenta has comperimus semideletas inscriptiones:

ΑΓΑΘΙΑ | ΚΡΑΤΩΝ ΕΤΜΕΝΟ[Τ]Σ ΔΑΜΑΣΙΛΑΣ |
ΚΑΛΛΙΣΤΩΝΟΣ ΔΗΜΟΝΙΚΟΣ ΑΡΜΟΔΙΟΤ | ΜΤΡΩΝ
ΑΣΚΛΑΠΩΝΟΣ ΔΑΜΑΤΡΙΟΣ ΟΝΑΤΙΧΟΤ |
ΛΤΣΙΜΑΧΟΣ ΝΙΚΑΝΩΡΟΣ ΤΙΜΑΙΟΣ ΖΕΝΩΝΟΣ[15]

20 Item apud Coroneam eodem in Suburneo Cheroneso:

ΑΝΤΩΝΙΟΣ ΣΕΒΗΡΟΣ ΑΝΤΩΝΙΟΣ ΡΟΤΦΟΣ |
ΑΝΤΩΝΙΟΣ ΑΧΑΙ[Κ]ΟΣ ΚΕΚΙΛΙΟΣ ΚΡΙΣΠΟΣ |
ΠΡΑΣΙΩΝ ΠΤΟΛΛΑΡΙΩΝΟΣ ΣΩΤΑΣ ΣΩΤΑ | ΜΗΝΑΣ
ΛΕΣΒΙΟΤ ΝΙΚΟΤΕΛΗΣ ΞΕΝΑΡΧΟΤ | ΔΑΜΙΩΝ
ΔΑΜΟΚΡ[Ι]ΤΟΤ ΕΠΙΓΟΝΟΣ ΑΠΟΛΛΩΝΙΟΤ[16]

21 Ad porphyreas huiusmodi figurae tabellas:

ΦΙΛΩΝΤΜΟΣ   ΣΩΦΒΕΑ ΦΙΛΟΤΜΕ|ΝΑ
  ΧΑΙΡΕ   ΧΑΙΡΕ[17]

[DRAWING]

land of vines," but now transformed quite appropriately into a Venetian colony. Ruling it with gubernatorial power on behalf of the Venetians, along with his consular colleagues, Marco Quirino and Bartolomeo ?Faliero, we found the distinguished Maffeo Bollani, a man of senatorial rank.

After they had received me most kindly, with their help and that of Marco Calergio, a learned noblemen from Crete, as guides, we found some remarkable [remains] of the ancient city, and in particular, at the peninsula which [situated as it is] in front of the city beside the sea they call the "island of Lebadea," we saw a good number of remnants of equal antiquity and most especially of ancient temples and an almost entire floor pavement, decorated on one side and the other with a most beautiful composition of outstanding artistry. And so we found among the marble stones and fragments of ancient bases these partially destroyed inscriptions: 19

Good [fortune]. Kraton son of Eumenes, Damasilas son of Kalliston, Demonikos son of Harmodios, Myron son of Asklapon, Damatrios son of Onatichos, Lysimachos son of Nikanor, Timaios son of Xenon . . .

Likewise in Corone on the same peninsula of Suburneum 20

Antonios Severos, Antonios Rouphos, Antonios Achaikos, Kaikilios Crispos, Prasion son of Ptollarion, Sotas son of Sotas, Menas son of Lesbios, Nikoteles son of Xenarchos, Damon son of Damokritas, Epigonos son of Apollonios [...]

On porphyry panels, figures that look something like this: 21

Philomenos, farewell.   Sophia Philoumena, farewell.

[DRAWING]

[The peninsula of Tainaron. "Pylos," i.e. Bitylos][18]

22   Ad Iduum Octobris diem ex Corone Taenarum[19] Laconicum insigne promuntorium[20] petens, ut et alia Laconicae Messaniacaeque regionis vetustatis insignia monumenta videremus, scapham ante diem conscendi, Johanne Rosea ducente Taenareo sollertissimo nauta, et antea quam sol caeli sextum conscenderet orbem, Messaniaco transiecto sinu, ad antiquam Messaniacam Pylon venimus, quam longevi Nestoris memoranda extitisse patriam, non nullis ab autoribus memoratur, tametsi Triphyleam Pylon ab Homero Aemathoenta dictam Straboni placuisse percepimus.

23   Extant enim adhuc nobilia oppidi monumenta ab extrema Taenari promuntorii parte c ferme stadiorum distantia, et non plus v stadiis a littore hodie arcem a posteris ex antiquis operibus conditam vidimus, ubi Ιωannem Palaeologum pro Spartano principe Constantino praefectum inveni. Ex quo honorifice susceptus, eo duce, aliquam in campo ex antiquis moenibus partem extare conspeximus et ad marmoream quam et in agro semidefossam comperimus basim hoc nostrum in Gordianum Caesarem epigramma consculptum invenimus, in quo Pylon a posteris Bitylon dictam, ut et Strabo ipse testatur, apparet:

ΑΤΤΟΚΡΑΤΟΡΑ ΚΑΙΣΑΡΑ ΜΑΡΚΟΝ ΑΝΤΩΝΙΝΟΝ |
ΓΟΡΔΙΑΝΟΝ ΕΤΣΕΒΗ ΕΤΤΤΧΗ ΣΕΒΑΣΤΟΝ | Η
ΠΟΛΙΣ Η ΒΕΙΤΤΛΕΩΝ ΔΙΕΦΟΡΩΝ ΤΩΝ ΠΕΡΙ
ΜΑΡΚΟΝ ΑΤΡΗΛΙΟΝ ΝΕΙΚΗΦΟΡΟΝ
ΠΡΟ|ΣΔΕΚΤΟΤ[21]

24   Vidimus et ingentes inibi antiqua manu fabresculptas cisternas et pleraque nobilia et ornata sculpturis sepulchra et eximia saxa.

[Dry]

25   Exinde eadem scapha et eodem ductitante scapharcho Rossea secus eiusdem promuntorii littora navigantes, ad villam Dryeam et

[The peninsula of Tainaron. "Pylos," i.e. Bitylos]

On the 15th of October, directing my course from Corone to the   22
noteworthy Laconian promontory of Tainaron in order to see
other noteworthy remnants of Laconian and Messenian antiquity,
I embarked before daylight on a small boat captained by Johannes
Rosea, a highly skilled sailor from Tainaron, and having crossed
the Messenian Gulf before the sun reached the sixth circle of
heaven, we came to Messenian Pylos, which is mentioned by several authors to have been the memorable fatherland of long-lived
Nestor, although, we noticed, Strabo decided that the Pylos called
emathoeis by Homer was in Triphylia.[7]

For there are still elegant remnants of the city approximately a   23
hundred stadia from the very tip of the Tainaron peninsula; and
no more than five stadia from the shore we saw a citadel built by
later inhabitants out of [materials taken from] ancient buildings,
where I found John Palaiologos, governor for the Spartan prince
Constantine. Received ceremoniously by him, we inspected under
his guidance the extant part, made up of ancient walls, in a field,
where we found this sculpted inscription to our emperor
Gordianus, in which it is evident that Pylos was called Bitylos by
later inhabitants, as Strabo testifies.[8]

> The city of Bitylos, through the overseers headed by Markos
> Aurelios Nikephoros son of Prosdektos, [honored] Emperor
> Marcus Aurelius Gordianus Pious Fortunate Augustus.

We also saw there huge cisterns carved out by an ancient hand   24
and many noble sarcophagi adorned with sculpture and some remarkable rocks.

[Dry]

From there, on the same light craft, guided by the same skipper,   25
Rosea, sailing along the shore of the same promontory, we came to

eiusdem nautae Lares venimus, ubi per diem morantes plerasque alias lata in planicie villas inspeximus cultis agris vinetisque et oliveis arboribus uberes, quas inter non nulla conspeximus antiqua Taenariae almae nobilitatis monumenta et eadem ipsa Dryea in villa antiqui colonum habitus marmoream imaginem huiusmodi figurae comperimus.

[DRAWING]

[Kharia]

26 Ad posteram vero diem, una eodem Rossea nauta comitante, ad x stadia proximam villam Καιρίαν nomine in aede Baptistae sanctissimi praecursori sacra antiquam et imaginibus ornatam comperimus aram ad eandem aedem a posteris ex antiquis operibus ornamento deductam. Ἐς Καιρίαν χωρίον πρὸς Ταινάρον ἐς Πρόδρομον:

[DRAWING]

ΚΑΛΛΙΚΡΑΤΙΔΑΣ ΓΟΡΓΙΔΑΣ ΩΦΕΛΙΑ ΝΙΚΟΙ ΧΑΙΡΕΤΕ[22]

[Kypariso]

27 Exinde vero extremas Taenarii promuntori partes videre desiderantes ad antiquas Cyparisseae nunc ab incolis vocitatae civitatis reliquias venimus, quam prope littora sitam, non Cyparisseam, ut aiebant, quin et Taenariam vetustam et olim nobilem Laconicam coloniam extitisse[23] plerisque ibidem compertis inscriptionibus cognovi. Nam ad altiorem civitatis partem eximia quam plura vidimus egregiae civitatis monumenta et innumeras hinc inde solo collapsas marmoreas et insignes nobilium quondam statuarum bases, quarum consculpta Graecis quoque litteris epigrammata hisce propriis characteribus ponam:

the village of Dry, the home town of the same seaman, where we lingered a day inspecting other villages on the broad plain, [villages] rich in cultivated fields, vineyards and olive trees, among which we noticed several ancient relics of the gracious Tainarian nobility; and in the very same village of Dry we found the marble image of a figure in the ancient dress of farmers [that looked] something like this:[9]

[DRAWING]

[Kharia]

The next day accompanied by the same Rosea, at the next village, 26
called Kharia, about ten stades away, in the sacred church of [John] the Baptist, the most holy Forerunner, we found an ancient altar bedecked with images, which had been removed by later inhabitants from ancient structures to adorn the same church. At the village of Kharia on Tainaron at [the church of the] Forerunner:

[DRAWING]   [PLATE V]

Kallikratidas, Gorgidas, Ophelia, Nikoi, farewell.

[Kypariso]

From there, desiring to see the very tip of the Tainarian promon- 27
tory, we came to the ancient remains of a city set by the sea that is now called Kypariso by its inhabitants, [though, as] I discovered from numerous inscriptions found on the same spot, it was not Kypariso, as they said, but the ancient and once famous Laconian colony of Tainaron. For at a more elevated part of the city we saw a rather large number of the splendid city's marble remains that had fallen to the ground here and there — countless noteworthy marble bases of once noble statues, whose inscriptions, carved in Greek letters, I shall write down in their particular script:

Η ΠΟΛΙΣ | Η ΤΑΙΝΑΡΙΩΝ Ω[ΛΟ]Ν²⁴ | ΟΦΙΛΛΙΟΝ
ΤΑΝΑΓΡΟΝ²⁵ | ΑΞΙΟΛΟΓΩΤΑΤΟΝ ΠΟΛΕΙΤΗΝ | ΤΗΣ
ΕΙΣ ΑΥΤΗΝ ΕΥΝΟΙΑΣ ΧΑΡΙΝ | Ψ̄Η̄. Β.²⁶

28   Ad aliam ornatam marmoreamque et eximiam basim:

ΤΟ ΚΟΙΝΟΝ ΤΩΝ ΕΛΕΥΘΕΡΟΛΑ|ΚΩΝΩΝ ΓΑΙΟΝ
ΙΟΥΛΙΟΝ ΛΑΚΩ|ΝΑ ΕΥΡΥΚΛΕΟΥΣ ΥΙΟΝ ΤΟΝ |
ΙΔΙΟΝ ΕΥΕΡΓΕΤΗΝ | ΔΑΜΑΡΜΕΝΙΔΑΣ
ΣΤΡΑΤΗΓΩΝ | ΕΠΕΜΕΛΗΘΗ²⁷

Euryclea vero Lacedaemonium, quem epigramma hoc superius La-
conis parentem commemorat, Caii Caesaris nostri amicissimum
fuisse Strabonem his dictis declarasse percepimus: Νεωστὶ δ'Εὐ-
ρυκλῆς αὐτοὺς ἐτάραξε, δόξας ἀποχρήσασθαι τῇ Καίσα-
ρος φιλίαι πέρα τοῦ μετρίου πρὸς τὴν ἐπιστασίαν αὐτῶν.
Εὐρυκλέα δε Λακεδαιμόνιον, ὃν τὸ ἄνωθεν ἐπίγραμμα τοῦ
Λάκωνος πατέρα μνημονεύει τῶι Γαίωι Καίσαρι ἡμετέρῳ
φίλτατον ὑπάρξαι τὸν Στράβωνα τοιούτοις λόγοις
δηλῶσαι ἴσμεν.

29   Ad aliam basim inscriptio:

Η ΠΟΛΙΣ | Η ΤΑΙΝΑΡΙΩΝ ΤΙΒΕΡΙΟΝ ΚΛΑΥΔΙΟΝ |
ΕΥΤΥΧΙΔΗΝ ΕΥΤΥΧΙΔΟΥ ΤΟΝ | ΑΞΙΟΛΟΓΩΤΑΤΟΝ
ΠΟΛΕΙΤΗΝ²⁸

30   Itemque ad eandem Taenariam acropolim ad aliam marmoream
basim:

Α ΠΟΛΙΣ Α ΤΩΝ | ΤΑΙΝΑΡΙΩΝ ΖΕΥΞΙ|ΠΠΟΝ
ΦΙΛΟΔΑΜΟΥ ΤΟΝ | ΙΔΙΟΝ ΑΠΟ ΠΡΟΓΟΝΩΝ |
ΑΡΙΣΤΟΝ ΠΟΛΕΙΤΑΝ ΙΑΤΡ|ΕΥΟΝΤΑ ΕΤΙ ΚΑΙ ΝΥΝ
ΕΥΝΟΙ|ΑΣ ΕΙΝΕΚΕΝ ΤΑΣ ΕΙΣ ΑΥΤΑΝ | Ψ̄Η̄. Β̄²⁹

The city of Tainaron [honors] Olos Ophillios Tanagros, a most worthy citizen, for his benevolence to her. By decree of the Council.

On an exceptionally embellished marble base: 28

The League of the Free Laconians [honored] Caius Julius Lakon son of Eurykles, their own benefactor. The chief magistrate Damarmenidas was responsible.

We noticed that Eurycles the Lacedaemonian, who the above inscription says was the father of Lacon, was a very close friend of our Gaius Caesar, according to this passage in Strabo:[10] "But recently Eurycles stirred them up, having apparently abused the friendship of Caesar unduly in order to maintain his authority over them."[11]

Inscription on another statue base: 29

The city of Tainaron [honors] Tiberios Klaudios Eutychides son of Eutychides, the most worthy citizen.

Likewise on the same acropolis of Tainaron on another marble   30 statue base:

The city of Tainaron [honors] Zeuxippos son of Philodamos, hereditarily its own best citizen, who is still serving as doctor, on account of his benevolence toward itself. By decree of the Council.

31   Ad aliam basim:

Α ΠΟΛΙΣ | ΤΩΝ ΤΑΙΝΑΡΙΩΝ | ΛΥΣΙΚΡΑΤΗ
ΔΑΜΑΡΜΕΝ[Ο]Υ[30] ΤΟΝ | ΙΔΙΟΝ ΠΟΛΙΤΑΝ
ΕΜΠΕΙΡΟΤΑΤΟΝ | ΤΩΝ ΝΟΜΩΝ ΑΡΙΣΤΑ
ΠΟΛΙΤΕΥΟΜΕ|ΝΟΝ | $\overline{\Psi H}$. $\overline{B}$.[31]

32   Ad aliam inibi eximiam basim:

Η ΠΟΛΙΣ | Η ΤΑΙΝΑΡΙΩΝ ΤΙΒΕΡΙΟΝ ΚΛΑΥΔΙΟΝ |
ΧΑΡΤΩΝΑ ΤΟΝ ΑΡΙΣΤΟΝ ΠΟΛΕΙΤΗΝ |
ΣΟΦΡΟΣΥΝΗΣ ΤΕ ΚΑΙ ΤΗΣ ΠΕΡΙ ΤΗΝ |
ΑΓΟΡΑΝΟΜΙΑΝ ΑΝΥΠΕΡΒΛΗΤΟΥ | ΦΙΛΟΤΕΙΜΙΑΣ
ΕΙΝΕΚΕΝ | $\overline{\Psi H}$. $\overline{B}$.[32]

33   Ad aliam basim:

Α ΠΟΛΙΣ | ΘΕΟΝ ΑΝΤΩΝΙΝΟΝ ΘΕΟΥ ΑΔΡΙΑΝΟΥ |
ΥΙΟΝ ΘΕΟΥ ΤΡΑΙΑΝΟΥ ΠΑΡΘΙΚΟΥ ΥΙΩ|ΝΟΝ ΘΕΟΥ
ΝΕΡΟΥΑ ΕΓΓΟΝΟΝ ΠΑΤΕΡΑ | ΤΩΝ ΜΕΓΙΣΤΩΝ
ΑΥΤΟΚΡΑΤΟΡΩΝ[33]

34   Ad aliam egregiam basim:

Α ΠΟΛΙΣ | ΑΥΤΟΚΡΑΤΟΡΑ ΚΑΙΣΑΡΑ Λ.
ΑΥΡΗΛΙΟΝ ΒΗΡΟΝ | ΣΕΒ. ΘΕΟΥ ΑΝΤΩΝΙΝΟΥ
ΥΙΟΝ ΘΕΟΥ ΑΔΡΙ|ΑΝΟΥ ΥΙΩΝΟΝ ΘΕΟΥ ΤΡΑΙΑΝΟΥ
ΠΑΡΘΙΚΟΥ | ΑΠΟΓΟΝΟΝ ΑΡΜΕΝΙΑΚΟΝ
ΠΑΡΘΙΚΟΝ ΜΗΔΙ|ΚΟΝ ΓΕΡΜΑΝΙΚΟΝ ΑΡΧΙΕΡΕΑ
ΜΕΓΙΣΤΟΝ ΔΗΜΑΡΧΙΚΗΣ ΕΞΟΥΣΙΑΣ ΥΠΑΤΟΝ $\overline{\Gamma}$.[34]

35   Item ad eandem Taenariam civitatem ad aliam marmoream basim in columnam cuiusdam religiosae aedis a posteris deductam:

Η ΠΟΛΙΣ | ΑΥΤΟΚΡΑΤΟΡΑ ΚΑΙΣΑΡΑ | Μ.
ΑΝΤΩΝΙΟΝ ΓΟΡΔΙΑΝΟΝ | ΕΥΣΕΒΗ ΕΥΤΥΧΗ
ΣΕΒΑ|ΣΤΟΝ | ΔΙΕΦΟΡΩΝ ΤΩΝ ΠΕΡΙ Μ. |

On another statue base: 31

The city of Tainaron [honors] Lysikrates son of Damar-
menos, its own citizen, most skilled in the law and excellently carrying out his civic duties. By decree of the council.

On another exquisite base: 32

The city of Tainaron [honors] Tiberios Klaudios Charton,
the best citizen, on account of his moderation and unsur-
passable munificence when he was in charge of the market.
By decree of the Council.

On another base: 33

The city [honors] the divine Antoninus, son of the divine
Hadrian, grandson of the divine Trajan, victor over Parthia,
descendant of the divine Nerva and father of the greatest
emperors.

On another fine base: 34

The city [honors] the Emperor Caesar Lucius Aurelius
Verus Augustus, son of the divine Antoninus, grandson of
the divine Hadrian, descendant of the divine Parthian victor
Trajan, victor over Armenia, Parthia, Media and Germany,
pontifex maximus, having the power of tribune and consul for
the third time.

Likewise in the same city of Tainaron, on another marble base 35
brought to use as a column of a certain religious building by later
inhabitants:

The city [honors] Emperor Caesar Marcus Antonius Gordianus, Pious Fortunate Augustus, through the overseers
headed by Markos Aurelios Thaliarchos son of Thaliarchos

ΑΥΡΗΛΙΟΝ ΘΑΛΙΑΡΧΟΝ | ΘΑΛΙΑΡΧΟΤ ΚΑΙ
ΕΠΙΜΕ|ΛΗΤΟΤ Μ. ΑΥΡΗΛΙΟΤ ΛΤ|ΣΙΞΕΝΟΤ ΤΟΤ
ΛΤΣΙΚΡΑΤΟΤΣ³⁵

36   Item prope forum ad marmoreum ornatissimum epistile:

ΛΤΣΙΚΡΑΤΗΣ ΚΑΛΛΙΚΡΑΤΟΤΣ | ΗΡΩΣ
ΣΤΡΑΤΗΓΗΣΑΣ³⁶

37   Ad alium epistile circulare:

ΔΑΜΑΡΧΙΣ ΕΤΕΑΡΧΟΤ | ΕΤΕΑΡΧΙΔΙ ΔΑΜΕΑ | ΤΗ
ΙΔΙΑ ΘΤΓΑΤΡΙ³⁷

38   Ἐπίγραμμα ἐν Σαλαμίνι ἐκ τοῦ Θουκιδίδου ἐξερευνομέ-
νον:

Ω ΞΕΝΕ ΕΥΤΔΡΟΝ ΠΟΤΕ ΝΑΙΟΜΕΝ ΑΣΤΤ
    ΚΟΡΙΝΘΟΤ
ΝΤΝΙ ΔΑΝΑΤΟΣ³⁸ ΝΑΣΟΣ ΕΧΕΙ ΣΑΛΑΜΙΣ³⁹

[Porto Quaglio, i.e. Chorasia]

39   Exinde equidem ad XIII Kalendas Novembris ex eadem Taenaria
civitate ad ipsam extremam promuntorii partem venimus. Et
prope Chorasiam villam secus portum quem Qualearum Latino
nomine nautae vocitant prope antiquas Neptuni templi reliquias
hoc primum comperimus epigramma:

ΑΡΙΣΤΟΤΕΛΗΣ ΙΕΡΕΤΣ | ΧΑΙΡΕ | ΠΡΤΑΙΟΣ
ΑΡΙΣΤΟΤΕΛΗΣ | ΙΕΡΕΤΣ ΧΑΙΡΕ | ΔΑΜΑΡΜΕΝΙΔΑΣ
ΑΡΙΣΤΟΤΗΛΟΤΣ | ΙΕΡΕΤΣ ΧΑΙΡΕ⁴⁰

40   Item ad quoddam religiosum Michaelis Archangeli sacellum ad
vetustissimam et semideletam tempore tabellam Cadmeis vetustissimis litteris inscriptio:⁴¹

[DRAWING]

ΚΑΙ Θ[Ε]ΟΔΟΡΟΣ ΤΙΟΣ ΤΟΤΤΟΙΝ ΦΙΛΟΤΑΤΑΣ

and through the financial officer Markos Aurelios Lysixenos son of Lysikrates.

Likewise, near the forum on a highly embellished marble archi- 36 trave:

The late chief magistrate Lysikrates son of Kallikrates.

On another curved architrave: 37

Damarchis daughter of Etearchos to Etearchis daughter of Dameas, her own daughter.

Epigram on Salamis drawn from Thucydides: 38

O stranger, once we lived in the well-watered city of Corinth, but now the unharmed island of Salamis holds us.[12]

[Porto Quaglio, i.e. Chorasia]

From there, on the 20th of October, we journeyed from the same 39 city of Tainaron to the very tip of the promontory; and near the village of Chorasia, close by the port which the sailors call by the Italian name of Quaglio, near the ancient ruins of a temple of Neptune, we first found this inscription:

Aristoteles the priest, farewell; Pryaios the priest, son of Aristoteles, farewell; Damarmenidas the priest, son of Aristoteles, farewell.

Likewise, at a religious chapel of Michael the Archangel, on a 40 very old tablet, partially effaced by the passage of time, an inscription in very ancient Cadmaean lettering:

[DRAWING]

[...] and Theodoros their dearest son. [PLATE VI]

319

41   Et ad ipsum portus eiusdem propinquiorem collem, in luco pri-
neis[42] exiguis arbuscolis denso, ad v stadiorum a littore abmotum,
ingens illud antrum comperimus, ex quo Cerberum ab inferis divum Herculem abstraxisse ferunt, tametsi eandem fabulam ab aliis
ex Herculea Pontica civitate Acherusiaque inibi spelunca traditam
novimus et locum illum anno nondum exacto conspeximus, ut et
superius nostra ex navigatione Pontica memoratum est.

42   Hic vero cum ad vestibulum et vastas baratri fauces accederemus, non draco, quem intus adesse indigenae agrestes pavidi nun-
ciabant, quin et abvolantum inde columbarum clangor, trepidantem sociorum animum percussit. Et denique tris e Porasia villa et
Taenaria civitate comitantibus accolis, saxeum per os ad interiorem speci partem descendi; et profundius demum Adr[iano?] Magola Iωanneque Tabulario sacerdote, per immania baratri viscera
accensis ceriis descendentes ad inextimabilem abyssi profundita-
tem antrum in abruptum[43] tendere percepimus.

43   Sed exeuntes ab eo cum iterum Taenariam civitatem revisissem,
has ad semifractum lapidem imagines comperi:

[DRAWING]

[Dry. The Laconian shore. Ruins of Amathea]

44   Postea equidem Dryea villa revisa et ex ea deinde per eiusdem
Taenarii promuntorii partes, indigenis comitatus colonis pedes,
plerisque per iter secus Messaniacum sinum oliviferis villis inspectis, tandem per vallem quae inter Taygeti montis colles ipsius Taenarii promuntorii Laconicum a Messaneaco sinu disterminantis isthmon facit, Laconicum ad littus venimus, ubi primum parvo in

And at the nearer hill of the same harbor, in a grove thick with   41
slender holm-oak saplings, at a remove of five stades from the
shore, we found that huge cave from which, they say,[13] the divine
Hercules dragged Cerberus out of the lower world—although we
learned that the same tale has been handed down by others from
the city of Heracleia Pontica, [that it was] from the Acherusian
cave there, and we saw that place less than a year ago, as is recorded above in the account of my voyage on the [Euxine] Sea.

Here, however, when we were approaching the forecourt and   42
the gaping mouth of the pit, it was not a dragon, which the timor-
ous rustic natives proclaimed was present within, but the racket of
doves flying out of there that startled the trembling hearts of my
companions. Finally, going down through the rocky entrance into
the interior of the cave, accompanied by three inhabitants from the
village of Porasia and the city of Tainaron, and eventually [ventur-
ing] with lit candles deeper into the vast interior of the pit along
with Adr[iano?] Magola and Giovanni Tabulario, a priest, we observed that the cave leads to a sheer drop.

When we had exited that cave and returned to the city of   43
Tainaron, I found these images [carved] on a partially broken
stone:

[DRAWING]

[Dry. The Laconian shore. Ruins of Amathea]

Afterwards, I revisited the village of Dry; and then, accompanied   44
from there on foot by farmers native to the area, [I journeyed]
through parts of the same peninsula of Tainaron, inspecting on
the way numerous olive-producing villages along the Messenian
Gulf. Finally, by way of a valley that creates a pass between the
heights of the Taygetus range of the Tainarian peninsula (which
itself separates the Laconian from the Messenian Gulf), we came
at length to the Laconian shore of the Tainarian peninsula, where

cheroneso Amatheae civitatis reliquias equidem exiguas vidimus. Nam pauca ibidem digna videntur nobilitatis praeter aliqua marmorea epistilia et columnarum non exigua quidem fragmenta atque nonnullas statuarum bases.

[Local customs described]

45 At et cum ex itinere pulchram et densis hinc inde vineis arboribusque et amoenis pratis virentem et placidissimam vallem hilari animo conspexissem, accolae mihi locum lapidibus ingenitis terminatum ostentarunt, quo quot annis indigena proxima quoque iuventus antiquo de more, positis a principe premiis, agonem exercent, quem ἀνδρόδρομον πεντοστάδιον quoque vocant; v scilicet stadiorum spatio virorum cursu contendunt, exutis quidem pedibus, et interiori linea tantum tunica induti et qui se primum signo velocius affert, aere x forte dragmarum quas *hyperpera* dicunt donatur; secundus vero v, tertius tris, et gradatim deinceps omnes, exiguo vel aere Hyrcinaeve carnis pondere, ita ut ex athletarum numero nullus non donatus abierit, quin et deteriorem ultimum princeps simul cepe donatum populoque ridiculum reddit.

46   Etenim hisdem locis homines, plurifariam modis antiquum servare ritum cognovimus, nam quisque suas per rura casas magnis polygonisque et antiqua arte compositis lapidibus aedunt; ac cisternas quoque manu longo tramite effodientes ingentibus et septipedum saxis protegunt. Ita et loquendi antiquum quodammodo servare morem cognovimus: mortuos nanque suos quosvecunque suae relligionis homines, ἐς τὸν Ἄδην, scilicet ad inferos, migrasse dicunt, dapes enim eorum fractae quoque fabae oleoque

we first observed, on a small promontory, the really scanty remains of the city of Amathea: for few items there seem worthy of note besides some marble architraves, fragments of columns — not scanty, I admit — and some statue bases.

[Local customs described]

And when on my journey I had viewed with pleasure a lovely valley green in every direction with close-packed vineyards and trees and pleasant meadows, and utterly tranquil, the locals showed me a place bounded by natural stones where every year the youths who live in the immediate vicinity engage by ancient custom in a competition, for which their prince provides the prizes, which they also call the *androdromon pentastadion*; that is, they compete in a men's footrace over a distance of five stadia, which they run barefoot, mind you, and dressed only in a linen undertunic; and whoever runs more swiftly and comes in first is given ten bronze drachmas, which they call *hyperpera*;[14] the second [is given] five; the third, three; and after that, all the others, in order of finishing, a little cash or a quantity of Hyrcanian meat, so that none of the athletes will have gone away unrewarded, except that the prince at once rewards the one who comes in last and makes him an object of popular ridicule with the gift of an onion.

And indeed we came to know that the people in these places observe an ancient practice in a variety of ways, for they all build their houses in the countryside with great polygonal stones put together according to an ancient technique; and, digging out cisterns by hand, each in a long line, they protect them with huge, seven-foot rocks; and we discovered that they somehow preserve an ancient manner of speaking, for they say that their dead, no matter what their religion was, have gone off "to Hades," that is, to the lower world. Also, their meals consist of snapped beans seasoned generously with oil, and their loaves are made from barley; their

45

46

conditae multo et ex ordeo panes sunt; potum vero aqua est, et raro vel nisi pro solemnibus laetis vinum gustant et panegyricis festis.

[Colochitea]

47 Ac inibi prope ut et caeteram fere per Greciam nostro quoque tempore omnes per alta montium et ardua saxis cacumina castella oppidave habitant, ut se a barbaris praedonumve incursionibus, tutiores potissimum reddantur. Sed in ea tantum promuntorii parte natura loci munita in planicie diversa floreaque per rura villas plerasque colunt. Hic vero ad eiusdem civitatis acropolim, quam Colochiteam vocant, arcem alto et arduo saxis in colle a posteris conditam ascendi, ubi ad semifractum lapidem antiquum et semideletum epigramma hoc comperimus:

ΣΩΖΟΜΕΝΟΣ ΕΝ ΤΕ ΛΟΓΩΙ | ΕΠΙΣΚΕΤΗ ΠΡΟΣ
ΜΕΝΗ ΕΤΓΕΝΕΣΤΑΤΗΣ | ΚΕΚΡΟΠΙΔΟΣ ΠΟΛΕΩΣ[44]

48 Item ad ipsam Amatheam maritimam civitatem:

[DRAWING]

[Karopolis]

49 Ex Amathea deinde progredientes, Caropolim venimus, Asineae antiquae civitatis vicum, ubi Solianum Georgi Stratopedarchi nomine pro Constantino despote praefectum comperimus, qui me quam digne subscipiens ad posteram diem, ad ipsam Asineam antiquam in Laconici sinus littore deletam civitatem duxit. Ubi pauca videntur adnotatione digna, tantae civitatis monumenta, praeter ingentes quasdam ex cocto latere thermarum reliquias et quas hodie vulgus locum ipsum ob non nullos extantes arcus camaras vocant. Extant et prope littus non nullae de marmore columnae ac alia vetustorum operum fragmenta. Sed nullis comper-

drink, however, is water. Wine they drink rarely, except on joyful festival days and on celebratory occasions that call for eulogistic oratory.

[Colochitea]

There, nearby, as also throughout almost all the rest of Greece 47 in our time, they all live in castles or settlements that are situated on steep, rocky mountain-heights, chiefly to insure greater safety from the attacks of barbarians and brigands. Only in the part of the promontory that is protected by the nature of the terrain do they reside in numerous villages on a remote plain, and in a flowering countryside. Here, however, on the acropolis of the same city, which they call Colochitea,[15] I climbed the citadel built by later generations on a steep and rocky hill, where we found the following inscription on a fragmentary and partially effaced ancient stone:

Sozomenos, in word [*unintelligible*] of the most noble city of Kekrops.

Likewise in the coastal city of Amathea: 48

[DRAWING]

[Karopolis]

Moving on from Amathea, we came to Karopolis,[16] a village of the 49 ancient city of Asine, where we found Solianos, son of George the *stratopedarches*,[17] administrator for the despot Constantine, who received me quite properly and led me the next day to the ruined city of Asine on the shore of the Laconic Gulf. There one sees few remnants worth recording of such a great city, other than some huge brick remains of the baths and the place the populace calls, the "vaults" because of some surviving arches. Also along the shore, some marble columns and other fragments of ancient structures survive. But since we found no inscriptions, we departed

tis litteris statim inde recedentes ea parum digna memoratione reliquimus.

[Gythion]

50 Ex ea vero ad diem posteram Gythion venimus, egregiam olim in Laconico littore civitatem et nobile Lacedaemonum urbis navale, ducenta ferme et XL stadia ab ipsa Spartana civitate disiunctum, cuius adhuc pluria suae antiquae magnitudinis monumenta extant et prope mare ipsius mirifici navistatii magna vestigia magnaque sub saxea rupe fabraefactae ingentes parietes, quarum primam C passuum longitudine et quattuor ac XXX altitudine metiti sumus.

51   Extant et aliqua ex parte integra sui magnifici theatri sedilia et parietum pars magnis quoque lapidibus erecta quod quidem eximium theatrum marmoreis sedilibus eximia magnitudine compositum, ad mare et australem in plagam versum non plus fere stadio a littore remotum constat.

52   Extant et inibi disiecta solo pleraque de marmore opera et magnorum aedificiorum vestigia thermarumque cocto ex latere reliquias inspexi et quas vulgum hodie ignarum Menelai palatia appellasse comperimus.

53   Extant et alia pleraque columnarum basiumque et epistilium atque nobilium statuarum fragmenta, quarum eximias binas ipsum prope theatrum hisce quoad licuit designandum delegi, quod et altera, quam pulcherrimis induta armis, caeteris praestare videtur. Menelai simulachrum esse accolae ibidem omnes, veteri fama vulgatum affirmabant.

[Arcasa]

54 Ex hinc inde, plerisque aliis eiusdem amplissimae civitatis per campos collapsis aedificiis inspectis, ex ea cum posteram ad diem recederemus, Arcaseam denique villam Spartanam venimus. In

from the site and left behind [ruins] not worthwhile enough to record

[Gythion]

On the next day we journeyed from there to Gythion, once an important city on the Laconian shore and a famous naval base of the city of Lacedaimonians, about 240 stades distant from the city of Sparta itself, where numerous reminders of her ancient greatness still survive and, by the sea, substantial remains of its remarkable naval station and, at the foot of a large, rocky cliff, massive walls wrought by craftsmen, the first of which we measured to be a hundred paces long and thirty four high. 50

Surviving also are some seats, in part intact, of a splendid theater and a portion of its walls, also built of large stones. This remarkable theater, made up of marble seats of remarkable size, still stands facing south towards the sea, no more than a stade away from the shore. 51

There also survive in that place numerous marble works scattered on the ground; and I examined the traces of large buildings and the brick remains of the baths, which we learned the ignorant populace of today called the palace of Menelaos. 52

Also surviving are numerous other fragments of columns and statue bases and architraves, as well as noteworthy statues; of the two most outstanding ones, near the theater itself, I elected, insofar as in me lay, to make the following sketch, because the second, which is dressed in most handsome armor, seems superior to the others. All the locals kept insisting that it is a portrait of Menelaos, according to a widespread ancient tradition.[18] 53

[Arcasa]

When, after inspecting in the fields on every side numerous other fallen structures of that same quite large city, we departed on the 54

planiciem ad orientales Taygeti montis radices — montem vero non usquam claro suo nomine Taygeton, quin Hagion Heliam late ab incolis vocitatum audimus — et ex ea niveos montis vertices prospectantes sacrum Heliae prophetae sacellum accolae ostentarunt; et quamvis per omnem Graeciam altiora montium cacumina hodierno quoque tempore Graeci eiusdem prophetae numini sacra colant, hoc precipue alto in vertice vivum et perennem Heliam habitare prophetam existimant et XIII Kalendarum Sextilium festo et sacro sibi panegyrico die rutilantes inter fulgido splendore nubes apparere visum affirmant tantum nostro quidem aevo incertos inter et vulgares homines et agrestes formidosa religio potest.

[Return to Mistra]

55   At et cum equidem inde Gemistei Platonici dilectissimi nostri gratia Laconicam Mysithratem revisissem et procul ex itinere Laconicorum ruinas nobilium quondam oppidorum animo revolvendo considerans, existimabam quippe quod etsi nobiles antiquas illas insignes et ornatissimas urbes undique fere per orbem collapsas penitus nostro tempore vel deletas videre dolendum esset, aegro magis animo ferendum censebam miserabilem ipsam humani generis calamitatem, quod et non tam graviter conspicua illa mundi oppida sacrave superis mirifica templa speciosaque simulachra, ac alia humanae quidem potentiae atque artis eximia ornamenta a prisco suo splendore cecidisse videmus, quam deteriorem in modum per omnes fere mundi regiones humanam illam priscam virtutem et animi inclytam probitatem corruisse visum, ac ubi olim magis floruerant, magis atque magis abierant.

next day from it, we came at length to the Spartan village of Arcasa. Gazing out from there onto the plain toward the eastern base of Mount Taygetus — the mountain is never called by its illustrious name, Taygetus, but rather we hear it widely referred to by the inhabitants as "St. Elijah" — and toward the snow-covered peaks of the mountain, the locals showed us a sacred chapel of the prophet Elijah; and, although throughout all Greece even in our own time Greeks revere the higher peaks of mountains as shrines of the same prophet, they think that the living, immortal Elijah dwells especially on this high peak; and on the 20th of July, his feast and festival, they assert that he appears, seen among the glowing red clouds in brilliant splendor — so powerful even in our own time is religious awe among the unstable, rustic common folk.

[Return to Mistra]

But when I had returned from there to Laconian Mistra in order 55 [to see] our very good friend Gemistos Pletho, while contemplating en route from afar the ruins of once-famous Laconian towns, mulling this over in my mind, I thought, naturally, of the fact that, even though one must grieve to behold those noble, ancient, distinguished and richly adorned cities, now in our time in a state of utter collapse or demolition almost everywhere throughout the region, one must endure with an [even] heavier heart, in my opinion, the pitiable ruin of the human race, because the fact that the world's outstanding towns, marvelous temples sacred to the gods, beautiful statues and other extraordinary trappings of human power and skill have fallen from their pristine grandeur seems not so serious as the fact that, throughout almost all the regions of the world, that pristine human virtue and renowned integrity of spirit has fallen into an [even] worse condition; and where they had once flourished most, there they had more and more departed.

329

56   Nam et generosum atque inclytum illud Spartanum genus,
olim non modo Graeciae, quin et Europae, totum vel per orbem,
militiae et virtutis omnigenae memorabile decus hodie ignave tur-
piterque sui degeneres homines a prisca illa Laconici moris Lace-
daemonumve inclyta probitate penitus cecidisse videntur. Quam
antea vero praeter quod ab iis Roma leges accipere non rubuit,
quanta eorum in armorum studiis exercita virtus et gloria fuerit
pluria quidem amittens ipsa in patria regione Orthryadam potentissimis Argis, Pausaniam vero in Boetia Persis, Lysandron Athenis, Asiae quidem Agesilaum, et in Africa utique nostris sane
Xanthippum ostentasse cognovimus. Ast enim vero hodie qui Laconicam regionem Spartanumve Taygeti montis collem, antiquo
posthabito nomine, Mysithra oppidum colunt, rem agrariam, mer-
caturam vel pauperem serviles artes et vilia quaeque mysteria exercentes, a barbaris vel externae nationis hominibus dominantur.

57   Verum equidem hoc unum minime pretermittam, quod et
quanquam memorata politica illa Lacedaemonum virtus disciplina
militiae et preclarae in gymnasiis virum ac nobilium mulierum
agonae, longo iam tempore ob incuriam destitutae aboletaeque
sint, natura tamen loci non penitus defecta videtur, cum ex se
quandoque homines gignit, suapte natura probos et ad virtutem
habiles atque idoneos. Namque[45] hodie dum Arcasana ex villa ad
ipsam Spartanam Mysithratem iter haberemus, nostros inter comites Spartanum quempiam vidimus iuvenem statura proceri ac
sane formosum, Georgium Chirodonta,[46] scilicet Apridenteum,

For that noble-spirited, renowned race of Spartans, once the   56
memorable triumph of every kind of military valor, not only in
Greece, but in Europe and throughout the whole world, [but]
nowadays a people feebly and basely untrue to their breeding,
seem to have fallen completely from that famous pristine moral integrity of the Laconian, Lacedaimonian way of life. Whereas in
the past, aside from the fact that Rome was not ashamed to bor-
row its laws from them, [and] leaving out the many achievements
in their own homeland, we know how great was their courage and
glory, practiced in the pursuits of war; [we know] that Orthryadas
manifested these qualities in powerful Argos, [as did] Pausanias in
Boeotia against the Persians, Lysander in Athens, Agesilaus in
Asia, and in Africa, certainly, Xanthippus against our [Roman]
forces. [I say this] because, in these our days, those who dwell
in the Laconian land, on the Spartan foothill of Mount Taygetus,
in the town of Mistra (which has discarded its ancient name),
men who practice a poor sort of agriculture or commerce or igno-
ble trades and every kind of worthless superstitious rite, are ruled
by barbarians or by foreigners.

For my part, however, I shall by no means pass over the follow-   57
ing single [exception], [proving] that, although the Lacedaimonians' much-talked-of political excellence, military training,
and the splendid contests of men and well-born women in the
gymnasia have been abandoned and have fallen into disuse
through neglect over a long period of time, still, the nature of the
place seems not totally to have waned, since it gives birth to human beings who are naturally honorable, able and suited to virtue.
For today, while we were traveling from the village of Arcasa to
Spartan Mistra, we saw among our companions a certain Spartan
youth, tall of stature and quite handsome, George, called by the
sobriquet Chirodontas, that is, "Boar's teeth," because, they say,
that once, while hunting in the forest, encountering a fierce boar,
he leaped onto its back, and pressing it down by sheer force, killed

cognomine dictum. Ipsum etenim quandoque per silvas inter venando, ferocem occurrentem aprum, saltu dorso desuper incumbentem, forti manu solo prosternatam feram exanimasse ferunt. Nec non aliquando bina hominum communia corpora prensa manu sub ulnis aliquot passuum transduxisse. Me quoque solatii loco et suae probitatis declarandae gratia ad cuiusdam parvi fluminis ripam manu prendens sub brachio ad ulteriorem amnis partem incolumem deposuerat. Et ad proximam villam manu ferream et tridigitum latitudine virgam detorquens, diversas in partes scidisse conspeximus.

58   Praeterea cum ad ipsam Spartanam arcem propinquius accederemus et campos Aurotaeque fluminis ripas atque verenda loca ubi Lacedaemonum civitas tam memoranda fuerat immensis adhuc undique conspersa ruinis procul attonitus aspexissem, illico collapsam e coelo Caliopen talia meo nomine Latio quoque nostro et laepidissimo idiomate canentem audivi:[47]

> Alma città laconica spartana,[48]
> gloria de Grecia, già del mondo exemplo
> d'arme e de castità, gymnasio e templo
> e d'ogni alma virtù specchio e fontana:
>   se politia, costumi e legge humana
> con l'altre[49] tue moral virtù contemplo,
> poi te remiro in Eurota, extemplo
> exclamo al chor de l'alma tua Diana:
>   "Dove è 'l tuo bon Lycurgo, ove Dioscori,
> diri gemelli, Castore e Polluce?
> Anaxandrida, Orthryada e Gylippo,
>   Euriste e Leonida? Ove demori
> Atride e Pausania? O chiaro duce
> Lysandro, Aristo, Agesilao e Xanthippo?"
>   "Non Roma, non Philippo,"

the prostrate beast; and [they say] that once he caught and held two men together under his arms and carried them several paces. In my case also, instead of reassuring me [verbally], and as a [physical] statement of his honesty, he caught me up with his hands on the bank of a certain small river, held me under his arm, and deposited me safely on the farther bank of the stream. And at the next village, we saw that, brandishing an iron rod that was three fingers thick, he had split it into separate parts.

In addition to that, when we were approaching closer to the 58 Spartan citadel itself and, stunned, I had viewed from afar the plains and the banks of the Eurotas river and the revered location where the city of the Lacedaemonians had stood, so memorable, [but] now scattered everywhere, its ruins still massive, at that very moment I heard Calliope, who had descended from heaven, singing, in my name and in our most delightful Italian tongue, the following song:

> Great Laconian city of Sparta,
> the glory of Greece, once example to the world
> of warfare and of chastity; gymnasium and temple
> and mirror and font of every noble virtue;
>   if I contemplate your constitution, customs
> and human law together with your other moral virtues,
> then gaze upon you on the Eurotas, suddenly
> I exclaim to your patron Diana's chorus:
>   "Where are your excellent Lycurgus, where the Dioscuri,
> the dire twins, Castor and Pollux,
> Anaxandridas, Orthryadas and Gylippus,
> Eurystus and Leonidas? Where do you dwell
> son of Atreus and Pausanias, o famous leader,
> Lysander, Aristo, Agesilaus and Xanthippus?"
>   "Neither in Rome, nor with Philip,"

dixe: "Ma è 'l saecol vil vostro. Adconfino
la volta in Mysithra, sub Constantino."

59 Ἐκ τῆς περὶ τῶν ζώων ἐδωδῆς ὑποθέσεως:
[Incipit] ζώων δ᾽ οὖν τῶν ἡμέρων . . .
[Explicit] . . . φθορὰν οἴκοθεν ὁρμάν.

[DRAWINGS]

60 ΜΕΛΙΚΡΕΑ ΑΦΡΟΔΕΙ|ΣΙΟΤ ΑΝΤΙΟΧΙΣΣΩ | ΧΡΗΣΤΗ
ΑΛΤΠΗ | ΧΑΙΡΕ[50]

61 ΚΙ[Ν]ΕΑΣ ΠΟΛΛΙΣ | ΔΕΞΙ ΧΑΙΡΕ[51]

62 Antiqua et eximiae artis composita Naupliae arcis moenia:

[DRAWING]

63 Apud eandem Naupliam arcem antiqua in lapidea tabella:

[DRAWING]

ΕΛΙΣΣΑ ΑΝΕΘΗΚΕ[52]

64 Ad alium lapidem semifractum antiquae Cadmeaeve litterae:

ΜΙΚΡΙΑΣ . ΘΕΟ[Ξ]ΕΝ . . . | ΙΣΧΡΟΝΟΣ ·
ΑΦΘΟΝΕΤ . . .[53]

65 Ad alium antiquum et semifractum ab ipso capite lapidem Doricis egregiis litteris inscriptio:

ΤΑΣ .ΕΙΣ . ΤΟΝ . ΔΑΜΟΝ ΤΩΝ ΤΡΟΖΑΝΙΩΝ ΚΑΙ |
ΤΑΣ ΕΙΣ ΠΡΟΤΕΡΟΝ ΔΩΡΕΑΣ ΔΕΔΟΜΕΝΑΣ ΕΙΜΕΝ
| ΑΤΤΩΙ ΔΕΔΟΣΘΑΙ ΔΕ ΑΤΤΩΙ ΚΑΙ
ΕΜΠΡΥΤΑΝΕΙΩΙ ΣΙΤΗΣΙΝ | ΚΑΙ ΕΣ ΤΟΤΣ ΑΓΩΝΑΣ
ΕΣΚΑΡΤΣΣΕΣΘΑΙ ΕΣ ΠΡΟΕΔΡΙΑΝ | ΑΤΤΟΝ ΚΑΙ
ΕΚΓΟΝΟΤΣ ΕΜΠΡΟΣΘΑΙ ΔΙΕΤΟΝ ΙΑΡΗΤΩΝ |
ΔΙΩΔΕΚΑ ΘΕΚΑ ΘΕΩΝ ΖΗΝΟΔΟΤΩΙ ΚΑΙ
ΕΚΓΟΝΟΙΣ | ΠΟΛΛΑ ΚΑΙ ΑΓΑΘΑ Ο ΚΑΙ

it said: "But it is your tawdry age. I assign
the turn to Mistra, under the leadership of Constantine."[19]

From the hypothesis of the treatise concerning the diet of ani- 59
mals:[20]

[DRAWINGS]

Melikrea from Antioch, daughter of Aphrodeisios: Dear 60
one, free from pain, farewell.[21]

Kineas, Pollis, Dexis, farewell. 61

The ancient walls of the citadel of Nauplion fashioned with ex- 62
traordinary skill:

[DRAWING]   [PLATE VII]

At the same citadel of Nauplion, on an ancient stone slab: 63

[DRAWING]   [PLATE VIII]

Elissa dedicated [this].

On another partially broken stone, ancient or Cadmean letter- 64
ing:

Mikrios, son of Theoxen[os] [...] son of Heschrion, Aph-
thonetos

On another ancient stone that is partially broken at the top, an 65
inscription in elegant Doric script:[22]   [PLATE IX]

[...] [his benefactions?] to the people of Troizen, and the
gifts which have been given in the past shall be his; he shall
be given public maintenance in the town hall and the right of
him and his descendants to the front seats in the games shall
be proclaimed in front of the temple of the Twelve Gods.

ΠΑΝΔΑΜΙΟΡΓΙΑ ΚΑΡΙΣΤΑΤΑΙ | ΚΑΙ ΕΙ ΤΙΝΟΣ ΚΑ
ΑΛΛΟΥ ΔΕΗΤΑΙ ΤΟΥ ΔΑΜΟΥ ΤΟΥ ΤΡΟ|ΖΑΝΙΩΝ
ΥΠΗΡΕΤΕΝ ΑΥΤΩΙ ΚΑΙ ΕΚΓΟΝΟΙΣ ΑΝ ΓΡΑ|ΤΑΙ
ΔΩΤΟ ΔΕ ΤΟ ΨΑΦΙΣΜΑ ΕΝ ΣΤΑΛΛΑΙ ... ΟΙΝΑΙ |
ΚΑΙΣ ... ΩΣΑΙ ΕΣ ΤΟ ΙΑΡΟΝ ΤΟ ΑΠΟΛΛΩΝΟΣ ΤΟΥ
ΘΕ|ΡΙΑΤΟΝ ΔΕ ΒΟΥΛΛΑΝΤΑ ΤΑΝ ΥΠΟΡΓΙΑΝ
ΠΑΡΕΧΕΝ | ΤΙΜΑΝ ΕΙ ΓΕ ΠΡΟΕΣΤΑΙ ΕΙ ΒΟΥΛΑΣ
ΔΑΜΕΑΣ ΑΡΚΦΙ | ΕΓΡΑΦΟ ΦΙΛΟ ΤΟ
ΚΑΛΟΔΑΜΟΥ⁵⁴

[*Nauplion, "Mycenae" (= Merbaka)*]

66 Ad x Kalendas Aprilium fausti resurrectionis humanati Iovis die-
previum cum Nauplium revisissem et Petrum Ranganum scribam
Iohannemque Bendramon amicissimos, magna cum hilaritate revisimus et postridie siquid deletae Mycenarum urbis nostram ad
diem reliquum extaret videre desiderans, iisdem comitantibus pleraque primum Argivo in campo vidimus veterum insignia monumenta et inter potiora non nullas pulcherrimarum imaginum candenti ex marmore tabellas, olim Iunonio ex antiquissimo templo
ex insignibus Polycleti ut putandum operibus, ad posteras relligionis nostrae aedes a Christicolis ornamento deductas quarum ad
primariam et praestantiorem ad semidirutum lapidem hoc Latinis
quoque litteris antiquum epigramma comperimus:

Q. CAECILIO . C.F . METELO . . . | IMPERATORI .
ITALICI . . . QVEI. ARGEIS. NEGOTIANTVR⁵⁵

67 Polycleti opus ex antiquo et diu iam deleto Argivae Myce-
neaeque Iunonis delubro et Argivo in campo ad sacram beatae
Virginis aedem a posteris et nostrae religionis hominibus ornamento deductum:

[DRAWINGS]

Many benefits for Zenodotos and his descendants as the
board of magistrates shall ordain, and if anyone asks anything else of the people of Troizen it shall be granted to him
and his descendants. This decree shall be inscribed on a
stone stele and set up in the temple of Apollo Thearios [...]
rendered this service. Timon spoke, Dameas son of Arkoias
presided over the Council; Philotas son of Kalodamos was
secretary.

[Nauplion, "Mycenae" (= Merbaka)]

On the 23rd of March, the eve of the blessed resurrection of the 66
incarnate Jove, when I had revisited Nauplion, we had a fully en-
joyable reunion with my very good friends, Pietro Rangano the
scribe and Joannes Bendramon, and on the next day, in company
with these same companions, desiring to see if anything of the destroyed city of Mycenae survived until our time, first of all we saw
on the plain a great number of remarkable remnants of antiquity
and, among the more important, some slabs of shining marble
[bearing] images of outstanding beauty that had been removed in
the past by Christians from a very old temple of Juno, thought to
be from among the masterpieces of Polyclitus, to adorn later
churches of our religion. On the principle and more outstanding
of these slabs, on a partially broken off stone, we found this ancient inscription in Latin script:

The Italians who do business in Argos to Quintus Caecilius
Metellus, son of Gaius, Imperator.

The work of Polyclitus that had been brought by later genera- 67
tions, men of our own religion, from an ancient and already long-
ruined temple of Argive and Mycenaean Juno to adorn the holy
church of the Virgin on the Argive plain:[23]

[DRAWINGS]   [PLATE X]

ΕΤΠΟΡΟΣ . ΕΤΠΡΑΣΙΣ . ΖΗ . ΑΝΤΕΡΩΣ[56]

68   Deinde vero veteres inter Argivas et desertas villas, vetusta Mycenarum monumenta perquirens Iunonii deleti jam diu delubri aliquod vestigium autumantes, tandem non longe ab eo et ab Argiva
urbe non plus ferme VII passum millia distantem, in Borealem
partem et a Nauplio minus XL stadiorum disiunctam, saxeum super et arduum collem, Mycenarum arcis reliquias vidimus et non
nullas antiquis suis e moenibus partes extare ac turrium porta-
rumque vestigia mira quidem et pulchra architectorum arte perspi-
cua atque nostri quoque spectatione praedigna. Ad quam cum una
iisdem solertissimis viris adscendere placuisset, eiusdem muri partem in Nauplium quoque spectantem hisce deponere figuratam
nempe delegimus.

69   Mycenarum antiquissimae arcis quae quidem nostro aevo moenia videntur saxeo in colle eximia arte magnis et plumbeo colore
lapidibus condita:

[DRAWING]

[Acrocorinth][57]

70   Cum ad XV Kalendas μαίας, faustum Mercuri diem e Spartana
arce Mysethrea Acrocorinthum revisissem, inibi Ἰωhannem Κατακουζινὸν magnificum ac regia de stirpe virum nec non pacis
bellique artibus praestantem pro Spartano rege Constantino Co-
rintheae provinciae praesidem comperimus. Qui cum me *ex Patra*
veterem novisset amicum *perquam* benigne suscepit et *munifice ex
venatu rediens magna cervi parte aliisque* haud indignis muneribus donavit.

71   Cuius vero ingenuum ac praeclarum filium Constantinum Comitem Palatinum Lateranensem, dum Aegium oppidum olim

Euporos, Eupraxis, Anteros

Then, while searching for ancient remnants of Mycenae among 68
old, uninhabited Argive villages that bespeak some hint of the
long-ago ruined temple of Juno, finally, not far from it and no
more than about seven miles away from the city of Argos, towards
the north and less than forty stadia from Nauplion, on a hill that
is rocky at the top and steep, we saw that remains of the Mycenaean citadel,[24] and some portions of its ancient walls survive, as well
as traces of towers and gates, conspicuous for the wondrously
beautiful craftsmanship of the architects and eminently worthy of
our scrutiny as well. When, along with the same highly experienced
men, we had decided to climb to it, we chose to set down here a
drawing of the part of the same wall that looks toward Nauplion.

The walls of the very old citadel of Mycenae, which are visible 69
even in our own time, built with extraordinary craftmanship on a
rocky hill of large, lead-colored stones:

[DRAWING]

[Acrocorinth][25]

When, on the 15th day before the Kalends of May, Mercury's 70
lucky day,[26] [we traveled] from the Spartan citadel of Mistra
and revisited Acrocorinth, we found there John Kantakouzenos, a
splendid man of royal lineage and outstanding in the arts of peace
and war, governor of the province of Corinth for the Spartan king
Constantine. When he recognized me as an old friend from
Patras, he received me with extravagant kindness and, since he was
returning from a hunt, generously bestowed on me a large portion
of a deer and other appropriate gifts.

We were in fact aware that his honorable and illustrious son, 71
Constantine, Count Palatine of the Lateran, while he was defend-
ing with praetorian power the once famous town of Aigion, now
called Vostiza, during the ruinous time of the upheaval between

Achaiae nobile *et quod Bostichiam vocant* praetoria potestate curaret pernicioso Teucrum Pannonumque motus tempore ex Peloponeso in Aetoliam Locridemve Ozoleam ac Parnaseam Phocidem loca urbesque diu iam a barbaris occupatas liberaturum nonnullis equitum peditumque cohortibus traductis apud Neopatriam et per arduos Pindi montis saltus in hostiles occurentes barbaros fortiter atque perstrenue pugnatum esse percepimus; ac inde superius antiquas *nonnullas Parnaseas* Dorieasque et Locreas[58] urbes *acceptas ipsa in Locride,* mediterraneam quidem unam Lydoriciam nomine, alteram vero maritimam, quam primum Euanthiam dixere,[59] nunc vero ab se Catacuzinopolim dictam *aliqua ex parte* moenibus arceque solertissime restituendas curasse

72   Ἐπειδὴ ἐς τὸ .ίε. καλενδῶν μαίου ὑπερηδίστου[60] μηνὸς εὐτυχὲς λαμπρόν τε καὶ Ἑρμαῖον ἦμαρ ἐκ τῆς Σπάρτης ἀκροπόλεως Μυζηθρᾶ Ἀκροκόρινθον ἀφικόμην, Ἰωάννην τὸν Κατακουζινὸν πανάριστον καὶ μεγαλοπρεπῆ βασιλικοῦ τε γένους ἄνδρα, διὰ τοῦ σπαρτιάτων ἄνακτος κορινθίας μέντοι Ἐπαρχίας ἡγεμονεύοντα εὗρον· ὃς ἐπεί με παλαιὸν ἔγνω φίλον, ἀξίως ἐδέξατο. καί με ἀξίαις δωρεαῖς ἐδωρήσατο.

73   Οὗτινος δὴ τὸν ἔξοχον καὶ περίκλυτον υἱὸν Κωνσταντῖνον, Κόμιτα Παλατῖνον τὸν Λατερανένσιον ἄξιον[61] ὑπὸ τοῦ αὐτοῦ Λακεδαιμονίων ἄνακτος Κωνσταντίνου Αἴγιον πόλιν πάλαι τῆς Ἀχαίας λαμπρὰν διαπρεπῶς διέποντα ἐν τῷ τῆς τῶν Τεύκρων καὶ Παιόνων κινήσεως χρόνῳ ἐκ Πελοποννήσου ἐς Αἰτωλίαν Λοκρίδα τε καὶ Παρνασσικὴν Φωκίδα στρατειὰν ἱππέων τε καὶ πεζῶν ἔλαυνων, ἵνα τὰς ὑπὸ τῶν βαρβάρων κατεχομένας πόλεις ἐλευθερώσειε, ἐς Νεοπάτραν καὶ ἐρυμνοὺς τοῦ Πίνδου λόφους κατὰ τῶν ἐπιόντων πολεμίων, λαμπρότατά τε καὶ μεγαλοπρεπῶς πολεμῆσαι. καὶ ἐκ τῶν Δωριέων πάλαι καὶ Λοκρῶν τῶν Ὀζολῶν πόλεων, μίαν μὲν μεσόγειον εἷλε Λυδωρικίαν λεγομένην, ἑτέραν[62] δὲ παράλιαν Εὐανθίαν πρίν, νῦν δὲ ὑπ᾽

the Turks and the Hungarians, transported some troops of cavalry and infantry from the Peloponnesus into Aetolia and Ozolean Locris and Parnassian Phocis in order to set free places and cities that had long been occupied by the barbarians, and fought bravely and vigorously against the onrushing barbarian enemy at Neopatras and throughout the steep passes of Mount Pindos. And [we know that] he then took care to bring about a highly skillful partial restoration of the walls and citadels of some ancient Parnassian and Dorian and Locrian cities that he had recovered: in Locris itself, one inland [city] named Lydoricia, the other, however, on the seacoast, originally called Euanthia, but now renamed after him Kantacouzenopolis.

When on the 15th day before the Kalends of the sweetest   72
month, May, Hermes' lucky and radiant day, [I traveled] from Mistra, the citadel of Sparta, to Acrocorinth, I found there John Kantakouzenos, an excellent and magnificent man of royal lineage, governing the Corinthian eparchy for the king of the Spartans. When he recognized me as an old friend, he received me appropriately and presented me with appropriate gifts.

We were aware that John's eminent, renowned son, Con-   73
stantine, deservedly [appointed] Count Palatine of the Lateran by the same King Constantine of the Lacedaemonians, when he was governing in distinguished fashion Achaea's once-glorious city of Aegium in the time of the disturbance between Turks and Hungarians, transported from the Peloponnesus to Aetolia and Locris and Parnassian Phocis an army of cavalry and infantry in order to set free cities that had been occupied by the barbarians and engaged the invading enemy at Neopatras and at fortified hilltops of Mount Pindus, as befits a great man, and he captured [two] cities of Dorians and Ozolian Locrians, one inland, called Lydoricia, the other by the sea, formerly named Euanthia, but now named

αὐτοῦ Κατακουζηνόπολιν ὀνομασθήσαν, τείχεσί τε καὶ
φρουρίοις ἀνεκαίνησεν ὡς διαπρεπέστατα.

: 46 :

DIANAE |PROSERPINAE | VENATIO | ACTIACA |
REGIA | ΘΗΡΑ | ΒΑΣΙΛΙΚΗ

Ex Kyriaco Anconitano[1]

[From Arta in Acarnania to the vicinity of Nicopolis]

1 Quom ad VI Iduum Septembrium, faustum Kyriaceumque et
beatae Dei parentis Mariae Virginis almae natalicium panegyri-
cumque dieμ, Karolus inclytus Acharnanum princeps, una dilectissimo suo cum nato Leonardo, magna nobilium stipante caterva,
ex Acarnanea nobili regia sua, occeanum petente Phoebo, exeuntes, Arachtheum per amnem et Ambraciacum aequor Pheacea veloci bireme et plerisque cymbis devecti, Cynthia e coelo clara lam-
pade comitante, lenis aspirantibus auris et Nereidum omnibus
2 iubilantibus Nymphis, ad eiusdem Ambraciaci sinus fauces ante
diluculum applicuissent, Actiaca demum ad littora Nicopolitanae
civitatis in conspectu desilientes in soluμ, ad surgentem serenum
pharetrigerae Dianae diem, Iacobo Ruphu nobili praefecto suo ex
Italia Leucatem nuper adventante, comperto viro nempe venationis
experto, Actiacos illos illico per campos et bina inter Actiaca nemora plerisque telis caeteris et venabulis armis muniti, veloces et

342

Kantacuzenopolis after him, and he restored their walls and citadels as magnificently as possible.

: 46 :

Diary fragment: Account of a royal hunt, 8–13 September [1448], Arta in Epirus

ROYAL HUNT ON THE ACTIAN COAST, TO DIANA AND PROSERPINA

From Cyriac of Ancona

[From Arta in Acarnania to the vicinity of Nicopolis]

On the 8th of September, a lucky Day of the Lord,[1] the feast of the Nativity of our fostering mother, Mary, Carlo, the noted ruler of the Acarnanians,[2] along with his best-loved son Leonardo and a large, thronging band of noblemen, departed from his noted Acarnanian palace as Phoebus was sinking into the ocean. As we sailed aboard a swift Phaeacian bireme and in several small boats along the river Arachthus and the Ambracian sea, the bright Cynthian lamp from heaven accompanied us and a light breeze was blowing and all the Nereid nymphs rejoiced. Arriving before dawn at the mouth of the Ambracian Gulf [and] finally at the Actian coast within sight of the city of Nicopolis, we leapt to the ground as the clear day of quiver-bearing Diana dawned. There we found Iacopo Ruphu, its governor, who was on his way to [the island of] Leukas from Italy, a man experienced in hunting in that Actian countryside. And it was in two Actian groves, that [the others] went hunting, armed with hunting spears and numerous other weapons, with swift, strong[3] Alcmanian hounds and wing-

3   Alcimos canes ac alipedes equos exercentes, venatum iere; et equidem, bonis avibus Diva Kaliope canante nostra, nostram hanc in
Dianam brevem orationem protulimus: 'Audi me, O regina multi
nominis ac Iovis filia cursoria, sagittis gaudens atque noctu ambu-
lans, diurna festina, hominum nutrix, puella daemon, quae habitas
confragosos montes, cervorum iaculatrix veneranda, accede, dea
Cynthia, ad omnes qui cupidi sunt fabulari Karuli filios, Acarneo-
rum duces, fortunam sibi secundam tuamque felicitatem praesta'
[...].[2]

4   [...] etenim vero postquam ad tris quidem posteros dies Myr-
thea Bondicianeaque et alia eiusdem sinus littora perlegentes,
proximis plerisque silvis solerti venatione discussis, quam plures
setigeros apros praedam[3] iuvenes principum ante ora duxere, e
quis itaque inprimis alteram a canibus vivas abrectam trepidantem
iuvenculam suem Karolus ipse genitor optumus et iucundissimus
princeps Leonardo filio praedigno, de quo maxima vel omnis ka-
rissimi parentis cura vigebat, antea e luco Catina Romano ad littus
regia tentoria repetenti praedigne alacri pro munere destinarat.

5   Verum equidem praeterea unum hoc minime praetereundum
censuimus, quod nostros inter nautas IIII animosos vidimus et me-
morabiles iuvenes, quos nuper ab usque occiduis Massalieis littori-
bus ex antiqua Niceaea magna animi et virtutis suae fiducia auden-
tes,[4] ut profunda undique maria legendi corali gratia scanderent,
parvula scapha devectos, Tyrrenum, Libycum, Sicanumque et Io-
nicum aequor transfretantes, Ceraunia nuper male fida passim
Phaeaceaque et Chaonia littoria perlegentes, denique Leucatem et
ipsum Ambraciacum sinum adventasse percepimus.

footed horses. As for myself, as our divine Calliope sang—a good   3
omen—I uttered the following brief prayer to Diana. "Hear me,
O queen of many names, swift-running daughter of Jove, who
dost rejoice in archery and going abroad at night, swift nurse of
men by day, virgin goddess whose dwelling is in the rugged mountains, revered thruster of the javelin, slayer of deer, come, O
Cynthian goddess, to all who are eager to become fabled; bestow
your good fortune and success on the sons of Carlo, leaders of the
Acarnanian folk" [...].⁴

[...] but after three days of traversing the Myrtean and Bon-   4
dician and other coastal lands of the same gulf and shaking out
numerous close-by forests with resourceful hunting, the young
men brought their prey, a number of bristly wild boars, for the
princes to see. [Choosing] from among these, their excellent and
most joyful prince, Carlo himself, as a father of course would, gave
the first award—another [catch], a quivering young sow that had
been ripped away alive from the hounds—as an eager gift to his
worthy son Leonardo, on whom the greatest, indeed all, the concern of his most beloved father centered, on his return to the royal
tent on the coast from the Roman grove [called] "Catina."

A personal observation that I think I should not leave out: 5
Among our sailors I noticed four lively, remarkable young men
who, I learned, with great confidence in their own spirit and courage, had sailed recently aboard a small skiff to plumb the deep seas
everywhere in search of coral to collect. All the way from the western shores of Marseilles they had come, from ancient Nicaea,
crossing the Tuscan, Lybian, Sicilian, and Ionic Seas; scanning the
promontory of Ceraunia, which is treacherous here and there,
Phaiakia, and the Chaonian coast, they had finally arrived at
Leucas and the Ambracian gulf itself.

[The peninsula of Caraconesia]

6   Nos vero iussu principum, quom ad pridie Idus Septembr. ad pis-
cosum exiguum cheronesum,[5] quem prope Arachthei fluminis os-
tia Καρακονήσιον vocitant, allaberemur, inibi, postquam per
noctem membra quievimus, sopnos per littora culices inter infes-
tos carpitantes, Venereo divo albescente die ad sacrum et conspicuum beatae Virginis sacellum, quod plerique Graeca religione
monachi colunt, sacris de more principibus coram exactis, breve
hoc marmoreum ad pavimentum epigramma antiquis et Atticis
quoque litteris Karolo ipso indicante rege comperimus:

ΚΛΑΤΔΙΑ | ΒΕΡΟΝΕΙΚΗ | ΕΤΩΝ Κ̅Δ̅ | ΧΑΙΡΕ.

Sic sonant Latine:

CLAUDIA VERONICE ANNORUM XXIIII SALVE.

7   Ast vero enim interim socii et regii quidem ingenii ex aula fa-
muli, solerti ipso curante Antonello ἀρχιτρικλίνα, quos iactis
sub unda retiis pingues c et varigenos pisces laquearunt, ad principes laeti detulere; et inde ante sacrum sacro ipso in diversorio religioso eodem Aphrodisio die perinde ac monastico et religioso
epulo sumpto, Arachtheam Acarnaneam ipsam regiam navigiis
equisque mari terraque intercedentibus, felicibus ipsis atque sere-
nis sequuti regibus felicissime nostri quidem voti compotes remea-
vimus:

ΧΑΙΡΕ ΑΚΑΡΝΑΝΩΝ | ΕΤΔΑΙΜΟΝ | ΠΑΤΡΙΣ.

[The peninsula of Caraconesia]

At the bidding of the princes, we sailed on 12th of September to 6
the narrow peninsula they call Caraconesia, abundant in fish, near
the mouth of the Arachthus river. There we rested our bodies
overnight, snatching sleep on the shore amidst an infestation of
mosquitos. When Venus' day was dawning, the liturgy was celebrated in the presence of the princes in the prominent chapel of
the Blessed Virgin, revered by very many monks of the Greek
Church. Afterwards, Duke Carlo pointed out to me in the marble
floor this brief inscription in ancient Attic lettering:

Farewell, Klaudia Veroneke, age 24.[5]

Meanwhile, the companions and talented royal servants from 7
the palace, under the supervision of Antonello, the resourceful
president of the banquet, casting their nets in the water, caught a
hundred fat fish of a variety of kinds and brought them cheerfully
to the princes. On the same holy day of Aphrodite, before [the celebration of] the liturgy, we made a meal of these in the inn itself
as though it were a monastic religious feast. Then, having most
happily attained our objective, we returned to the Acarnanian
royal residence by the Arachthus, successfully negotiating the intervening distance over sea and land by ship and horse in the train
of the calmly assured princes.

Hail, blessed fatherland of the Acarnanians!

: 47 :

1 Exemplum litterarum ex Paschale de Sorgo Raguseio nobili, qui est cum despote Serviae inter primores et fuit in exercitu Pannonorum cum transnarent Danubium. Scripsit ad Nicolaum Ansalonem Siculum equitem clarum apud Arachteam Acarnanum Regiam.

2 *Incipit:* Ut notificem tibi de novis istis in partibus contingentibus, clarus eques noster Comes Iohannis sive Coniati Janus regni Hungariae, etc.

3 *Explicit:* e felicibus Christianissimisque castris, III Idus Septembris 1448.

: 48 :

De Morte Karuli Regis[1]

1 Ad xv Kalendas Novembris Lucae evangelistae sanctissimi sacrum Venereumque diem, ex eadem Arachthea ἀστείᾳ[2] Acarnanum regia, Karolo inclyto principe abusque pridie Kalendas Octobris defuncto et Leonardo regnante regulo annuente, una Hermodoro nostro comitante liberto, Dodoneam per silvam Acherontei ad fluminis ripas Dodonem antiquam venimus, antiquissimo Dodonei Iovis oraculo memorabilem urbem, ubi iam longevae et almae suae

: 47 :

Letter to Niccolò Ansalone from Pasquale Sorgo, 11 September 1448, seen by Cyriac in Arta and copied in his own hand

Copy of a letter from Pasquale de Sorgo, a noble of Ragusa, who 1
is with the despot of Serbia in the front ranks and was in the
Hungarians' army when they crossed the Danube. He wrote it to
Niccolò Ansalone, a distinguished Sicilian knight at the court of
the Acarnanians in Arta.

[*The letter begins:*] "To inform you about what is happening 2
in these parts, our distinguished knight, Count John, or János
Hunyadi of the kingdom of Hungary," etc.

[*It ends:*] "from the successful, most Christian camp, 11 Septem- 3
ber 1448."

: 48 :

Diary fragment: Dodona and Rhogous, 18 October [1448]

On the death of King Carlo

On Friday, the 18th of October, the feast of the most holy evan- 1
gelist Luke, I departed from the same urbane palace of the
Acarnanians by the Arachthus. With the consent of Leonardo,
who reigned as prince, the famed Prince Carlo having died not
long before on the 30th of September, and accompanied by my
freedman Hermodorus, I journeyed through the forest of Dodona
to ancient Dodona on the banks of the Acheron river, a historic
city because of its very ancient oracle of Dodonean Jove. There, of

veternitatis monumenta non nulla nostra utique conspicitur aetas et inter potiora suis et turritis et mirificis moenibus non equidem exiguam partem extare comperimus.

2   Et itaque ad arcem, quam hodie accolae Rhogum vocitant, Basilio amico veteri nostro favitante praefecto, ad sacram eiusdem Evangelistae metropolitanam aedem vetusto in loculo sacrum suum revisimus et venerabile corpus, nec non Annae, almae Virginis genetricis, beatissimum preciosum et honorabile caput ac recolendum Chrysostomi Iωannis religionis nostrae per Graeciam doctoris et facundissimi Theophori pedem. Quibus denique visis et alia inter sacra relicta nobis monumenta divum praedignissime veneratis sacris et deinde Graeco de more religiose peractis, ad pacendum eiusdem Karoli principis pientissimi Manes hanc in eundem Lucam luculentissimum Evangelistam Latio idiomate piam orationem habuimus:

Oratio

Inclyto, sancto e celestial Thoro,
evangielista, medico e pictore,
de l'incarnato Verbo almo scriptore,
dal buon principio al fin del gran lavoro;

    tu, da gusto exornando el verbo loro,
Sybilla, ornasti el buon roman valore,
nel cui imperio, humanato il Redemptore,
Iove mostrasti in terra far dimoro.

    Dignate, ordunque, o glorioso Luca,
che del tuo car fidel, despote Karlo,
l'anima in ciel de la tua luce, luca.

    [E 'l] Qual in Dodonea sua vol exornarlo,

350

course, our past is visible in some remnants of its age-old, fostering antiquity; and among the more important of these I personally found that a not inconsiderable portion of its towered, admirable walls survives.

And so, on to the citadel that today the locals call Rhogous, 2 through the kindness of my old friend Basil, its chief magistrate. In the holy metropolitan church of the same Evangelist, in an ancient nook, I visited again his holy and revered body as well as the most blessed, precious, and venerable head of Ann, the mother of the fostering virgin and the foot of John Chrysostom, Doctor of our faith and most eloquent God-bearer, an object of devotion throughout Greece. When I had seen these relics and afterward, when, among other sacred remains of the saints left behind to us, the liturgy was celebrated for the repose of the soul of the same most devout prince Carlo, very appropriately [in Latin] and then in the customary Greek rite, I composed in the Italian language the following devout prayer to the same the most luminous Luke the Evangelist:

Prayer

Illustrious, holy and celestial Bull,[1]
evangelist, physician and painter,
holy writer of the Incarnate Word,
from the wondrous birth to the end of the great labor;
    you, desiring to embellish the Word,
Sybil-like, exalted the great value of Rome,
in whose empire, once the Redeemer was incarnate,
you revealed Jove to be dwelling on earth.
    Grant now, therefore, o glorious Luke,
that of your faithful devotee, Lord Carlo,
the soul in heaven may be illumined by your light.
Let he who wishes to pray in his own Dodona

del sacro corpo tuo hor si conduca,
nel regno del cielo a<d a>compagnarlo;
e di gratia a dotarlo
    ch' el veggia doppo lui, con pio riguardo,
con sua prole regnar el suo Leonardo.

Per eundem Kyriacum

    Inclyta maiestà trina; alma electa
Vergine excelsa; e voi, substantie pie;
angielice superne hierarchie;
e tu, gran precussor più che propheta
    con tua patriarchal sede secreta;
quel gran legista, il cuor di prophetie;
e 'l buon cantor de le cui psalmodie
omne sacra ede <è> per l'orbe repleta;
    e tu, del sancto Agnel buon sodalitio
Piero con gli altri; e 'l vaso electo, Polo;
e chi testò col sangue el gran supplicio
del nostro Pelican nel terren sòlo;
e gli Animal che al fin del primo initio scripse;
e de' confessori el grande stuolo;
    e 'l bel verginal bruolo,
con tutte alme salite a l'alte rote:
ricevan l'alma di Karlo dispote.

Deprecatio per eundem

Aeterno Padre, or tua gran pietà surga,
nel buon dì quarto, nona di novembre,
verso l'alma che, sciolta da le membre,
la già concreta labe al foco purga
    sì che dal gran supplicio omai risurga.
Vedi ben come par che si dismembre,

for him, look to your sacred body
to accompany him to the kingdom of Heaven;
   and to endow him with the grace
to see, within godly limits,
Leonardo and his descendants living after him.

By the same Cyriac

Glorious, Triune majesty, elected soul
of the sublime Virgin and you, holy Substances,
angelic, supernal Hierarchies,
and you, renowned precursor, O more than prophet
   with your patriarchal secret abode;
that great legislator, the source of prophecy;
and the excellent cantor, of whose psalmody
every sacred temple throughout the world is filled;
   and you, good companion of the holy Lamb,
Peter, and the others and Paul the chosen vessel,
and whoever testified with his blood the great sacrifice
   made by our Pelican here on earthly soil;
and the Creatures who at the end of the new beginning
wrote, and the great multitude of confessors;
   and the lovely garland of virgins
together with all the souls raised to the highest spheres:
let them receive in welcome the soul of Carlo the Lord.

Invocation by the same [Cyriac]

Now, Eternal Father, let your great mercy spring forth
on the auspicious fourth day, the nones of November,
towards the soul that, freed from its body,
is already purging in the fire its hard dross
   to be born again through such harsh punishment.
Note well how wracked by torment it does appear,

porgiendo in te le brace tutte insembre,
perche, tua gran bontà lor colpa expurga.
Per questo, la tua Madre, ognor constante,
con l'una e l'altra celestial corte
porgie lor prieghe in te, sacre e divote,
Per questo, Sancta Chiesa supplicante
pulsa de Olympo l'alte e sacre porte
con Leonardo, per Carlo dispote.

: 49 :

1 Scripsi ad te pridie, karissime Aegidi, hac ex parte quam paucis; et
paucos post dies barbarorum quidem relatu audivimus XVI Kalendas Novembris Pannonum primas peditum cohortes certamen
cum Theucris inisse et atroci pugna per diem dimicantes omnes
denique orientales peditum ordines magna cum strage fudisse non
absque ingenti utique victoris caede; et posterum ad diem Teucrum omne cum equitatu ex Amasia utique auxiliatorum ad XV
equitum milibus adiunctis magno impetu pugnam cum hostibus
integrasse; et per biduum dubio eventu inexplicabili cum utro-
2 rumque militum clade accerrime pugnatum esse; et quamquam
barbarorum et numero et recentiori milite praestare visum, demum eximia ducis Iani virtute solertia et quoiusque militaris rei
peritia et providentia constantia et animi fortitudine nec non sui
exercitus probitate, innumeris barbaris caesis et potissimum ex or-

as it stretches out towards you both its arms
for your great compassion to cleanse of sin.

    For this one, your ever constant Mother,
in the name of the one and the other Court of Heaven,
offers up their prayers, sacred and devout, to you.

    For this one, Holy Church as supplicant
beats against the high and sacred Olympian portals
along with Leonardo, for Carlo the Lord.

: 49 :

To Egidio of Megara, after 19 October 1448, ?Arta

I wrote to you from here on the day before the last, my very dear 1
Egidio, with little news. But a few days ago I heard this, actually
from a Turkish report:[1] On the 17th of October, the first contin-
gents of Hungarian infantry had joined battle with the Turks and,
fighting throughout the day in fierce combat, had finally put to
flight the ranks of oriental infantry with a great slaughter, though
not without a huge loss of life on the part of the victors. On the
next day, the Turk, reinforced by all his cavalry from Amasia, actually about fifteen thousand mounted auxiliaries, resumed battle
against their foe with a great push. For two days they fought with
great ferocity with the outcome in doubt, with an indescribable
slaughter of soldiers on both sides; finally, although the barbarians 2
seemed to have the upper hand in numbers and fresher troops,
still, owing to Captain John [Hunyadi's] extraordinary valor, skill
and experience in every kind of military action, and his foresight,
persistence, and mental fortitude, as well as the quality of his
army, countless barbarians were killed; and most importantly, very
many line officers and senior officers were slain. The Hungarians,

dinum principibus militumque tribunis plerisque obtruncatis, Pannones barbaros superantes, Teucrum cum reliquis suis re non ad summum exacta ex pugna secedere collesque repetere coegisse; eumque truculenta[1] ex victoria suos intra vallum ad castra reduxisse.

3   Haec autem hactenus percepimus et deinceps ut superi piam in rem omnia bene vortant optamus. Oratores, quos e Theucro expectare diximus, iterum expectamus, e quis nos certiores fieri melioraque intelligere speramus.

4   Vale, vir Alchatone *charope*; decoratum augusta felicitate et deditum respice virum.

gaining the upper hand over the barbarians, compelled the Turk, with the rest of his army, to withdraw and head for high ground while the issue was [still] not fully decided, [then] to pull his men back to their camp within its breastwork, away from [what would have been a] devastating [Hungarian] victory.

This is what we have learned up to now. We pray that in the fu- 3 ture the heavenly powers will turn all this to a good and holy consequence. We are again expecting emissaries, the ones from the Turk that I said we were expecting, by whom we hope to be informed and to have a better understanding of the situation.

Farewell, fiercely courageous Megarean,[2] and take heed of a 4 dedicated man, honored by venerable good fortune.

1   Chiriacus Anconitanus Roberto Valturio, Ariminensi patrio et oratori insigni salutem dicit.[1]

2   Heri et eodem quo die concessimus vɪɪɪ Kalendarum Iuliarum, serenissimo die, praeclare Roberte, Ravennam, antiquam et insignem venimus Boiorum urbem, Nereidum nostrarum omnibus secundantibus nymphis, ubi Mapheum Contarenum virum pernobilem, inclytis pro Venetis Ravennatum praefectum honorificum et

3   veterem nobis amicum, comperimus; qui cum me perhumane suscepissset, una cumque aliis plerisque egregiis sociis dignis suis et civibus claris pleraque revisimus tantae civitatis insignia; et inter quae nobiliora comperimus hoc, quod ad portam quam auream vocant Latinis magnis et aureis litteris olim ornatissime consculptis epigramma videtur, hisce tibi ut tuae dignum spectationi rescribendum transmittendumque curavimus. Nam divum ipsum Tiberium Claudium Caesarem praeclarissimarum plerumque legum conditorem exornatoremque fuisse novisti:

TI. CLAVDIVS DRVSI F.AVG GERMANICVS PONT
MAX. TR.| POT. II. DESIG. III. IMP. III. PP. DEDIT.

4   Iamque vale et Karolo nostro viro claro caeterisque tuis meo nomine salutem plurimam dicit Kyriacus Anconitanus tuus.

24 June to 8 July 1449
Return to Italy

: 50 :

To Roberto Valturio, 24 June 1449, Ravenna

Cyriac of Ancona greets Roberto Valturio, native of Rimini and   1
distinguished orator.

Yesterday, the same day I departed, June 24th, a very clear day,   2
excellent Roberto, I arrived in Ravenna, an ancient and distinguished city of the Boioi with the help of all our Nereid nymphs,
where I found Maffeo Contarini, a nobleman, honored *podestà* of
the people of Ravenna on behalf of the Venetians, and an old
friend of mine.[1] When he had received me most cordially, along   3
with his numerous other distinguished worthy associates and famous citizens, I went back to see a number of the important features of the city, and among the more noteworthy that I found,
one sees at the gate they call "golden" this inscription in large,
gilded letters, at one time so beautifully carved that we took the
pains to copy and pass it on to your excellency. For you know that
the divine Tiberius Claudius Caesar authored numerous brilliant
laws as well as enhancing [the city]:

> The Emperor Tiberius Claudius Germanicus son of Drusus,
> High Priest, with the power of tribune twice, designated for
> the third time, hailed as *imperator* three times, father of his
> country, gave [this].

Farewell now. Your Cyriac of Ancona sends [his wishes for]   4
good health to our celebrated Carlo and to the rest of your
[family?].

1   SEX. VIBIO GALLO [T]RICINARIO PRIMO PILARI
PRAEF. | KASTROR. LEG. XIII GEM. DONIS
DONATO AB IMPERA|TORIBVS HONORIS
VIRTVTISQ. CAVSA TORQVIS AR|MILLIS
PHALERIS CORONIS MVRALIBVS III VALLARI|BVS
II AVREA I VEXILLIS II [SEX.VIBIVS COCCE|ANVS.
PATRONO | BENEMERENTI]¹

2   Vides iamque, elegantissime Roberte, Ariminensium insigne
decus, antiqua hac inscriptione ab me nuper nostra ex Pontica
navigatione comperta, Latini nominis hominem Gallum Tricina-
rium² a Cocciano liberto ob egregiam eius rei militaris virtutem et
res in Pontica expeditione bene gestas statua quondam ex aere vel
marmore honoris causa donatum.

3   Et perinde ac apud Aulum Gellium³ nostrum te quandoque lec-
titasse non dubito Licinium Dentatum, Tribunum Plebis ob ingentem et perstrenuam militiae virtutem et fortitudinem Achillem
Romanum appellatum innumerisque coronis et militaribus ornamentis decoratum, ita et eundem ipsum Gallum plerisque coronis
et insignibus exornatum fuisse percipies, lapideo ipso epigrammate

4   ad nostram usque diem luculentissime declarante; ad te quidem
igitur nunc hisce benivolentiae tuae eam ipsam inscriptionem rescribendum delegi, quia eam ipsam antiquam virtutem et praeclaram disciplinam, tam longo aevo ob antiquarum nobilium rerum

: 51 :

To Roberto Valturio, after 24 June 1449, Ravenna

To Sextus Vibius Gallus [T]ricinarius, Senior Centurion,   1
Camp Commander of the 13th Legion, XIII Gemina, honored with gifts by emperors for his prowess and courage with
collars, arm bands, metal discs, three times with turreted
crowns [for being the first to scale a wall], twice with crowns
[for being the first to cross an enemy's earthwork], once with
a golden crown, twice with a military banner [dedicated by
Sextus Vibius Cocceanus to his well-deserving patron].

And now, most elegant Roberto, manifest glory of the people of   2
Rimini, you see from this ancient inscription I discovered recently
during my travels in the Black Sea that a person with a Latin
name, Gallus [T]ricinarius, was honored with a statue of bronze
or marble by Coccianus, a freedman, for his outstanding courage
in military service and his exploits in the Black Sea campaign.[1]

I am sure you read in our Aulus Gellius at one time or another   3
that Licinius Dentatus, a Tribune of the People, was called the
Roman Achilles and bedecked with numerous crowns and military
decorations for his vast and vigorous valor and courage in battle.
In a similar way you will learn from this very stone inscription,
which right down to our own times clearly affirms it, that the
same Gallus [just mentioned] was adorned with numerous crowns
and decorations. Indeed, out of good will towards you I chose to
have this same inscription copied here and now because you also,
in our own age, have chosen to resurrect by your assiduous writings that most ancient valor and storied discipline which has been
neglected over so long a time among our people and among foreigners, and completely banished from mind because of a lack of

incuriam nostros inter et externos homines neglectam et penitus abolitam, tua tu nostro quoque tempore virtute, solertia et animi magnitudine et eximia praeclaraque ingenii praestantia et nobilitate diligentissime litteris in lucem revocare, oportune quidem et benemerite Sigismundi Pandulphi inclyti et perstrenui principis nomine, delegisti.

: 52 :

1   Nivea Paros, de marmor candente,
Cycladum decus aequoris Aegei
honor de artisti, de heroi et de ideis
che di te si fa 'l mondo splendente.
     Ornasti Apollo in Delpho et l'Oriente
per Cyrro et per Alcide, Indi et Sabei;
Minerva Athene, et Iove i campi alphei;
Alexandro, Austro et Cesar[e] l'Occidente.
     Di Phydia et Polycleto el gran valore
mostrò qual fusti de natura pari;
da te Lysippo e gli altri hebbe splendore.
     Hor per Nencio et Donato a' nostri mari,
Nicolò Baroncielli en tuo decore,
fa Leonel col patre al mondo clari.
     Ornasti il quinto già papa Martino,
sculpto in Milan, per man di Iacobino.
ΧΑΙΡΕ . ΕΣΤΙΕΩΝ. ΑΓΑΤΗ. ΦΥΛΗ

2   Epigramma strenuissiimi et fortissimi imperatoris Stephani Gatamelatae:

interest in the noble achievements of the past. [You have done this] opportunely indeed and deservedly under the patronage of the famous, vigorous prince Sigismundo, son of Pandolfo.[2] because of your own courage, skill, and greatness of heart and the outstanding and illustrious excellence and nobility of your natural gifts.

: 52 :

On Donatello's statue of Gattamelata, ?June, 1449, Padua

Snow-white Paros, of the shining marble,   1
glory of the Cyclades in the Aegean sea,
honor of artists, heroes and of the gods:
the world is made radiant by you.
    You added lustre to Apollo at Delphi and to the Orient
through Cyrus and Heracles, to Indians and Arabians;
to Minerva in Athens and to Jove the plains of the Alpheus;
to Alexander the East and to Caesar the West.
    The great prowess of Pheidias and Polykleitos,
equal to Nature's, demonstrated your worth;
from you Lysippos and the others drew their splendor.
    Now, within our seas, through Nencio and Donato,
Nicolò Baroncielli in your honor
gives worldly splendor to Leonello together with his father.
    You adorned the late pope, Martin V,
sculpted in Milan by the hand of Iacobino.
    Hail, noble family of the Este!

Inscription [for the statue of] the most energetic and valiant   2
general, Stefano il Gattamelata:

Stephanus Catamelata Narnius, Veneti exercitus imperator maximus. In Flaminia ecclesiae socia arma iungens Brutios fudit; Perusinos reliquasque hostium copias inopinata victoria profligavit; bello Ligurico Nicolaum Picininum hostem, prospero proeliorum eventu ferocem trans Athesim persequendo coercuit traductaque in Benacum per abruptos Penede montis colles ingenti classe, vindicata Veronae defectione, Bergomo Brixia obsidione liberatis, Venetam rem publicam multiplici clade concussam atque labantem stabilivit. Huic senatus in monumentum fidei et virtutis statuam hanc equestrem faciundam decrevit anno divi Christi Humanati MCCCCXLVII.

: 53 :

Rugerius Brugiensis Pictorum Decus

1   ΑΓΑΘΗΙ ΤΥΧΗΙ. Rugerius in Bursella, post praeclarum illum Brugiensem picturae decus Ioannem, insignis nostri temporis pictor habetur, cuiusce nobilissimi artificis manu apud Ferariam VIII Iduum Quintilium die, Nicolai Quinti Papae Anno III:

2   Leonellus Hestensis princeps illustris eximii operis tabellam nobis ostendit, primorum quoque parentum ac e suplicio humanati Iovis depositi pientissimo agalmate circum et plerumque virum mulierumque moestissime deploratum imaginibus, mirabili quidem et potius divina dicam quam humana arte depictam.

364

Stefano da Narni, il Gattamelata, captain general of the Venetian army: joining his forces with those of the Church in Reggio Emilia, he put the Abruzzesi to flight; the Perugians and the rest of the enemy forces he crushed in an unexpected victory; in the Ligurian war he checked his enemy, Niccolò Piccinino, pursuing him across the Adige in the successful aftermath of the battle; and he punished the defection of Verona after portaging a huge fleet over the steep hills of Mount Penede to [Lake] Garda, having freed Bergamo and Brescia from siege. He stabilized the Venetian republic when it was battered and left staggering by numerous defeats. To him, in remembrance of his loyalty and courage, the [Venetian] senate commissioned this equestrian statue in the year of the divine Incarnate Christ 1447.[1]

∶ 53 ∶

In praise of Rogier van der Weyden, 8 July 1449, Ferrara

Rogier of Bruges, the Ornament of Painters

GOOD LUCK. Rogier in Brussels is held to be the outstanding   1
painter of our time after the distinguished Jan of Bruges,[1] the ornament of the art of painting. [A work] by the hand of this noblest of artists, [seen] at Ferrara, 8 July in the third year of the reign of Pope Nicholas the Fifth:

The illustrious Leonello d'Este showed us a painting of extraor-   2
dinary workmanship, a representation of our first parents and of the incarnate Jove taken down [from the cross] after his most holy [act of] atonement; and round about him a number of men and women mourning with consummate sorrow, painted with wondrous—indeed, I would say with divine rather than human—skill.

3   Nam vivos aspirare vultus videres, quos viventes voluit ostentare mortuique similem quem defunctum, et utique velamina tanta
plurigenumque colorum palulamenta et laboratas eximie ostro
atque auro vestes virentiaque prata, flores, arbores, et frondigeros
atque umbrosos colles nec non exornatos porticus et propylea auro
aurum simile margaritis gemmas et cetera omnia, non artificis
manu hominis, quin et ab ipsa omniparente natura inibi genita di-
ceres.

4   Cuius nempe inclytae artis et eximii artificum ingenii egregium
equidem imitatorem, Angelum Parrisium, quoque Senensem, re-
cens picturae in Latio specimen vidimus[1] inclyti eiusdem Leonelli
Marchionis paradiseum nobile diversorium, quod ad v stadiis extra civitatis moenia Belflorem vocitant. Musarum divis imaginibus
suiscumque sacris insignibus et ornamentis praeclaris ac eximiis
plurigenis picturis perbelle quidem atque mirifice exornantem.

5   At enim vero Clio Melpomeneque, quarum iam absolvisse figu-
ras vidimus: illa quidem ostro auroque elaborata chitona ac caelesti
colore chlamyde insignis, dextera tubam, laeva quidem apertum librum ostentans, modesta quadam vivi vultus hilaritate, divino
quodam nutu sub ciliis annuendo homines ad gloriam excitare
perspicitur.

6   Sed quas una ex parte ad ?orchestrae basim e fulvo coloris auro
leves globosas ?imminentes margaritas gemmasque nitentes in-
spexeram ab altera vero parte planae et expolitae eas aequato colore tabellae videre vehementius equidem pictoris ingenium admi-
rari cogor.

For you would think you were looking at the living, breathing   3
faces of those that he wanted to portray as living, while he whom
[he wanted to portray as] dead [appears] dead; and such cos-   4
tumes! especially cloaks of many kinds of colors and vesture
superbly executed in purple and gold; and the green meadows,
flowers, trees; and the leafy and shaded hills; and the decorated
porticoes and the gateways; the gold like [real] gold and jewels
[like real] pearls and all other details — you might say that these
were not [created] by a human artisan, but inwardly begotten by
Nature herself, the parent of all.

To be sure, we did see in Latium a recent example of [this kind   4
of] painting,[2] [by?] a remarkable imitator of famous art and of the
extraordinary genius of artists, Angelo from ?Ferrara, also from
Siena, [at?] the same Margrave Leonello's noble pleasure-ground
which they call Belfiore, about five stades outside the city walls.
This he has adorned beautifully indeed and marvelously with inspired representations of the Muses, each with her own sacred attributes and with striking ornamentation and extraordinary paint-
ings of all kinds.

But as for Clio and Melpomene, whose figures, we saw, had al-   5
ready been completed: the former, remarkable for a chiton worked
out in purple and gold and a cloak the color of the sky, displaying
in her right hand a trumpet [and] in her left, an open book, with a
kind of modest joy on her lifelike face, appears to inspire men to
glory, signaling her approval with a subtle glance beneath lowered
eyelids.

But beholding, on one side [of the composition], towards the   6
base of the ?orchestra, the smooth, round pearls, tawny yellow in
color, and the shining gems that I observed hanging down; and
seeing them on another side of the flat, burnished panel with
matching color, I am compelled to marvel all the more strongly at
the genius of the painter.

7   Altera vero aurea tunica et ab humeris purpureo amita paluda-
mento manu levem pulsando citharam *theoidea* facie in Olympum
ad parentem versa, honesta gravique quadam alacritate, ut chorde
melodemati concordem paeana cantu perbelle quidem καὶ φιλο-
τιμώτατα modularet, roseis labiis vocem formare visa; et denique
ut plura tam mirandi operis ammittam, nitentes varios quos inibi
ornamento hinc inde virides per herbas perpulchre conspexerat,
flores tam naturae similes aspexi, ut suo quandoque fulgore apes
nempe solertes decepturos puto.

8   Clio hoc ad basim ex Guarino nostro epigramma conscriptum
habet:

Historiis famamque et facta vetusta reservo.

The other Muse, dressed in a gold tunic and a purple cloak 7
[draped] from her shoulders, strokes a smooth lyre with her hand
as she turns her face toward her parent on Olympus, [moving]
with a certain virtuous and dignified vivacity to sing most beautifully and most eagerly a peaceful hymn with a charming melody.
She seems to shape her voice with rose-red lips; and finally, to
leave out more detail of so wondrous a work, I beheld varied,
bright flowers very beautifully [scattered] here and there as an
adornment throughout the green grass that she gazed on, so like
nature that I think that they will surely sometimes deceive the
skillful bees with their splendor.

[The statue of] Clio has this inscription, composed by our 8
Guarino written on its base:

I reserve both fame and ancient deeds to the histories.

Biographical Notes

The following is an alphabetical list of the most important personages that appear in Cyriac's letters and diaries, with brief biographical sketches. For the identity of other persons mentioned in these documents, see the Notes to the Translation.

GIULIANO CARDINAL CESARINI (1398–1444; Letters 2 and 16). Born of a poor but noble Roman family, Cesarini studied at Perugia, taught canon law at Padua, and served on diplomatic missions to Germany and France before he was created cardinal by Pope Martin V. After having served as legate for a crusade against the Hussites in Bohemia (1431), as president of the Council of Basel (1431–1438), and then as Pope Eugene IV's most forceful representative at the Council of Ferarra/Florence (1437–1441), he was privileged to read out the Latin text of the Decree of Union from the pulpit of Florence's cathedral on 6 July 1439. He was sent to Hungary (1 March 1442) to settle the contested succession to the Hungarian throne and to organize a crusade against the Ottoman Turks, who had invaded Transylvania and now threatened Belgrade, their only obstacle to penetrating into Hungary. It was his diplomacy that welded together the previously individual efforts at resistance of Ladislas II, King of Poland and Hungary, John Hunyadi, *voivode* of Transylvania, and George Branković, the dispossessed *despotes* of Serbia.

FRANZESCO DRAP(P)ERIO (Letter 38). Franzesco (di) Drapieri dal Bancho, as he is called in the account-book of Giacomo Badoer,[1] was the most famous member of a wealthy Genoese family whose presence in Galata/Pera, the Genoese suburb of Constantinople, is attested as early as the beginning of the fourteenth century and extended to at least the middle of the seventeenth. The surname seems to be an occupational designation: "draper" or "mercer," from *drappo*, cloth.[2] Franzesco, a rich and influential banker with a considerable palace outside the walls of Galata/Pera,[3] was from 1437 to 1447 the lessee of Foglia Nuova (Nova

Phocaea, *Turk.* Yeni Foça), a strongly fortified port built in the fourteenth century six miles from ancient Phocaea at the foot of the mountain where most of the alum used in Europe was mined. The alum was so important to the dye trade and the textile industry, so profitable to the Genoese merchants of Chios who monopolized it, and so vulnerable to attack at its source, that its revenues were farmed out to some powerful noble who would in turn reside there and maintain a strong garrison of mercenaries.[4] There is a record of Drapieri's selling a "truly prodigious quantity" of alum to two Florentines in 1437.[5] Even after his tenure as lessee of the port, Franzesco is known to have dealt in alum—in 1449, through an agent on Chios, Cristoforo Giustiniani,[6] and on 28 October 1452.[7] Because Drapieri was on good terms with both Murad II and Mehmed II, the unfortunate sobriquet, "traitor of Constantinople" has been attached to him.[8]

During 1444 and 1446 Cyriac was frequently in the company of Drapieri, who proved very useful to him. On 1–2 April 1444 they traveled together from Chios to Foglia Nuova. On 22 May 1444 Cyriac was present in Adrianople when Murad II received Drapieri in an audience and accepted from him purple garments worked with gold. On 17 April 1446 he was with Drapieri at Manisa (ancient Magnesia) in Asia Minor when Murad II, temporarily in retirement, received Drapieri in his private chambers; shortly after, on 4 May, they set out for Manisa from Foglia Nuova to meet Murad, who had been summoned back to the throne and was about to return to Adrianople. They accompanied the sultan as far as Pergamum and Ayasmend, transacting their business with him along the way, before returning to Foglia Nuova on 11 May. The fruit of these negotiations was a much-coveted safe-conduct through Turkish lands for Cyriac, who had Drapieri's influence to thank for it. On 15 August 1446 he witnessed in Galata/Pera the wedding of Franzesco's daughter, Elizabetta Maria, to a young Genoese, Tommaso Spinola.

FRANCESCO III GATTILUSIO (documents in Diary II), lord of the island of Thasos, to whom his father, Dorino I, had recently made over the island. In November 1444, during his first visit to Thasos, Cyriac recorded

in his diary an inscription commemorating the restoration by Francesco
of some portion of the ancient city, probably the walls (Diary II, §33),
and made a drawing of an ancient marble statue that represented allegor-
ically the council of Thasos (Diary II, §35).[9] Francesco wrote one of the
letters that helped Cyriac gain admission to the Grand Lavra monastery
on Mount Athos on 26 November 1944 (Diary II, §70). On Christmas
Day, 1444, toward the end of his second stay in Thasos, Cyriac composed a long inscription honoring the young prince as *ingenua Palaeologum
proles*, "noble offspring of the Palaeologi" — Francesco was distantly related to Emperor John V Palaeologus, whose sister had married his
great-grandfather, Francesco I, and he was brother-in-law to Constantine
Dragases Palaeologus — and expressing the hope that Francesco would
win back "from the cruel tyranny and oppression of the barbarians," all
the cities, towns, lands, and sacred places of mainland Thrace that had
once been under the dominion of Thasos (Diary II, §81). This was the
kind of cooperation he sought from the Gattilusi on Thasos and elsewhere in the northern Aegean. On New Year's Day, just before leaving
for Ainos, Cyriac composed an Italian sonnet in Francesco's honor (Diary II, §82).

ANDREOLO GIUSTINIANI-BANCA (Letters 3 to 9, 12, 13, 15, 21 to 24, 27 to
37, 40 to 43, 45). Cyriac's humanist friend on the island of Chios, to
whom the bulk of these letters are addressed, was a member of the
Genoese *Maona*, a company of merchants who monopolized the nearby
alum mines of Foglia and its port of Foglia Nuova. All the sharehold-
ers took the same surname, Giustiniani. That Andreolo sometimes
trafficked in antiquities is clear from the correspondence cited by Silvio
Giuseppe Mercati,[10] and from letters 7 and 26 in this volume. Andreolo's
wife, Carenza, whose name Cyriac consistently latinizes as Clarentia,[11]
was the elder daughter of Errico Simone Giustiniani-Longo, Drapieri's
predecessor as lessee of Foglia Nuova (1427–1437), and the sister of
Paride, its last contractor. Andreolo and his wife had seven daughters, all
of whom married prominent *maonesi*, and six sons. Niccolò, their eldest
son, and Angelo, their fifth, are mentioned in the letters.

JOHN (JÁNOS) HUNYADI (JOANNES CORVINUS), (ca. 1387–1456; Letters 10 and 11). Half-Wallachian, half-Romanian, son of a noble of the Hungarian court, this redoubtable warrior was trained in his art by two years of service as a mercenary of Filippo Maria Visconti, duke of Milan. In 1439 the youthful King Ladislas III made him *voivode* (regional administrator) of Transylvania as a reward for his support in the struggle for the throne of Hungary and in recognition of his military capability to defend a frontier province that the Ottoman Turks were menacing, having already established themselves in Bosnia and Serbia in their attempt to take advantage of Hungary's internal struggles. In 1441 and 1442 Hunyadi won a series of great defensive victories over three Turkish armies; and in July 1443 he joined with Ladislas and George Branković, the dispossessed despot of Serbia, in the first great offensive against the Turks of the fifteenth century, the so-called "Long Campaign," which was to last until the following January 1444, when stiffening resistance by the enemy, the bitter cold, and lack of supplies would force them to withdraw. By 3 November they had invaded Bulgaria and had occupied the city of Niš, which he was using as a base of operations. It is to this success that Cyriac refers in a letter written to Cesarini just one month later (Letter 2). Hunyadi's successes in 1441–1443 caused hopes to rise in the West, and Pope Eugene IV pressed King Ladislas for a new campaign to drive the Turks out of Europe in fulfillment of his promise to the Greeks that the union of the Greek and Roman churches effected at Florence would be followed by a serious attempt to rescue Constantinople from the Turkish threat. At the same time, because Sultan Murad II's Asian empire was being threatened by the rebellion of his son-in-law, Ibrahim Beg, prince of Karaman, the largest province of Ottoman Anatolia, Ladislas was compelled to negotiate a ten-years' peace with Ladislas, Hunyadi, and Branković, as reported by Cyriac in his letters from Adrianople. Two letters in this collection (10 and 11), although they do not bear the name of the addressee, are almost certainly addressed to Hunyadi, to judge from their contents.

EMPEROR JOHN VIII PALAIOLOGOS (1392–1448; Letter 1). Almost an exact contemporary of Cyriac, John was the eldest of the six sons of

Manuel II Palaeologus, with whom he was co-*basileus* from 1421 until his father's death in 1425. He had inherited a moribund empire, the healthiest part of which, the Morea (i.e., the Peloponnese), was under the quasi-independent rule of his brothers. His own portion — Constantinople and bits of coastland along the Black Sea and the Propontis — he was desperately trying to save with the help of the West. To this end he went to Hungary as early as 1422–23 to solicit the aid of the Emperor Sigismund, and later he initiated negotiations with the papacy which resulted in the Council of Ferrara/Florence, where the leaders of the Greek and Roman churches were momentarily reconciled (July 1439). It was understood by both sides that the pope would reciprocate by mounting a crusade for the relief of Constantinople, which had already been besieged once by Sultan Murad II in 1422. Pope Eugene IV did his best to persuade the Christian princes of the West to unite in this cause, but, except for Burgundy and Ragusa (Dubrovnik), only those nations responded that were immediately threatened, i.e., Hungary, Poland and Wallachia. In the winter of 1443–44, because of the success of the Hungarian "Long Campaign," there was high optimism that the Hungarian and Serbian forces, along with the fleet being assembled in the Arsenal of Venice, might drive the Turks out of Europe. It is in this context that Cyriac's dealings with John occurred.

GEORGE SCHOLARIOS (ca. 1403–ca. 1472; Letter 17) later the Orthodox Patriarch Gennadios II, claimed to be self-taught in rhetoric, philosophy and theology, and very soon became interested in Western theology, particularly that of Thomas Aquinas, which he studied, first in Greek translations, then in Latin. He opened a school in Constantinople in which Latin philosophical and theological works were required reading because he felt that Latin scholarship was more advanced than Greek. He wrote commentaries, translations and summaries of Aquinas' works and was well acquainted with the writings of Augustine, Peter Lombard and Duns Scotus. By 1438 he was an official *didaskalos* or public teacher, a member of the Senate, and General Judge. He favored union with the Roman church before and during the Council of Ferrara/Florence, where as an adviser to the emperor, he delivered an impassioned plea for the

Greeks to accept as legitimate the Latin addition of *Filioque* to the creed. At the time of the letter written to him by Cyriac on 29 September 1444, Scholarios was back in Constantinople, where he had reopened his school and had resumed his imperial position of General Judge. In addition, although he was still a layman, he now preached every Friday at court before the Senate and people. He was at this time maintaining a careful neutrality in the controversy between unionists and anti-unionists that raged in Constantinople after the Greek delegation returned from the council, and Cyriac's news in Letter 17 about the papal fleet, which the traveler had found patrolling the Hellespont in fulfillment of its role in the promised crusade, was undoubtedly meant to win back Scholarios' support for the union, the Greek acceptance of which depended on the ability of the West, under papal leadership, to rescue Constantinople from the Ottoman menace.[12]

ROBERTO VALTURIO (1405–75; Letters 50 and 51), worked briefly as papal abbreviator (or drafter of papal correspondence), but spent most of his career in his native Rimini in the service of its lord, Sigismondo Malatesta, the famous condottiere. Among his duties was that of serving as ambassador (*orator*) representing Malatesta, and Cyriac's use of the epithet "distinguished orator" to describe him probably refers to this function, rather than to his speaking abilities. Valturio was most famous as the author of a classicizing treatise on the art of war, the *De re militari libri XII*, which is sometimes seen as a forerunner to the work of Leonardo da Vinci and Machiavelli. It is to this interest that Cyriac is plainly responding in conveying to him inscriptions that document the military decorations given by the ancient Romans to their soldiers.

NOTES

1. Badoer, passim.

2. Babinger 1950, p. 233, note 4.

3. Marked on Cristoforo Buondelmonti's map of Constantinople in his *Liber insularum archipelagi*: See Paris, Bibliothèque Nationale, MS nouv. acq. lat. 2382.

4. His trade was not restricted to alum, of course. Heers, p. 285, cites a document giving information on the dealings of Drapieri ("admittedly one of the most powerful in the East") in soap, cloth, mastic, and wines from Chios to Phocaea, in exchange for which he received cotton, alum, and grains. The figures in this document are for trade done on his account by Niccolò de Sestri over several years: "Even if Drapieri has inflated them to suit his needs, these figures are still eloquent. . . . This document, despite all its imperfection, shows the considerable importance of Drapieri's trade" (and it deals with the activities of only one of his agents).

5. Singer, p. 114.

6. Argenti, 1: 488–489.

7. ibid. 3: 658, an agreement about alum and cloth.

8. Hopf, pp. 71–72.

9. Ashmole 1957.

10. Silvio Giuseppe Mercati, "Lettera inedita di Giovanni Argiropulo ad Andreolo Giustiniani," in *École Française de Rome, Mélanges d'Archéologie et d'Histoire* 39 (1921–1922): 153–163.

11. Cf. ibid., p. 153.

12. C. J. G. Turner, "The Career of George-Gennadius Scholarius," *Byzantion* 39 (1969): 420–455, and idem, "George-Gennadios Scholarius and the Council of Florence," *Journal of Theological Studies*, n.s. 18 (1967): 83–103; Joseph Gill, *Personalities of the Council of Florence* (New York, 1965), pp. 79–94; and Setton, 2: 66 and 88.

Note on the Texts

꽃뿣꽃

The bulk of the letters occurring in this volume are preserved in only one manuscript, Florence, Biblioteca Nazionale Centrale, Palazzo Targioni 49, paper, 15th c. (**Fn8**). Most of these are addressed to Cyriac's humanist friend Andreolo Giustiniani-Banca, who lived on the Genoese-owned island of Chios. Andreolo must have saved these letters, probably in a loose pile in no particular chronological order, and it is likely that they were copied in Chios by an itinerant scribe in the last third of the fifteenth century, when there seems to have been widespread interest in Cyriac's literary remains, especially his copies of Greek inscriptions. Were one tempted to name that scribe, a likely candidate might be Nicola Ugolino (or Ugolini), who on June 2nd, 1473, was in Chios, where he copied, dated and signed Poggio's two books *De miseria conditionis humanae* (Florence, Biblioteca Laurenziana, Plut. 89 inf. 35, paper, 15th c., fols. 110r-144v). In the same year, in the same gothic cursive hand, which resembles that of **Fn8**, Nicola copied, signed and dated a version of Cyriac's *Naumachia Regia* that the traveller had left behind in Galata/Pera, the Genoese suburb of Constantinople (ibid., fols. 44r-48v; see Monti Sabia, p. 22).

That **Fn8** was once part of a larger codex is clear from the old foliation in ink on fols. 53 to 90. Whereas it is clear from the old numbering that one folio (87) is missing, the new, stamped numbers run without interruption from 1 to 36 without indicting a break between fols. 33v and 34r, where a considerable amount of text has been lost. The letters themselves were later numbered in a darker black ink according to their occurrence in the bound manuscript, but since this numeration does not reflect their true chronological sequence, these are generally not referred to in the notes to this text. **Fn8** survived the disastrous flood of November 1966 that inundated the basement and ground floors of the Biblioteca Nazionale, but it had to be rebound, so that no codicological study of the slim codex has been possible. Giovanni Targioni Tozzetti, who donated the manuscript to the Biblioteca Nazionale, published substantial sec-

tions of the letters in his *Relazioni d'alcuni viaggi fatti in diverse parti della Toscana* (TT).

The letters that relate to the negotiations between Sultan Murad II and the representatives of King Ladislas II of Poland and Hungary are, all except one, preserved in a single manuscript: **Lc,** fols. 454r–465r, a miscellany written in several hands. These texts have been the object of intense historical and philological scrutiny by Pall 1937, 1938, Halecki and Dabrowski (see Abbreviations). See also Bodnar 1988.

Others of the letters included in this volume occur as drafts in the fragmentary travel diaries, clearly Cyriac's custom. A few are found in **T.** For the letters to Roberto Valturio, see the introductory note to nos. 50 and 51.

The Travel Diaries, except for V (the Peloponese), as presented in this collection, have been patched together from manuscript sources that are named and characterized in their introductory notes where they occur in this volume. For a full discussion of the rationale behind the edition of Diaries I and II, see BM, Introduction, pp. 1–13. For the manuscripts from which Diary III has been reconstructed, see Bodnar 1998. The Cretan Diary (our IV) is pulled together mainly from two manuscripts, **VL5,** an autograph selection made by Cyriac himself, and **VL7,** which represents an independent tradition, as explained in the introductory note to that diary.

Finally, the sole witness to Diary V, **Ma5,** is a precious one: the only extant autograph portion of Cyriac's travel diaries that escaped (hypothetically) the fire that in 1514 destroyed the Sforza library in Pesaro. For the definitive study of this manuscript see Sabbadini 1910, 1933.

In general, the spelling of the chief manuscript source has been followed, while punctuation and capitalization have been modernized throughout. Sigla of manuscripts are indicated in bold type, other abbreviations in normal type. Italics (other than in the titles of works of literature) indicate text that has presumptively been added or changed by hands other than that of the author of the document. Glosses, headings and elipses added by the present editor are indicated by square brackets; textual emendations by angle brackets; textual deletions are noted in the apparatus.

The texts of the inscriptions are given for the most part as they occur in the manuscripts, despite numerous errors. Some obvious scribal errors have been corrected and the corrections indicated in square brackets. The translations, however, in order to make consistent sense, have been based on current editions and tacitly correct any misreadings. References to their most recent, edited publications are given in the Notes to the Text. Vertical lines indicate the divisions of lines in the manuscript, which often differ from the line divisions on the actual stones, where the stones exist and a comparison can be made.

SIGLA OF MANUSCRIPTS

These sigla are extracted from an unpublished master list of known mss. containing Cyriacan texts. The first letter signifies the city, the second the library (in lower case except for where lowercase "l" can be confused with the number 1), and a number. Thus **Ma1** signifies Milan, Biblioteca Ambrosiana (the first of several mss. containing Cyriacan texts).

B1	Berlin, Staatsbibliothek (Haus Zwei), Hamilton 254, s. XV, 15th c., fols. 81–90 autograph
E	Eton College 141, 15th c., Cyriac's Strabo, with autograph marginal notes
Fr3	Florence, Biblioteca Riccardiana, Ricc. 996, 16th c.
FL5	Florence, Biblioteca Laurenziana, Plut. XLVI 3, 15th c.
FL14	——, Ashb. 1174, 15th c.
Fn8	Florence, Bibloteca Nazionale Centrale, Pal. Targ. 49, 15th c.
Lc	Lucca, Biblioteca Capitolare 555, 15th c.
M1	Munich, Staatsbibliothek, clm 716, 16th c. (a. 1504)
Ma1	Milan, Biblioteca Ambrosiana, A 55 inf., 15th c.
Ma5	——, Trotti 373, 15th c., fols. 101–124 autograph
N5	Naples, Biblioteca Nazionale, V.E.64, 18th c.
O2	Oxford, Bodleian Library, Canon. misc. 280, 15th c.
O6	——, Lat. misc. d. 85 (Ashmole), 15th c.
P1	Paris, Bibliothèque Nationale, Par. gr. 425, 15th c.
Pp	Parma, Biblioteca Palatina 1191, 15th c.

Ra	Rome, Biblioteca Alessandrina 253, 15th c., autograph
Rc	Rome, Biblioteca Casanatense 3636, 15th c., autograph
Rv	Rome, Biblioteca Vallicelliana, G.47, 15th–16th c.
T	Treviso, Biblioteca Capitolare, I-138 (no. 37), 15th c.
Vb2	Vatican City, Biblioteca Apostolica Vaticana, Barb. lat. 4424, 16th c.
Vg1	———, Vat. gr. 1309, 15th c.
VL5	———, Vat. lat. 5237, 15th c, autograph.
VL6	———, Vat. lat. 5250, 16th c.
VL7	———, Vat. lat. 5252, 15th c.
V2	Venice, Biblioteca Nazionale Marciana, Marc. gr. 481 (coll. 863), 14th c., but fols. 1–123 are 15th c.
V3	———, Marc. gr. 517 (coll. 886), 15th c., autograph
V5	———, Marc. lat. VIII 29 (coll. 2498), 15th c.

Notes to the Text

꙰ꙮ꙰

Lc, fols. 454r–455v; Fabricius 1754, cols. 12a–13b (= 1858, cols. 634a–635b); Pall 1937, pp. 50–53 (= 1938, pp. 58–61); Halecki, pp. 82–85 (see pp. 79–82 and Setton, 2: 70, note 110). This letter is placed first in **Lc,** *although it was written after Letter 2, for the same reason that it is placed first in the present collection: because it relates Cyriac's itinerary from the very beginning.*

LETTER 2

Lc, fols. 458v–460v; Fabricius 1754, cols. 16b–17b (= 1858, cols. 638a–639a); Pall 1937, pp. 15–16 (=1938, pp. 23–24); Halecki, pp. 82, 84.

1. *After* provinciam, *the scribe writes:* Repetitum reliquum epistolae superioris [= *Letter 1*] ad Ioannem Palaeologum Imp. Aug.

2. ἐκ φανεστάτων *ms.*   3. ductitare *ms.*   4. venumdare *ms.*

LETTER 3

Fn8, fols. 6r–7r, in TT, pp. 439–441, from the manuscript, with omissions; Michaelis, text volume, pp. 334, from TT with suggested emendations; translated (in part) by Bodnar 1970, pp. 99, 100–101, 191; Mitchell 1974, pp. 114–116. Cf. Setton, 2: 234–235.

1. fabrefactam *ms.*   2. litteras *ms.*   3. columnas *ms.*

4. ipse *ms.*   5. proferemus *Pliny.*

6. caelavit . . . parmae] caelavit intumescente ambitu, in parmae *Pliny.*

7. videntur *ms.*

LETTER 4

Fn8, fols. 11v–12v, no. 7; ed. in part only by TT, pp. 436–437.

1. quam *ms.*   2. Nereyda Loto] Nereia Doto *Vergil.*

3. spumantem *Vergil.*

LETTER 5

Fn8, fol. 24r, no. 26. TT, p. 450, omits all except the date and place.

LETTER 6

Fn8, fol. 27r–v, no. 30; ed., with omissions, by TT, pp. 451–452. **Fr3,** *fols. 58r–72r, contains inscriptions from Foglia Vecchia, Magnesia, Sardis, and Philadelphia (inscrr. nos. 10–18, 21–27 in the edition of Riemann). De Rossi, 373a, rightly infers that the whole series was recorded by Cyriac during this trip.*

1. Sardis, no. 47. *The copies of this inscription in* **Fr3** *and* **FL2** *are slightly better than those of* **Fn8** *and a number of their readings have been employed by the editors of* Sardis.

LETTER 7

Fn8, fols. 19v–20r, no. 19; ed., with a few omissions, by TT, pp. 452–453; cf . de Rossi, p. 373, who places it in 1446 (but see also the notes to Letter 6, in the Notes to the Translation).

LETTER 8

Fn8, fol. 19r, no. 17; ed. TT, p. 422 (only a brief summary); Pall 1937, pp. 48–49 (= 1938, pp. 56–57) from the manuscript (entire); Halecki, p. 86, no. 3, from Pall; cf. Babinger, pp. 29–30; Halecki 1943, p. 15; Pall 1937, p. 17 (= 1938, p. 25), and Setton, 2: 79.

LETTER 9

Lc, fols. 455v–456r; Fabricius 1754, cols. 13b–14a (=1858, cols. 635b–636a); Pall 1937, pp. 53–54 (= 1938, pp. 61–62); Halecki, pp. 86–87 (from Pall); translated in part by Setton, 2: 78.

LETTER 9A

Lc, fol. 456r–v.

LETTER 9B1

Lc, fols. 456v–457v; Fabricius 1754, cols. 14b–15a (=1858, cols. 636b–637b) and Pall 1937, pp. 55–56 (=1938, pp. 63–64); Halecki (from Pall), pp. 88–90, no. 5.

LETTER 9B2

Fn8, fols. 17r–18r; ed. TT, p. 432 (only the covering note); Pall 1937, pp. 49–50 (= 1938, pp. 57–58); Halecki, pp. 88–90, no. 5 (printed parallel to Letter 9b1, without the covering note; cf. Setton, 2: 79).

LETTER 10

Lc, fols. 457v–458r, ed. Fabricius 1754, p. 15 (=1858, p. 637), and Pall 1937, pp. 56–57 (= 1938, pp. 64–65); Halecki (from Pall), pp. 90–91, no. 6.

LETTER 11

Lc, fol. 458r–v; Fabricius 1754, cols. 15b–16a (= 1858, cols. 637b–638a); Pall 1937, pp. 57–58 (= 1938, p. 66); Halecki, pp. 91–92, no. 8.

LETTER 12

Fn8, fol. 26r–v; ed. TT, pp. 66–69; Belgrano, pp. 977–979), who mistakenly dates it 18 July. See also Pall 1937, pp. 34–35 (= 1938, pp. 42–43); Halecki, pp. 25–26; Setton, 2: 82. The initial salutation was probably at the bottom of the previous page (fol. 78v in the old numbering), which is missing from the manuscript.

1. domos *ms.*   2. septigeros *ms.*   3. cum *ms.*
4. diὼrican *ms.*   5. natum *ms.*   6. vastum *ms.*
7. molem *ms.*

LETTER 13

Fn8, fol. 11r–v; ed. TT, p. 423. Dated 21 July [1444], from Constantinople ('hac ipsa in regia civitate').

1. CIL III, 139, no. 740.

DIARY I

Diaries I and II are presented as composite texts based, as far as possible, on **VL6,** *fols. 1r–22r — the fullest of several manuscripts in which various segments of these diaries are preserved — but with recourse to the other manuscripts, as assembled and edited with a critical edition in BM. The other manuscript sources for both diaries are:* **Rc,** *fols. 122v–135r and 141–145 (and* **N5,** *fols. 3r–17v, 18th c., copied from Rc or from a common source);* **T,** *fols. 139r–154v; for the drawings,* **O6,** *fols. 132v–141r;* **FL14,** *fols. 119v–125r;* **Ma1,** *fols. 69r–70r, 71r. For a full discussion of the manuscripts see BM, pp. 1–8. I have reproduced here the text in BM, but not its critical apparatus, to which the interested reader is referred. Since the various segments of these diaries, as they occur in the manuscripts, are not in chronological order, BM rearranged them in the interest of readability into what appears from internal evidence to be their chronological order, without thereby meaning to imply that this was the original order of Cyriac's lost autograph record. I have kept BM's order of presentation, but without their division headings (I, a, b, II, III, etc.); and have replaced the line numbers with paragraph numbers. Also, the two diaries are treated here as two distinct documents. Diary I, the Propontic Diary, occurs in BM on pp. 21–33 (and figs. 1–6); the North Aegean Diary on pp. 33–60 (figs. 7–24). The inscriptions were edited by Dumont, Mommsen and Ziebarth 1897. The text was prepared by both Bodnar and Mitchell; the translations are Bodnar's alone except for the inscriptions, which were translated by Clive Foss, and the Prayer to Mercury, which owes some of its language to Charles Mitchell. Because of the requirements for volumes in this publication series, detailed references to the manuscript sources of the individual segments of the assembled text are not given here. The reader is referred to the corresponding sections in BM.*

1. BM 21.1; Mommsen, no. 1.   2. BM 22.2; CIG 2020.
3. BM 22.3; Mommsen, no. 4.
4. BM 22.4; Dumont, no. 72a (=Mommsen, no. 28), 72g, 72h.
5. BM 23.5, otherwise unpublished?   6. BM 23.6; CIG 2024.
7. Ad portum *in the manuscript is erroneously placed after the seventh line of the following inscription.*
8. BM 23.7; Dumont, 72e; Ziebarth 1897, no. 28.
9. BM 25.8; Dumont, 72g.   10. BM 25.9; Dumont, 72h.
11. BM 25.10; Dumont, 72i.
12. BM 25.11; Dumont, nos. 72k, 72j; CIL III, 731 (Dumont, no. 74k).

13. *BM* 25.12; *Dumont, 72j.*   14. *BM* 26.13; *CIL III, 731; Dumont, 74k.*

15. *BM* 26.14; *Cagnat, 797.*   16. *BM* 26.15; *Dumont, 64a.*

17. *BM* 26.16; *Kaibel, no. 228.*   18. *BM* 26.17–19; *Ziebarth 1897, no. 26.*

19. *BM* 27.20 = §19, *above.*   20. cuius ergo *VL6:* cum ego *Rc.*

21. insignem *Rc:* ingentem *VL6.*   22. vultus *Rc: om. VL6.*

23. sua . . . canens *Rc: om. VL6.*   24. Inque *Ovid.*

25. millium *Pliny.*   26. quod *VL6:* quam *Rc.*

27. *It is clear that Cyriac regarded* paries *as a feminine noun.*

28. enim *Rc:* cum *VL6.*   29. suo *Rc:* eius *VL6.*

30. inlaesae . . . intactae *mss.*   31. pedum *Rc: om. VL6.*

32. immanes *Rc:* inanes *VL6.*   33. IIII *edd.:* III *VL6.*

34. *BM* 29.1; *Reinach, no. 2.*   35. *BM* 29.2; *Reinach, no. 4.*

36. *BM* 29.3; *Reinach, no. 5; Loewy, no. 281.*

37. *BM* 29.4; *Reinach, no. 6.*

38. *BM* 29.5; *Reinach, no. 7.*   39. *BM* 29.6; *Reinach, no. 3.*

40. serpentino *Rc:* Propontico *VL6.*   41. IIII *Rc:* XIII *VL6.*

42. *This paragraph is from* **Pp,** *f. 62v, which gives only the Latin translation of the inscription.*

43. *Ashmole 1956, 187–188 and Pl. 37a.*   44. *BM* 31.7; *Reinach, no. 1.*

45. *BM* 31.1; *Mommsen, no. 5.*

46. *BM* 32.2; *Dumont, 72d; Mommsen, no. 6.*

47. *The manner of dating this passage and the fact that the text is preceded by two inscriptions suggest that it is part of a letter, addressee unknown.*

LETTER 14

Only in **Rc;** *ed.* **BM,** *p. 32.*

1. **Rc** *places a blank space between* venimus *and* et primo, *indicating that the missing expression was in Greek.*

DIARY I, CONTINUED

1. *BM* 33.1, *Dumont, 72f.*

LETTER 15

Fn8, *fol. 14r–v; ed.* TT *(from the beginning to* revisimus *only), p. 23.*

LETTER 16

Lc, *fols. 460v–461r; Fabricius 1754, col. 18 (= 1858, cols. 639b–640a); Halecki, pp. 92–93, no. 9, from Fabricius, without the postscript (which is, however, summarized); Setton, 2: 87, who paraphrases much of the letter and translates two sentences; Pall 1937, pp. 37–38 (= 1938, pp. 45–46).*

DIARY II

1. BM 34.1, *otherwise unpublished?*   2. BM 35.2; IG XII.8, 110.
3. BM 35.3; IG XII.8, 115.   4. BM 36.4; Ziebarth 1906, p. 406, note 1.

LETTER 17

Rc, *ff.127v–129r; ed. BM, pp. 36–37, from both manuscripts; ed. Ziebarth 1906, pp. 405–6, from* **N5;** *Neuhausen and Trapp; Pall 1937, p. 38 (= 1938, p. 46); Setton, 2: 87–88 and note 22.*

1. Et *om. Vergil.*

LETTER 18

VL6, *ed. Ziebarth 1906, p. 406; BM, p. 37.*

DIARY II, CONTINUED

1. BM 39.1; IG XII.8, 253.
2. BM 39.1; CIL III, 713; Ziebarth 1906, no. 1.
3. BM 39.2, IG XII.8, 165.   4. BM 40.3; IG XII.8, 182.
5. IG XII.8, 172; Ziebarth 1906, pp. 112–113, no. 4 (cf. CIL III, 713).
6. BM 41.5; CIL III, 714. **Ma1,** *fols. 69r–70r, adds three inscriptions (IG XII.8, 259, 211, 214) and drawings of the stele and Medusa's head, as in* **O6** *and* **FL14.**
7. auri sacra fames *Vergil.*   8. BM 42.1, *otherwise unpublished?*
9. BM 44.1; IG XII.8, 270.
10. BM 44.2; CIL III, 131. *The stone was found by Photios Petsas in Salonica* (Ἀρχαιολογικὴ Ἐφήμερις *1950–51, pp. 65–66, no. 8.*)
11. BM 44.3; IG XII.8, 467.   12. BM 44.4; IG XII.8, 418.
13. molo *T.*   14. BM 45.1; IG XII.8, 394a.

15. *BM 46.2; IG XII.8, 263.*   16. *BM 47.1; IG XII.8, 553.*

17. *BM 47.2; IG XII.8, 525.*   18. *BM 47.3; IG XII.8, 502.*

19. *BM 47.4; CIL III, 131.*   20. *BM 47.5; IG XII.8, 553.*

21. *BM 48.6; IG XII.8, 403.*   22. *BM 48.7; IG XII.8, 529.*

23. *BM 48.8; IG XII.8, 555.*   24. *BM 48.9; IG XII.8, 557.*

25. *BM 48.10; IG XII.8, 556; CIL III, 131.*

26. *BM 49.11; IG XII.8, 458.*

27. *BM 49.12; IG XII.8, 482.*   28. *BM 49.13; IG XII.8, 474.*

29. *A space was left in the manuscript here for a Greek word.*

30. **VL6**, **T**; *ed. Colucci, p. CXXXV, from* **T** *(down to* habebat inscriptionem*); Graeven, pp. 212–13, from* **VL6** *and Colucci; BM, p. 52.*

LETTER 19

T, fol. 13; ed., with obscurities unresolved, by S. Lampros, Νέος Ἑλληνομνήμων *18 (1924): 10–12, from a transcript by the librarian of the Capitular Library in Treviso communicated to him by William Miller.*

1. molo *T.*   2. cursus *Vergil.*

LETTER 20

Fn8, fol. 35v; ed. TT, p. 459.

LETTER 21

Fn8, fol. 16v; ed. Kaibel, p. 52, no. 151.

1. *IG XII.8, 38.*

LETTER 22

Fn8, fols. 14v–15r; ed. TT, p. 437.

1. *ID, no. 1597.*

DIARY III

Excerpts from the journal recording Cyriac's visit to Mykonos, Delos, Naxos, and Paros in April 1445 are preserved in two quite different manuscripts, **VL7** *(done in the first person, with dates and personal references) and* **M1** *(written in the third*

person, without dates or personal references). Since neither of these could have been copied from the other, they represent two distinct traditions, both possibly originating with Cyriac himself or some early copyist. For the purposes of this publication series, the two have been compressed into one account that necessarily does some violence to each tradition.

*On the supposition that the personal, dated journal from which the excerpts in **VL7** were made represents Cyriac's original diary, and that **M1** represents a later redaction, this editor has preferred the personal forms of **VL7** (e.g. venimus) except where an entry or section has been preserved only in **M1** (as in the section on Naxos). A detailed study of the relationship between these manuscripts and of other instances of depersonalization in the Cyriacan corpus may be found in Bodnar 1998, pp. 49–70. A third manuscript (**Fr 3**), which contains only inscriptions excerpted from the Cycladic diary, has been helpful.*

1. IG XII.5, 377.   2. ID, no. 1597.   3. EAD xxx.55.

4. EAD xxx.306.   5. ID, no 1560, extant.   6. ID, no. 1821.

7. ID., no. 1723, extant.   8. ID, no. 1558.

9. nigerrimo **M1**: integerrimo **VL7**. *The reading of* **M1** *conforms better to the description of the extant stone in* ID *as* pars antica marmoris nigricantis.

10. IG XI.4, 1100.   11. ID, no. 49.   12. IG XI, 1084. Extant.

13. ID, no. 2344.   14. Ziebarth 1897, p. 412, no. 22.

15. ID, no. 2343.   16. ID, no. 1866.   17. plenissime **M1**.

18. *This and the following Delian texts are preserved only in* **M1**.

19. ID, no 1755.   20. ID, no. 1693 bis; CIL III, 484, and Suppl. I, 7220.

21. ID, no. 1858 bis; CIL III, 485 and Suppl. I, 7219.   22. ID, no. 2092.

23. *The words in square brackets are supplied or corrected from Mommsen's edition of the text of Solinus. The phrase in italics was added by Cyriac or the scribe of* **M1**.

24. EAD xxx.92.

25. *The prayer to Mercury and the entire section on Naxos occur only in* **M1**.

26. *Analogy suggests that* venitur *and* visuntur *in this section of the diary (preserved only in* **M1**)*, *as well as similar impersonal verbs in §§28–38, represent changes from* venimus, visimus *and other personal verbs in the "personal" journal on Naxos (***VL7***).*

27. IG XII.5, 96.   28. *emended to* beatae: Ban [sic] **M1**.

29. IG XII.5, 55.   30. IG XII.5, 84.   31. IG XII.5, 86.

32. stom *M1 (a transliteration of the Greek στόμα?).*   33. *IG XII.5, 43.*

34. *Words and phrases in square brackets are supplied or corrected from Mommsen's edition of Solinus.*

35. Strongile *M1.*   36. debetur *M1.*   37. portus *Vergil.*

38. *ID, no. 49.*   39. Aranodori *M1.*

40. ΑΡΑΝΟΔΩΡΟΣ *M1.*

41. *Text and translation based on VL7, fols. 23r–v and 14r–15v. The parallel texts on Paros in M1 occur on fols. 41v–52rv, assuming with Rubensohn that the series of full-page drawings of sculptures on fols. 46v–52r belongs to the Parian journal.*

42. XIII *VL7: om. M1.*   43. claram *M1.*   44. conspicitur *M1.*

45. memoriae et *VL7:* memora *M1.*   46. epistilium *(gen.) M1.*

47. heroum *M1.*   48. *IG XII.5, 267.*

49. *The personal reference,* Quod. . . . subscriptis *is omitted in M1.*

50. *Apparently unpublished.*

51. *This second title of the entire diary appears at this point in the ms.*

52. *IG XII.5, 464.*   53. *IG XII.5, 154.*

54. *In this paragraph M1 changes the personal* Vidimus *to* Videntur, *reads* plereque *to agree with the now nominative* bases *(forgetting to change the case of* suffossas), *omits* diversorum *and converts* simulachra *to* simulacrum *(the archaic genitive, of which Cyriac was fond), which now goes with* bases; *he omits the personal reference,* et e nobis . . . revulsas, *substituting for it the adverb* noviter, *(but forgets to change the case of* deductas); *finally, he changes the personal* epigrammata comperimus *to* tale compertum epigramma.

55. *IG XII.5, 165.* ΚΑΙ.ΥΓΙΕΙΑΙ *added by M1.*   56. *IG XII.5, 167.*

57. *IG XII.5, 160.*   58. *IG XII.5, 166.*   59. *IG XII.5, 172.*

60. *IG XII.5, 163.*   61. *IG XII.5, 171.*   62. *IG XII.5, 315.*

63. *IG XII.5, 320.*   64. *IG XII.5, 442.*   65. *Rubinsohn, 355.*

66. *IG XII.5, 321.*   67. *IG XII.5, 422.*   68. *IG XII.5, 345.*

69. *The following passage is from VL7, fol. 15v–16r. In M1 it is depersonalized in the first sentence by the omission of* Ad posterum . . . principe *and by replacing* venimus *with* venitur, mirificas *with* mirificae, vidimus *with* videtur, *and* marmifodinas *with* marmifodinae. *In the second sentence it replaces* malueram *with* mavult *and* explicarem *with* licet explicare. *In the third sentence, it leaves out the personal reference,* Cursino ipso comite, *replaces*

penetravimus *with* penetratur, *and* patuisse percepimus *with* patere gnoscitur. *In the next sentence,* binas alias *becomes* binae aliae, perscrutavimus *is replaced with* visuntur, *and* latomias *becomes* latomiae. *Finally, in the sentence that begins,* Quod et tam inmensum, miror *is replaced by* mirandum est.

70. primam *M1:* prima *VL7.*   71. abrutam *VL7:* obruptam *M1.*

72. undique *M1.*   73. consculptum patet *M1.*

74. *IG XII.5, 245.*

75. *This and the following drawings and inscriptions occur in* M1 *on ff. 46v–58r.*

76. *IG XII.5, 350.*   77. *IG XII.5, 425.*   78. *IG XII.5, 423.*

79. *IG XII.5, 301.*   80. *IG, XII.5, 315.*   81. *IG XII.5, 320.*

82. *IG XII.5, 249.*   83. *IG XII.5, 302.*

84. Orion *M1. Cf. Herodotus 1.23, Vergil, Ecl. 8.56.*

LETTER 23

Fn8, fol. 32r–33r, no. 33; ed. Mitchell 1962, pp. 293–295, 299, and Tav. XXVIII; cf. TT, p. 460 (part only; dated wrongly to 1446).

1. constitutum *ms.*   2. Cnososque . . . pharetras *Lucan.*

3. Gortyna *Lucan.*   4. antiqua *repeated after* omnium.

LETTER 24

Fn8, fols. 33v–34r in the modern stamped foliation = old fols. 86v–88r (old 87 is missing); ed. TT, pp. 455–456.

1. *After* villam *a folio (= old fol. 87) is missing from the manuscript. The more recent, stamped foliation does not indicate the break. Unless there were drawings on old fol. 87, we can assume that as many as 70 lines of the text of this letter are missing,*

DIARY IV

These journal entries, which supplement the letters pertaining to Crete (Letters 22–25 and 27), are preserved in two manuscripts which complement each other. The first manuscript is found in a parchment quarto (234 × 162 mm.), bound in

*at the end of Vat. lat. 5237 (**VL5**). An autograph of Cyriac, it is a compilation, excerpted from his Cretan diary, probably designed for presentation to potential patrons as a specimen of his work. This collection of excerpts from Cyriac's travel-di-
aries was first identified as an autograph of Cyriac by de Rossi. (For this and other
such "presentation copies," headed by the inscription on the arch of Trajan in
Ancona, see de Rossi 1888, cols. 375b–376a, and Bodnar 1960a, pp. 55–56, note 2.)
It includes the Latin verses honoring Cyriac and his mother, in §§9–11 of the
Cretan Diary, and Letter 26. The parchment leaves of the Cyriacan fragment are
numbered as fols. 517–521 of the entire codex, but they have in addition an older
numbering, fols. 137–144. All the text is legible (de Rossi, 2: 372a). Fols. 137r–138v
preserve inscriptions §§4–8 of the Cretan diary (§§4–7 also occur in **V2**). Folio
142 (518 of the manuscript) contains, also in Cyriac's hand, fragments of a correspondence between Brutus and Damas of Pergamon, with Latin translations. On
the verso, Cyriac copied the Greek text of a letter from Chion of Heraklea to
Matris and the beginning of a Latin translation. The Latin translation breaks off
in mid-sentence, indicating that the following page is missing, despite the consecu-
tive numbering of the manuscript, both old and new. Other excerpts from the
Cretan diary (Part II, below) are preserved in Vat. lat. 5252 (**VL7**), fols. 9v–10v.
This manuscript is a compilation of Cyriacana made by Pietro Dolfin in Ancona
and Rimini in 1458 and 1464. The Cretan excerpts supplement the contents of
VL5 with only one overlapping, the inscription on the seal-stone of Eutyches (cf.
Letter 26).*

1. CIL IX, 5894.   2. Guarducci I, p. 197, n. 28 (=n. 29).
3. Guarducci II, p. 203, n. 14.   4. Guarducci III, p. 60, n. 16.
5. Guarducci III, p. 61, n. 17.   6. Guarducci III, p. 59, n. 12.

LETTER 25

O2, fol. 70v; ed. Mitchell 1962, pp. 288–289 (photograph on Tav. XXV).

1. *Reading* Litton *for O2's* litteram, *since this partially defaced inscription from
the site of ancient Lyttos (below, §8), was already recorded in Cyriac's Cretan journal (Diary IV, §3), a better copy of the same inscription than the one contained in
this letter.*

2. *Guarducci, 1: 197, no. 28.*

LETTER 26

VL5, fols. 515v–516r (= 139v–140r); ed. G. B. de Rossi in the Bulletino dell'Instituto di corrispondenza archeologica, *1853, p. 54, from the manuscript. Cf. Vittorio Poggi, "La gemma di Eutiche,"* Atti della società ligure di storia patria *13, 1 (1884), pp. 7–53, text on pp. 12–13, note 3 (from de Rossi); and Ashmole, pp. 38–40 (with a translation).*

1. tenuissimus *ms.*

DIARY IV, CONTINUED

1. procha *ms.*
2. excaturientem *ms.* = excataruentem, i.e., ἐκκαταρνέντα? Cf. κατάρρυτος ὕδωρ, "flowing water" in Olympiadorus' commentary on Aristotle's *Metaphysics.*
3. angustas *ms.*
4. *The last item in* VL5, *fol. 516r (142v), is the beginning of a Latin translation of the letter of Chion to Matris. The next folio is not numbered, is only three-quarters of the height of the other pages, and is clearly an insert. On the recto is a short Greek text containing the beginning of a description of the gods going forth in battle, probably not in Cyriac's hand. The verso is blank. (This information from J. M. Paton's notes on the manuscript).*
5. VL7, fols. 9v–10v.   6. adgnoscere *ms.*

LETTER 27

Fn8, fol. 22r–v; TT, p. 459, no. XXII, prints only Ex Candida . . . 7 Idus Novembris, *dismissing the contents of the letter as unimportant.*

LETTER 28

Fn8, fol. 16r–v, no. 13; ed. Rubinsohn, pp. 357–358, from a copy made for him from the manuscript; TT, pp. 423–424 (part only); cf. Miller, pp. 423 and 605; Setton, 2: 92–93.

1. iocundum *ms.*

LETTER 29

Fn8, fol. 5r–v, no. 2; ed. TT, pp. 425–426 (part only).

1. honestius *ms.*　　2. imponere *ms.*　　3. omne *ms.*

LETTER 30

Fn8, fols. 28r–31r, no. 31; ed. TT, pp. 429–434 (with omissions).

1. *The following poem also occurs in* Nova Fragmenta, *p. 68.*
2. di *ms.*
3. *CIG 2895.*　　4. *Riemann, pp. 287–8, no. 64, from* **Fr3.**
5. sedem **Fn8**: aedem **Fr3** *(a mosque?).*
6. *Riemann, p. 288, no. 65, from* **Fr3.**
7. Γεροτα *ms. Cf. Cyriac's heading for the same inscription in* **Fr3:** Extra urbem Milesiam ad locum qui a priscis Tridymus dictus est, nunc γέροντα ex antiqua pa(latia) appella(tur). *Cf. Riemann, p. 288, no. 66.*
8. *CIG 2852.*

LETTER 31

Fn8, fol. 35r; ed. TT, p. 459 (only the initial greeting, and the first and last sentences).

1. *This heading was probably added by Andreolo or the copyist of* **Fn8.**

LETTER 32

Fn8, fols. 9v–10v; ed. TT (part only), pp. 447–448.

1. Sed quod *ms.*　　2. Johannem *ms.*

LETTER 33

Fn8, fol. 19r–v; ed. TT, p. 449 (only the greeting and the first and last sentences).

LETTER 34

Fn8, fol. 17r; ed. TT, p. 449 (with omissions).

LETTER 35

Fn8, fols. 21r–22r; ed. TT, p. 450, in part (first paragraph to curabimus *and the indication of place and date at the end).*

1. VIII *ms. Although the date here at the end reads* VIII Iduum Aprilis *(6 April),* Eugenii papae anno XVI *(=1446), in the body of the letter he refers to* hodie *as* VI Iduum *(= 8 April), a Friday (*Venereo . . . die*). April 8 fell on Friday in 1446, so the numeral* VI *is correct and the numeral* VIII *must be emended to* VI.

LETTER 36

Fn8, fol. 15r–v; ed. TT (part only), pp. 450–451.

LETTER 37

Fn8, fol. 20r–v; ed. TT (part only), p. 453.

LETTER 38

T, fols. 155v–156v; ed. Colucci, pp. 142–143.

LETTER 39

Fn8, fols. 1r–4v, and VL7, fols. 24r–34r; ed. (from Fn8) by Belgrano, pp. 979–986; ed. (excerpts only) from Fn8 by TT, pp. 416–418, who notes the existence of the copy in VL7 but does not use it. The text offered here is based on Fn8 except where a reading in Fn8 is clearly the scribe's idiosyncratic spelling. Although the text in VL7 is arguably a later revision, possibly supervised by Cyriac himself, possibly copied directly from Cyriac's autograph with insertions and omissions by a Venetian scribe, this editor chooses to print the earlier version because (1) it is more complete and (2) it belongs to the time of his actual visit to Pera/Galata in the summer of 1446 when Cyriac was moved to honor Maruffo, the current podestà of the Genoese colony, and to commemorate a particular achievement of Maruffo's tenure in office, an especially fine stretch of wall added to Pera's defense perimeter along its maritime shore.

1. consuevissent *VL7: om. Fn8.*

2. πέραν *VL7: Fn8 leaves a space for the Greek to be added.*
3. invenissem *VL7: om. Fn8.*   4. ad *VL7: a Fn8.*
5. honoris *VL7:* honori *Fn8:*   6. epigrama *VL7: om. Fn8.*
7. *Belgrano, p. 981, and Tavola XIX (photograph of the actual inscription).*
8. Praetereo Ponticam . . . manduliferam Thason *om. VL7.*
9. ab *VL7: om. Fn8.*   10. preciosissima *Fn8.*
11. una cum Venetis Pisanisque *added after* victores *VL7.*
12. et dexterae manus palma[m] quam Veneti miro omni honore obser-
vant *added after* colit *VL7.*
13. sui . . . cives *om. VL7.*   14. dictionis *Fn8:* ditionis *VL7.*
15. perspicacem . . . omnigenum *om. VL7.*
16. dicta dedit *after* ubi *deleted.*
17. Nam et primum . . . colonos *om. VL7. The text breaks off at this point.*

LETTER 40

Fn8, fols. 7r–9v; ed. TT, pp. 441–445.

1. *Cagnat, p. 265, no. 916.*

LETTER 41

Fn8, fol. 22v; ed. TT (short excerpt only), p. 447.

1. pontificem] pintas *Fn8.*

LETTER 42

*Fn8, fols. 13v–14r; ed. TT (in part), pp. 435–36, who incorrectly places this letter in 1445. Ash Wednesday (*religioso Mercuri nostri atque excolendo christicolis die*) fell on 22 February in 1447.*

1. splendida *Fn8.*   2. gratiam *Fn8.*   3. extimandum *Fn8.*
4. P.que (*sic*) *Fn8, but Antonio's father's name was Giorgio.*

LETTER 43

Fn8, fols. 12v–13v; ed. TT (in part), p. 454.

1. peritissimum *ms.*   2. confecta *ms.*   3. vestram *ms.*

4. rubore *ms.*   5. delexit *ms.*

6. πεπαλόεσσαν *and* πεπαλοέσσηι *ms.*

LETTER 44

Fn8, fol. 35r–v; ed. TT, p. 460 (one paragraph only).

1. tali **Fn8.**   2. gnotum **Fn8.**

LETTER 45

Fn8, fols. 22v–23r; ed. (only part of the first sentence) TT, p. 425.

1. et *after* nepos *ms.*   2. quia: quam **Fn8.**

DIARY V

Ma5. *This is the only portion of Cyriac's* Commentaria *surviving in his own hand. As is the case with most of the Cyriacan manuscripts, the folios are in disorder chronologically; the present text follows the order established by Sabbadini (see the Note on the Text). Cross references are given below to Moroni's* Epigrammata reperta, *which contains several entries from this diary that are based on a different manuscript, now lost; and to Cyriac's copy of Strabo, E, in the margins of which he copied four of the inscriptions that he also recorded in this journal. Cf. Bodnar 1960a, pp. 118–119.*

1. *Also in Moroni, no. 251.*   2. *IG V.1, 555a.1.*

3. *Also in Moroni, no. 267.*   4. *IG V.1, 529.*   5. *IG V.1, 494.*

6. NOΩN *ms.*   7. *IG V.1, 560.*

8. *IG V.1 505; also in Moroni, no. 252.*

9. *IG V.1, 471.*   10. *IG V.1, 569.*

11. *Also in the margin of E, fol. 223a, with the lemma:* ἐγὼ δὲ Κυριακὸς εἰς Ἰθώμην μεσσηνίων ἀκρόπολιν τόδ᾽ ἐπίγραμμα εἰς λίθον εὗρον. *("I, Cyriac found this inscription on a stone in Ithome, the citadel of the Messenians.")*

12. *IG V.1, 1469, extant.*   13. *IG V.1, 1455.*

14. *IG V.1, 505. All of §18 also occurs in in Moroni, p. xxxxiii.*

15. *IG V.1, 1407.* ΞΕΝΩΝΟΣ *Moroni.*

16. IG V.1, 1408. Also in Moroni, no. 268.   17. IG V.1, 1416.

18. §§22 and 23 occur also in Moroni, p. xxxxiiii.

19. Terrarum Moroni.   20. promontorium Moroni.

21. IG V.1, 1294. Copied by Cyriac into **E**, f. 222b, with the lemma: Τόδ᾽ ἐγὼ Κυριακὸς εἰς μεσσηνιακὸν Πύλον ἐπίγραμμα εὗρον· καὶ νυνὶ δὲ ταύτην ἐλαττομένην πύλιον πόλιν Βείτυλον καλοῦσιν. ("I, Cyriac, found this inscription by the Messenian Gate; but now they call this the gate to the diminished city of Bitylos"). Moroni's text lacks the inscription.

22. IG V.1, 1334a.   23. Changed in manuscript from fuisse.

24. ΩΑΝ ms. The corrected reading is from the stone.

25. ΤΑΝΑΤΤΙΓΡΟΝ ms. Corrected reading is from the stone.

26. IG V.1, 1247, extant.

27. IG V.1, 1243, extant. Copied by Cyriac into **E**, fol. 226a, with the notation: καὶ ἡμεῖς εἰς Ταινάρον περὶ αὐτοῦ υἱοῦ Λάκωνος τόδ᾽ ἐπίγραμμα εὗρον. ("In Tainaron I found this inscription concerning the very son of Lacon.") His copies of the text are accurate to the extant stone, including the leaf decoration, but neither has the correct division of lines.

28. IG V.1, 1248, extant. This inscription was copied by Cyriac into **E**, f. 222b.

29. IG V.1, 1245.   30. ΔΑΜΑΡΜΕΝΕΥ ms.   31. IG V.I, 1244.

32. IG V.I, 1246. Copied by Cyriac into **E**, f. 224b (Cf. Richard Foerster, "Zur Handschriftenkunde und Geschichte der Philologie IV: Cyriacus von Ancona zu Strabon, Rheinisches Museum, N.F. 51 (1896): 481–491 at 483.)

33. IG V.1, 1237.   34. IG V.1, 1239.   35. IG V.1, 1241.

36. IG V.1, 1250.   37. IG V.1, 1257.

38. Modern editors of Plutarch read νῦν δ᾽ἄμ᾽ Αἴαντος, correcting νῦν δ᾽ἀνάματος of the mss.

39. IG I² 927.   40. IG V.1, 1236.

41. IG V.1, 1225. For the inscription, see Plate VI.

42. From πρῖνος, "holm-oak."

43. abruttum ms. Cf. the Cycladic diary, §59, where the same mistake occurs.

44. IG V.1, 1224.

45. The following passage is also in Moroni, pp. xxxxii–xxxxiii.

46. Chirodonta is formed on the Greek word for "boar", χοῖρος.

47. The personal names in this poem are glossed in Greek between the lines by Cyriac himself, e.g., Lycurgo is glossed by ὁ Νομοθέτης.

48. *This poem occurs also in Florence, Biblioteca Nazionale Centrale, MS Naz. II.IV.128, fols. 108v–110r. Moroni's* Epigrammata *preserves, in addition to the Italian text (p. 43), a Greek translation of lines 1, 3, 5, 7, 9, 11, and 13 (p. 42), a clear indication that in Moroni's exemplar, the odd-numbered lines occurred on the verso of one folio and the even-numbered lines on the recto of the next folio. See Sp. Lambros,* κυριακοῦ τοῦ Ἀγκωνίτου ἐπίγραμμα εἰς τὴν Σπάρτην ἐπὶ Κωνσταντίνου Παλαιολόγου, *in* Παλαιλόγεια καὶ Πελοποννησιακά *(Athens, 1930), pp. 99–101.*

49. *Possibly a corruption of* alte.   50. *IG V.1, 809.*   51. *IG V.1, 808.*

52. *Published in* Bulletin de correspondance hellénique *68/69 (1945–46): 395–96.*

53. *Ibid.*   54. *IG IV, 748.*

55. *CIL I, 595; III, 531, extant. In the ms., the inscription is pictured accurately as broken on the right side: after* METELO *in the first line, after* ITALICI *in the second line, and after* NEGOTIA *in the third, with* -NTVR *added beyond the break in the stone.*

56. *IG IV, 539, extant.*

57. *The italicized words in the Latin text of §§70 and 71 are omitted by Cyriac in his translation of these two paragraphs into Greek.*

58. Lucreas *ms. (cf. the Greek translation).*

59. ipsa in Locride . . . Euanthiam dixere *in the margin.*

60. *Not in the Latin text.*

61. *The words* Κόμιτα . . . ἄξιον *were added afterwards in the margin, corresponding to the later addition of the initials* C.P.L *in the Latin text.*

62. *The words* μεν μεσόγειον — ἑτέραν *were added later in the margin to correspond to the previous correction introduced into the Latin text.*

LETTER 46

T, fols. 120v–121r, 124r–125v (fols. 122 and 123 are missing from the manuscript); ed. Ziebarth, "Κυριακός ὁ ἐξ Ἀνκῶνος ἐς Ἠπείρῳ," Ἐπειροτικὰ Χρονικά *1 (1926):114–117; omitted by Colucci: cf. p. 109: "perche del tutto informe, sebbene inserito nel codice medesimo Trivigiano."*

1. *Added by the scribe, Felice Feliciano.*

2. *Two folios are missing from the manuscript at this point.*

3. praeda *ms.*   4. audientes *ms.*   5. heronesum *ms.*

LETTER 47

Ra, fols. 13v–16r. Although the full text of Sorgo's letter is preserved in the ms., only the incipit *and* explicit *are given here.*

LETTER 48

T, 126r–128r; ed. Colucci, p. CX, who wrongly dates it to 1438; cf. Miller, p. 424; Bodnar 1960a, pp. 28–29 (for Cyriac's earlier visit to Arta) and pp. 64–65; Setton, 2: 97–98.

1. *A misleading title, possibly by the scribe Feliciano, for what is clearly an excerpt from Cyriac's travel diary.*   2. *Astaio ms.*

LETTER 49

T, fols. 166v–167r; ed. Colucci, p. CXLVII; cf. Jacobs, p. 197; Pall, 1937, pp. 44–45 (=1938, pp. 52–53) and Bodnar 1960a, p. 64.

1. *truculenti ms.*

LETTER 50

FL5, fol. 196r; V5, fol. 183r; ed. (from FL5) Bandini, 2: 375; ed. (from FL5) Calogerà in Nuova Raccolta d'opusculi scientifici e filologici, *vol. 38.1 (Venice 1783), p. 134 (not seen); cf. de Rossi, p. 358; Jacobs, p. 198.*

1. *FL5 omits this heading.*

LETTER 51

FL5, fol. 49r–49v; V5, fol. 183r; for editions see the note on the preceding letter.

1. *The bracketed phrase is omitted in the mss.*
2. *RICINARIO mss. Cyriac was fooled by the ligature of T and R at the beginning of the word.*
3. *Gallius ms.*

LETTER 52

FL5, fol. 196r; V5, fol. 183r. For editions see above, Letter 49, note.

LETTER 53

T, fols 157r–158v; ed. Colucci, pp. CXLIII–CXLV.

1. vicimus *ms.*

Notes to the Translation

༄༅༄

ABBREVIATIONS

Argenti
Philip Argenti. *The Occupation of Chios by the Genoese and their Administration of the Island, 1346–1566.* 3 vols. Cambridge, 1958.

Ashmole 1956
Bernard Ashmole. "Cyriac of Ancona and the Temple of Hadrian at Cyzicus." *Journal of the Warburg and Courtauld Institutes* 19 (1956): 179–191.

Ashmole 1957
Idem. "A Lost Statue Once in Thasos." In *Fritz Saxl 1890–1948: A Volume of Memorial Essays from his Friends in England*, ed. Donald James Gordon. Pp. 195–198. London, 1957.

Ashmole 1959
Idem. "Cyriac of Ancona." *Proceedings of the British Academy* 45 (1959): 25–41. (Italian Lecture, delivered in 1957.)

Atti
Ciriaco d'Ancona e la cultura antiquaria dell'Umanesimo. Atti del Convegno Internazionale di Studio, Ancona 6–9 febbraio 1992. Accademia Marchigiana di scienze, lettere ed arti, Collana "Progetto Adriatico," 2. Ed. Gianfranco Paci and Sergio Sconocchia. Reggio Emilia, 1998.

Babinger 1950
Franz Babinger. "Von Amurath zu Amurath, Vor- und Nachspiel der Schlacht bei Varna (1444)." *Oriens* 3 (1950): 229–265.

Babinger 1978
Idem. *Mehmed the Conqueror and His Time*, ed. William C. Hickman, tr. Ralph Manheim. Princeton, 1978.

Badoer
Il libro dei conti di Giacomo Badoer (Costantinopoli 1436–1440), ed. Umberto Dorino and Tommaso Bertelè. Rome, 1956.

Bandini
Angelo Maria Bandini. *Catalogus codicum latinorum Bibliothecae Mediceae Laurentianae*, vol. 2. Florence, 1776.

Belgrano   T. Belgrano. "Documenti riguardanti la colonia
               genovese di Pera." *Atti della Società Ligure di Storia
               Patria* 13 (1877–1884): 99–336, 977–1003 *Documenti
               riguardanti la colonia genovese di Pera.* Genoa, 1888.
Bergstein   Mary Bergstein. "Donatello's *Gattamelata* and its
               Humanist Audience." *Renaissance Quarterly* 55:3
               (2002): 833–868.
Bodnar 1960a   Edward W. Bodnar. *Cyriacus of Ancona and Athens.*
               Collection Latomus 43. Brussels and Berchem, 1960.
Bodnar 1960b   Idem. "The Isthmian Fortifications in Oracular
               Prophecy." *American Journal of Archaeology* 64 (1960):
               165–171.
Bodnar 1970   Idem. "Athens in April, 1436." *Archaeology* 23 (1970):
               96–105, 188–199.
Bodnar 1972   Idem. "A Visit to Delos in April, 1445." *Archeology* 25
               (1972): 210–215.
Bodnar 1973   Idem. "A Quarry Relief on the Island of Paros."
               Archaeology 26 (1973): 270–277.
Bodnar 1988   Idem. "Ciriaco d'Ancona and the Crusade of Varna: A
               Closer Look." *Mediaevalia* 14 (1988): 253–280.
Bodnar 1998   Idem. "Ciriaco's Cycladic Diary," in *Atti*, pp. 49–70.
               Reggio Emilia, 1998.
BM   Edward W. Bodnar and Charles Mitchell, eds. *Cyriacus
               of Ancona's Journeys in the Propontis and the Northern
               Aegean, 1444–1445.* Memoirs of the American
               Philosophical Society, 112. Philadelphia, 1976.
               References in the form "34.1" mean "page 34, first
               inscription."
Cagnat   René Cagnat, ed. *Inscriptiones Graecae ad res Romanas
               pertinentes, auctoritate et impensis Academiae
               Inscriptionum et Litterarum Humaniorum collectae et
               editae.* Rome, 1964.
CIG   August Boeck et al., eds. *Corpus inscriptionum graecarum,
               auctoritate et impensis Academiae litterarum regiae
               borussicae.* 4 vols. Berlin, 1828–77. Supplemental

volumes published under the authority of the
Akademie der Wissenschaften, Berlin, 1863–1905.

CIL   *Corpus inscriptionum Latinarum, consilio et auctoritate*
Academiae Litterarum Regiae Borussicae editum. Berlin,
1862–. Vol. I: *Inscriptiones Latinae antiquissimae ad C.*
Caesaris mortem, ed. Th. Mommsen (1863). Vol. III:
Inscriptiones Asiae, provinciarum Europae Graecarum,
Illyrici Latinae, ed. Th. Mommsen. Pts. 1–2 (1873),
and Supplementum. Fascs. 1–5 (1889–1902). Vol. IX:
Inscriptiones Calabriae, Apuliae, Samnii, Sabinorum,
Piceni Latinae, ed. Th. Mommsen (1883).

Colucci Giuseppe Colucci. *Antiquità Picene.* Vol. 15. Fermo,
1792.

Cornelius Cornelius Flaminius. *Creta sacra, sive de episcopis*
utriusque ritus graeci et latini in insula Cretae. Vol 1.
Venice, 1755.

Dabrowski Ian Dabrowski. "L'anneé 1444." *Bulletin international de*
l'Académie polonaise des sciences et des lettres (Polska
Akademia Nauk), classe de philologie — classe d'histoire et
de philosophie. Numero supplémentaire 6 (1951).
Cracow, 1952.

Diller Aubrey Diller. "A Lost Manuscript of Nonnus'
Dionysiaca." Classical Philology 48 (1953): 177.

Dölger Franz Dölger. *Mönchsland Athos.* Munich, 1943.

Dumont Albert Dumont. *Inscriptions et monuments figurés de la*
Thrace. Paris, 1876.

EAD   École Française d'Athènes. *Exploration Archéologique de*
Délos. 39 vols. Paris: 1909–2001.

Fabricius 1754 Joannes Albertus Fabricius. *Bibliotheca latina mediae et*
infimae aetatis, cum supplemento Christiani Schoettgenii.
Editio prima italica, ed. J. D. Mansi. Padua, 1754.

Fabricius 1858 Idem. *Bibliotheca latina mediae et infimae aetatis, cum*
supplemento Christiani Schoettgenii, jam a patre Joanne
Dominico Mansi . . . e mss. editisque codicibus correcta
illustrata aucta, post editionem patavinam an. 1754, nunc

denuo emendata et aucta, ed. Gustavo Camillo Galletti. 6 vols. Florence, 1858–59.

Foerster   Richard Foerster. "Zur Handschriftenkunde und Geschichte der Philologie IV: Cyriacus von Ancona zu Strabon." *Rheinisches Museum,* n.f. 51 (1896): 481–491.

Graeven   Hans Graeven. "Cyriacus von Ancona auf dem Athos." *Centralblatt für Bibliothekswesen* 16 (1899): 209–215 and 498–500.

Guarducci   Margherita Guarducci. *Inscriptions Creticae, opera et consilio Friderici Halbherr collectae.* 4 vols. Rome, 1935–1950.

Halecki   Oskar Halecki. *The Crusade of Varna: A Discussion of Controversial Problems.* Polish Institute Series, 3. New York, 1943.

Heers   Heers, Jacques. *Gènes au XVe siècle, activité économique et problèmes sociaux.* (Texte intégral. École pratique des hautes études, VIe Section.) Paris, 1971.

Hercher   Rudolf Hercher, ed. *Epistolographi graeci.* Paris, 1873.

Hopf   Carl Hopf. *Les Giustiniani.* Paris, 1888.

IG   *Inscriptiones graecae, consilio et auctoritate Academiae Litterarum Regiae Borussicae editae.* Berlin, 1873–. Vol. IV: *Inscriptiones Argolidis* (1902). Vol. V, pt. 1: *Inscriptiones Laconiae et Messeniae* (1913). Vol. XI: *Inscriptiones Deli* (1912–1914). Vol. XII: *Inscriptiones insularum maris Aegaei praeter Delum.* Pt. 5: *Inscriptiones Cycladum* (1903–1909). Pt. 8: *Inscriptiones insularum maris Thracici* (1909).

ID   Felix Dürrbach, et al. *Inscriptions de Delos.* 7 vols. Paris, 1926–.

Jacobs   E. Jacobs. "Cyriacus von Ancona und Mehmed II." *Byzantinische Zeitschrift* 30 (1929–30): 197–202.

Janin   Raymond Janin. *Constantinople Byzantine, développement urbain et répertoire topographique.* 2nd edition. Paris, 1964.

Kaibel	Georg Kaibel, *Epigrammata graeca ex lapidibus conlecta*. Berlin, 1878.
Lehmann 1973	Phyllis Williams Lehmann. *Samothracian Reflections: Aspects of the Revival of the Antique*. Princeton, 1973.
Lehmann 1977	Eadem. *Cyriacus of Ancona's Egyptian Visit and its Reflections in Gentile Bellini and Hieronymus Bosch*. Mary Flexner Lecture, Bryn Mawr College. Locust Valley, N.Y., 1977.
Loewy	Emanuel Loewy. *Inschriften griechischer Bildhauer*. Leipzig, 1885. Reprint, Osnabrück, 1965.
Luttrell	Anthony Luttrell. *The Maussolleion at Halikarnassos*, Vol. 2, Part II: *The Later History of the Maussolleion and its Utilization in the Hospitaller Castle at Bodrum*. Jutland Archaeological Society Publications, XV:2. Copenhagen, 1986.
Mercati	Silvio Giuseppe Mercati. "Lettera inedita di Giovanni Argiropulo ad Andreolo Giustiniani," *École Française de Rome, Mélanges d'Archéologie et d'Histoire* 39 (1921–1922): 153–163.
Michaelis	Adolf Theodor Friedrich Michaelis. *Der Parthenon*. Leipzig, 1870–71. With a separate volume of plates.
Miller	William Miller. *Latins in the Levant. A History of Frankish Greece, 1204–1566*. London, 1908. Reprint, New York, 1964.
Mitchell 1962	Charles Mitchell. "Ex libris Kiriaci Anconitani." *Italia medioevale e umanistica*. 5 (1962): 283–299.
Mitchell 1974	Idem. "Ciriaco of Ancona: Fifteenth-Century Drawings and Descriptions of the Parthenon." In *The Parthenon*, ed. Vincent J. Bruno, pp. 111–123. New York, 1974.
Mommsen	Theodor Mommsen, "Observationes epigraphicae. XXI. Cyriaci Thracica." *Ephemeris epigraphica* 3 (1877): 235–236.
Monti Sabia	Liliana Monti Sabia, ed. *Kyriaci Anconitani Naumachia Regia*. Istituto Nazionale di Studi sul Rinascimento Meridionale, Studi XI. Pisa and Rome, 2000.

Moroni   [Carlo, Moroni, ed.] *Epigrammata reperta . . . a Cyriaco Anconitano.* [Rome, ca. 1660].

Neuhausen   K. A. Neuhausen and Erich Trapp. "Sprachliche und
and Trapp   Sachliche Bemerkungen zu einer neuen Ausgabe des Cyriacus von Ancona." *Humanistica Lovaniensia* 32 (1983): 45–74 and 33 (1984): 22–70.

Nova Fragmenta   Annibale Olivieri degli Abati, ed. *Commentariorum Cyriaci Anconitani Nova Fragmenta notis illustrata.* Pesaro, 1763.

Pall 1937, 1938   Francesco Pall. *Ciriaco d'Ancona e la crociata contro i Turchi.* Valenii-e-Munte, 1937. Also published in *Académie Roumaine, Bulletin de la section historique* 20 (1938): 9–68.

Pall 1941   Idem. "Autour de la croisade de Varna. La question de la paix de Szeged." *Académie Roumaine, Bulletin de la section historique* 22 (1941): 144–158.

PL   Jacques-Paul Migne, ed. *Patrologiae cursus completus, series latina.* 221 vols. Paris, 1844–91.

Raby   Raby, Julian. "Cyriacus of Ancona and the Ottoman Sultan Mehmed II." *Journal of the Warburg and Courtauld Institutes* 43 (1980): 242–246.

Reinach   Théodore Reinach. "Temple d'Hadrien à Cyzique." *Bulletin de correspondence hellénique* 14 (1890): 517–545.

Riemann   Othon Riemann. "Inscriptions grecques provenants du recueil de Cyriaque d'Ancône." *Bulletin de Correspondance Hellénique* 1 (1877): 81–88; 134–136; 286–294.

de Rossi   Giovanni Battista de Rossi. *Inscriptiones christianae urbis Romae septimo saeculo antiquiores.* 2 vols. Rome, 1861–1888.

Rubensohn   Otto Rubensohn. "Geschichte der wissenschaftlichen Erforschung von Paros." *Athenische Mitteilungen* 25 (1900): 341–372 (Ciriaco 349–364) and Tafel VI.

Sabbadini   Remigio Sabbadini, "Ciriaco d'Ancona e la sua
1910, 1933   descrizione autografa del Peloponneso trasmessa da Leonardo Botta." In *Miscellanea Ceriani,* pp. 183–247.

	Milan, 1910. Republished without the illustrations in his *Classici e umanisti da codici ambrosiani*, pp. 1–52. Fontes Ambrosiani, 2. Florence, 1933.
Sardis	W. H. Buckler and D. M. Robinson, eds. *Sardis* 7, 1: *Greek and Latin Inscriptions*. American Society for the Excavation of Sardis. Leiden, 1932.
Scalamonti	Francesco Scalamonti. *Vita viri clarissimi et famosissimi Kyriaci Anconitani*, edited and translated by Charles Mitchell and Edward W. Bodnar. Transactions of the American Philosophical Society, vol. 86, part 4. Philadelphia, 1996.
Setton	Kenneth M. Setton. *The Papacy and the Levant*. Vol. 2: *The Fifteenth Century*. Memoirs of the American Philosophical Society, vol. 127. Philadelphia, 1978.
Singer	Charles Singer. *The Earliest Chemical Industry*. London, 1948.
TT	Giovanni Targioni-Tozzetti. *Relazioni d'alcuni viaggi fatti in diverse parti della Toscana*. Vol. 5. Florence, 1773.
Wolters	Wolters, Paul. "Cyriacus in Mykene und am Tainaron." *Athenische Mitteilungen* 40 (1915): 91–100.
Ziebarth 1897	Erich Ziebarth. "Cyriaci Anconitani inscriptiones graecae vel ineditae vel emendatae." *Mitteilungen des Deutschen Archäologischen Instituts, Athenische Mitteilungen* 22 (1897): 405–414.
Ziebarth 1906	Erich Ziebarth. "Cyriacus von Ancona in Samothrake." *Mitteilungen des Deutschen Archäologischen Instituts, Athenische Mitteilungen* 31 (1906): 405–414.

LETTER I

This letter, though written later than Letter 2, is placed first because it contains information on Cyriac's travels and activities prior to those referred to in Letter 2 (which stands first in the manuscript).

1. The union of the Greek and Roman churches, proclaimed at the Council of Florence on 6 July 1439.

2. As stipulated by the Treaty of Terracina, signed 14 June 1443.

3. Domenico Capranica, cardinal 1426–1458.

4. Not extant.

5. The so-called "Crusade of Varna" against the Turks in Europe, the purpose of which was to liberate Constantinople from the Turkish threat, was proclaimed by Pope Eugene IV in January 1443. Giuliano Cardinal Cesarini (see Biographical Notes) was the papal legate in overall charge of the land army sent from Hungary. The reference here is to the nearly successful "Long Campaign" of July 1443 to February 1444. See Setton, 2: 82–107.

6. The Turks, variously referred to in these documents as *barbari* ("barbarians," "strangers," "foreigners"), *Parthi* ("Parthians," "Persians"), and *Teucri* ('Trojans"). *Teucri* is the word regularly used for Turks in the Venetian archival documents cited by Setton, 2, *passim*. Cyriac uses it throughout. For the political overtones of these terms, see James Hankins, "Renaissance Crusaders: Humanist Crusade Literature in the Age of Mehmed II," *Dumbarton Oaks Papers* 49 (1995): 111–207, esp. 135–144.

7. A proverb borrowed from Pliny the Younger, *Epist.* 1.8.1.

8. The so-called *Hexamilion*, a six-mile-long fortification wall across the Isthmus of Corinth, built first in antiquity and destroyed and rebuilt several times in its history. See Bodnar 1960b.

9. The channel between the island of Euboea and the mainland of Greece.

10. *Cyothalani* in the manuscript.

LETTER 2

1. For the omitted passage see Letter 1, §§3–7.

2. The subject of this sentence is inferred from the parallel sentence in Letter 1.

3. Ladislas the Jagiellonian, King of Poland (1434–1444), King of Hungary (1440–1444).

4. See Michael Kritoboulos, *History of Mehmed the Conqueror* (ed. V. Grecu), 1.4.2. Kritoboulos was an acquaintance of Cyriac's.

5. Previous travels of Cyriac in Turkish-occupied lands are recounted in Scalamonti, *passim*.

LETTER 3

This document, usually referred to as a letter, has all the earmarks of an excerpt made by Cyriac from his travel journals for presentation to his good friend in Chios, the humanist Andreolo Giustiniani-Banca, to whom most of the letters in this series are addressed. Its date, 29 March, then, must be the date of the presentation, not of Cyriac's actual visit to Athens, which falls logically within the course of his journey in January and February 1444 across the mainland of Greece, as described in letter Letter 1. Thus he would have visited in succession Patras, Corinth, the Isthmus of Corinth, then Athens, before crossing the Euripus to Chalcis and Oreos in Euboea, and on to Asia Minor via the Cyclades.

1. The Parthenon in Athens, actually the third of the three monuments described in this excerpt.

2. The Horologion of Andronikos, popularly known as the "Tower of the Winds."

3. Copies of Cyriac's drawings of these Athenian monuments, lacking in **Fn8,** occur in two other manuscripts: **B1** (Cyriac's autograph presentation sample of his drawings and inscriptions to Pietro Donato, bishop of Padua) and **Vb2** (the architectural sketchbook of Giuliano da Sangallo). See Plates I and II.

4. Cyriac reports the inscribed names (two of which are incorrect) of the winds as he moves counter-clockwise around the eight-sided monument: Lips (SW), Notos (S), Euros (SE), Apeliotes (E), Aparktias (N, instead of Kaikias, NE), Boreas (N), Thraskias (NW, instead of Skiron, also NW), and Zephyr (W), See Bodnar 1970, 192.

5. The Propylaea, which had been converted into the ducal residence.

6. The deep west porch had been converted into the main hall of the palace.

7. Pseudo-Aristotle, *De mundo* 6.399b: the reference is to the cult-statue rather than to the building.

8. Pliny the Elder, *Hist. nat.* 36.4.18.

LETTER 4

1. The first of April fell on a Wednesday in 1444. Cyriac looked on Hermes/Mercury as his *genius*, and on Wednesday (*mercoledì* in Italian, *dies Mercurii* in Latin) as Mercury's day. *Genius* in the old Roman sense is difficult to translate in a single word, and the difficulty is compounded by the need of expressing Cyriac's syncretistic understanding of the term. The nearest concept might be that of patron saint, or better a guardian angel or protective spirit/deity.

2. Chios.

3. The Genoese *nave* (cog), a huge (*cetea*, "whale-like") merchant ship, whose massive proportions were designed with bulky cargoes of alum in mind, held between 750 and 1,000 tons of cargo. The mythological fantasy of this letter involving the mother ship and two trailing skiffs or dinghies, one of which is larger than the other, presupposes the *nave* as the "mother" ship, which normally carried on deck, besides the traditional small boat, called a *barca*, a much larger one as well, called a *lembo*.

4. Franzesco di Drapieri dal Banco (see Biographical Notes), the current lessee of the alum mines on the coast of Asia Minor near ancient Phokaia as well as of the new trading mart (*Ital.* Foglia Nuova; *Turk.* Yeni Foça); the other two men mentioned are Andreolo's brother-in-law Paride and Visconte Giustiniani da Pagana.

5. Cyriac was obsessed by the sea-nymphs, of whom he regarded Cymodocea (*Gr.* Κυμοδόκη, "Wave-Receiver") as his special patron. They recur often in these documents.

6. Vergil, *Aen.* 9.102–103.

7. Federico of Montefeltro, Duke of Urbino (1422–1482).

LETTER 5

1. The *Maona* was a company of Genoese merchants, all of whom took the name Giustiniani, who essentially owned shares in the island of Chios.

LETTER 6

The year is not given. De Rossi, p. 373a, places it and Letter 5 in 1446; but both letters fit better into the chronology of Cyriac's travels for the year 1444. If he was in Manisa on April 9th and 10th, this would have given him ample time to get to Sardis, Philadelphia, back to Manisa, and over to Lesbos before returning to Foglia Nuova on April 24th. If Letter 7, written from Foglia on 4 May, is also placed in 1444, we have filled most of the gap in de Rossi's chronology between April 2 (Letter 4) and May 22 (Letter 8).

1. Dorino I Gattilusio, lord of the island of Lesbos.

2. Leonardo Giustiniani, soon (1 July 1444) to be named Archbishop of Mytilene.

3. In Hellenistic times, this was a two-celled temple of Zeus and Artemis. Cyriac saw twice as many standing columns as did the next recorded travelers, in the seventeenth century. By 1910 only two complete columns, with their capitals, remained standing. The actual height of the columns is slightly over 58 feet and the actual circumference is 20 feet.

4. Segments of the late Roman wall ran along the east bank of the river.

5. See Strabo 13.4.5.

6. I.e., Franciscan.

LETTER 7

1. Possibly one of many ancient cities names Chryse or Chrysa, usually in association with a nearby deposit of gold ore. This one had to be within a short journey's distance from Foglia Nuova.

2. A favorite topic of Cyriac's. See Scalamonti, §99.

3. Probably a bronze coin. This image is frequent on coins of Greek cities from the sixth to the third centuries B.C.

4. *Iliad* 12.200–297; see also *Aeneid* 11.751–756.

LETTER 8

1. Turkish Edirne, the European capital of the Ottoman Turks before the capture of Constantinople in 1453.

2. The prince at Murad II's side was the twelve-year-old Mehmed II Çelebi, his recently designated successor, who nine years later would capture Constantinople.

3. A region of Assyria.

LETTER 9

Halecki, pp. 81–82 and Pall 1941, p. 3, note 1, suggest the addressee is Andreolo Giustiniani even though the text is not included among the letters in **Fn8.** Another possibility may be Franzesco di Drapieri. See Letter 10.

1. Atanasije Frašak, Metropolitan of Semendria. The Chancellor's name was Bogdan. See Setton, 2: 78.

2. A stronghold of exceptional strategic importance as a gateway to Hungary. *Golubac* seems to be a corruption of *Columbarium*, which in turn is the Latin translation of the Greek word for "dove-cote", περιστερεών.

3. Ibrahim Bey, prince of Karaman, the sultan's brother-in-law.

4. Murad II's grand vizier.

LETTER 9A

A letter of credence carried to the sultan by Ladislas' representative to the peace negotiations at Adrianople, Stojka Gisdanić, an almost unknown Serb or Wallachian. (See Halecki, pp. 16, 21–25). This document and Letter 9b1 (and possibly 9b2) were undoubtedly enclosed with Letter 9.

1. This and the next two headings may be editorial additions by the scribe of Lc and are treated as such here.

2. The letter itself is dated 24 April. The feast of St. George occurred on 23 April.

LETTER 9BI

1. Mehmed I (sultan 1413–21).

2. Branković.

3. Vlad II Dracul was *voivode* or prince of Wallachia from 1436 to 1447, except for a brief interval in 1442–43. He was a vassal of the Holy Roman Emperor, but he was also tributary to Sultan Murad II. His son, Vlad III, was the infamous Dracula.

4. Suleiman Beg, the Turkmen ruler of two states in central Anatolia, commanded a large army.

5. For the controversy over whether Ladislas ever actually swore to this ten years' peace, see Setton, 2: 83, note 5.

LETTER 10

1. The contents point clearly to Hunyadi, the Hungarian captain of the crusader army, as the addressee. See Pall 1941, p. 3, note 1; and Halecki, pp. 80–81.

LETTER 11

The manuscript does not name the addressee of Letters 10 and 11; but if 10 was to John Hunyadi, as seems likely, then 11 was also to him. See Pall, 1937, p. 28 (=1938, p. 36) and 1941, p. 3, note 1; and Halecki, pp. 80–81.

1. Galata, also called Pera because it was situated across ($\pi\epsilon\rho\alpha\nu$) the Golden Horn and could be reached only by ferry (*perenterea cymba*), was the prosperous colony of Genoese merchants opposite the Golden Horn from Constantinople.

2. The pronoun *haec* would seem to indicate a document enclosed with Letter 11 and must refer to our Letter 10, which Cyriac seems to have car-

ried with him to Galata/Pera rather than posting it from Adrianople, the Ottoman European capital, carefully phrased though it is.

3. Babinger, p. 31, translates: "I wrote what was possible from Edirne, most Christian prince, in a moderate form, in order to avoid certain destruction at the hands of the barbarians."

4. Essentially, Bulgaria and Serbia.

5. The defeats of the so-called "Long Campaign" of 1443. What Cyriac predicted did come true. Murad put down the rebellion in Karamania more quickly than anticipated, crossed back to Europe, not via the Hellespont, which was blocked by the fleet, but over the Bosporus, which was not, and went on to annihilate the crusader army at Varna in present day Bulgaria.

6. Understanding *occupaturum* to be a mistake for the passive form, *occupatum iri*.

LETTER 12

The addressee is very probably Andreolo, since it occurs in his collection. The honorific title *tuae beatitudini*, used toward the end of this letter, is repeated in other letters that are definitely addressed to Andreolo.

1. The term *despotes* means "lord" or "master," roughly the same as *dominus* in Latin, and does not connote what the English word "despot" does. Theodore was *despotes*, lord, of Selymbria, near Constantinople. See Setton, 2: 69–70.

2. Probably Apameia, a fortified inland village in Thrace (modern Bosnaviran), northwest of Hebdomon, a port on the Sea of Marmara seven miles from Constantinople. Situated on a height from which one could see the Byzantine capital, it contained the ruins of an imperial villa. See Janin, pp. 405–406.

3. Boruele Grimaldi was *podestà* of "Peyre" at this time: Belgrano, pp. 208–209.

4. For this translation of the Latin *baiulus*, see Giulio Rezasco, *Dizionario del linguaggio italiano storico ed amministrativo* (Florence, 1881), p. 78b, s. v. BALIO (BAJULO), VI: "Console veneziano . . . in Costantinopoli,

il quale titolo i Veneziani dettero un tempo a tutti i loro Consoli in qualunque parte del Levante." The Venetian quarter in Constantinople extended along the south coast of the Golden Horn from the Drongariou Gate to the Perama Gate. See Janin, pp. 237–239.

5. Thursday (*giovedì* in Italian, *dies Jovis* in Latin).

6. The noble Venetian family of the Giustiniani should be distinguished from the Genoese *albergo* (association) of the same name on Chios.

7. *argironem*: perhaps a corruption of *anguineum*, "lizard-like."

8. διώρυχα (accusative of διῶρυξ, a trench, conduit, or canal), translated here as "channel." They seem to have followed the river down to one of the large cisterns that supplied water to the city (*lacus*), then sailed along the shore (*marittimum litus*) to the southwest corner of Constantinople. The tower of Narlikapi is near the monastery of St. John ὁ Πρόδρομος τῶν Στουδίου, often incorrectly referred to simply as "the Studion."

9. Ovid, *Fasti* 1.455–456.

10. Introduction to a dream-narrative. Thalia and Calliope are Muses, but Cyriac included the Muses among the Nymphs, as we know from his drawing of thirteen Samothracian dancing maidens whom he interpreted as "Nymphs of Samothrace," while labelling nine of them with the Muses' names. See Lehmann, 1973, pp. 100–108, 111–115, and figures 28–33; BM, p. 89, figures 21–22.

11. See inscrr. nos. 10–18, 21–27 in the edition of Riemann. The wording here is strikingly similar to that of other passages in which he reports having seen the giraffe. Since this encounter with a giraffe seems to be narrated as occurring in a dream, it is unlikely that there was an actual giraffe within the city walls of Constantinople. Cyriac did, however, see a giraffe during an earlier visit to Egypt and the "Memphitic Babylon" (i.e., Cairo: see Lehmann, 1977, p. 12), possibly in September, 1436 (ibid., p. 29, note 66), and made drawings of it. For a detailed study of this Egyptian visit see, ibid., pp. 9–13 and notes 65–96. Cyriac's word, *zoraphan*, written here in Greek characters, is close to the Arabic *zaraphah*, which the Italians made into *giraffa*. A drawing similar to his other drawings of the giraffe must have accompanied this letter.

DIARY I

1. Modern Silivri. Cyriac seems to think of the Pontic (i.e. the Black) Sea as extending as far as Heraclea Perinthus (see §2).

2. Modern Marmarareğlisi, which, however, lies, not on an isthmus, but on a blunt peninsula.

3. Emperor from A.D. 610 until his death in 641.

4. Drawing not extant.

5. Abridged in Latin; full text in Greek.

6. Text defective.

7. St. John the Baptist.

8. A list of names, classified by their place of origin.

9. A fragmentary list of victories in games.

10. The drawing is now lost.

11. Ovid, *Tristia* 1.10.29–30.

12. Pliny the Elder, *Hist. Nat.* 36.22.98.

13. For Cyriac's visit to, and drawings of the Cyzican temple of Hadrian, see Ashmole 1956, pp. 179–191 and plates 334–39; Lehmann 1973, pp. 45ff., and Reinach (q.v.). For his earlier visit to Cyzicus, in 1431, see Scalamonti, §§81–83, where it is called a temple of Jupiter.

14. Corrected by the editor because the 3rd of August 1444 (the date given in the manuscript) fell, not on a Sunday (*Kyriaceum diem*), but on a Monday.

15. The translation of this and the next paragraph is mostly that of Ashmole 1956, p. 187.

16. I.e., seventy feet.

17. This sentence is a heading to the drawings in O6, fols. 132v–136v (See BM, p. 62, note 33, figs. 1–6).

18. Translated from the original Greek text.

19. Translation of the same inscription from Cyriac's Latin version.

LETTER 14

1. Raffaele Castiglione was a wealthy Genoese merchant residing in Heraclea Perinthus on the northern shore of the Sea of Propontis (the Sea of Marmara), in a position to help the papal navy obtain provisions for its operations in that location. For his surname see below, §49 of the resumed Propontic diary. For Castiglione's possible importance to the crusader fleet see Bodnar 1988, pp. 260–262.

2. A phrase in Greek has been omitted by the copyist.

3. See Vergil, *Aen.* 6.670–671.

4. Çorlu was rather close to Perinthus (Marmara, Ereğli), north and slightly west.

5. Probably his detailed drawing of the temple of Hadrian at Cyzicus.

DIARY I, CONTINUED

1. A clearly symbolic, intentionally didactic gesture related to the crusade that was then under way. See Cyriac's gift of a gold coin of Trajan (the "good" emperor) to the emperor-designate, Sigismund, in 1433 (Scalamonti, §97), which was in turn a conscious imitation of Petrarch's presentation of a gold and silver coin of Augustus to Emperor Charles IV in 1354.

LETTER 15

Year and place not indicated. De Rossi, p. 369b, places it in 1444, where it fits well with our chronology. It could also fit into 1446.

1. See Homer, *Od.* 10.302–306, esp. 304–5.

LETTER 16

1. In the manuscript this letter follows immediately after Letter 2, also to Cesarini. This accounts for the expression "the same *(eundem)* Giuliano" in the heading, supplied by the compiler rather than by Cyriac.

2. These two letters have not survived.

3. Cardinal Francesco Condulmer, nephew of Pope Eugene IV, since 1431 vice-chancellor of the Church, and since 8 May 1443 apostolic delegate in Greece in command of the fleet that was to act in concert with the land forces coming from Buda.

4. Another play on Cesarini's designation as *cardinalis Sancti Angeli*, ἄγγελος being the Greek word for messenger.

5. The crusader army crossed the Danube on 20 September (Setton, 2: 88 and note 24).

6. To the best of my knowledge he never again saw Cesarini, who was killed in the battle of Varna in November 1444.

DIARY II

1. Lodovico (Luigi or Alviso) Loredan, commanding the Venetian galleys of a papal fleet sent in the Crusade of Varna to support the army coming down from Hungary. The fleet's mission was to prevent Sultan Murad II from crossing from Asia to Europe with the bulk of his army, a mission that failed.

2. Hermodoros Michael Kritoboulos, from Imbros, historian and later panegyrist of Mehmed II.

LETTER 17

1. Georgios Scholarios, later Gennadios II, Patriarch of Constantinople (1453–1459). See Biographical Notes.

2. Vergil, *Aen.* 7.208

3. Inscription not extant.

LETTER 18

1. For this inscription see Ziebarth 1906, p. 406, note 1.

DIARY II, CONTINUED

1. Vergil, *Aen.* 7.208

2. Modern Chora.

3. Plutarch, *Life of Alexander*, 2.1.

4. The drawing is lost.

5. A decorative motif incorporating the heads of cattle.

6. The drawing is lost.

7. The heading is given in both Greek and Latin, with the phrase "by the sea" left out in the Greek.

8. Modern Enez.

9. The phrase is quoted from Pomponius Mela 2.25.

10. Vergil, *Aen.* 3.57

11. The manuscripts have not preserved these inscriptions.

12. Pomponius Mela 2.16; 2.9.

13. Pomponius Mela 2.25.

14. See Ashmole 1957.

15. A list of names, all qualified as "Friend of Caesar and of their Country."

16. Latin version of the Greek inscription in §55.

17. Greek version of the Latin inscription in §49.

18. The manuscript leaves space for a Greek word, probably προη-γούμενος, abbot.

19. Now **Vg1**, containing Plutarch's *Moralia* and 256 Greek letters in two volumes. On fols. 210v–211r, the unknown fifteenth-century purchaser notes that he acquired this manuscript from Cyriac's nephew. On the last folio (318r), there is an autograph note by Cyriac stating that he bought the manuscript on 25 November ἐκ τῆς ἰβερίας ἱεροτάτης μονῆς ἀπὸ τοῦ ἱερομονάχου Ἰαχόβου Στρυμονίου, τοῦ ἀξίου αὐτῆς ἐκκλησιάρχου, εἰς τὸ .ζ. καλενδῶν Δεκέμβρ. ("from the most holy monastery of Iveron from the holy monk Iakonos, its worthy sacristan from the Strymon valley, on the 25th of November"). The purchaser made a list of other books he saw in Cyriac's library in Ancona. For this list and other references, see BM, pp. 66–68, note 119.

19. Morphinou no longer exists; see Dölger, *Mönchland Athos* (Munich, 1943), p. 56.

20. Athanasios of Trebizond founded the Grand Lavra in A.D. 961–963.

21. Cf. the *Oxford Dictionary of Byzantium*, s. v. "Lavra": "The word originally meant a narrow lane or alley in a city." Later it came to mean "a monastery in which everyday life is individual, but social life is directed to the common purpose of loving God."

22. An *incipit* is the first few words of a text; it is used to identify texts, which often circulated under a variety of titles.

23. Now Paris, Bibliothèque Nationale, MS Coislinianus 173 (Diller, p. 177).

24. Now Moscow, Russian State Library, MS 473 (Diller, p. 177).

25. Although the text Cyriac saw, or its exemplar, was written in two columns, with the odd lines on the verso of one folio and the even ones on the recto of the next folio, our manuscript preserves only the odd lines. In the only other manuscript known to contain this poem, Florence, Biblioteca Laurenziana, Plut. 32, 16, the poem is similarly arranged. See Diller, p. 177. In the following translation, the missing lines are supplied from H. J. Rose's translation in the Loeb Classical Library.

LETTER 19

1. Since Pedemontano was a pedagogue (he was the tutor of Francesco Gattilusio), Cyriac attempts an ambitiously literary letter with an avalanche of quotations from, or allusions to the *Iliad*, the *Aeneid*, Ovid's *Fasti*, and Pomponius Mela (identified in BM ad loc.), and we encounter the usual coterie of nymphs, including the ever-present Cymodocea. The combination of Cyriac's bombast, which strained his sometimes uncertain hold on the language, and Feliciano's eccentric copying invites more emendations than usual and demands a readable translation that is still faithful to the original (in so far as that shows through Feliciano's haze).

2. Francesco III Gattilusio.

3. Vergil, *Aen.* 3.516.

4. Vergil, *Aen.* 7.8–9.

5. See Pomponius Mela 2.25. Cyriac alludes to this story in above (Diary II, §30) when recounting his voyage from Maroneia to Thasos. A copy of his Mela, which he was clearly carrying with him on this journey, survives in Oxford, Bodleian Library, MS Canon. misc. 280, fols. 78 ff.; see Mitchell 1962, pp. 290 and 297.

6. Vergil, *Aen.* 9.103.

7. I.e., Ainos. See Pomponius Mela 2.25.

LETTER 20

1. Boruele Grimaldi was Baldassare Maruffo's predecessor as *podestà* of Galata/Pera (1443/1444). See Jacobs (q.v.).

2. This is Cyriac's *Naumachia Regia*, an account of the battle of Ponza, fought on 5 August 1435. Cyriac carried an improved version of this *libellus* with him to Pera in 1444; a copy of it, made in Pera at that time, was the basis for Nicola Ugolini's extant copy, made almost twenty years later in Pera. See Monti Sabia, passim.

LETTER 21

The date of 1445 is a natural sequence if he was coming to Lemnos from Ainos. De Rossi, p. 373b, dates this visit to 1447, but Cyriac was in Foglia Nuova as late as 20 February 1447 and most probably as late as the 22nd (see below, Letters 41 and 42), whereas there is room in 1445 for a visit to Lemnos on 25 February after his stay in Ainos in January of that year, and many weeks before his Cycladic tour in April 1445.

LETTER 22

1. Departure from Chios was on April 2nd, with arrival at Mykonos on the 3rd.

2. Bessarion of Trebizond.

3. I.e., Ancona.

DIARY III

1. The text in Greek is followed by a Latin translation.

2. The "Sacred Lake." Cyriac thought it was one of the artificial lakes the Romans sometimes created for staging mock naval battles. This inscription was found northeast of the lake, near the "Palaestra of the Lake."

3. The unlabelled drawing of this statue, which was already in two broken parts and separated from its large base when Cyriac saw it, appears in M1, but out of sequence, on fol. 31r. It is not in VL7 at all. See Bodnar 1972, pp. 210–213.

4. This inscription is the later in date of the two inscriptions on the base. In M1, fol. 32v, it is written across the bottom of the drawing, below the base. In the drawing of the base, in both VL7, fol. 18r, and M1, fol. 32v, the plinth is depicted as pulled out of its seating and still bearing the feet of the statue. See Bodnar 1972, pp. 210–13.

5. Found *in situ* south of the prytaneum.

6. Found outside of and to the south of the gymnasium. The copy of Cyriac's drawing in M1, fol. 33v, has written on the doorway, not *Id quod supra graece scriptum est*, as in VL7, but the first few words of the inscription.

7. Actually, the arched cisterns behind the stage-building which were part of the theater's drainage system. See Bodnar 1972, p. 215.

8. Actually, the grotto-shrine of Herakles on the west slope of Mount Kynthos. On the drawing are written the measurements: *p. VII, p. VIII,* and *p. XII.* See Bodnar 1972, pp. 210–13.

9. See Bodnar 1973, pp. 310–13.

10. For the location, see note 2, above.

11. Solinus 11.18.

12. δῆλος in Greek means "visible."

13. See Bodnar 1972, p. 214; Mitchell 1962, pp. 284–5, 297–8, and Tav. XXI (another manuscript copy of this drawing is in O2, fol. 68r).

14. Vergil, *Aen.* 3.125.

15. The drawing of this building, now considered to be a temple of Herakles, shows the walls, with lifting bosses, up to a considerable height, whereas now there is nothing left except some foundations and the majestic doorway on which Cyriac remarks here.

16. Solinus 11.28 (= p. 76, lines 7–11 of Mommsen's edition).

17. Vergil, *Aen.* 3.124–126.

18. Ovid, *Met.* 3.636–7.

19. VL7's date, 19 April, seems impossible in the light of the other dates mentioned in the text.

20. Or possibly, "made memorable and celebrated by the poets," stretching the meaning of *memor*.

21. Ἀγουτα in the manuscript, probably to be identified with Naousa, on the northeast coast of Paros, the nearest port to Naxos.

22. Probably sarcophagi.

23. Seen by Rubinsohn, pp. 351–2, note 3, in the southeast side of the tower of the Venetian castle, so high up that it could be read only with binoculars from the roof of a neighboring house. It is an epistyle block, not a statue base.

24. Pliny the Elder, *Nat. Hist.* 36.19; 29.84 ff.

25. For the drawing of the relief mentioned in the text as accompanying the inscription and preserved only here in an altered copy, see Bodnar 1973, pp. 270–77.

LETTER 23

1. Niccolò Zancarolo was a Venetian living in Cydonia, Crete.

2. Isidore of Seville: a condensed paraphrase of *Etym.* 14.6.15–16.

3. *Etym.* 18.8.1.

4. Cf. Pindar, *Pyth.* 5.41.

5. *Phars.* 3.184–186.

6. *Aen.* 12.856–9. H. R. Fairclough's translation in the Loeb Classical Library.

7. Ovid, *Met.* 8.22 (Loeb translation).

8. Apuleius, *Met.* 11.5. See Mitchell 1962, p. 294.

9. This would make the legendary date of the founding of Venice A.D. 421, or 116 years earlier than the earliest documentary evidence, i.e., Cassiodorus' letter to the lagoon-dwellers (*Variae* 12.14).

10. *Aen.* 8.704–706 (Loeb translation).

11. Drawing of Apollo the Archer; see Mitchell 1962, p. 299, Tav. XXVIII. See Macrobius *Sat.* 1.17.47.

LETTER 24

1. The Greek inscription omits the slighting reference to the "Greek neglect of past priests."

2. The missing folio (= old fol. 87) seems to have described at least one excursion away from the bishop's country house.

3. Taking *oppidum* to be the archaic genitive plural, a favorite affectation of Cyriac.

4. Thursday, 15 July (or, less likely, 22 July).

DIARY IV

1. A meticulous copy of the Latin inscription on the arch of Trajan at Ancona, which Cyriac seems to have used as a *sphragis*, or seal of authenticity on several of his collections of excerpts intended as representative samples of his work. See de Rossi 1888, 2:375b–376a and Bodnar 1960, pp. 20 and 55, note 2.

2. Today at least, "Pediada" is the designation for the district in which Lyttos was located.

3. I.e., Lappa.

4. The remains, mostly Roman, of the ancient city of Lappa, also called Lampaia, lie southwest of Rhethymnon at the modern village of Arguropolis (Guarducci 2:191).

5. Ancient Hierapytna.

6. Leonardo Dati (b. 1408), a humanist poet who wrote in Latin and Italian, worked for various popes from Calixtus III to Sixtus IV; he was most famous as the author of *La sfera*, a Italian metrical version of an astronomical treatise by Sacrobosco. Antonio Beccadelli (1394–1471), called "il Panormita" from his birthplace of Palermo *(Panormus)*, was most famous for his collection of pornographic poems in Latin known as *Hermaphroditus*. He spent most of his career as a counselor to the kings of Naples.

LETTER 25

1. Bandino was a priest of the Knights Hospitallers of Rhodes. See Luttrell, p. 180, note 30.

2. 12 August fell on a Thursday in 1445.

3. It is not known if Cyriac carried out this promise to visit Rhodes again.

4. Vergil, *Aen.* 6.848.

5. An indication that Cyriac sometimes included in his collection of inscriptions copies made for him by others.

6. The Latin translation is incomplete.

LETTER 26

1. Although the heading for this excerpt from Cyriac's letter refers to him in the third person, both the heading and the excerpt are in his own hand. He therefore chose to include only this portion of his letter to Lepomagno in these excerpts from his Cretan diary. For a photograph of the intaglio, see Ashmole 1959, Plate XIVa.

2. The figure on the tiny gem (three and a half centimeters high), which Cyriac probably could not see very well in the dim light of the captain's cabin, was not that of Alexander the Great, but of Athena (Ashmole 1959, p. 38) and "The Molossian hounds are griffins, and the cloak with elaborate designs along the top is the aegis with its snaky edge." (ibid., p. 39, note 1).

3. Ashmole 1959, p. 39, translates: "When you hold up the thick part of the gem right towards the light, where the breathing limbs are seen to shine out in wondrous beauty with complete solidity, and with luminous crystal shadows in the hollows, we learn who is the maker of so splendid a thing by the Greek letters — very ancient ones, too — carved above."

DIARY IV, CONTINUED

1. Assuming that demogorgon = δγμιουργός, the "world-artificer" of Plato's *Timaeus*.

2. *spondalis* seems to be a coinage, perhaps pertaining to σπονδή, "libation," "treaty," and in the Christian context "baptismal."

3. An inscription, apparently composed by Cyriac, to commemorate the restoration of the Venetian arsenal in Candia and naming those responsible. Although it is dated 16 January 1446, this does not necessarily prove that Cyriac was actually in Crete until that time, since he could have composed it earlier and left it with the authorities to be inscribed and set up; and it is unlikely that he was in Crete as late as the middle of January; see Letter 29, written from Chios shortly after 13 January 1446.

4. In Greek, followed by a Latin translation. Cf. Hercher, p. 183.

5. In Greek, followed by a Latin translation. Cf. Hercher, p. 183.

6. In Greek, followed by a Latin translation. Cf. Hercher, p. 183.

7. In Greek, followed by a fragmentary Latin translation. See Ingemar Düring, ed., *Chion of Heraclea, A Novel in Letters* (New York, 1979), pp. 58–59.

8. Modern Iraklion, the port of prehistoric Cnossos.

9. Latin hexameters, possibly the beginning of a longer narrative poem about a great Hungarian victory over the Turks. But note the date: *after* the disastrous rout of the Hungarian army on 10 November 1444.

10. Cyriac's actual departure from Crete was in fact delayed until 7 November (see Letter 25). His destination was Constantinople, where he planned to confer with Cardinal Francesco Condulmer, legate in charge of the papal fleet: see Letter 25, where he spoke of a Hungarian thrust

against the Turks (*in Teucros Pannoniae gentis motum*) as his reason for the projected visit. In the lines of the Latin poem cited above he celebrates a victory over the Turks. This is almost the *anniversary* of the the Turks' crushing defeat of the crusaders at Varna, in present-day Bulgaria, on 10 November 1444, largely because the papal fleet was unable to prevent the vastly more numerous main Turkish force from crossing into Europe. See Bodnar 1988, pp. 263–264.

11. This is the gem belonging to Giovanni Dolfin that was described in Letter 26. Here its Greek inscription is given, with a Latin translation, in the context of Cyriac's homage to another Venetian ship captain named Dolfin, Bertutio.

12. In Greek, followed by a Latin translation.

LETTER 27

1. Possibly = *Negropontine*, i.e., from Negroponte, the Venetian colony on the Euripus.

LETTER 28

1. The letter from Naxos is not extant. For Cyriac's visits to Naxos and Paros in April 1445, see the Cycladic diary above.

2. The epithet is from Vergil, *Aen*. 3.196.

3. Paulinus of Nola, *Poemata* 18.128 (*PL* 61.493).

4. Crusino Sommaripo, duke of Naxos and Paros.

5. Vergil, *Aen*. 6.848.

6. The year is not given, but 1445 fits in with the rest of Cyriac's itinerary. Paros is half-way between Crete, whence he sailed before a south wind on 7 November 1445 (Letter 27) and Chios, where he landed on Wednesday, 12 January 1446 (Letter 29). On the way to Paros from Crete he had stopped at Naxos.

7. Cyriac's own device: K(yriacus) A(nconitanus).

LETTER 29

1. It is impossible to convey in translation the word-play in *claritati* (*intellectual* brilliance of Andreolo), *claram* (the brilliant *physical* whiteness of the island of Andros), and *praeclaram* (the brilliant *reputation* of the island of Chios).

2. Letter 28, dated 25 December [1445].

3. The official designation of the Dominican Order.

4. Understanding *Nereydum* (*sic*) as a partitive genitive.

5. Known as Cape Mastico in the Middle Ages (Heers, p. 276).

6. The drops of mastic are tear-shaped.

7. *Homeric Hymn to Apollo* 38.172.

LETTER 30

1. Pythagoras was born in Samos

2. Vowels representing the seven Archangels.

3. In Greek, followed by a Latin translation.

4. I.e., the people of Palati, the village near the ancient site.

5. The drawing of the temple in Didyma has not survived.

6. I.e., Cyriac's Latin rendering of the preceding Greek inscription.

7. The letter breaks off here without a conclusion.

LETTER 31

1. I.e., of Candia. See Letter 25.

2. *meliore lapillo*: Persius 2.1; Martial 9.52.5, referring to "the custom (in magic) of recording days as good with white or bad with black pebbles" (*Oxford Latin Dictionary*, s.v. *lapillus*.)

LETTER 32

1. For *nauclerus* = "mate," see F. C. Lane, *Venice and History* (Baltimore, 1966), p. 267.

2. Presumably the rowers were called into play, since the sails were of little use in a calm.

3. Monday, February 28th.

4. Shrove Tuesday (also known as "Fat Tuesday"), the last day before the beginning of Lent. In 1446 it fell on February 29th.

5. Lodixius de Borlascha. See Argenti, 3: 657.

6. The term *regio* is used loosely, since the *podestà* governed the island in the name, not of a king, but of the Commune of Genoa.

LETTER 33

1. Letter 32. Notice that the word *pridie* refers to a date four days previous (2 March).

2. Aeolus.

3. Paraphrased from Vergil, *Aen.* 7.32–34.

LETTER 34

1. Dorino I Gattilusio, lord of Lesbos, 1428–1449.

2. The complete sense of this sentence cannot be determined until the code is deciphered. A string of initial letters such as this sometimes stands for a literary quotation in Cyriac's writings: see Letter 19, the quotation from Vergil, *Aen.* 3.516–518.

3. I have been unable also to decode this string of initials.

4. Cyriac first visited Lesbos in 1431, as related in Scalamonti §§86–87.

LETTER 35

1. A salutation possibly added by the copyist.

2. Sultan Murad II.

3. For this cryptic apophthegm of Andreolo see Letter 34.

4. Friday, 8 April [1446].

5. The treaty of 19 February 1446 which allied Ancona with Florence and Venice against the papal-Neapolitan-Milanese axis.

LETTER 36

1. Reading *vellem . . . abs te me fieri certiorem* in the manuscript as equivalent to *vellem . . . abs te fieri certior.*

2. Easter Sunday, 17 April 1446.

LETTER 37

1. The letter referred to here is one that has not survived, but it is clear from the context that it was written before 5 May. Therefore, in this case *pridie* has to mean at least "a week ago."

2. On the coast opposite Lesbos: see Babinger 1978, p. 45.

3. The future Mehmed II, conqueror of Constantinople in 1453.

4. 11 May fell on a Wednesday in 1446.

LETTER 38

1. The fifteenth of August fell on a Monday in 1446.

2. Vergil, *Aen.* 1.498–501.

LETTER 39

A *laus urbis* (praise of a city), in epistolary form, of the Genoese colony of Galata/Pera. The genre was a popular one during the late middle ages and Renaissance. No date or place of origin for this text is indicated, but it is clear from internal evidence that the original version was written shortly after 21 August 1446, in Pera/Galata.

1. Baldassarre Maruffo was Genoese *podestà* of Galata/Pera, 1445/46.

2. It was 879 years from the founding of Constantinople to the treaty between the Genoese and Emperor Andronikos II.

3. After the disastrous rout of the Christian army at Varna in November 1444, Constantinople, with whose fate Galata was intertwined, was virtually under siege *(expugnatio)* and would fall to the Turks seven years later.

4. The last phrase is repeated in Greek.

5. See Letter 38, §2, above.

6. Lover of antiquity.

7. The image seems to be that of a statue (ἄγαλμα: in **VL7**, *conam* = *?iconem*), personifying Galata in the Hellenistic manner and standing in a row of such statues of famous ancient cities.

8. The trading marts of the Phocaeans are Foglia and Foglia Nuova; Thracian Samos is Samothrace.

LETTER 40

1. Probably the feast of the Conversion of St. Paul, 25 January.

2. 29 January fell on a Sunday in 1447.

3. Setton, 2: 95–96 and note 57; Bodnar 1988, pp. 264–265.

4. On the northwest coast of Lesbos, above the Bay of Kalloni.

LETTER 41

Although the year is not given, this letter fits well into the series of those written on Cyriac's return from Byzantium in 1447, in which case the expression, *nudius tertius* refers to our Letter 40, dated 13 February [1447], also from Foglia Nuova.

1. If Pope Eugene IV is meant, this was written just three days before that pontiff's death (23 February 1447).

LETTER 42

1. The name Adorno is echoed and reechoed in this paragraph by various applications of the adjective *adornus* (= *adornatus*). Because this conceit would be lost if the adjective were to be translated differently each time appropriately to the character of its noun, it is translated each time "adorned" with quotation marks. The same principle was applied to *hilari . . . Hilarione*, though "cheerful" would be more appropriate than "hilarious" as applied to a ship's captain.

2. Ash Wednesday.

LETTER 43

1. Cyriac uses the Greek superlative *diaprepestata*, which can also mean "most magnificent."

2. *Homeric Hymn to Apollo*, 38.172.

LETTER 45

1. The year is not given. De Rossi 1888, p. 374a, places it in 1447 without explanation.

DIARY V

1. Son of Emperor Manuel II, prince of Achaea, 1432–1460.

2. Constantine Palaiologos, despot of the Morea (the Peloponnesus) 1428–1448, brother of Thomas and of Emperor John VIII.

3. George Gemistos Plethon, the Greek Platonist philosopher, teacher of Cardinal Bessarion. He was accused of being a pagan by George Scholarios and George Trebizond. He spent the last years of his long life here at the court of Constantine, where he died on 26 June 1452.

4. Cyriac had visited the ruins of Sparta once before, on 24 September 1437. See Bodnar 1960a, p. 48, and Moroni, pp. 37–38.

5. Paulinus of Nola, *Poemata* 18.128 (*PL* 61.493). Cyriac quotes the same phrase in Letter 28, §2.

6. Ithome: see §14 below.

7. Strabo 8.3.7. ἠμαθόεντα as an epithet of Pylos in Homer is generally translated as "sandy," but see Strabo 3.7.14 for another, false derivation.

8. Strabo 8.4.4.

9. Drawing now lost.

10. This sentence is repeated in Greek after the quotation from Strabo.

11. Strabo 8.5.5 (Loeb translation).

12. Actually from Plutarch's *Moralia* (*De mal. Herod.* 39.870e); the second line, after correction by modern editors, may be translated, "Now Salamis, isle of Ajax, holds our dust."

13. Strabo 8.5.1.

14. This is a regular term for a Byzantine coin "tested by fire," i.e. pure, usually employed for gold coins.

15. Modern Phlomochori.

16. Modern Las. See Strabo 8.5.2.

17. For this title in the fourteenth and fifteenth centuries see *The Oxford Dictionary of Byzantium*, vol. 3, s.v.

18. The drawings mentioned here are missing from the manuscript.

19. Cyriac spent the winter of 1447–1448 in Mistra. Here, in addition to the Ode to Sparta, and the excerpts from Greek medical texts preserved in **Ma5** (see below), he composed in Greek, on 4 February 1448, a schema of the Roman calendar dedicated to the despot of the Morea, Constantine. The latter was shortly (12 March 1449) to succeed his brother John VIII as emperor, after having been crowned in Mistra the previous 6 January 1449. For editions of the calendar from the autograph (**V3**, fols. 129–132), see Castellani, "Un traité inédit en grec de Cyriaque d'Ancona," *Revue des études grecques* 9 (1896): 225–330, and Sp. Lambros, "Κυριακοῦ Ἀγκωνίτου Μηνῶν τοῦ ἐνιαυτοῦ τάξις ἀφιερουμένη εἰς τὸν Κωνσταντῖνον Παλαιολόγον," *Palaiologeia kai Peloponnesiaka* (Athens, 1930), 4: 96–98. V3 also preserves on fol. 118r-v an exchange of Strabo readings between Cyriac and Plethon; see A. Diller, *The Textual Tradition of Strabo's Geography* (Amsterdam, 1975), pp. 110–123. Here, too, he wrote in Greek a summary of the *Bellum Troianum* by Dictys of Crete (see A. Diller, "The Autographs of Georgios Gemistos Pletho," *Scriptorium* 10 (1956): 30–31), which also appears in Moroni's *Epigrammata*, p. 42; in **Vg2**, f. 17r-v; and Munich, Bayerisch Staatsbibliothek, cgm 495, fol. 155v.

20. From a commentary on the *Prognostica* of Hippocrates.

21. The location of this inscription is probably Nauplion, though the account of his journey from Mistra to Nauplion is missing from the manuscript. See Wolters, p. 104n. The third of these drawings is clearly a representation of Dionysos wearing a faunskin (*nebris*). On the verso of fol.

113, which is an isolated page and out of order, is a drawing of the walls of Nauplion.

22. Cyriac found this inscription either in Nauplion, in which case it had been misplaced, or on the Saronic island of Kalauria (modern Poros), near Troizen. (From *IG* IV, 848, inscribed in the margin of his Strabo manuscript, he is known to have visited that island).

23. All three reliefs are from the Panaghia church in Merbaka. The first was stolen in the nineteenth century and is still missing.

24. Not Mycenae, but Katsingri. See Wolters, pp. 91–100.

25. §§70 to 73 appear in the manuscript first in Latin, then in Greek, both texts presumably composed by Cyriac.

26. I.e., Wednesday, April 17th.

DIARY FRAGMENT 46

1. September 8th fell on a Sunday in 1448.

2. Carlo II Tocco, despot of Epirus and tributary to the Turks.

3. Alcimos = Greek ἄλκιμος, "strong, swift."

4. Two folios are missing from the manuscript at this point.

5. In Greek, followed by a Latin translation.

DIARY FRAGMENT 48

1. The iconographical symbol of the evangelist Luke.

LETTER 49

1. A report of the Second Battle of Kosovo, Oct 17–19, 1448, usually seen by historians as a crushing defeat for the Hungarians.

2. Pall 1937, p. 42 (= 1938, p. 52), suggests that Alcaton = Alkathoe or Alkatho, the poetic name of Megara. Charope (Greek χάροψ -οπις) means "bright-eyed" or "fiercely courageous."

LETTER 50

1. Maffeo Contarini was *podestà* of Ravenna from 5 June 1448 to 31 August 1450.

LETTER 51

1. Cyriac's text here presupposes the last three lines of the inscription, SEX.VIBIVS COCCE|ANVS. PATRONO | BENEMERENTI, which were therefore omitted, not by Cyriac, but by the copyist of the manuscript.

2. Sigismondo, son of Pandolfo Malatesta, lord of Rimini, a famous condottiere; he was so much hated by Pope Pius II that the pontiff "canonized" him to hell.

LETTER 52

Although this document is dated 1447, it is unlikely that Cyriac composed it before 1449, when, as we have seen, he was in the Venice-Ravenna-Rimini area, which includes Padua. The statue was not actually erected until 1453 and Cyriac's text was not used for its inscription. See Bergstein (q.v.), who gives a text and translation for the sonnet "Nivea Paros" and for the inscription.

1. This text was never inscribed on the base of the statue. See Bergstein for discussion, especially pp. 845–852.

LETTER 53

1. Jan van Eyck.

2. The text of paragraphs 4 through 6, as preserved in **T,** appears to be defective. The translations here are tentative and conjectural.

Bibliography

Ashmole, Bernard. "Cyriac of Ancona." *Proceedings of the British Academy*, 45 (1957): 25–41.

Bergstein, Mary. "Donatello's *Gattamelata* and its Humanist Audience." *Renaissance Quarterly* 55:3 (2002): 833–868.

Bodnar, Edward W. *Cyriacus of Ancona and Athens*. Collection Latomus, 43. Brussels and Berchem, 1960.

———. "Ciriaco d'Ancona and the Crusade of Varna: A Closer Look." *Mediaevalia* 14 (1988): 253–280.

———. "Ciriaco's Cycladic Diary." In *Ciriaco d'Ancona e la cultura antiquaria dell' Umanesimo, Atti del Convegno Internazionale di Studi, Ancona, 6–9 febbraio 1992*, edd. Gianfranco Paci and Sergio Sconocchia, pp. 49–70. Reggio Emilia, 1998.

Bodnar, Edward W., and Charles Mitchell. *Cyriacus of Ancona's Journeys in the Propontis and the Northern Aegean, 1444–1445*. Memoirs of the American Philosophical Society, vol. 112. Philadelphia, 1976.

Brown, Beverly Louise, and Diana E. E. Kleiner. "Giuliano da Sangallo's Drawings after Ciriaco d'Ancona: Transformations of Greek and Roman Antiquities in Athens." *Journal of the Society of Architectural Historians* 42 (1983): 321–335.

Miller, William. "The Genoese in Chios." In *Essays on the Latin Orient*, pp. 298–312. Cambridge, 1921, repr. New York, 1983.

Mitchell, Charles. "Archeology and Romance in Renaissance Italy." In *Italian Renaissance Studies*, ed. E. F. Jacob. London, 1960, pp. 455–483.

Scalamonti, Francesco. *Vita viri clarissimi et famosissimi Kyriaci Anconitani*. Edited and translated by Charles Mitchell and Edward W. Bodnar. Transactions of the American Philosophical Society, vol. 86, part 4. Philadelphia, 1996.

Vickers, Michael. "Cyriac of Ancona at Thessaloniki." *Byzantine and Modern Greek Studies* 2 (1976): 75–82.

Weiss, Roberto. *The Renaissance Discovery of Classical Antiquity*. 2nd Edition. Oxford, 1988.

Index

❧❧❧

References to letters are by arabic letter-number and arabic paragraph-number. References to diaries are by roman diary-number and arabic paragraph-number; "n" after an arabic number refers to a note to the translation attached to that numbered paragraph. Thus, 1.1 indicates Letter 1, paragraph 1; I.1 indicates Diary I, paragraph 1, and I.1n indicates a note to the English translation of Diary I, paragraph 1. Personal names occurring in inscriptions are too numerous to be included in this index.

Abaris, letter, manuscript of, II.65

Abruzzesi, 52.2

Acarnania, Acarnanians, 46.1; 46.3; 46.7; 48.1

Acciaiuoli, Nerio, 3.3

Achaea, 1.9

Acheron river, 48.1

Acherusian cave, near Porto Quaglio, V.41

Achilles, V.18

Acrocorinth, V.70, V.72

Acropolis of Athens, 3.3

Actian coast, countryside, groves, 46.2

Adiabene, 8.3

Adige river, 52.2

Adorno, Gregorio, Marquis, 42.3

Adrianople (Edirne), 8.5; 9b1.7; 9b2.9; 10.3, 10.5; 11.1; 16.2; 37.2

Aeacus (Aiakos), IV.22

Aegean islands, 16.5; 39.14

Aegean Sea, 1.10; 3.10; 4.2–4; 28.5; 30.3; 38.9, 38.13; II.1; 17.3; III.27

Aeneas, 19.6; II.22

Aeolus, king of the winds, 30.3; 32.9; 33.2n; 39.17; 40.3

Aeolus, "temple" of. See "Tower of the Winds"

Agamemnon, V.18

Agauousia Modatia, a village in Crete, IV.12; IV.14

Agesilaus, a Spartan, V.56, V.58

Agouta. See Naousa

Aiakos. See Aeacus

Aigion (Vostiza), V.71, V.73

Ainos in Thrace (Enez), 19.1–2; 20.3; II.22–27, II.61, II.70

Aitolia, V.71, V.73

Ajax, V.38n

Akakios, monk of Vatopedi, II.61

Albanians of Colchis, 29.3; II.75

Alexander the Great, 52.1; II.11; intaglio of, see Athena

Alexandrian fleet of Venice, IV.23

Alexandridas, a Spartan, V.58

Alfonso V "the Magnanimous," King of Naples 1.3; 2.2; 16.4; 20.2; 35.4

Alphaeus river, 28.5; 52.1

Amasia, 9.1

Amastris, on the Black Sea, 39.13

Amathea, on cape Tainaron, V.48, V.49

Amazons, 3.8, 39.13

Ambracian sea, gulf, 46.1–2, 46.5

Amisos in Pamphylia, 39.13

Ampelusium, harbor of Cnossos, 25.2

Amphitrite, 4.4; 19.5; 30.3

Anacharsis, letters, manuscript of, II.65

Anastasium, II.81

Ancona, Anconitans, 22.5n; 28.5; 29.5; 30.3; 35.4, 34.6, 34.7, 34.10; 37.6; 39.2, 39.10, 39.20; 40.4; treaty with Florence and Venice, 35.8n

Andromache, 29.5

Andronikos II, emperor of Byzantium, 39.4n

Androusa, Ithomean, estate of Thomas, V.16

Andros, 29.1

Angelo, a painter, 52.4

Angelo, son of Andreolo Giustiniani-Banca, 43.2

Angels, 48.4

Ansalone, Niccolò, 47.1

Anthaeus, 23.1

Antiochus, king, 30.12

Antonello, president of the banquet, 46.7

Antoninus Pius, I.3

Antonio, Franciscan friar, 6.7

Apameia (Bosnaviron), 12.1n

Aphamnia, 12.1

Apollo, Actian, 23.11

Apollo, Phoebus, 19.1; 23.2; 28.5; 33.3; 39.20; 42.3; 43.6; 46.1; III.27; Pythian, 23.1; of Rhodes, coin showing, 25.4; coin of, 23.2; colossal statue of, on Delos, III.9, III.10, III.37; Hymn to, 43.6; temple of?, 32.8; on Delos, III.11, III.17, III.20; temple of, at Didyma, 30.12–15; of Delphi, 52.1

Apollo's Hill and Apollo's River, on Naxos, III.33; the archer, drawing of, 23.10

Apostles, church of, I.16

Apuleius, *Metamorphoses*, 23.8

Arabs, 23.11; 29.3; 52.1

Arachthus river, 46.1, 46.6–7; 48.1

Arcasa, a Spartan village, V.54, V.57

Arduini, 19.7

Argos, 30.3; V.56, V.68

Arguropolis, Crete, IV.4n

Aristo, a Spartan, V.58

Aristotle, manuscript of, II.72. *See also* Pseudo-Aristotle

Arsenios, a monk of Vatopedi, II.61

Artace. *See* Erdek

Artemon, ruler of Rhodes, 25.4, 25.6

Artemis. *See* Diana

Asine, ancient. *See* Corone

Assumption of the Virgin Mary, feast of, 38.2; 39.7

Athanadoros, ancient ruler of Rhodes, III.38

Athanasios, a monk, 22.3

Athanasios of Trebizond, founder of the Grand Lavra, II.69

Asan, Demetrios, 1.9

Asan, Manuel, 17.4; 18.1; II.8

Asclepius, temple and inscriptions of, on Paros, III.44–55

Ascoli in Picenum, 1.3

Athena (Minerva), 28.5; 52.1; intaglio of, 26.1–4; IV.24; statue of, 3.5–7; temple of, *see* Parthenon

Athenian, V.4

Athens, 3.1–10; 28.5; 52.1; V.56

Athos, Mt., II.59–80

Attic lettering, 46.6

Ayasmand in Phrygia, 37.2

Augustus Caesar, 29.5; I.38, I.49n; III.41–42; month of, 39.7

Aulus Gellius, 51.3

Ayia, territory in Crete, 24.1

Azov, Sea of, 29.3

B., a Franciscan priest, 35.10

Babylonians, 29.3

Bacchus. *See* Dionysos

Bactrians, 29.3

Balduo, P., governor of Crete, 23.1

de Bancha, Antonio, 42.5

de Bancha, Giorgio, 42.5

Bandino, Melchiore, 25.1

Barbadico, Daniele, consul in Crete, 23.1

Barneote, a seaman, 21.2

Baroncelli, Niccolò, 52.1

Basil, a Cretan, 14.7

Basil, chief magistrate of Rhogous, 48.2

Beccadelli, Antonio, "il Panormita," IV.9, IV.11

Belfiore, 53.4

Bellerophon, IV.9

Bendramon, Joannes, V.66

Bergamo, 52.2

Bessarion of Trebizond, "Cardinal of Nicaea", 22.3; V.2n

Bithynia, 14.2

Bitylos = Pylos, V.2

Black Sea, 14.2; 29.3; 39.13; 40.2, 40.8; 41.2; 51.2

Boccone, Antonio, 5.2; 7.3; 15.2; 35.10

Boeotia, V.56

Bogdan, chancellor of Serbia, 9.1n

Boii, 50.2

Bondician lands, 46.4

Boreas, 33.2

de Borlasca, Lodixius, 32.6

Bosnaviron. *See* Apameia

Bosporus, II.3n; 16.2; 29.3; 39.3–4; 39.12; 40.2; 40.3

Branas, Theodore (= Vranas?), 21.2

Branković, George, *despotes* of Serbia, 2.7; 9.1; 9b1.3; 9b2.4; 10.3

Brescia, 52.2

Britain, 45.4

Britons, 29.3

Brutus, letters, manuscript of, II.65; IV.16–18

"Bubularia" caverns, II.27

Buda, 9a.4

Bulla, Alberto, 40.9
Bulgaria, 11.3n
Buonaccorso, secretary of Candia, 25.2; 31.1
Byzantium (Constantinople), 1.6, 1.10; 9.1; 9b2.11; 11.1n, 11.4; 12.1; 12.8; 14.3; 16.2; 17.2; 25.3; 34.4n; 35.3; 38.2; 39.1, 39.6, 39.7; 40.2, 40.3; 41.2; I.1; II.2; IV.23n

Cadiz, 29.3
Cadmean alphabet, V.40, V.64
Caesar, 2.2; 2.5; the Caesars, III.40; statues of in Crete, 28.5; 39.13; 52.1; IV.5–7; V.28
Caesaria in Syria, 39.16
Calendar, Roman, Cyriac's Greek schema of, V.58n
Calergio, Marco, V.19
Cairo, 12.5
Calirachium, II.81
Calliope, a Muse, 12.5; 30.2; 32.30; 33.2; 35.9; 36.2; 36.6; 39.20; 42.3; 43.6; 46.3; V.58
Callixtus III, pope, IV.9n
Calvo, Francesco, II.22, II.27
Canabuzios, Crytes, 6.5, 6.6
Candia (Iraklion), Crete, 25.2; 27.4; IV.20; IV.23; arsenal in, IV.15
Cape Mastico, Chios, 29.1n
Capelli, Carlo, 12.4
Cappadocians, 29.3
Cappaneo of Selymbria, I.1
Capranica, Domenico, Cardinal of Fermo, 1.3n

?Capsalum, on Samothrace, II.15
Caraconesia, peninsula, 56.6
Carlo duke of Nania. See Tocco
Carmeno, Iacopo, 30.8
Carra, village on Naxos, III.30
Castiglione, Raffaele, 8.2; 14.1–4; I.48
Castiglioni, the, 42.4
Castor and Pollux. See Dioscuri
?Catalans, 1.10
Catanio, Luca, 40.4
Catina, gulf of, 46.4
Catrinelli, Iacopo, 40.4
Ceba, Niccolò, 20.2
Çelebi. See Mehmed II
Cembalo, 39.12
Ceraunia, promontory, 46.5
Cerberus, V.41
Ceres and Persephone, temple of, IV.8
Cesarini, Giuliano, Cardinal of Sant'Angelo, 1.4; 2.1; 16.1
Ceteyam, Manuel, Cretan monk, 32.2
Chalcis, 1.10; 3.1n
Chalkokonyles, Laonikos, V.2, V.4
Chaonia, 46.5
Chariotissa, church of, on Naxos, III.30
Charles V, emperor, I.49n
Chavaro, Ciriaco de, ship's mate, 32.3
Chersonese, Byzantine, I.2
Chersonese, Thracian, 17.3
Chinarum, II.81

Chion, letters, manuscript of, II.65; IV.19

Chian baths, 37.4

Chion of Heraclea, IV.19

Chios, 1.10; 3.10; 20.2; 22.2n; 28.2; 29.1–5; 30.3; 31.2–4; 42.3; 43.2; 43.6; 44.4; 45.4

Chirodantas, George, V.57

Chora, a town on Samothrace, II.10n

Chorasia, a village near Porto Quaglio, V.39

Christians, 40.6; 42.6; 45.4; 47.3

Christmas, II.81

Christophoros, a friend of Cyriac's, V.16

Chrysonea, 7.2

Cicada, Cosmo, 36.3

Cilicians, 29.3

Cimmerian, 39.12

Circe, 15.3

Clio, a Muse, 32.3; 53.5–6, 53.8

Clotho, a nymph, 37.4

Cnossos, 23.5; 23.6; 25.2; IV.20n, IV.22

Coccianus, a sculptor, 51.2

Colchis, Colchians, II.75; 29.3

Colochitea, on Cape Tainaron, V.47

Condulmer, Cardinal Francesco, 16.2; 25.3; IV.23n

Constantine Dragas. See Palaiologos

Constantine, Flavius, Roman emperor, 39.3

Constantinople. See Byzantium

Contarini, Maffeo, *podestà* of Ravenna, 50.2

Contarini, Pandolfo, IV.15

Corinth, 1.9; 3.1n; province (eparchy) of, V.70; V.72; Isthmus of, 1.9; 3.1n; 40.5

Çorlu in Thrace, 14.3

Corone in Messenia (Koroni; ancient Asine), V.16; V.18–22; V.49

Cosmas, 34.4

Crete, Cretan, 23.1–9; 25.5; 27.1–5; 31.1; chancellor of, 44.4; IV.1–24

Crimea, 39.12; 40.8

Croesus, 6.2; 6.4

Cyclades, 1.10; 3.1n; 21n; 28.5; 52.1; III.1–70

Cydonia (Khania), Cydonian, 23.1–2; 23.9; 24.1; 40.7; IV.22

Cymodocea, a nymph, 4.2; 17.5; 19.5; 30.3

Cyothalani, 1.10n

Cynthian lamp. *See* Diana

Cynthus, Mt., on Delos, 38.2; 39.7; 42.3

Cyril, manuscript of, II.72

Cyprus, king of, 39.13; 42.4

Cyrus, 28.5; 52.1

Cyzicus, I.26; I.31; I.39; temple at, *see* Hadrian

Daedalos, IV.22

Daniel, abbot of the Grand Lavra, II.70

Damas of Pergamon, correspondent of Brutus, IV.16–18

Danube river, 9.3; 16.4n
Dardanelles. *See* Hellespont
Dati, Leonardo, IV.9
Daulis, 1.9
David, abbot of Karakallou, II.68
David, monk of Vatopedi, II.62
Delfino, Giovanni, 26.3
Delos (ancient Ortygia), 1.9; 1.10;
    22.2; 22.5; III.3–27; III.33–34;
    III.36
Democritos, II.29
Dentutuo, Cristoforo, II.22; II.24
Dernixio, Urbano, 40.8
Diana (Artemis), 38.2; 39.7; 46.3;
    IV.14; her day = Monday,
    38.2; 39.7; 40.11; 46.2; her lamp
    (= the Moon), 46.1; prayer to,
    46.3; Delian, 23.1; Diktaian,
    IV.12; IV.22; Ephesian, 30.2
Dictys of Crete, *Bellum Troianum*,
    Greek summary of, V.58n
Didyma, 30.12–15
Diomedes, 19.4; II.30
Dionysias, old name of Naxos,
    III.34
Dionysios the Areopagite, manu-
    scripts of, II.62; II.72
Dionysos (Bacchus), III.34;
    III.36; temple of on Naxos, *see*
    Hercules; image of, V.60n
Dioscuri, V.58
Disypatos, Alexios, 17.3
Dodona, 48.1; 48.3; II.2
Dolfin, Bertutio, IV.23
Dominicans. *See* Order of
    Preachers
Domitian, emperor, I.3

Don river, 29.3
Donat, Andrea, IV.15
Donatello, 52.1–2
Donato, Pietro, bishop of Padua,
    3.2n
Donysa, III.35
Dorians, V.71
Doric script, V.65
Doris, a nymph, 19.5; 30.3
Dositheos, sacristan of the Grand
    Lavra, II.70
Doto, a nymph, 19.5; 30.3; 37.4.
    See also Loto
Dracula. *See* Vlad Dracul
Drapieri, Franzesco di, 4.2; 7.5;
    8.2; 8.4; 9.1n; 9b2.10; 32.11;
    35.2; 36.4; 36.6–7; 37.2–3; 37.7;
    38.1
Drapieri, Elisabetta Maria di,
    daughter of Franzesco, 38.2;
    39.7; 39.20
Drongariou Gate (Byzantium),
    12.2n
Dry, village on the Tainaron pen-
    insula, V.25; V.44
Dryads, 32.5
Dubrovnik. *See* Ragusa

Easter Sunday, 36.4
Edirne. *See* Adrianople
Egidio, 49.1
Egypt, 12.5; 16.7; 23.11; 29.3
Elisabetta Maria. *See* Drapieri
Elysian Fields, 29.5
Emmanuel, 34.3
Enez. *See* Ainos
Epidaurus, ancient. *See* Ragusa

Epirus, 2.11; letters 46–49
Ephesus, 30.2; 30.3; 40.11
Erdek (Artace), I.26–27; I.39
Este family, 52.1; Leonello d'Este, 53.2–3
Ethiopians, 29.3
Euanthia. See Kantakuzenopolis
Euboea, 1.10–11; 3.1n
Eugene IV (Gabriele Condulmer), 1.3; 1.4n; 2.12; 12.8; 23.10; 35.10; death of, 41.2n; IV.23
Euripides, letters, manuscript of, II.65
Euripus, the, 1.10; 3.1n
Eurotas river, 39.7; V.58
Eurupontine (= Negropontine?), 27
Eurystus, a Spartan, V.58
Eusebius, manuscript of, II.72
Eustathius' commentary on the Iliad, II.67; manuscript of, II.73
Euthimos, former superior of Iveron, II.76
Eutyches, intaglio by, 26.2; 26.3; IV.24
Eutycles the Lacedaimonian, V.28
Euxine Sea, V.41

Faliero, Bartolomeo, Venetian consul of Koroni, V.18
Famagusta, 39.13; 42.4
Fauns, III.60
Faunus, shrine of, on Thasos, II.45
Federico of Montefeltro, duke of Urbino, 4.6n
Fermo, Cardinal of. See Capranica

Ferrara, 53.2–3
Florence, 2.2; IV.9; Council of, 1.2n; treaty with Ancona and Venice, 35.8n
Foça. See Foglia
Foglia (Vecchia; ancient Phocaea), 4.2
Foglia Nuova (Yeni Foça), 4.2; 4.6; 6.6–7; 7.5; 21.1n; 35.4; 35.7; 35.10; 36.3; 37.2; 37.4; 37.5; 37.7; 40.10–11; 41.2–3; 42.2; 42.3; 42.5
Foroflaviniano, Bartolomeo, 40.4; 40.7
Foscari, Francesco, doge, IV.15
Franchi, Andronico, 12.4
Franchi, Gerolimo, 39.9
Frankish, V.16
Frašak, Atanasije, metropolitan of Semendria, 9.1n
Fridiman, Johann, 32.9

Gaius Caesar, V.28
Galaphatos, A., 28.6
Galata/Pera, 11.4; 12.2; 12.4; 16.3; 20.2n; 38.2; 39.1; 39.4–6; 39.10–12; 39.20; 40.2
Galatea, a nymph, 4.4; 19.5; 39.4
Galatia, 8.3
Galen, manuscript of, II.72
Gallipoli, 17.3; 40.3
Gallus Tricinarius, 51.2
Garamanians, 29.3
Garda, lake, 52.2
Gattamelata. See Stefano da Narni
Gattilusi, the, of Lesbos, 39.3; of Thasos, 19.3

Gattilusio, Dorino I, son of Palamede, prince of Lesbos, 6.2; 34.2–3; II.22, II.81

Gattilusio, Francesco, prince of Thasos, 19.1; II.35; II.70; II.80–83

Gattilusio, Giorgio, son of Palamede, II.22

Gattilusio, Palamede, prince of Ainos and Samothrace, 19.6; II.10; II.14–15; II.22; II.70

Gaul, 45.4

Gauls, 29.3

Gennadios II, patriarch of Constantinople. *See* Scholarios

Genoa, Genoese, 5.1n; 11n; 16.7; 29.5; 39.4; 39.6; 39.10–12; 39.15–20; 41.2; 43.2; Genoese ships, 4.2n; 29.3; 39.5–6; 39.10–13; 42.3; comune of, 32.10n

George F., 45.4

Georgians, 29.3; II.75

Germans, 29.3

Geronimo R.B., 45.2

Geronta (= Miletus), 30.12

Ghiberti, Lorenzo, called Nencio, 52.1

Gisdanić, Stojka, 9.1; 9a.2–3; 9b1.2–5; 9b2.3

Giustiniani, Leonardo, archbishop of Mytilene, 6.3; 15.2; 34.3; III.43

Giustiniani, Niccolò, 12.4

Giustiniani-Banca, Andreolo, son of Niccolò, 3.1; 3.10; 4.1; 5.1; 6.1; 7.1; 8.1; 9b2.1; 12.1; 13.1–2; 15.1–4; 20.2; 21.1; 22.1; 22.6; 28.1–2; 29.1; 30.1; 31.1–3; 32.1–2; 33.1–2; 34.1–2; 35.1–2; 36.1–2; 37.1; 37.4; 40.1; 40.4; 41.1; 42.1; 43.1; 45.1–2

Giustiniani-Banca, Angelo, son of Andreolo, 45.4

Giustiniani-Banca, Carenza, Andreolo's wife, 7.5; 27.3; 28.4; 35.10; 41.3; 45.4

Giustiniani-Banca, Niccolò, Andreolo's son, 37.4–5

Giustiniani-Banca, Paride, Andreolo's brother in law, 4.2; 5.2; 15.2; 27.2; 28.4; 32.10; 45.4

Giustiniani da Pagana, Visconte, 4.2; 6.8

Glauke, a nymph, 19.5; 30.3

Glycadea, a valley on Thasos, II.58

Golubac (Peristerion), 9.3; 9.5

Good Friday, 36.6

Gordianus, emperor, V.23

Gortyn, IV.22

Grand Lavra, monastery, II.68–74; library, II.72–74; II.76

Greek, Greeks, IV.22; 29.5; captives, 40.5–6; monks, 46.6; rite, 48.2

Gregory, patriarch of Constantinople, 38.2; 39.7

Grimaldi, Battista, 35.7–9

Grimaldi, Boruele, 12. 2; 20.1; 39.5

Grimaldi, Carlo, II.37; II.41

Grimaldi, Oberto, 4.2

Grimaldi, Paolo, 12.4

Grimaldi ship, 22.3

Grimani, Buonaccorso, secretary of the Cretans, 31.1

Grimani, Domenico, 44.1; 44.3

Grimani, Luca, 24.1–3

Guarino Veronese, 53.8

Gubbio, 40.8; 41.2

Gyilippus, a Spartan, V.58

Gythion, in Laconia, V.50–53

Hadrian, temple of, in Cyzicus, 14.3; I.28–43

Haghia Sophia, church of, in Constantinople, 39.7; on Samothrace, II.9

Halil Pasha, 9.4; 11.2

Hebdomon, 12.1n

Hellespont (Dardanelles), 11.2; 11.3n; 11.4; 16.2; 17.3; 19.8; 29.3; 40.3–4; II.1–2; II.65

Hephaisteia, on Lemnos, 21.2

Heracleia. See Perinthus

Heracleia Pontica, V.41

Herakles. See Hercules

Heraclius, Roman emperor, I.3

Hercules, II.30; Herakles, 28.5; 44.2; 52.1; III.60; V.41; grotto of on Delos, III.19n; temple of, on Naxos, III.28

Hermes. See Mercury

Hermodorus, Cyriac's freedman, 48.1

Hermus river, 37.3

Herodotus, manuscript of, II.72–73; 29.5

Hexamilion, the, 1.9n

Hierapetra (ancient Hierapytna), Crete, IV.5; IV.8; IV.12

Hierasimos, abbot of Iveron, II.63; II.75

Hierasimos, monk of Philotheou, II.66

Hilarion, a sea captain, 42.3

Hippocrates, letters, manuscript of, II.65; II.72; *Prognostica*, commentary on, V.59n

Hircanians, IV.22

Homer, 7.4; 29.5; *Iliad*, commentary on, II.66; *Odyssey*, 15.3n; manuscript of, II.61; 39.14; V.18; V.22; temple of? 32.8; tomb of, on Chios, 43.2–4; on Pylos, V.23n

Homeric Hymn to Apollo, 29.5n; 43.6n

Homerica, a village on Chios, 43.2–3; 43.6–7

Horologion of Andronikos. See Tower of the Winds

Hunyadi, John, 1.6; 2.6; 9.1–2; 10.1; 11.1; 16.3; 47.2; 49.2

Hungarians, 19.8; 25.3; 40.6; 49.2; IV.21; V.71; V.73

Hungary, 9.5; 9b1.1; 47.2; IV.21n

Hyrcanian hide, 24.7

Hyrcanians, 23.1; 29.3

Iacobino, 52.1

Iakovos, sacristan of Iveron, II.63; II.76; II.77

Ialissos, on Rhodes, 25.3; 35.8

Iberi. See Georgians

Ibrahim Beg, prince of Karaman, 9.4n

Ida, Mt., in Crete, 25.2; IV.22

Ignatios, monk of Vatopedi, II.61
Illyricum, 1.7; 2.11; 29.3
Imbros, 16.5; 17.3–5; II.22
India, Indians, 23.11; 28.5; 29.3;
    52.1
Ionia, 30.6; 30.12
Ionian Sea, 29.3; islands, 39.14;
    46.5
Ionians, 29.5
Ionic lettering, 30.2
Iraklion, Crete. *See* Candia
Iris, Jove's messenger, 32.9
Irish, 29.3
Isfendijar Beg, 8.3
Isidore of Seville, 23.2
Ismail Beg, 8.3
Italy, 29.3; 45.4
Ithome in Messenia, V.12–15; V.16
Iveron, monastery, II.63–65; II.75;
    II.76

John of Novara, II.43
Jove, his day = Sunday, 24.6;
    25.2; III.59; father of Diana,
    46.3; statue of at Olympia, 3.7;
    temple of, at Sardis, 6.4;
    Cretan, 25.2; IV.22; Dodonean,
    48.1; = (Christian) God, 4.2;
    37.2; 39.14; I.29; II.81; "incar-
    nate" = Jesus Christ, 8.2; 28.6;
    36.6; 39.18; 48.3; 53.2 II.81; V.66
Juno, 30.2; Argive, temple of,
    V.66–68
Jupiter Ammon, 26.3

Kaffa, 39.12; 40.8
Kalauria (Poros), island of, V.65n

Kallistos, abbot of Philotheou,
    II.66
Kalloni, gulf of, 33.2–4; 34.2;
    40.10n
Kamiros, on Rhodes, 25.3
Kantakouzenopolis (Euanthia),
    V.71; VI.73
Kantakouzenos, Constantine, son
    of John, Count Palatine of the
    Lateran, V.71
Kantakouzenos, John, governor
    of the province of Corinth,
    V.70
Kantakouzenos, Thomas, son of
    George, I.1, V.70
Karakallou, monastery of, II.68
Karaman, the, 9.4; 11.2; II.3
Kardhamila, a port of Chios, 32.3;
    32.9–10; 33.2–4
Karopolis, near ancient Asine,
    V.49
Katsingri, V.68n
Khania, Crete. *See* Cydonia
Kharia, village on cape Tainaron,
    V.26
Knights Hospitallers of Rhodes,
    25.1n
Koroni. *See* Corone
Kritoboulos, Michael, 2.5n; II.4
Kydones, governor of Perinthus,
    14.2
Kypariso (ancient Tainaron),
    V.27; V.42

Lacedaimonia, Lacedaimonians.
    See Sparta, Spartans
Lacon, son of Eutycles, V.28

Laconia, Laconian, V.1; V.22; V.27; Laconian Gulf, V.44; V.49; Laconian Mistra, V.55–56; Laconian Sparta, V.58

Ladislas III, King, 1.6; 2.5; 9.1; 9a.1; 9b.1; 9b1.7n; 9b2.2

Lampea. See Lappa

Lampsacus (Lapsaki), 17.3

Landino, 37.6

Lappa, Crete, IV.4

Lapsaki. See Lampsacus

Laskaris, Ioannes, II.10

Las, a village near ancient Asine, V.49n

Latin name, 40.4; 40.6; Latin rite, 48.2

Latins, 29.5

Latium, 30.3; 35.4; 39.10; 53.4; IV.9

Lebadea, 1.9

Lebadea, island of, V.19

Legio, M., IV.15

Lemnos, 16.5; 17.4; 21.2; II.2

Leondari, V.1

Leonidas, a Spartan, V.58

Lepomagno, M., 26.2

Lesbos, 6.2; 19.7; 32.2–4; 33.2; 34.3–4; 35.3–4; 36.2; 39.13; 40.10; 42.3; II.81–82

Lethe river, 34.2

Libanius, manuscript of, II.73

Liber. See Dionysos

Libyan sea, 29.3; 46.5

Licinius Dentatus, 51.3

Ligurian coast, 39.11; travel diary, 39.16; war, 52.2

Lindos, on Rhodes, 25.3

Locris (Ozolean), V.71; V.73

Loredan, Alvise (or Luigi), II.3

Loto, a nymph, 4.4. See also Doto

Lucan, 23.5

Lucius Flavius Pollio, bronze statue of, 40.4

Lydia, 6.2; 6.5; 35.3; 36.6; 37.2

Lysippos, 28.5; 52.1

Lycia, 42.3

Lycurgus, V.58

Lydia, 40.6

Lydoricia, V.71; V.73

Lysander, a Spartan, V.56; V.58

Lyttos, Crete, IV.3; 25.5

Macedonia, 2.10–11; 9b2.2; 40.6; 45.4; II.59; II.75

Macrobius, Saturnalia, 23.10n

Maeotis, Lake, 39.12

Magnesia-ad-Sipylum. See Manisa

Magola, Adriano, V.42

Makarios, prior of Vatopedi, II.61

Malatesta, Sigismondo, son of Pandolfo, 51.4

Manisa (Magnesia-ad-Sipylum), 5.3; 6n.2; 35.3; 36.2; 36.5; 36.6; 37.2

Mantua, IV.10

Manuel, 32.10

Manuel, a fowler, 12.4

Manuel, an Imbriot sailor, II.8; II.10

Manuel of Crete, O.P., 29.1

Maona, 5.1; 29.5

Marmara, Sea of. See Propontis

Marmareğlisi. See Perinthus

Maroneia in Thrace, II.28–30

Marruffo, Baldassarre, *podestà* of
  Galata/Pera, 39.1–2; 39.5–6;
  40.2; 40.9; 42.3; 42.5
Marruffo, Barnaba, 40.9
Marseilles, 46.5
Marshal, 31.2n
Martin V, pope, 52.1
Masiella, Cyriac's mother, IV.11
Matris, correspondent of Brutus,
  IV.19
Maximos, commentator, manu-
  script of, II.62
Meander river, 30.9
Mediterranean sea, 29.3
Megarean, 49.4
Megarid, 1.9
Mehmed Beg, father of Murad II,
  9b1.1; 9b2.2
Mehmed II Çelebi, son of Murad
  II, 8.2; 9.4; 11.2; 19.8; 35.2n;
  37.3; II.1;
II.4n
Mela, Pomponius, 19.4n; 19.6n;
  II.27; II.30
Melpomene, a Muse, 53.5; 53.7
Memphis, pyramids of, III.59
Memphitic Babylon; cf. Cairo
Menelaos, so-called palace of, and
  portrait of, in Gythion, V.52;
  V.53
Merbaka, V.68; V.69
Mercury (Hermes), 4.2; 7.4; 15.3;
  19.5; 23.2; 23.9; 23.10; 24.7;
  25.7; II.1; V.2; prayer to, III.27;
  Mercury's day (Wednesday),
  1.10; 4.2; 29.1; 32.10; 42.6;
  V.70; V.72

Messene, V.16–17. *See* also Ithome
Messene, gulf of, V.18; V.22;
  V.44
Messenia, Messenian, V.22–23
Michael, *podestà* of Lesbos, 32.6
Michael the archangel, tower of,
  in Galata/Pera, 39.5; chapel of,
  near Porto Quaglio, V.40
Miletus, Milesian, 30.2; 30.5–12
Minerva. *See* Athena
Minerva, temple of. *See* Parthenon
Minoa (ancient Paros), 28.5
Minos, IV.22; 28.5
Miscea in Crete, 24.3
Mistra (Spartoboune), 1.9; V.1;
  V.55–58; V.70; V.72
Mithridates, 39.13; letters, manu-
  script of, II.65
Moesia. *See* Serbia
Moisetta Catania, 39.15
Molin, Maffeo, 1.10
Molossian hounds, 26.4
Montefeltro, Federico. *See* Urbino
Morea, the. *See* Peloponnesus
Morphinou, monastery of, II.68
Mudacio, Luca, consul in Crete,
  23.1
Mulasanio, Giovanni, 43.2
Mulazana, Niccolò, 30.8
Murad II, sultan, 2.6; 8.2; 9a.1;
  9b1.1; 9b2.2; 10.3; 11.2; 11.3; 19.8;
  35.3; 36.7; 37.2–3; 38.3; 39.8;
  40.5, II.3n, II.63
Muses, 3.1; 12.5; 36.6; IV.21 of
  Picenum and Rhodes, 25.1. *See*
  also Nymphs
Mycenae, V.66

Mycenae, so-called ruins of. *See* Katsingri

Mykonos, 22.2; 22.4; III.2–4

Myliadema, 12.4

Mysistrate. *See* Mistra

Mytilene, 6.2; 19.7; 32.2; 34.2–3; 35.3; 35.6; 36.3; 39.13; 42.3; II.81

Namni or Nani, Francesco, 22.2; III.27

Naos, area in northern Chios, 32.8

Naousa (Agouta), III.39n

Nature, parent of all things, 39.14

Naumachia Regia, manuscript of, 20.2

Nauplion, V.60n; V.65n

Napoleone, 9b2.12

Narlikapi, tower of, in Byzantium, 12.5n

Nauplion, V.62–63; V.66; V.68

Naxea, city of, III.29–33

Naxos, 28.2; III.28–39

Nencio. *See* Ghiberti

Neokastro, port of Thasos, II.81

Neopatras, V.71

Neophytos, prior of the Grand Lavra, II.71

Neptune, 17.3; 17.5; 18.2; 19.4; 30.3; 32.9; 39.17; 40.10; II.9; IV.22

Neptune's Samos. *See* Samothrace

Neptune, temple of? on Chios, 32.8; temple of, on Samothrace, II.13; temple of, near Porto Quaglio, V.39

Nereids, daughters of Nereus. *See* Nymphs; Sirens

Nereus, 30.3

Nestor, V.22

New Rome. *See* Constantinople

Nicholas V, pope, 53.2

Nicopolis, 46.2

Nicaea, cardinal of. *See* Bessarion

Nicaea = Nice, 46.5

Nigro, Bartolomeo, 40.8

Nigrone, Benedetto, 39.16

Nikandros, abbot of Pantokrator, II.62–63; II.77

Nile river, 12.7

Nonnos, *Dionysiaka*, manuscript of, II.73

North Wind, 30.3

Nymphs, 4.3–4; 12.5; 17.5; 29.1; 32.5; 37.4; 40.10; of the Bosporus, 39.4; Chian nymphs, 29.3; 30.3; 32.2–4; 33.3–4; = women of Galata/Pera, 38.2; 39.7; of Kardhamila, 32.9; nymphs of Lesbos, 32.4; 32.9; 33.2–4; Thasian nymphs, II.82; III.27; III.60; Thracian nymphs, 39.9; 50.2; IV.20

Ocean, 29.3

Odysseus, 15.3

Old Town, on Imbros, 17.4; on Samothrace, II.10; II.16

Olearos, a Cycladic island, III.35

Olympias, II.11

Order of Preachers, 40.8

Oreades, 29.4; 32.5; 38.2

Oreos on Euboea, 1.11; 3.1n

Orpheus, II.82
Orthryadas, a Spartan, V.56; V.58
Ortygia, ancient name for Delos, 39.7; III.35
Ovid, *Fasti*, 12.5; *Tristia*, I.27; *Metamorphoses*, 23.7; III.36
Ovid, Greek translation of, II.61

Pactolus River, 6.6
Padua, bishop of, 3.2n
Padua, city of, 52n
Palace of Nerio Acciaiuolo. *See* Propylaea
Palaestra of the Lake, on Delos, III.7n
Palaiopolis. *See* Old Town
Palaeologus, Andronicus II, emperor, II.60
Paleologus, Constantine Dragaš, *despotes*, of the Morea, 1.8–9; 40.4; V.2; V.23; V.49; V.58n; V.70–72; V.73
Paleologus, John, governor of Bitylos, V.23
Paleologus, John VIII, emperor 1.1; 12.1; 16.3; 16.5; 21.2; V.48n
Paleologus, Theodore Porphyrogenitus, *despotes* of Messenia, 1.8; 1.9; 12.1; I.1; V.1
Paleologus, Thomas, prince of Achaia, brother of Constantine and John, V.1
Palati, the village near Miletus, 30.8
Pallas. *See* Athena
Panaghia church in Merbaka, V.67n

Pangiotis, Philippos, 27.2
Pannonian. *See* Hungarian
Panopea, a nymph, 19.5; 30.3; 37.4
Panormita. *See* Beccadelli
Pantheo, Valentino, a seaman, 30.2; 30.5
Pantokrator, monastery of, II.62; II.77–79
Pausanias, a Spartan, V.56; V.58
Paros (Minoa), 28.1–6; 29.1; 30.13; 52.1
Parthenon, 3.1; 3.5–10
Parthians, 23.1; 23.6; 29.3; IV.22; = Turks, 1.7; 2.5; 18.2
Patras, 1.9; 3.1n; V.70
Paulinus of Nola, *Poemata*, 28.2; V.2n
Pedasos, ancient name of, V.18
Pedemontano, Giovanni, 19.1
Pediada, an estate or district in Crete, IV.3
Pelican, as symbol of Christ as Eucharist, 48.4
Peloponnese, 1.9; 40.6; V.71; V.73
Penede, Mt., 52.2
Pera. *See* Galata
Perama Gate, in Byzantium, 12.2n
Pergamon, 37.2
Pericles, 3.9
Perinthus (Marmarareğlisi; Heracleia), 14.1–4; I.2; I.26; I.46–48
Peristerion. *See* Golubac
Persians, 29.3; 40.7; V.56
Persius, 31.2n
Perugians, 52.2
Petrarch, I.49n

Peyre. *See* Galata/Pera

Phaeton, IV.22

Phalaris, letters, manuscript of, II.65

Phanourian coast of Crete, III.35; III.39–70

Phantasios, a Cretan sailor, II.28

Phaeacia, 46.5; Pheaecian trireme, 46.1; IV.12

Pheidias, 3.1; 3.5; 3.7; 28.5; 52.1

Philadelphia, 6.2

Philip of Macedon, II.11; V.58

Philotheou monastery, II.66–67

Philotheos, holy founder of Philotheou, II.66

Phlomochori. *See* Colochitea

Phocaea, ancient. *See* Foglia Vecchia

Phocaeans, ancient, 39.13

Phocas, dedicator of the Grand Lavra monastery, II.69

Phocis (Parnassian), V.71

Phoebus. *See* Apollo

Phoenicians, 40.7

Picenum, 2.3; 25.1; 25.2; 25.5; 30.3; 35.4; 40.8

Piccinino, Niccolò, 52.2

Pierides (= the Muses). *See* Nymphs

Pindar, 23.4

Pindos, Mt., V.71

Pius II, pope, 51.4n

Plato, manuscript of, II.72; his dhmiourgo/j in the *Timaeus*, IV.13n

Platonic tradition, V.2

Pletho, Georgios Gemistos, known also as, V.2n; V.55; V.58n

Pliny the Elder, 3.5; 3.7; I.28; III.59

Pliny the Younger, 1.8n

Plutarch, *Alexander*, II.11; *Moralia*, V.38n; manuscript of, II.64

Poggio, Iacopo, 40.4

Pollux, 44.3

Polycarp, manuscript of, II.72

Polyclitus, 52.1; V.66; V.67

Polydorus, II.23

Pol(yh)ymnia, a Muse, 12.5; 32.5; 39.10; 39.15

Polykleitos, 22.5

Polymnestor, II.24

Polyrrhenia, 24.6

Pontic Sea, so-called, I.1–2

Pontus, IV.19

Ponza, battle of, 20.2n

Porasia, a village, V.42

Poros. *See* Kalauria

Porto Quaglio, V.39

Poseidon. *See* Neptune

Poseidonia, on Chios, 43.2

Potamium, II.81

Precursor, *Prodromos. See* St. John the Baptist

Priam, II.23

Proconnessos, 17.2; I.26; II.2

Propontis (Sea of Marmara), 12.1n; 14.2; 40.3; II.1–2

Propylaea of the Athenian Acropolis, 3.3–4

Proserpina, so-called temple of. *See* Hadrian, temple of, in Cyzicus

Pseudo-Aristotle, 3.5; 3.6n
Pulseverio, presumed ship owner, 40.3
Pythagoras, Pythagorean, 30.4; Pythagoras, letter, manuscript of, II.65

Quintus Metellus, IV.22
Quirino, Marco, Venetian consul in Corone, V.8
Quirinus, 29.5

Ragusa (Dubrovnik; ancient Epidaurus), 1.6; 1.8; 2.12; 10.3; 47.1
Rangano, Pietro, V.66
Ravenna, 50.2
Reggio Emilia, 52.2
Rethymnon, Crete, IV.4
Rhadamanthos, IV.22
Rhodes, Rhodians, 16.7; coin of, 23.1; 25.2–4; 25.6; 44.5; III.38
Rhogous, citadel of, 48.2
Rimini, 51.2
Rocea, P., secretary of Chios, 35.3
Roman Achilles, 51.3
Rome, 2.5; 39.2; 39.11; 39.17–18; 40.8; 48.3; IV.9; IV.22; V.56; V.58
Rosea, skipper of a light craft, V.25–26
Ruphu, Iacopo, 46.2

Sabaeans, 23.11
Saced Lake on Delos, III.7n

Sacrobosco, IV.9n
St. Alexander, martyr, church of, 21.2
St. Athanasios, patron of the Grand Lavra, II.69; tomb of, II.71
St. Athanasios (archbishop of Alexandria), manuscript of, II.72; II.77
St. Basil, ms of, II.72
St. Demetrios, martyr, church of, on Samothrace, II.17
St. Elijah, Mt. See Taygetus
St. Francis of Assisi, church of on Mikonos, 22.3; church of in Galata/Pera, 38.2; 39.7; prayer to, 36.4; 36.6; 36.7
St. George, St. George, feast of, 9a.4; patron of Genoa, 39.18
St. Gregory (Nazianzen?), manuscript of, II.72
St. John the Baptist, 35.9; church of, I.11; on Mykonos, III.2; body of, in Genoa, 39.17; church of, in Kharia, V.26; monastery of, see Studion
St. John Chrysostom, manuscript of, II.72; foot of, 48.2
St. John the Evangelist, II.81; chapel of, on Chios, 43.4
St. Luke the Evangelist, 48.1–3; bull as symbol of, 48.3n
St. Mark the Evangelist, IV.15
St. Paul, 48.4; feast of, 40.3; chapel of, in Crete, 24.8
St. Peter, 48.4
St. Theodore, church of, I.15

Sts. Peter and Paul, patrons of Karakallou, II.68

Salamis epigram, V.38

Salimbene, George, 9b2.11

Samonium, IV.20

Samos, 30.4

Samothrace, 17.4–5; 18.2; 39.13; II.8; Nymphs of, 12.5n

Sant'Angelo, cardinal of. See Cesarini

?Saracen, ?a kind of fish, 40.9

Sardis, 6.2; 6.5; 6.6

Samos, 30.2–4

Sangallo, Giuliano da, 3.2n

Sarmatians, 28.3

Saturn's day = Saturday, 30.2; 43.2

Scalamonti, Francesco, *Vita . . . Kyriaci*, 2.9n; 34.3n; I.49n

Scholarios, George, 17.1–2; V.2n

Scots, 29.3

Scylla, gem depicting, 4.6

Scythians, 23.1; 29.3

Seleucus, king, 30.12

Selvatico, Benedetto, 12.4; 39.9

Selvatico, Lisabetta, 39.10

Selymbria (Silivri), I.1; 12.1n

Serbia (Moesia), Serbian, 2.7; 2.11; 9.1; 11.3; 47.1; II.68

Seriphon, promontory, II.28

Sibyl, 2.5; 48.3

Sibylline inscription, I.46

Sicilian sea, 46.5; knight, 47.1

Sidonian skill, 39.15

Siena, 53.4

Sigismund, emperor, I.49n

Signoria of Venice, IV.14

Sigrion, 40.10

Silivri. See Selymbria

Simon, 35.7

Sinop, 8.3

Sirens, 33.4; II.67; II.82; IV.22; Nereid Sirens, 28.3

Sixtus IV, pope, IV.9n

Skyathos, 16.5

Skopelos,16.5

Skyros, 16.5

Soldajal, town of, 39.12

Soliano, son of George the *stratopedarches*, V.49

Solinus, 29.5; III.25; III.33

Sommaripa, Crusino, duke of Naxos and Paros, 28.2; 28.5; III.39

Sorgo, Pasquale de, 47.1

Spaniards, 29.3

Sparta, Spartans, V.2; V.4–11; V.50; V.56–58

Spartoboune. See Mistra

Spinola, Branca, 42.4

Spinola, Cristiano, 34.2

Spinola, Francesco, 39.16

Spinola, Tomasso, 38.3; 39.8

Squarciafico, ship owner, 45.2

Stefano, secretary of Chios and Foglia, 36.2; 37.7

Stefano da Narni, called Gattamelata, 52.2

Studion, monastery of the (*Prodromos tou Stoudiou*), 12.5

Strabo, 6.6n; manuscript of, 40.3; V.58n; on the location of Pylos, V.22; on Eutycles, friend of Gaius Caesar, V.28; V.41n

Stragile, town of, on Naxos, III.34

Strymon river, II.63

Suburneum, peninsula of, V.20

Suleiman Beg, 9.5; 9b1.7; 9b2.8; 10.3

Sulmo. *See* Ovid

Superanzio, Marino, father of Niccolò, 12.2

Synesios, manuscript of, II.73

Superanzio, 12.2

Syrians, 29.3

Tabulario, Giovanni, a priest, V.42

Tainarian nobility, relics of, V.25

Tainaron, ancient city of. *See* Kypariso

Tainaron, peninsula of, V.22–48

Tauric Chersonese, 39.12

Taurico, Lorenzo, 43.2

Taygetus, Mt. (Mt. St. Elijah), V.1; V.44; V.56

Tenedos, 40.9

Tenos, III.27

Terpsichore, a Muse, 32.3

Terracina, Treaty of, 1.3n

Tethys, 4.4

Teucer, IV.22

Thales, 30.6

Thalia, a Muse, 12.5

Thasos, 19.1–4; 39.13; II.31–59; II.70; II.80–83

Thasos, Council, statue of, II.35

Thebes, Thebans, 1.9; 28.5

Thessalonica, II.67

Thetis, 30.3

Thomas, a monk of Vatopedi, II.61

Thrace, 2.10; 9.4; 9b2.2; 11.3; 12.1; 14.2; 14.4; 19.1; 19.8; 29.3; 37.2–3; 39.13; 39.20; 40.6; 45.4; I.3; II.22–30; II.81

Thracian Samos. *See* Samothrace

Thrasyxenos, statue of, 28.2

Thucydides, 29.5; V.38

Thule, 29.3

Tiberius ClaudiusCaesar, 50.3

Tocco, Carlo II, duke of Acarnania, 46.1; 46.4; 46.6; death of, 48.1–5

Tocco, Leonardo, son of Carlo II, 46.4; 48.1; 48.3; 48.5

Tortorino, Francesco, 40.9; 41.2; 42.3–5

Tortorino, Giorgio, father of Francesco, 42.4

Tower of Christ, in Galata/Pera, 39.5–6

Tower of Michael the Archangel, in Galata/Pera, 39.5

Tower of the Winds, 3.2

Trajan, emperor, 22.5; 25.5; 25.8; I.49n; III.2; arch of, in Ancona, IV.1

Trebizond, George, V.2n

Triphylia, location of Pylos, V.22

Troizen, island of, V.65n

Turcummale, I.47

Turks, 1.4n; 1.7; 2.5; 2.10; 25.3; 34.4; 39.5; 40.5; 49.1–2; I.19; IV.21n; V.71

Tuscan sea, 46.5

Ugolini, Nicola, scribe, 20.2n
Umbriaci, Iacopo; 38.3; 39.8
Umbro, Tomasso of Gubbio, Do-
    minican vicar, 40.8; 41.2
Urbino, prince of, 4.6n
Urania, a Muse, 35.9; 39.15; 39.20

Vahtang, king of Macedonia, II.75
Valturio, Roberto, 50.1; 52.2
Van der Weyden, Rogier, 53.1–8
Van Eyck, Jan, of Bruges, 53.2n
Varna, 11.3n; battle of, 16.6n;
    39.5n; IV.21n; crusade of, 1.4n
    and passim
Vatopedi, monastery of, II.60–61;
    II.71; II.76; II.80
Venice, Venetian, 12.2; 23.1; 23.9;
    25.2; 35.4; 50.2; 52.2; III.4;
    III.43n; IV.14–15; IV.23; V.18;
    treaty with Ancona and Flor-
    ence, 35.8.
Venus' day = Friday, 35.8; 46.6–
    7; month = April, 35.8
Vergil, Aeneid, 14.2; 17.4; 19.3–5;
    23.6; 23.10; 28.2; 33.2n; 38.2
    II.8; III.28; III.35; IV.4; IV.10
Verona, 52.2
Vespasian, I.3; coin of, I.48; atria
    of, in Perinthus, I.19
Vesta, 39.15
Viario, Fantino, IV.15
Virgin Mary, II.81; feast of the
    Assumption of, 38.2; 39.7; feast
    of the Nativity of, 46.1; Virgin

Mary, church of I.46; on
    Naxos, called Chariotissa,
    III.30; cathedral church of, in
    Ayia, Crete, 24.1; 24.5; church
    of the Annunciation, monastic
    church of, Vatopedi, II.60–61;
    of Philotheou, II.66; on Naxos,
    III.31; chapel of, on
    Caraconesian peninsula, 46.6;
    48.4; church of, on the Argive
    plain, V.67
Visconti, Filippo Maria, duke of
    Milan, 39.16
Vitislao, 9.1
Vlad, voivode of Wallachia, 9b1.4–
    5; 9b2.5
Vlad III Dracul, 9b1.4n
Vladislav. See Ladislas
Vostiza. See Aigion
Vranas (= Branas?), 9.5

White Mountains in Crete, 24.1;
    24.4; 24.6
Wisdom, Church of the Bounti-
    ful, in Constantinople, 38.2;
    39.7

Xanthippos, a Spartan, V.56; V.58

Yeni Foça. See Foglia Nuova

Zancarolo, Niccolò, 23.1–2
Zeus and Artemis, temple of, in
    Sardis, 6.4n

Publication of this volume has been made possible by

The Myron and Sheila Gilmore Publication Fund at I Tatti
The Robert Lehman Endowment Fund
The Jean-François Malle Scholarly Programs and Publications Fund
The Andrew W. Mellon Scholarly Publications Fund
The Craig and Barbara Smyth Fund
for Scholarly Programs and Publications
The Lila Wallace–Reader's Digest Endowment Fund
The Malcolm Wiener Fund for Scholarly Programs and Publications